D1568228

THE CLASSICS OF WESTERN SPIRITUALITY
A Library of the Great Spiritual Masters

Elijah Benamozegh
ISRAEL AND HUMANITY

TRANSLATED, EDITED AND WITH AN INTRODUCTION BY
MAXWELL LURIA

PREFACE AND APPENDIX ON
"KABBALAH IN ELIJAH BENAMOZEGH'S THOUGHT" BY
MOSHE IDEL

PAULIST PRESS
NEW YORK • MAHWAH

Cover art: The painting, Third Allegory, is one of BEN SHAHN's most expressive religious works. Having rejected religion in his early youth, he began to rediscover it in middle age, no longer regarding it as "a trap" (his earlier designation), but as a fundamental human need. He delighted in the Hebrew myths and lore that, despite his early skepticism, he knew so well. He executed numerous works—books, paintings, prints and the like and many drawings—all expressing his love and enjoyment of the beliefs, the stories, the rare ritual objects of his hereditary faith. But, as an adult, he looked upon all religions in the same light: he was awed by the Catholic mass; he cherished the Greek religious myths; he was acutely aware of the broad dimension that religion, as such, has added to the human community—the music, the art, the exquisite churches, temples and cathedrals and, above all, the principles of humanity, tenderness and justice. Not infrequently, he commented upon the quiet presence of the Ten Commandments in the American Declaration of Independence, the Bill of Rights, the Constitution itself. He executed many versions of the Ten Commandments—the Decalogue—including the one just above the lamb in this painting. Third Allegory celebrates the Hebrew Seder, the Feast of the Passover, which itself commemorates the release of the Children of Israel from captivity in Egypt.

Third Allegory © 1994 Estate of Ben Shahn/Licensed by VAGA, New York

Excerpts from the TANAKH: The New JPS Translation According to the Traditional Hebrew Text. Copyright 1985 by the Jewish Publication Society. Used by permission.

The publisher and translator are grateful to Association Menorah, Paris, France, for permission to translate this text from *Israël et l'Humanité*.

Library of Congress Cataloging-in-Publication Data 2/98

Benamozegh, Elia, 1823–1900.
    [Israël et l'humanité.   English]
    Israel and humanity / Elijah Benamozegh ; translated, edited, and
with an introduction by Maxwell Luria.
        p.   cm. — (Classics of Western Spirituality)
    Includes bibliographical references and index.
    ISBN 0-8091-3541-8 (pbk.)—ISBN 0-8091-0468-7 (cloth)
    1. Judaism. 2. Judaism—Relations—Christianity. 3. Christianity
and other religions—Judaism.   I. Luria, Maxwell, 1932–   .
II. Title. III. Series.
BM560.B347313   1995
296.3—dc20   94-34906
                                                                   CIP

Published by Paulist Press
997 Macarthur Boulevard
Mahwah, New Jersey 07430

Printed and bound in the United States of America

Contents

CONTENTS

Editor and Translator of this Volume
MAXWELL LURIA was born in Trenton, New Jersey and was educated at Rutgers, Pennsylvania, and Princeton universities. He is a
medievalist and professor of English at Temple University. Dr. Luria
has translated and edited French and English texts and written exten-
sively about the literature and philosophy of the Middle Ages. His
publications include *Middle English Lyrics, A Reader's Guide to the Roman
de la Rose,* and studies of the philosophy of Hugh of St. Victor, Renaissance manuscript glosses on the *Roman de la Rose,* the poetry of
Caedmon, Chrétien de Troyes, Chaucer, Shakespeare, and the letters
of A. Edward Newton. He lives at present in Tokyo.

Author of the Preface and the Appendix
MOSHE IDEL, Professor and Chair of the Department of Jewish
Thought at the Hebrew University in Jerusalem, Israel, was born in
Rumania in 1947. He is a graduate of the Hebrew University, where he
also received his Ph.D. An editor of *Jerusalem Studies in Jewish Thought,*
he is the author of numerous articles and books on the history of
Kabbalah and Jewish Renaissance thought.

To the memory of my mother
Etta Gurney Luria

פיה פתחה בחכמה ותורת־חסד על־לשונה

Os suum aperuit sapientiae,
Et lex clementiae in lingua eius

Foreword

I

Israël et l'Humanité was given to the world in 1914, fourteen years after the death of its author, the Italian rabbi, theologian, philosopher, and Kabbalist Elijah ben Abraham Benamozegh.[1] Though it was a principal occupation of his last years and constitutes a synthesis of his religious thought, he left the work in an unpublishable state, and its eventual editor, Benamozegh's student and disciple Aimé Pallière, was obliged to impose shape on an enormous mass of manuscript and to reduce it to publishable dimensions.[2] The Introduction that Pallière wrote for his edition, included in the present volume, provides an interesting account of his editorial procedure along with a survey of the author's life.

But the work thus issued in 1914 comprises nearly 800 large, closely printed pages, and this was sufficient reason for undertaking a further substantial reduction when another edition was called for in 1961. Émile Touati, its editor, describes the rationale of this second edition:

> Some time before his death (1949), Aimé Pallière himself wished to see published "an abridged edition of this essential work, which might be more accessible to the public." . . . In keeping with the wishes of Aimé Pallière, whose decisive role in bringing Benamozegh's work to the attention of readers we happily acknowledge, we have done all in our power to make his monumental *Israël et l'Humanité* more accessible while yet remaining faithful to his inspiration, style, and ideas. We have thus eliminated as much as possible the repetitions and digressions, condensed those passages which were too prolix,

and removed protracted discussions of technical or obsolete
scholarship which were too dependent on certain preoccupations of late nineteenth-century biblical criticism. When possible, we took the liberty of correcting certain expressions or
awkward locutions in French, which were certainly excus-
able in an Italian author who was determined to write in our
language. But in all essentials, we have scrupulously respected the characteristic style, thought, and logic of Benamozegh, a task all the more delicate as we are dealing here
with an unfinished work which had already been revised by
Pallière. Readers will not be surprised, then, to find that we
have sometimes retained certain weaknesses in the exposition, or somewhat circuitous procedures of explanation. Such
imperfections are inherent in a work which was not altogether finished, but of such great richness, embracing so
many ideas, synthesizing so much knowledge, that in its development it tended to become a veritable *summa* of Judaism.
It was not possible, in any case, to convert this English park
into a French-style garden.[3]

There have been two translations. The first, a freely abridged and
often paraphrased Hebrew version of Touati's edition, was brought out
in 1967 by Dr. Simon Marcus as *Yisroel v'ha-Enoshut*, under the imprint
of the Mossad ha-Rav Kook in Jerusalem. This version has merit but
must be used with care, for Marcus's editorial procedures are sometimes casual. He does not acknowledge the paraphrastic character of
his translation; silently omits material from the original; adds new—
usually Midrashic or kabbalistic—amplifications, equally without notice; fails to distinguish between his own notes and those of the original
editors; and offers no editorial explanation of his procedures. Nevertheless, his documentation of Benamozegh's sources is fuller than the
original, and I have used it with profit.

In 1990, Marco Morselli published an Italian translation of the
second edition: *Israele e l'umanità* (Genoa: Marietti, 1990). This version
includes most of the French notes, with some bibliographical amplifications, and a thoughtful introductory essay by Martin Cunz on Benamozegh's ideas and their vitality.

The present English version presents the unabridged text of Émile
Touati's second French edition of 1961.

FOREWORD

II

In his *Avertissement* to *Israël et l'Humanité*, Elijah Benamozegh remarks that he cannot claim wholly to have triumphed over the challenges of writing in a language not his own. What, then, induced him to compose this work, as he did several others (most notably, *Morale juive et morale chrétienne* [Jewish and Christian Ethics], 1867), in French rather than in Italian or Hebrew? The answer is simply put: "The need to be read." He adds modestly: "I beg the reader to distinguish the work from its author and not to scorn its contents on account of the form in which they appear."

As we have seen, both of Benamozegh's French editors, Pallière in 1914 and Touati in 1961, chose to rationalize and trim the vast, inchoate, and unpolished manuscript left by the author. In addition, each felt impelled to clarify his idiosyncratic French. Despite these editorial changes, however, which appear to have been executed in a spirit of discreet respect, the language of *Israël et l'Humanité* is by no means always clear or idiomatic. Moreover, Benamozegh's occasional predilection for very long, complex sentences, with clause hanging uneasily from clause, and his fondness for diffusive rhetorical questions as a means of exposition—echoes, no doubt, of decades of pulpit oratory—provide a challenge to the conscientious translator who wishes to adhere scrupulously to his original while making it as accessible as he can to his reader.

I have tried, therefore, to achieve fidelity to Benamozegh—in substance and spirit always, in letter as consistently as I could—but never to sacrifice essential clarity for a strictly literal rendering or ordering of words. I have thus allowed myself, on those relatively few occasions when my twin objects seemed to demand it, to break up or recast awkward sentences, to modify their sequence, to transpose material from Benamozegh's notes to his text (with acknowledgment of this transposition in an endnote), to divide paragraphs, omit repetitions, compress or amplify, substitute one simile for another, expand biblical citations, and revise the use of italics and parentheses. Nothing, however, of substance has been silently omitted or replaced or added. When, in a few instances, the cause of clarity has required me to amplify Benamozegh's text in a more substantial way, my amplification is enclosed in square brackets and identified by an endnote. All other bracketed interpolations are from the French original, or are minor amplifications for the sake of clarity.

FOREWORD

I have retained Benamozegh's distinction between "Judaism" and "Hebraism," which, together with the more obvious contrast between "Mosaism" and "Noachism," is (as the reader will soon discover) central to his religious philosophy.

III

The least satisfactory feature of the French editions of this book is their documentation of Benamozegh's hundreds of citations and allusions. Pending study of the manuscript (which is now in the library of the Technion at Haifa), we cannot know much about Benamozegh's method of composition. Specifically, we cannot be sure to what extent the footnotes in the first edition are Benamozegh's own rather than by Pallière or his assistants. Whatever their origin, these notes are seriously inadequate by the standards of modern scholarship. Many of Benamozegh's references to ancient or modern materials are left undocumented, and the others are not infrequently documented incorrectly or imprecisely. Even biblical quotations are occasionally misascribed. Most surprisingly, this faulty annotation does not appear to have been subjected to any correction whatever when the second edition was prepared; and though they must have been noticed by readers during the half century between editions, the errors and lacunae of 1914 were taken over unhesitatingly into the edition of 1961.

In his Hebrew version of 1967, Dr. Marcus has corrected a number of these faulty ascriptions, filled in some of the gaps, and substantially amplified the documentation of Talmudic, Midrashic, and kabbalistic themes. Though his editorial procedure is faulty, as I have already noted, his documentation is much superior to that of the French editions, and I have freely used his notes in preparing my own.

Benamozegh is fond of attributing ideas without specificity to "the sages" (*les Docteurs*), "the rabbis," "the Kabbalah," and so on. It has not been possible (nor, I think, essential) to document all such general references or obiter dicta. Apart from other considerations, this would have burdened the book with an inflated apparatus of notes inappropriate to its broadly philosophical, mystical, exhortatory character. Besides scrutinizing and correcting all the French notes, I have tried instead to pin down the significant undocumented citations and allusions, and in a few instances have adduced sources that could not have been known to the author but which strengthen his case. Wherever possible, I have cited recent, available editions and English translations.

FOREWORD

The French editions do not always differentiate clearly among quotations, compressed summaries, and paraphrases, but are apt to use quotation marks for all three. This imprecision is particularly egregious in the Talmudic citations. I have tried in all such instances to clarify the proper distinctions and provide accurate citations, even when this required some expansion of Benamozegh's material. Most such translations are adapted from the volumes of the *Soncino Talmud*, edited by Rabbi Dr. Isidore Epstein.

Biblical citations are more problematic still, owing to the obscurity of many biblical passages as well as Benamozegh's frequent use of kabbalistic or Midrashic interpretations of his proof-texts. For the sake of consistency, I have used the Jewish Publication Society's new translation (1985) throughout, even when it does not emphasize that particular potentiality of the text with which Benamozegh is concerned. In cases where the divergence is significant, I have cited multiple translations, including of course Benamozegh's own.

Altogether, then, the annotation comprises, in a single sequence, four kinds of notes: (1) documental notes, referring to texts or sources, and based on those in the French editions and in Dr. Marcus's Hebrew version, corrected and supplemented; (2) authorial footnotes from the first edition that explain or amplify the text, identified here as Benamozegh's; (3) editorial footnotes from the French editions, identified here as Pallière's; (4) a small number of explanatory notes by the present editor.

Identifications of names and terms that may be obscure to the reader unfamiliar with Benamozegh's sources are gathered in the Glossary.

IV

Much of the research for this book was accomplished in the Jewish Division of the New York Public Library and in the Speer Library of Princeton Theological Seminary. I am deeply indebted to these superb institutions, and their admirably courteous and professional staffs, for allowing me many hours of happy and productive labor. I am also under obligation to the libraries and librarians of Yeshiva, Temple, and Princeton Universities. My work was completed in Tokyo, where the Jewish Community Center's fine Judaica Library was put at my disposal by Rabbi Moshe Silberschein, who generously shared with me his learning as well as the books in his charge. His successor, Rabbi James Le Beau, has been equally kind and helpful.

FOREWORD

The Notes and Bibliographies will reveal my indebtedness to published scholarship. Three names require special notice here. Louis Ginzberg's great monument, the seven thickly printed volumes of *Legends of the Jews*, proved to be an invaluable source of Midrashic and Talmudic references. The copious writings of Gershom Scholem are, of course, the starting point for nearly all modern work in Jewish mysticism, and I have referred often to his many publications on Kabbalah, including his articles in the *Encyclopaedia Judaica*. Among contemporary students of Kabbalah, no name is more respected than that of Moshe Idel, and no scholar's publications are more indispensable. Professor Idel's Appendix on Kabbalah in Benamozegh's Thought forms a significant contribution to the present volume.

The name of Aimé Pallière, which has already been mentioned, will figure further in the pages ahead. His fascinating spiritual autobiography, *Le Sanctuaire inconnu* (Paris: Rieder, 1926), provided my introduction to Benamozegh himself, and will interest anyone who is attracted by Benamozegh's thought and excited by adventures of the human spirit in search of transcendence. I cannot now recall how I came upon the English translation of Pallière's book, *The Unknown Sanctuary*, or why I chose to bring it along to read on the plane to France several summers ago. But I was enthralled by it; and finding myself a few weeks later in the noble city of Lyon, where Pallière was born and in which the most dramatic episodes of his spiritual drama were enacted, I was naturally drawn to the imposing, somewhat forbidding Synagogue on the Quai Tilsitt. Here, in 1892, during the closing hours of Yom Kippur, Pallière's odyssey began, and here I determined to learn something about this man's inspired teacher, Rabbi Elijah Benamozegh of Leghorn. The present volume is the result; and my obligation to the disciple is eclipsed only by that to his master.

V

I have received precious help and encouragement from several friends and colleagues, whose names I acknowledge with gratitude, even as I absolve them from responsibility for any errors or extravagances that remain: Yerachmiel Altman, Richard Brewer, Rachel Cohen, Charles Dyke, J. David Davis, Aryeh Gallin, Louis Gordon, David Green, Hanoch Guy, Gabriele Bernhard-Jackson, Karl Kalfaian, Violet Ketels, Aaron Lichtenstein, Benjamin Pinker, Donald Rosenthal, Ida Cohen Selavan, Pearl Selwyn, David Welker, and Her-

FOREWORD

bert C. Zefren. Jean-Pierre Vlaminck vetted my translation and helped
me around numerous linguistic traps. Without his aid this book would
be a poorer thing. Donald Walter identified several scriptural and literary allusions that had puzzled me. Rabbi Marc Gopin and Rabbi David Shluker supplied important information of various kinds. Rabbi
David Riceman, Rabbi Yosef Serebryansky, and Rabbi Moshe Silberschein helped me identify some of the scores of undocumented
rabbinical and kabbalistic references scattered through Benamozegh's
pages. Professor Moshe Idel was kind enough to read the manuscript
and to suggest amplifications of the documentation and improvements
of the text, for which I am deeply grateful. The scope of my obligation
to Rabbi Benjamin Holczer and Rabbi Joel Finkelstein, my friends and
teachers, would be difficult to measure.

My profoundest debt for whatever merit may be found in this
presentation of Benamozegh's masterpiece is beyond calculation, and is
recorded in the dedication.

Preface

*E*lijah Benamozegh was a very erudite and prolific writer, whose creativity was broad and multifaceted. However, one major theme permeates most of his important writings: the centrality of kabbalistic ideas, which are conceived of, not only as representing a highly evolved form of religiosity, the quintessence of Judaism, but also as the sources for both Christianity and Gnosticism. For him, Kabbalah is "an abundant source of noble and profound doctrines." Time and again these presuppositions inform his historical and phenomenological discussions. His insistence on these points qualifies him for the title of Kabbalist. But Benamozegh was a rather peculiar type of Kabbalist.

Kabbalah has often been colored by the cultural ambience within which the various Kabbalists have composed their writings. In the East, a kabbalistic-Sufi synthesis can be discerned; in Italy, an openness toward philosophical theories was much more conspicuous and significant than in Spain, or elsewhere in general. This is evident in the writings of the first Kabbalist who produced a significant corpus of writings in Italy, Abraham Abulafia. It is also present in the works of Pico della Mirandola's companion, Yohanan Alemanno, and in several sixteenth-century Kabbalists, like Rabbi Berakhiel Qafman or Abraham Yagel. This trend, which can be described as universalistic, is still evident in some of the writings of Kabbalists in the seventeenth century who, though writing outside Italy, had spent time there and absorbed Renaissance culture.

It is within this context that we can identify the particular attitude to Kabbalah found in the writings of Elijah Benamozegh. Though he did not interpret the mystical lore in accordance with philosophical terms, he repeatedly drew correspondences between the two types of discourse. By doing so, he was confident that he did not impose an alien mode of thinking on Kabbalah, nor did he think that he had discovered its sources. On the contrary, by pointing out the resemblances between kabbalistic ideas on one the hand and Neoplatonic and Gnostic ones on the other, he assumed that he was able to make a decisive argument in favor of the traditional claims as to the antiquity of this Jewish lore. Though he made use of philological and comparative arguments, Benamozegh was mainly concerned with an historical question: Is Kabbalah an ancient Jewish wisdom that, at the same time, also faithfully represents the essence of Judaism? Unlike the orthodox Kabbalists, who embraced this view as a matter of fact and attempted to counteract any opposition to it solely by means of material found in classical sources, Benamozegh combined this approach with methods taken from classical studies. Well-acquainted with many of the available texts of antiquity, in their Greek or Latin originals and also in translation, his writings constitute a *sui generis* type of erudition in Judaism, not only in the nineteenth century. He represents the most substantial instance of the impact Kabbalah had on a significant Jewish thinker who also drew much from the general culture.

A strong allegiance to kabbalistic ideas is conspicuous in Benamozegh's writings. It is not only a matter of defending the "ancient lore" against its critics, but also of advancing a more mystical vision of Judaism in general. Kabbalah contributed much to Benamozegh's own formulations concerning the nature of religion. Therefore, the questions must be asked: What is Kabbalah in Benamozegh's view? And what were the kabbalistic writings that served as the background for his thought? As far as I could check in Benamozegh's very voluminous writings, he never gives a clearcut definition of Kabbalah. This seems initially rather bizarre, given the polemic situation which provoked the writings that were produced as responses to critiques addressed to this lore. However, the absence of an elaborate definition of Kabbalah may not be so surprising. It is still a question whether modern scholarship has been able to provide a single definition that covers all the variegated types of kabbalistic literature. It is also very frustrating for the scholars who attempt to "summarize" Kabbalah as a literature in itself, to find that most of the Kabbalists themselves defined their lore as being in deep relationship to other bodies of Jewish writings. Many of their definitions have a relative component: Kabbalah is regarded, for example, as the mystical meaning of the Bible, or is conceived of as constituting part of the Oral Law. When envisioning their lore as an interpretation, most of the Kabbalists did not assume that it was an additional layer, grafted on the original or canonic text by the Kabbalists, but rather that it was the disclosure of a dimension inherent in, and crucial for, the spiritual meaning implicit in the sources. Therefore, for the Kabbalists (and I consider Benamozegh to be one of them) to define Kabbalah is to define the most spiritual aspects of the texts that constitute classical Judaism.

Like other Kabbalists, Benamozegh operates with rather broad concepts. He is less inclined to base his phenomenological and historical analysis of texts upon the strictly philological approaches adopted by modern scholarship. In other words, it is not the existence of an ancient body of writings that use a certain type of uniquely kabbalistic vocabulary that preoccupies Benamozegh, but the existence of more vague sets of ideas, either in Jewish or in non-Jewish ancient writings. For Benamozegh, the recurrence of mystical and mythical ideas in ancient Jewish texts would be conceived of as a proof of the antiquity of Kabbalah. He was not interested in creating or debating proposals concerning historical sources of Kabbalah or distinctions among kabbalistic schools.

Though he wrote in the nineteenth century, Benamozegh's style is reminiscent of some of his Italian predecessors among the Christian Kabbalists who composed their books at the end of the fifteenth and in the early sixteenth centuries. The search for the correspondence between Jewish Talmudic and mystical writings and those non-Jewish views that he considered to be influenced by them was a problematic task for a traditional Jew, as we learn from a discussion in his early *'Eimat Mafgi'a*. When addressing the question of the divine unity that is possible even on the basis of the assumption that there are ten *sefirot*, Benamozegh mentions the fact that Pythagoras asserted that the ten numbers are united to the Monad, while Plato assumed a multiplicity of ideas within the divine wisdom, and presupposed a single Demiurge. This comparison provoked a rather apologetic footnote, where he mentions that Jewish scholars, like Rabbi Menasseh ben Israel and Abraham Kohen Herrera, had already resorted to pagan authorities so that he should not be blamed for this practice. Therefore, Benamozegh explicitly identified himself, rather early in his literary career, with the style and way of thought of some of his predecessors who wrote under the influence of Renaissance culture.

It should, nevertheless, be emphasized that despite the strong resemblance between Benamozegh's pointing out affinities between ancient pagan sources and Jewish mystical ones, and those resemblances put forth by Pico della Mirandola or Johann Reuchlin, he never mentioned these Renaissance predecessors in his polemical writings. I assume that this "ignorance" is a deliberate move, one which attempted to counteract the criticisms of Kabbalah's influence on Christians. Still, to a great extent, Benamozegh's project, while structured as a direct answer to the details of the critiques of post-Renaissance authors, betrays the impact of Ficino's translations of Neoplatonic texts for the reinterpretation of Kabbalah, and it does so in a way similar to that found in the Christian Kabbalists. In fact, the philological tradition of the humanistic period encountered, in Benamozegh's response, the Florentine approach to religious truths as expressed in different versions by various religious systems. From the very beginning of Christianity the philological approach has tended to uncover religious forgeries, to construct historical schemas, and has been little inclined to seek for conceptual affinities among different religions. The Florentine thinkers and their followers, on the other hand, were less interested in historical sequences and possible forgeries, placing strong emphasis on the unity of truth. In a way quite similar to the Florentine thinkers who wrote in the Renaissance period, Benamozegh saw the *hebraica veritas* as the initiating source that influenced many of the cognate ideas found in various religions.

The Renaissance view that assumed the unity of truth seems to me to be the starting point of Benamozegh's more comprehensive and less apologetic theological project: *Israel and Humanity*. It is in this book that the universalistic tendencies that characterized the spiritual life of many of the Italian intellectuals bloomed in a very special manner. The basis of this universalism was, as in the case of the Renaissance thinkers, deeply informed by the religious faith of the author. In this case, Kabbalah, the ancient and undistorted mystical lore, is conceived of as the ideal religiosity, that was not only the pristine religion of the Jews, but also the perfect religious solution of the future. In other words, Benamozegh's universalism was of a limited type, one which reflected, nonetheless, a rather uncommon accord in the Jewish orthodox camp. It assumed a static phenomenology, that is, not so much an evolving process, but a synthesis that contains within itself the most perfect form of religion. Unlike the other European Jewish intellectuals of the eighteenth and nineteenth centuries, who saw the sublimity of Judaism in its rationalistic aspects (similar to the Western *Aufklärung*), Benamozegh emphasized the universalistic and unifying aspects of the mythical components of Judaism, understood as constituting the Kabbalah. Together with A.

PREFACE

Franck and F. Molitor, he adumbrated the twentieth-century reevalua-tion of Jewish mysticism as a vital constituent of Judaism.

(The complete version of this essay is to be found in the Appendix to this volume.)

Translator's Introduction

*I*n early April of 1919, Henry Morgenthau, Sr., the well-known financier and former United States ambassador in Constantinople, received the following letter:

> Dear Sir:
>
> By request of Mr. Emmanuel Banamozegh [*sic;* the author's son], of Livorno, Italy, I took the liberty of mailing you today under separate cover one copy of "Israel et l'Humanite," by the late Elie Banamozegh, Rabbi of Livorno, prefaced by Pere Hyacinthe, the celebrated French preacher.
>
> In sending you this work, Mr. Emmanuel Banamozegh expects to interest you in this most remarkable study on the problem of universal religion. It is to be regretted that the fact that this work is published in the French language only makes it inaccessible to the majority of the English reading public. The publication of this great humanitarian study in the English language would be of great importance, and Mr. Banamozegh would be willing to make arrangements for its translation and publishing in America.
>
> Yours very truly,
> Jacob N. Chester

What response if any this letter elicited is not known. Ambassador Morgenthau, a prominent figure in New York's Jewish community, was about to be appointed by President Wilson as chairman of a U.S. commission to investigate treatment of Jews in Poland; perhaps therefore he never got around to addressing a matter which must at least have piqued his interest.¹ At any rate, the volume arrived, and Morgenthau laid in it the letter from Jacob Chester. (Book and letter eventually found a home in the New York Public Library.) But the younger Benamozegh was to be disappointed in his wish to see a translation, and *Israël et l'Humanité* has remained inaccessible to the English-reading public till this day.

Its author, Elijah ben Abraham Benamozegh—*Eliyahu* in Hebrew, *Elia* in Italian, *Élie* in French—was born in Leghorn, in 1823, to Moroccan parents from Fez, members of a wealthy family of rabbis and merchants. A brilliant student of Torah, omnivorous for secular learning as well, he would eventually serve the important Jewish community of Leghorn for fifty years as rabbi and become widely known for his provocative, highly original writings in Hebrew, Italian, and French: biblical commentaries; studies in theology, law, history, and ethics; polemical works in defense of the Kabbalah, and its principal text, the Zohar; and the present volume, a grand synthesis of his ideas about Judaism and its place in the world, which occupied him for a decade and more but was still unfinished when he died in 1900.

To appreciate this remarkable man and his work, it is necessary to know something about the city where he spent his long and fruitful life. Leghorn was the youngest of the major centers of Jewish settlement in Italy—by contrast, most notably, with Rome, whose continuous Jewish presence is perhaps exceeded only by that of Jerusalem. Leghorn was itself a relatively new city. Sponsored by the Medicis of Florence in the mid-sixteenth century, it became the principal port of Tuscany, and from the start extended a warm welcome to Jewish exiles from Spain and Portugal. The community of Jews that grew there was for more than three centuries distinguished for art and wealth, scholarship and Kabbalah. These fruits of urban civilization and Jewish culture flourished in an atmosphere almost uniquely free of the hostilities and compulsions that then beset Jewish life elsewhere, even to a degree in Italy; for alone of the major cities where Jews lived in that relatively tolerant land, Leghorn never had a closed ghetto, and by 1800, its five thousand Jews formed fully an eighth of its population. Its superb synagogue, started in the sixteenth century, lovingly enhanced in the generations following, finally completed in 1789, was the most admired in Italy, and until its destruction by the Germans, was rivaled in Europe for architectural merit only by the great synagogue of Amsterdam.²

Such was the place in which Benamozegh lived and worked. The genial civility of Leghorn, the freedom from oppressive and demeaning restrictions, the relative ease with which Jews and Christians lived together—all this penetrated his spirit. A proud and visionary Jewish thinker with an exalted conception of his people's history and destiny, an austerely Orthodox and deeply learned rabbi devoted without qualification to Torah, Talmud, and Midrash, a penetrating mystic who consistently affirmed his perception of the centrality of Kabbalah in Jewish thought—he was, nevertheless, fully at home with Aristotle and Plotinus, Dante and Victor Hugo, Fichte and Renan. Even more strikingly, the Christian Scriptures, saints, Fathers, and modern theologians were part of his intellectual universe, part indeed of his spiritual world. No Jewish thinker of his century asserted stronger claims for the "chosenness" of the Jews and their unique importance in the religious life of mankind; but neither did any relate to the "Gentiles," especially the Christians, with greater warmth, respect, and sentiment of kinship.

In one sense, this generous perspective identifies Benamozegh as a Jew of Italy.[3] Born into a diaspora community of extreme antiquity—older, in fact, than Christianity—he shared the acculturation that was a result of over two millennia of continuous Jewish life in the same land. Unlike many of his counterparts in northern and eastern Europe, he did not fear secular learning as a threat to his Jewish orthodoxy; there was no obligation or even impulse for such an Italian Jewish thinker to have to choose between *Haskalah*—the modernizing movement which welcomed secular studies—and traditional rabbinical values. To be sure, Plato or Bossuet must necessarily occupy an inferior position to that of Torah, but they were nonetheless precious minds to be engaged, not perceived as threats to Jewish existence. In one way, this attitude may call to mind the Christian humanism of Pico della Mirandola and his friends in the fifteenth century—which also was made possible by the exceptional continuity of Italian culture and its consequent self-assurance. The parallel between Benamozegh and the *quattrocento* humanists extends to their relative tolerance of other religions—not, of course, in the sense that such religions were seen as equally valid alternatives to one's own, but rather that all serious creeds were felt to embody universal truths and could therefore be encountered with civility and even respect instead of the relentless hostility and fear that had characterized interreligious relations in the West since the triumph of Christianity.

Anyone surveying this book, however cursorily, will see at once

TRANSLATOR'S INTRODUCTION

that it is unlike other books by Orthodox rabbis. In fact, *Israel and Humanity* carries the clear stamp of its Italian ambiance. Greek philosophers and German theologians appear here alongside Maimonides and Mendelssohn, comfortably and without a trace of awkwardness; and St. Paul, or one of the Gospels, may suddenly appear, not necessarily in order to be refuted. Such a cosmopolitan perspective does not surprise us in the writings of Liberal-Reform thinkers in the two centuries since Jews began to enter the main current of European life, for the agenda of these men was precisely to pull down the barriers between what they perceived as the impoverished intellectual ghetto of medieval Judaism and the great world of European ideas and culture. Such a perspective was highly unusual, however, in an author of deeply Orthodox credentials and commitment. Even today, one does not often encounter Orthodox rabbinical thinkers who appropriate classical and Christian texts with as little self-consciousness as Benamozegh. Tone is nearly as important as substance in this matter—is, indeed, part of substance—and one is not likely to miss Benamozegh's implication that the Socratic *Dialogues* or the Pauline Epistles are neither alien nor dangerous—that whatever may be our reservations with respect to their contents or claims, we need not fear nor condescend to them—even as our attitude toward our own tradition need not be one of humble apologia, nor of that uncompromising assertiveness which is an expression of insecurity and fear, but one rather of easy self-assurance and receptivity. It is the stance of the Western humanist from ancient times forward: *Nihil humanum me alienum puto.*[4] It is Italy's best lesson to the world.

Thus Benamozegh did not feel obligated to keep at a distance the influence of such contemporary philosophers as Gioberti, Rosmini-Serbati, and Bergson, as well as Fichte and Spinoza.[5] His respect for Ernest Renan and other nineteenth-century Christian religious authors is apparent on many pages. (It is often his procedure to quote them to summarize points in his own argument.) Though the large preponderance of his citations and allusions is naturally to Torah and classic Jewish texts, among authors from his own period, it is mainly Christian thinkers whom we meet. (Mendelssohn, Friedenthal, and one or two other near-contemporary Jewish authors appear here, but they are exceptional.) This is partly a strategy, which may be explained, as we shall see presently, by Benamozegh's overall design in this work; but it contributes to the book's depiction of a Judaism firmly joined to the world of nations, not isolated from or set against this world—yet a

4

TRANSLATOR'S INTRODUCTION

Judaism that is historically authentic and ontologically unique, the Judaism of the Torah that was revealed at Sinai and its authoritative amplifications in the ongoing experience of Israel. If, therefore, his point of departure seems in one way similar to that of nineteenth-century Liberal-Reform thinkers, his conclusions are drastically and categorically different. And it is this union of traditional historical Judaism with a sophisticated embrace of universal learning—encouraged, as we have already suggested, by the singular character of the Jewish historic experience in Italy, and also by the cosmic consciousness of Kabbalah, which declared not mankind only but the entire universe the necessary object of Jewish concern—it is this spacious perspective that marks Benamozegh's life and work, and finds ultimate expression in *Israel and Humanity*.

Most Orthodox Jewish intellectuals in Benamozegh's day as for generations past, though devoted to the same rabbinically shaped culture as he, viewed Jewish life and destiny from a more restricted vantage, the consequence surely of historical memories from centuries of Jewish existence in largely hostile societies. (In significant measure, this remains true, for the parochial impulse has been reinforced, especially among religious youth and *ba'alei teshuvah*—religiously alienated Jews who have "returned" to traditional ways—by nationalistic emotions engendered by decades of struggle between restored Israel and its enemies.) It is therefore not surprising that his work has occasionally been received in traditional circles with hostility. The most notable instance of this was the condemnation of his commentary on the Torah, *'Em la-Mikra* (1862), by the Orthodox rabbinical establishment in Jerusalem and Damascus. Benamozegh discusses this episode in his Preface to Eliahu Hazan's *Zikhron Yerushalayim* (see Bibliography of Further Readings, below).[6] *Israel and Humanity* itself may even now, at least initially, jar the sensibilities of some readers unused to its author's Italian habits of mind and eclectic frame of reference. If so, we hope that reading further into the book will reveal that its Jewish Orthodoxy is as unimpeachable as its originality and contemporary relevance.

At the heart of this originality and contemporaneity is the scope of Benamozegh's sympathy, his refusal to exclude from his concern any part of the divine creation, least of all the human. This disposition, in the form it assumes in his work at any rate, is essentially kabbalistic. His perspective is universal. His subject, affirmed in the subtitle of the original edition, is religion as a human and not solely a Jewish phenomenon.[7] *Israel and Humanity* addresses itself to both Jews and Gentiles,

5

whom its author seeks to reconcile with one another in the frame of what he calls "catholic Israel." His essential thesis can be stated thus: Judaism, the recipient and guardian of God's unique, eternal revelation, has been ordained to communicate to the nations of mankind the universal essence of this revelation, which is crystallized in the Seven Commandments of the Sons of Noah. In order to fulfill this vocation, Judaism must at all costs preserve the purity of its own identity. It must form, as it were, a priesthood, a consecrated elect, to serve mankind's religious needs. This is the meaning of Israel's election; and this is why Israel itself has been given not seven but 613 laws, or *mitzvot*, many of them difficult, obscure, seemingly arbitrary, which together are intended to preserve Israel's separateness, and thus its historical identity, so that it may pursue its providential task in the common interest. This task is, in fact, the only reason for Israel's existence and persistence. Judaism itself, therefore, cannot possibly constitute "universal religion" but it must be the source and touchstone of that which validates the religion or religions of the nations. Israel and the rest of mankind are thus two entities, but the difference is one of function, not of merit. Ideally, Israel and mankind will relate to each other in a mutually advantageous symbiosis: Israel performing the awesome task of channeling God's *mitzvot* to men, serving as proximate source of authentic religion (and inversely as censor of the inauthentic); the nations of men pursuing their own diverse lives, each perhaps excelling (and providing for) the rest of mankind in its own way, as Israel does with respect to religious inspiration; all acknowledging the central "Noachide" core of God's universal Revelation or Law as the essence of the divine intention for man, and relating to one another, as they all stand before God's throne, as absolute equals.

The book in which Benamozegh fleshed out this thesis was to be the last work in a long life of creativity; and the vast unpolished manuscript he left behind became a kind of recapitulation not only of his own thought in sixty years of preaching and publishing, but of Judaism itself. As such it has been read, used, and praised.[8] The dynamic principle of its argument is complementarity, and its style is sometimes polemical and apologetic, as Benamozegh speaks to the three kinds of readers about whom he is chiefly concerned: (1) Jews, whom he wants to wean in some measure from the particularist bias of their culture and make perceive the universal sympathies it also embodies, especially through the medium of the insufficiently appreciated but liberating mysticism of Kabbalah (he is never quite explicit about this part of his intention, but it is manifest, and of the highest importance); (2) Christians, whom he wishes to persuade that Judaism, far from being obsolete and of only historical interest, contains the germ of universal religion, which can help them to renovate their own crumbling religious structures and attain a higher, juster level of faith, purified of the corruptions that came in the wake of their separation from the mother religion; and (3) those he calls "critics"—the rationalists and secularists, whom he seeks perhaps not so much to persuade as to counter, in the interest of his effort to reach Christians and Jews.

It is this agenda that dictates, or at least justifies on polemical grounds, Benamozegh's extensive use of ancient and (especially) modern, Christian sources (even for the documentation of Jewish rites), Kabbalah, and the methods of comparative religion. But, of course, no such justification or agenda really needs to be postulated, for, as we have seen, Benamozegh's own breadth of sympathy, allowed or encouraged by the humane, tolerant Italian culture into which he was born, disposed him to precisely this kind of comprehensive vision and method. One of his most characteristic and memorable pages is the one in his Introduction in which he affirms that "certain passages of the Gospels" never fail to move him deeply, that "the simplicity, grandeur, infinite tenderness which these pages breathe out overwhelms us to the depths of our soul." Similarly, in invoking, as he often does, nineteenth-century philology, comparative religion, archaeology, and other historical disciplines, he is in effect addressing the "critics" in their own language.

In his attempt to rehabilitate mystical Kabbalah, in his focus on the universalist strains in Tanakh, and in his recurring defense of the Pharisees from the historically unjustified condemnation of Christian apologetics, Benamozegh is on one level providing still another document in the centuries-long debate between Synagoga and Ecclesia. We may recall that Boethius, thoughtful Christian and sensitive philosopher, chose to keep all trace of religion out of the *De Consolatione Philosophiae*, the better perhaps to draw pagan readers to basic axioms of spiritual truth in the language they were prepared to comprehend. So Benamozegh, whose design in *Israel and Humanity* is hardly less ambitious, seeks to address committed Jews as well as committed Christians, and has crafted a dialectical language to serve this object. No reader of either kind who does not already share the author's major premises will probably be entirely happy with the result. Christian readers will find Benamozegh a warm, sophisticated, and outreaching interlocutor, but they will note that in his assessment of their theology he is uncompromisingly Jewish. Jewish readers will find him startlingly free of traditional Jewish defensiveness with respect to other religions as well as to the perceived threat to Jewish survival in "Hellenism"—sometimes unsettlingly comfortable with both, in fact—at the same time that he is obviously an authentic rabbi and profound mystic, perhaps even (as Émile Touati says of him) "incontestably in the great line of the Sages of Israel."[9]

II

Benamozegh's writings are unmistakably the work of such a man as we have been describing, nourished by such a society, embracing such a culture, advancing such a world view. His copious *oeuvre* in three languages amply reveals the breadth of his interests, though we find there a few repeated themes and characteristics that define the special shape of his thought. Inevitably there are Hebrew biblical commentaries: *Ger Tsedek* (1855), a gloss on the Aramaic version of the Torah (Targum Onkelos); *Nir le-David* (1858), a commentary on Psalms; and his principal work in this genre, a five-volume philological and philosophical commentary on the Torah, *'Em la-Mikra* (1862), which, as we have already noted, agitated the more conventional Orthodox rabbinate of Eretz Yisroel. His major work in ethics is a study in comparative religion, *Morale juive et morale chrétienne* (1867)—like the present volume and a number of shorter pieces, composed in French, which he saw as the European language of philosophy and science likely to make his work most accessible. There are other works in French and Hebrew of more modest scale, including Hebrew-language tracts on liturgical and ritual subjects and instructional material on the Oral Law for the use of students in his yeshiva at Leghorn. But most of his publications are in Italian, and deal with a broad range of historical, liturgical, and theological subjects, especially Kabbalah.

Benamozegh's pastoral life as a community rabbi, teacher, and polemicist is naturally reflected in his publications. Most of these were issued at Leghorn, often under the imprint of his own name as publisher; many appeared as occasional fascicles. *Storia degli Esseni* (*History of the Essenes*, 1865) is his principal effort in historiography. Of a projected multivolume work in dogmatic theology (*Teologia dogmatica e apologetica*), a single volume (*Dio*) was published in 1877, though the author left other portions in manuscript, where they remain, except for excerpts published in 1904. Also in manuscript, among numerous other writings, is a book on the origins of Christian dogma, which Josué Jéhouda considered "of exceptional importance."[10]

If there is a single thread, however, that runs through all of Benamozegh's work from start to finish more visibly than any other, it is Kabbalah, and the primary kabbalistic text, the Zohar. For nearly half a century he affirmed in his books and essays the exalted position he believed Jewish mysticism had occupied historically and ought to occupy in contemporary estimation. At a time when this tradition was widely neglected or depreciated, he defended it relentlessly whether against attacks by the eminent seventeenth-century Italian rabbi Leone Modena (*'Eimat Mafgi'a*, 1855) or against Samuel David Luzzatto's rejection of the antiquity of the Zohar (*Ta'am le-Shad*, 1863).

Luzzatto (1800–1865) was a versatile scholar, philosopher, and biblical exegete. He and Benamozegh have been called the most distinguished intellects Italian Jewry produced in the nineteenth century. The one was as unsympathetic to Kabbalah as the other was enthusiastic, and their controversy can be traced in a series of publications, including a volume of Benamozegh's letters to Luzzatto (1890). But the importance to Benamozegh of Kabbalah reveals itself in all his major works and in many of the lesser ones. In *Israel and Humanity*, as the reader will discover almost at once, it figures conspicuously, and is invoked very often in support of the conception of Judaism that Benamozegh develops here in such loving and elaborate detail.

What is missing from this conspectus of the writings of the preeminent rabbi of Italy in his time is a focus on halakhah per se, in isolation from its implications. It is not that the subject was less important to him than to his peers in Vilna or Jerusalem, or that his work does not continually address the Oral and Written Law of Israel—but it does so within the frames of those disciplines he found most congenial and in which he was best able to address his vision of Jewish life and destiny: biblical commentary, philosophy, comparative religion, theology, and mysticism. These are the modes of discourse in which his religious imagination most freely expressed itself, nowhere more memorably than in *Israel and Humanity*.

III

Everyone agrees that we are in the midst of a great religious crisis. This reveals itself in three ways. The conflict between religion and science is in an acute state, and therefore occupies us the most; but to this must be added the antagonism among the religions themselves, and the evolutionary changes which are occurring simultaneously at the heart of each religion.

So begins the long, provocative Introduction to this book, which Benamozegh published by itself as early as 1885.[11] In its original form, this Introduction is some two-and-a-half times as long as the version included in the complete published text, though the structure of its argument and a good part of its language are the same. He sets forth here many of the ideas the book is to develop. At the same time he outlines those contemporary crises, the principal conflicts in the religious and intellectual life of his time and place, as he perceives them, that the book is to address. To be sure, the importance of this book—or of any product of the human mind or spirit—is not necessarily contingent on the special circumstances that inspired it; but it is convenient to note these circumstances, if not simply because of their instrinsic interest, then because knowing what has brought a book into being helps us recognize the essential shape of its argument.

Benamozegh was no cloistered philosopher, despite the exotic aura of some of his mystical ideas. To the contrary, he was firmly grounded in the social, religious, and intellectual life of his time, and his occasional publications touch on such immediate public matters as controversies about pantheism or cremation, or a movement in 1870 to outlaw war. (The most intriguing of such titles is a short paper called "Bimetallism and monometallism in the Mishnah."[12]) In the documentation of *Israel and Humanity*, he often cites articles in general intellectual periodicals like the *Revue des Deux Mondes* and comparable publications of the time in France and Italy. There are dozens of references in this book to nineteenth-century European thinkers whose reputations, once green, have long ago decayed and disappeared—together, of course, with names such as Ernest Renan, Max Müller, William James, and J. S. Mill, which are still remembered and esteemed. But if we are no longer much concerned with the views of, say, Pietro Emilio Tiboni, or Joseph Salvador, their enshrinement in Benamozegh's pages and notes ensures a certain contemporaneity of reference, while we can evaluate for ourselves the merit of their ideas. And their presence here is one reason—but only one—why this book, for all its dependence on other books (principally of course Torah, in all its manifestations), never smells of library dust nor seems more literary than it should.

10

TRANSLATOR'S INTRODUCTION

The reader will notice a number of instances in which influential nineteenth-century disciplines such as ethnology, philology, linguistics, and biology leave their mark, now perhaps somewhat dated, on this book. Benamozegh is more likely than we to appeal to racial or national character to explain cultural phenomena, or to impose linguistic categories such as "Aryan" or "Semitic"—the first of these names having long ago given way to "Indo-European"—on entire cultures. He is intensely aware, in a now rather old-fashioned way, of "rationalist critics" (by which he often refers to the Higher Criticism of the Bible) as a threat to believers that must be countered. The metaphor of organic development, drawn from the immensely influential language of biology, permeated much discourse in all fields in the later nineteenth century, and Benamozegh is of his age. So we read:

> For Judaism, history is not a succession of events without connection, but rather an organism which develops, a world which acquires form, which has at its start, chaos . . . and at its end, Shabbat (the name given to palingenesis, or cyclical rebirth, in imitation of the Shabbat that followed the six days of creation).[13]

Elsewhere, he speaks of Hebraism's "theory of the natural selection of ideas." None of this is at all exceptional; and while Benamozegh's unashamed embrace of the language and discourse of his age, even as he seeks to describe what is eternal and universal, will sometimes date a sentence or an expression and remind us of his time and place, it does no violence to the vitality of his argument.

Nor, as the opening sentences of his Introduction, quoted above, show, is Benamozegh less sensitive a register of the great preoccupations and intellectual crises of his age than of its language and images.

In the 1870s and 1880s, there erupted in Germany the *Kulturkampf*, and similar agitations in Italy and France: conflicts between the new imperial, monarchical, and republican regimes and the Roman Catholic Church with respect to the church's power in society, particularly in education. At the same time, the assault on religious faith generated by recent discoveries in geology and biology proceeded without abatement throughout the Christian world, even as socialism and other rationalistic ideologies hostile to religion continued to gain adherents. In the Vatican, under the staunchly conservative Pius IX, the response to this multiple crisis was the reaffirmation and amplification

11

of traditional doctrine, as evidenced most dramatically in the Vatican Council's promulgation of the dogma of Papal Infallibility and condemnation of atheism and materialism—at the very moment that the Franco-Prussian War, which was to bring the unification of Germany and Italy and consequent consolidation of secular nationalism in both countries, exploded upon Europe. All these tremors were keenly felt by the Jews of Leghorn, we may be sure. Jewish life itself registered some of the same conflicts, and, in addition, there were the unsettling effects of the Haskalah movement in its various ramifications; the expanding influence of Liberal Judaism, with its rejection of the rabbinically sanctioned principles of scriptural and oral revelation; the still controversial challenges to normative rabbinism of the Hasidic movement. Altogether, there was ample reason for Benamozegh to begin his book by speaking of a great contemporary crisis in religion. The outlines have shifted since his day, of course, but a century and a quarter later the crisis remains, and Jews and Christians—the peoples with whom Benamozegh is most directly concerned—are perhaps no less in need of a reevaluation of their religious identities, including their perceptions of each other.

Somewhat more elusive, from our perspective at the end of the twentieth century, is Benamozegh's interest in what he calls "universal religion." The subtitle of the present work in its original edition was "Étude sur le problème de la religion universelle et sa solution" (A study of the problem of universal religion and its solution), and the author's point of departure is revealed in his third paragraph:

> Yet although it is generally agreed that religious unity is desirable, there is no consensus with respect to the authentic religion. Having long ago triumphed over ancient paganism, Christianity has not yet managed to attract all members of the human family. We are not speaking of the great Eastern religions, nor of pagan cults. . . . It is not to these that the future belongs. The religions to be reckoned with are those which have descended from Hebraism.

In our day "religious unity" is likely to connote collaboration or union among the separated branches of a particular faith—"ecumenism" is the term most often used in recent decades by Christians—but the notion of a single universal (let alone uniquely authentic) religion for all men has long since passed from serious intellectual discourse, at least in the West. In the nineteenth century, however, the matter evoked a good deal of discussion[14]—perhaps as a reaction to the fragmentation and perceived decline of Christianity, perhaps in part as a deist response to the rationalist critique of faith, and perhaps too (in some circles at least) as an expression of European political and cultural imperialism and its attendant racialism and missionary impulse. Benamozegh himself, in the passage cited above and elsewhere, seriously undervalues the vitality of the oriental religions, and even of paganism. His perspective here is Eurocentric and, as we should say, Victorian. He could not have suspected how attractive certain varieties of Buddhism and Hinduism would presently become to many in the West seeking transcendence, nor how ghastly—above all, to the children of Israel—would be the twentieth century's encounter with paganism disguised as social ideology.

We can see in the interest that the idea of universal religion aroused in Benamozegh's generation the convergence of several nineteenth-century attitudes: meliorism, optimism, rationalism, cosmopolitanism. For Benamozegh, however, the concept fitted neatly with two intellectual systems to which he was devoted, each of which plays a very prominent role in the argument of *Israel and Humanity*. One is Noachism, or adherence to a code of basic *mitzvot* that are regarded as incumbent on all mankind. This scheme is derived in the Talmud from passages of Scripture describing God's covenant with Noah. Benamozegh called this "the Noachic religion,"[15] and its very conception requires it to be a "universal religion." The other system is Kabbalah, the ancient discipline of Jewish mysticism, which embraces mankind, all of creation, and the Creator in a complex pattern of cosmic values and relationships. Both Noachism and Kabbalism are universal systems, which appealed to Benamozegh's fondness for the metaphysical, the synthetic, and the speculative. His love of the grand synthesis in particular is a kabbalistic trait. So in choosing to address the issue of universal religion, Benamozegh was seizing an opportunity to propose those two systems of Jewish thought that expressed some of his deepest convictions.

IV

Kabbalah, the essential tradition of Jewish mysticism, appears for the first time in the late twelfth century, in Provence, from which it very soon migrates to Spain.

Roughly speaking, the history of Kabbalah has been regarded
as including two main stages: the Spanish one, from the beginning of the thirteenth century until 1492 when the Jews
were expelled from Spain, and the Safedian one, which flourished [in the Safed community of Palestine] during the second and third quarters of the sixteenth century. The most
important kabbalistic systems were composed in one or another of these centers, and from there they radiated throughout the entire Jewish world.[16]

This is not the place to try to summarize even its main ideas, or to
survey the scholarly controversies surrounding their antiquity and
sources, even with respect to the Zohar, the most influential kabbalistic
text, which in its received form dates from the late thirteenth century,
though tradition declares it to have originated in the second.[17] (The
interested reader should start with Gershom Scholem's important articles in the *Encyclopaedia Judaica* and proceed to the authoritative works
by Scholem and by Moshe Idel, which are included in the Bibliographies to this volume.)

Benamozegh, for whom Kabbalah was an absolutely fundamental
part of Jewish thought, was confident of its extreme antiquity. One of
his differences with S. D. Luzzatto, to which reference has already
been made, was on the question of the dating of the Zohar. It has been
pointed out that Kabbalah was particularly important in the culture of
the Moroccan Jews, the community from which Benamozegh's family
came, and that he may have inherited some of his interest from this
source.[18] In any event, he became, in the words of Moshe Idel, "the
nineteenth-century thinker most sympathetic to Kabbalah."[19] For
Benamozegh, the attribution "the rabbis say . . . " refers to the sages
of Mishnah, Talmud, Midrash, *and* Kabbalah, who together, in his
view, constitute the authentic postbiblical expression of Torah.

But his was a decidedly uncommon point of view among Jewish
historians and thinkers of the last century, to many of whom—
influenced by the rationalistic currents of the age, some of which found
expression in the historiography of *Wissenschaft des Judentums*—Kabbalah seemed hopelessly compromised by Gnostic mystifications and
dubious theological superstitions, unworthy of their century of science
and enlightenment, and an embarrassment to a Jewry that had only
lately emerged from the ghetto to take its place in the modern world.
To traditional Orthodox thinkers, on the other hand, the Kabbalah's

elaborate conception of Deity as a dynamic hierarchy of emanations or *Sefirot* often appeared alien to the Torah, and perhaps even perilously close to violation of the supremely important principle of the unity of God. A complicating matter was the connection between Kabbalah and the zealous but erratic enthusiasm of Hasidism, which itself seemed to many in the last century both heterodox and superstitious. Even Benamozegh on one occasion (see below) seems to refer to this movement with a touch of disdain.

As Aimé Pallière points out in his Preface to the First Edition, Benamozegh's close embrace of Kabbalah undoubtedly damaged his standing in certain Orthodox circles. In *Israel and Humanity*, he often feels obliged to defend it, as though he fears that for some of his Jewish readers, his kabbalism diminishes his credibility.

> We are convinced that those who would take the trouble to examine carefully this question of the relation between Judaism and philosophical freemasonry, and the mysteries in general, would be less disposed to hold the Kabbalah in disdain, and would even consider seriously the possible role which Kabbalistic theology may have to play in the religious developments of the future. Instead of seeing in it only what the *hasidim*, the miracle-working rabbis of Russia and Poland, have prepared them to recognize, they might better perceive the real value of a teaching whose importance and antiquity are being revealed by the modern study of comparative religions. We shall not tire of repeating that the Kabbalah contains the key to the fundamental problems of modern religion. At the same time, it offers a solution for the difficulties which are encountered by the many mutually hostile Christian sects which share a concern for the reform of Christianity.[20]

Benamozegh is unyielding on this issue, which affects his essential categories of religious classification. Thus, when he wishes to cite the authentic, comprehensive tradition of Jewish thought, he usually uses the word "Hebraism" rather than "Judaism." As Pallière remarks, for Benamozegh, "Hebraism" denotes "the totality of Judaism, including, as authentic embodiments, the written and oral Law—i.e., the Bible and Oral Tradition—as well as the Kabbalah, which is the highest theological expression of both."[21]

Benamozegh invokes Kabbalah dozens of times in this book, frequently in connection with his most original and daring speculations. Kabbalah, he asserts, embodies concepts that in Judaism are esoteric though in other systems commonplace. The most significant and startling of these is the multiple manifestations of Deity:

> For the Jews (apart from the Kabbalah) the single, indivisible divine personality is always infinitely above the material creation. The Gentiles, however, feel the need to humanize the gods, to see an embodiment of the divine even on the lower stages of the scale of being. The Kabbalah allows us to see how these two impulses—the latter embodied in the plural name of Divinity (*Elohim*), the first in the uncommunicable name of the one God—are joined in the religious synthesis of Hebraism.[22]

And if God may be found in surprising places, so also may less exalted manifestations of Truth be found. Thus Kabbalah forms a bridge between Israel and mankind because it has preserved, and acknowledges, elements of primal truth that had been obscured in *exoteric* Judaism, though retained, perhaps in a corrupt form, by the "Gentiles."

> Kabbalism regards the long sojourn of the Hebrews in Egypt as a means used by divine Providence to *restore* to the religion of Israel—to incorporate in it through a selective process—all that was good and true in Egyptian religion. It points out the resemblance between the words *Mitzrayim*, Egypt, and *metzarim*, frontiers or limits, to indicate that Egypt was the nearest country to Palestine, not only geographically but also from a religious perspective.[23]

It is safe to say that most ordinary Jewish or Christian readers will have assumed that there was *nothing* that need be thought "good and true" in ancient Egyptian religion. But, declares Benamozegh, by acknowledging, long in advance of modern historians and anthropologists, that sparks of true religion had been received and preserved by the nations, even in the midst of their pagan corruptions, and that their separation from Israel was therefore relative and partial, not absolute, Kabbalah gives Israel the means of defending itself against rationalist critics, who, rejecting as unreasonable the notion of Israel's total uniqueness and postulating ideas such as the "reciprocal influence of Egypt and

Israel," are merely giving scientific authority to what "the rabbis" had long known.[24]

> Jewish enemies of Kabbalah sinned . . . in substituting a false notion of divine oneness for the authentic doctrine, for the true God is One only if He fills all beings, or, to put it better, if we worship in Him being itself, just as His universally venerated name [i.e., the Tetragrammaton] indicates.[25]

Kabbalism teaches that we must always be gathering fragments of truth wherever and in whomever we find them scattered. Thus, proselytes can instruct us as well as learn from us.[26]

Benamozegh's conclusion to this part of his discussion is more breathtaking still.

> Authentic Judaism . . . is connected to a certain extent with the pagan mysteries. The authentic Jewish tradition acknowledges both the immanence and the transcendence of God, and thus links monotheism with the reasonable element in pantheism. Belief in the unity of God, as Israel preserves it, therefore harmonizes the demands of science and the needs of religious faith. One day it will be able also to reconcile the divided churches.[27]

Kabbalah ignited or provided the occasion for Benamozegh's most provocative speculations and comprehensive claims, along perhaps with a certain heedlessness of the upsetting effect these were likely to have on more conventional religious sensibilities—unless, indeed, in adopting the methods of hyperbole, paradox, and shock that some of the ancient rabbis share with certain masters of Zen, he actually intended to agitate his readers. Those complacent in their inherited (and sometimes unexamined) conviction that between Israel and the rest of mankind is a solid barrier of faith or providential design might just respond to the sweeping grandeur of Kabbalah's great system more readily than to ordinary discourse. Whatever his intention, and however we may finally regard one or another of his kabbalistically based affirmations (or even his claims for Kabbalah itself), we may find as we read this book that Kabbalah often gives him a powerful tool for shattering that barrier, and a voice vibrating with the authenticity of centuries of intense Jewish mystical devotion.

V

But once the barrier is shown to be largely illusory, what then? If the true relation between Israel and mankind is not one of radical unlikeness, what is it? In Benamozegh's view, the answer is firmly and clearly embedded in Torah itself—and pregnant with important implications for the religious life of mankind. It is what we may perhaps call radical complementarity. It is God's design that the life of Jews be anchored in the Law of Moses, and the life of Gentiles in the Law of the Sons of Noah, based on the covenant that God established with surviving humanity after the Flood (Gn 9). But the two laws are doubly interlocking—the Noachide Law is part of the Mosaic Law (though it was of course given to all men earlier), *while the Mosaic Law as a whole has as a primary object the preservation and propagation of Noachism among the Gentiles*. That is to say, there is but a single fundamental "Law," or essential ethico-religious system, for all men, and it is distilled in the Noachide *mitzvot*. If the Jews are bound not by "seven" but by "613" *mitzvot*—the traditional numbers are perhaps in some sense arbitrary or emblematic, and the seven Noachide laws are really expansible categories—this is in significant measure because God wants to hedge round Jewish identity with such elaborate and inviolable particularism that Jewish group survival will be ensured, enabling the Jewish mission to be accomplished. The Jews are, as it were, the priests of mankind, and not only their Mosaic Law but their very group existence and survival have as their object the guarding and disseminating among men of the essentials of true religion and morality. And the divinely proposed role of the Gentiles—that is, "humanity"—in this cosmic religious drama is to enshrine Noachism at the core of their religion or religions, so that however diverse these may otherwise be (in keeping with the natural diversity among human cultures), the differences will be of the margin rather than of the essence, and *all humanity will in fact be "Noachide."*

This astonishing doctrine or myth is the mainspring of *Israel and Humanity*. Although Benamozegh affirms it to be an authentic expression of Torah, he acknowledges that it has often been obscured or ignored, and is even now not very widely understood by Jews themselves. The *locus classicus* is tractate Sanhedrin of the Babylonian Talmud, especially folios 56a–60a, where the validity of the general conception is assumed: "Our Rabbis taught: Seven precepts were the sons of Noah commanded: social laws [i.e., courts of justice]; to refrain from

18

blasphemy, idolatry, adultery, bloodshed, robbery, and eating flesh cut from a living animal" (Sanhedrin 56a).[28] The rabbis disagree on many of its details, but the code itself, which they find asserted and implied in a variety of places in the written Torah, and ordained by God for all men, is not in doubt. Equally taken for granted is that the "seven precepts" are titles merely, rubrics, which, like the Mosaic *mitzvot* in the Torah, require clarification and amplification. Thus, in the rabbinical view, Israel and "mankind" (despite deep differences of vocation) are equally the recipients of a divine code or Law. And according to R. José b. Hanina, the Mosaic Law includes in its entirety the Noachide: "Every precept which was given to the sons of Noah and repeated at Sinai was meant for both [Noachides and Israelites]" (Sanhedrin 59a).

The conception appears in rabbinical literature throughout the subsequent centuries. One such discussion of particular importance—Benamozegh refers to it often—is in the *Mishneh Torah* of Maimonides, who emphasizes its scriptural authenticity and traces most of the Noachide code back to the creation:

> Six precepts were given to Adam: prohibition of idolatry, of blasphemy, of murder, of adultery, of robbery, and the command to establish courts of justice. Although there is a tradition to this effect—a tradition dating back to Moses, our teacher, and human reason approves of those precepts—it is evident from the general tenor of the Scriptures that he [Adam] was bidden to observe these commandments. An additional commandment was given to Noah: prohibition of eating a limb from a living animal. So it was until Abraham appeared, who, in addition to the aforementioned commandments, was charged to practice circumcision.[29]

Maimonides adds to his account of these *mitzvot* a crucial corollary, also derived from Torah:

> Moreover, Moses, our teacher, was commanded by God to compel all human beings to accept the commandments enjoined upon the descendents of Noah. Anyone who does not accept them is put to death. He who does accept them is invariably styled a resident alien [*ger-toshav*]. . . . A heathen who accepts the seven commandments is a "righteous heathen," and will have a portion in the world to come, provided

that he accepts them and performs them because the Holy
One, blessed be He, commanded them in the Law and made
known through Moses, our teacher, that the observance
thereof had been enjoined upon the descendents of Noah
even before the Law was given. But if his observance thereof
is based upon a reasoned conclusion, he is not deemed a
resident alien, or one of the pious of the Gentiles, but one of
their wise men. [30]

Acceptance of the Noachide Law is as incumbent on the Gentile as the
Mosaic Law is on the Jew, and "Moses" is commanded to enforce it and
to impose the most rigorous justice on those who reject or violate it. (At
least in theory; for Maimonides does not discuss Moses' failure or
inability—let alone that of his descendants—to fulfill this awesome
charge.)

It seems quite possible that these Noachide traditions going back to
the Tannaim represent some kind of institutional reality in the ancient
world. We know that during the period when the Jews were eager and
highly successful proselytizers (fourth century B.C.E. to first century
C.E.), there is mention of a class of Gentile "sympathizers," sometimes
called in Greek "God-fearers" or "God-sympathizers" (*phoboumenoi*,
sebomenoi ton theon), who are alluded to in classical and Christian literature. How numerous they were, what role if any they played in the life
of the Temple or Synagogue, how closely they approximated the subsequent traditions of Noachism—such matters are the subject of intense
scholarly debate. [31]

Whatever may have been the precise shape of Noachism in Torah
tradition or in historical experience, the idea has periodically excited
the interest of writers concerned with the religious relationship between Israel and the Gentiles. In his recent volume *Jewish Ethics for a
Lawless World*, a work of importance, the late Rabbi Robert Gordis
stresses the universalism and truly revolutionary pluralism of the
Noachide conception:

> [The] doctrine of the Noachide Laws is extremely interesting
> from several points of view. It represents in essence a theory
> of universal religion which is the heritage of all men. Charac-
> teristically Jewish is its emphasis upon right action rather
> than right belief as the mark of the good life. Its spirit is
> epitomized in the great rabbinic utterance: "I call Heaven and

earth to witness that, whether one be Gentile or Jew, man or woman, slave or free man, the Divine spirit rests on each in accordance with his deeds" (*Yalkut Shimoni* on Jgs, sec. 42). In its all-encompassing sweep, this passage recalls the famous words of Paul: "There is neither Jew nor Greek, nor bound nor free, there is neither male nor female, for you are all one in Christ Jesus" (Gal 3:28). [But] significantly, the equal worth of all men in the rabbinic formulation does not derive from common doctrinal belief, nor does it depend upon it; it requires only loyalty to a code of ethical conduct. . . . By requiring no credal affirmation, the Noachide Laws prepare the ground for freedom of conscience.[32]

It was Benamozegh's enthusiasm for Noachism that brought him his most famous disciple, Aimé Pallière, who became his posthumous editor and, for half a century, his articulate advocate. But Benamozegh did not only revive and disseminate a fascinating though neglected Talmudic tradition. In his hands Noachism became an instrument for projecting his matured beliefs about the meaning and destiny of Judaism and the complementary meaning and destiny of Christianity (and, to a smaller degree, the other religions)—a way of reconciling the uniqueness of Israel, which is expressed in the idea of Israel's election, with the precious doctrine of Israel as a light unto the nations, with his deep-rooted universalist convictions, and with the demands of modern science and society. In his philosophy of religion, he moved Noachism from the margin to the center, seeing it not merely as a God-given yet theoretical obligation for ancient "heathens" but as an urgently necessary desideratum for modern "Gentiles," and not as a self-flattering and largely conceptual doctrine for Jews but as the very justification for Jewish existence. In this emphasis lies the daring originality of Benamozegh's encounter with the Laws of the Sons of Noah.

VI

The theme appears prominently in his Introduction, again in the ten chapters of Parts One ("The God of Israel") and Two ("The Hebraic Idea of Man"), and is elaborately developed in the climactic chapters of Part Three ("The Law").

Benamozegh's long Introduction, as we have noted, is the only section of the book to have been published during the author's lifetime, in a somewhat different form, as *Israël et l'Humanité. Démonstration du cosmopolitanisme dans les dogmes, les lois, le culte, la vocation, l'histoire et l'idéal de l'hébraisme. Introduction* (Leghorn: Benamozegh, 1885). It is a forceful apologia, parts of which are addressed directly to Christian readers, seeking to show that Judaism, so often depreciated in Christian apologetics as a strictly national religion, now largely irrelevant, in fact has a universal dimension or potentiality. Christian doctrine would often assume that since the chief function of Judaism, the preparation for Christianity, has long since been accomplished, from a Christian perspective Judaism is now of merely historical interest. This view Benamozegh counters with an elaborate, impassioned argument. Noting, for instance, that most men know of Jewish doctrines and ideals only from Christian sources, he questions whether this is reasonable:

> When it is a question of knowing the true nature of Judaism, does common sense allow us to assume that the successors of the young innovator, mostly of pagan origin, should be preferred to the authentic representatives of the ancient religion? And if the world should conclude, rightly or wrongly, that the progress of human intelligence has at certain points passed beyond the Christian ideal, is it fair to include that of Israel in the same judgment? Elementary fairness, simple logic, respect for truth, and the very interest of our religious future alike must reject such a confusion. So what, then, is in fact that Judaism which had apparently been well understood for centuries? It is only a second-hand Judaism, deposed, torn away from the source of its life, and exposed in the most crude way and without the smallest circumspection to the grossly distorting and deleterious action of the prejudiced, of doctrines and civilizations which had nothing in common with it.[33]

Benamozegh is attempting to demonstrate that Judaism, far from being self-contained and isolated, actually includes within itself the universal Noachide Law, which may in future turn out to be more relevant to the religious needs of the generality of mankind than Christianity in its present form. Thus, he anticipates his main thesis, though in an apologetic and polemical voice that is for the most part absent from the rest of the work, where he addresses himself primarily to Jews.

Pending study of the manuscript, it seems reasonable to assume that this Introduction, published fifteen years before the author's death, was the first part of *Israel and Humanity* to have been written. The body of the book follows a contracting or descending path, starting with the transcendent—God, particularly His universal nature in authentic Hebraic thought, then Man, seen from the many perspectives of Hebraic tradition; and finally Law, both Mosaic and Noachide, by which men relate to God and to one another. At last, to round out Benamozegh's elegant scheme, there is a compact Conclusion, which complements and balances the Introduction, addressing itself chiefly to Jews, and ending with an emotional peroration:

> Have courage, then, people of God. Hold firmly to your faith in the truth which has been entrusted to you. Surrounded by passion and error, you have always found in your pure ideals reasons to fight on and incentives to keep hoping. You have triumphed peaceably over attacks, traps, persecutions. Continue to refute fallacy with the teaching of your simple and luminous Law. If the learned men of today persist in condemning you, you must make your appeal to the wise men of tomorrow. The past has shown you right; the future too will justify your immortal hopes and the predictions of your Prophets.[34]

Between these fervent appeals to the two classes of readers whom he principally envisioned and about whose religious ideas his book is largely concerned, Benamozegh provides a wonderfully rich exploration of religious history, traditions and ideas, mystical concepts and biblical evidences, creation myths and messianic expectations, against a background of anthropology and ethnology, philological analysis, Talmudic and Midrashic and kabbalistic lore, European philosophy, and more. Benamozegh's agile mind is endlessly roving, comparing, touching down where it sees a likely idea or speculation. Frequently impassioned, never condescending, alert to the science of his day as to the wisdom of the ages, properly respectful of the opinions of all men, he may on occasion seem baffling or simply wrong but he is never dull.

The encyclopedic diversity of *Israel and Humanity* is especially conspicuous in the original edition of 1914, where there are long digressions or entire chapters—sometimes multiple chapters—on Kabbalah, biblical rites, angelology, pagan mysteries and initiations, primitive monotheism in "Semitic" and "Aryan" cultures, the implications of holy names when subjected to analysis, and a number of other recondite, interesting, intrinsically important matters. Much of this material is retained but a good deal is omitted from the revised edition of 1961. This second edition, here translated *in toto*, keeps the organization of 1914, though its editor Touati shifted about several chapters and parts of chapters to improve clarity. It is less than half as long as Pallière's 776-page text, which had itself been excavated from a much larger manuscript; but even so, our present text may not necessarily be less faithful to Benamozegh's intention. As Pallière points out in his Preface, Benamozegh's manuscript had become a kind of repository of his half-century of religious reflection and had never received anything like definitive editing. Alive as he was to the needs of his readers, Benamozegh would probably have approved reduction of his *summa* to a volume of practical dimensions that might serve as an introduction to his thought. Nevertheless, in due course, some or all of the material excised by Pallière, and that which was later omitted by Touati, must be brought into print and into translation: A new edition will have to be prepared from the manuscript, and modern scholarship will then be able to evaluate and if necessary revise Pallière's achievement, and take a truer measure of Rabbi Benamozegh's.

VII

Digressive as this book may be, eager as its author is to illuminate obscure corners of religious history and to disclose recondite concepts from Kabbalah, it remains a book with a clearly defined thesis, which Benamozegh unfolds with a fine clarity. The digressions—both those omitted from the second edition and those retained in it—are all of them germane to the dominant ideas; and it is with respect to Benamozegh's espousal of these ideas that the work, and its author, have mainly been remembered. William Wolf states the matter accurately:

> His fame rests . . . on his revival of Jewish "Noachism." Based on the Talmudic doctrine—and its elaboration—of the seven Noachitic laws which, unlike the rest of the Torah, were revealed as the universal law of all mankind, Benamozegh held, in the words of his famous disciple Aimé Pallière, that "Judaism is not a particular religion whose position needs to be defended against competing cults whose

errors must be demonstrated. Judaism is religion *par excellence:* all other religions, like so many special manifestations responding to the needs of different peoples, group themselves around it in more or less close relation." To the extent to which the latter have deviated from Noachism they have fallen into error and must be restored to their Biblical purity. For the rest, however, let "all the nations walk each in the name of its God. As for us, we shall walk in the name of the Lord our God forever and ever." (Mi 4:5) In this way will be brought about the spiritual unification of mankind, the fulfillment of the Messianic promise.[35]

We may ask what effect if any these Noachide conceptions have actually had on the religious life of mankind, what effect they may conceivably have in the future. To the extent that it forms an advocacy of Noachism, is *Israel and Humanity* destined to remain a theoretical construct, as distant from actual social institutions as, say, Plato's *Republic?* The question put in this form does honor to Benamozegh (who, we are told, was sometimes called by his admirers a Jewish Plato)[36] and virtually answers itself: of course, there has never been such a polity in all its particulars outside Plato's pages, as Plato perfectly well expected and in effect says; but like all great and influential conceptions, its influence over centuries on the minds of men, and therefore on their institutions, has been incalculable, even when, as in our day, some of Plato's prescriptions seem more deserving to be shunned than imitated, for he has turned out to be a grim prophet as well as an inspiring teacher. Benamozegh's philosophy, like Plato's, may have valuable lessons to teach even detached from his overarching system. But in fact, Noachism has not always been—nor, especially, is it today—solely a matter of theory.

We have already referred to the "God-fearers" of Second Temple times. It is true that over the centuries, neither Israel nor the Gentiles have rushed to embrace Noachism, as a doctrine or as a religion, though its concept has for many centuries been available in the Talmud, and from time to time its tremendous implications have surfaced to tantalize men's spirits. Benamozegh's lifelong advocacy did indeed give impetus to these ideas, and his follower Pallière espoused them vigorously, and not without effect, until his own death in 1949. But information about Noachism in Europe or elsewhere in the first half of this century is hard to find. A generation ago, we learn from Touati, there was a Noachide kibbutz at Pardailhan, near Béziers in Provence; but we know little more.[37] The matter deserves study.

In recent years, however, particularly in the last decade, Noachism has attracted more attention perhaps than ever before in modern times.[38] As of 1992, there were active groups of men and women in North America and Europe—possibly elsewhere as well—who were studying the Seven Laws, often under Orthodox rabbinical guidance, seeking to embody them in their lives, and attempting the soul-stirring project of establishing a Noachide religion. These modern Noachides number in the thousands, have congregations and leaders, assemble periodically, issue publications, are noticed in the press, and are becoming more and more visible to the world at large. It seems certain that Benamozegh, directly or indirectly, has been a significant influence on them; and although it remains to be seen how considerable or durable this fascinating religious experiment will prove, it can no longer be ignored by anyone who is interested, like Benamozegh, in the "religion of the future."

But Noachides do not simply appear spontaneously *ex nihilo*. In current reality, as in Benamozegh's conception, they are for the most part Christians or former Christians who are trying to modify or reform or adjust their ancestral religion—itself sprung from Judaism, and thus embodying already at the earliest stage of its formation the sparks of Noachism. From a crucial perspective—Benamozegh's own—the theme of Judaism and Noachism is actually the theme of Judaism and Christianity. Josué Jéhouda speaks directly to the issue:

> The chief merit of Benamozegh is to have located Israel in relation to Christianity and Christianity in relation to Israel. No Jewish thinker before Benamozegh had dared attempt, with such intellectual vigor and moral candour, this double historico-philosophical clarification. For good reasons, Jewish literature has traditionally remained silent with regard to the Christian schism; this is a taboo subject which Jewish authors cannot take up with a light heart. And yet, in order to understand the meaning of universal history as conflicts of the spirit which occur in every age, and nowadays are conducted under constantly changing labels, it is indispensable to start clarifying the ideological conflict which separates Israel from Christianity, since their interdependence, often involuntary, is sealed by an identical origin and confirmed by history.[39]

Noachism as Benamozegh conceives and advocates it is no mere
interfaith geniality, no perfunctory nod of approval toward a vacuous
"Judaeo-Christian brotherhood," no politically correct but inane formula. If, as he and other sages going back to Tannaitic times have
believed, it is founded in the Torah, and so, for Jews and Christians
alike, must embody in some way the divine will, it is also, as it
appears in Benamozegh's work, a radically upsetting conception,
which neither Christian nor Jew can seriously encounter without a
seismic shock to old assumptions and hallowed traditions. But one
can hardly imagine a more appropriate advocate; for if Jews are asked
to consider that the worship and beliefs of "Goyim," once they con-
form to Noachide principles, will be altogether as pleasing in God's
sight as their own, and—scarcely less startling—that Jews exist as
Jews mainly for the purpose of preserving and communicating the
Noachide *mitzvot* to these Goyim, it is an irreproachably Orthodox
rabbi, for whom the truth of Torah is Truth itself, who asks them to
consider these shocking notions. For though he shares with the
Liberal-Reform thinkers of his century a deep interest in Christianity
and in the relation between Jew and Christian, and is thoroughly at
home in secular learning, no one should be misled by this, for he is
essentially unlike them in his unqualified devotion to Orthodox rabbinic Judaism, which he has not the smallest wish to modify. And if
Christians and others are to be asked to reform their priorities according to a program of universal religion contained in the Torah, the
asking may as well be attempted by an Orthodox rabbi who is in
certain ways sympathetic to Jesus and to Christianity (which is, as he
points out, linguistically equivalent to a word no more alien to Jews
than "Messianism")—is deeply moved by the Sermon on the Mount,
and looks on followers of Christ without fear, hostility, or condescension, as particularly close brothers in the family of God's children.[40]
Of course, if one reads him with attention, such a man is likely to
disturb practically everyone, as did the Prophets; but perhaps like
them, he has a chance of being heard.

Heard by whom? By Christians, perhaps, whom Benamozegh
addresses in his Introduction, whose notion of Judaism may have been
painfully distorted by the terrible reproaches seared into their tradition, some of which have indeed by now been expunged or neutral-
ized. Far from having superseded Israel once and for all, such people,
Benamozegh believed, are more than ever in desperate need of Israel's
teaching.

TRANSLATOR'S INTRODUCTION

Heard equally by Jews, some of whom—ignited by the flames of their piety, enmeshed in their ancient, necessary particularism, traumatized by the Holocaust, inspired by their reborn nation—are yet disabled from relating to "humanity" in the spirit of their finest traditions. For such young Jews especially, the tolerant, pious Italian bearing his message of Jewish destiny as priestly service, who is altogether at home only in Torah but still on excellent speaking and loving terms with all his human brethren in their search for God—such a man may be a timely guide and model, may be able to open eyes to hitherto unconsidered options.

Heard finally by all of Adam's or Noah's children who have attained that stage in the unfolding of their humanity where they require the illumination of transcendence.

Such hopes may be quixotic in a world in which passionate intensity, today as ever, is encountered more often than reason, and spiritual inertia more often than either. But the line between prophecy and quixoticism is rarely fixed and never clear.

We may suppose that Rabbi Benamozegh would not have been dismayed to know that this translation of his ultimate book into the language that in our day is read by more Jews and Christians than any other comes from a publishing house with essential Christian associations, and that it appears in a series called The Classics of Western Spirituality. For Benamozegh, all human life is life of the spirit, and this life quite literally knows no limits. Cherished categories like "Jew" or "Christian" (for which we might read "Buddhist" or "Moslem") refer to functions merely, providentially arranged by the Creator to accommodate the circumstances of post-Babel mankind. "Western" and "Eastern" are distinctions of convenience. As God is one, so His creation—especially that part of it which most conspicuously shares His nature—is one; and the holy Law through which man collaborates with God in elevating himself and his world to Him is also, in its essence, one.

Israel and Humanity teems with the excited discoveries and communicated enthusiasms of a mystic for whom, in Blake's unforgettable expression, the doors of perception were uncommonly clear, and for whom, therefore, everything appeared as it is: infinite.[41] If in such a book the reader finds some extravagances and exaggerations among the innumerable provocative insights and perceptions about God, man, and Law, about religion and culture and history, he should not allow these to obscure the larger vision.

And those readers who cannot for whatever reason embrace as an agenda Benamozegh's soaring Vision of the Sons of Noah and the Sons of Israel may come to it as we come to the visions of Plato and Blake and other great seers: as a potent myth, rich with truth and trembling with possibility.

Preface to the First Edition (1914) by Aimé Pallière

I

A few preliminary remarks may be welcome with respect to the remarkable personality of the author, the subject which he addresses in this book, and the way it was composed and revised.

Elijah Benamozegh was born in 1823 in Leghorn. His family had come to Italy from Fez, and it has been suggested, with some reason, that these Moroccan roots may have provided significant nourishment to the intellectual development of a man who would eventually be called the Plato of Italian Judaism.[1] It is certain that despite his exceptionally thorough assimilation of European culture, both his work and his cast of mind always retained an oriental stamp.

His father died when he was young, and he was brought up in a deeply religious atmosphere by his mother, a woman of almost matriarchal faith, for whom he always had a touching reverence. (He evokes her precious memory in the opening pages of *Morale juive et morale chrétienne*.[2])

He was originally intended for a business career, but though he had at his disposal the means to achieve success in the field, he turned aside, while still young, to the religious and secular studies for which he felt an irresistible attraction. He was introduced to Jewish learning by Rabbi Yehuda Coriat, his mother's brother. But it would be correct to say that the young student, impelled by a passion to explore all branches of human knowledge, was his own teacher. His exceptional intelligence compensated for the lack of any precise method in his self-instruction.

PREFACE TO THE FIRST EDITION (1914)

At the age of sixteen, he contributed a preface to Rabbi Coriat's *Ma'or va-Shemesh* (Leghorn, 1839), which even then provided evidence of his precocious talent;[3] and several years later he completed his rabbinical studies with particular brilliance. Remaining in Leghorn, he devoted himself for the next half-century to a rabbinical career which was perhaps never adequately appreciated by his contemporaries.

What this man succeeded in reading and writing in his lifetime is truly astonishing. In his fragile body there burned a spirit of extraordinary power. There is no branch of knowledge that remained closed to him, no domain of intellect where his indefatigable curiosity did not enter. Authors whom he might reasonably regard as adversaries were as familiar to him as those who shared his convictions. Their ideas crowded together profusely in his prodigious memory. Indeed, if his own publications—or those writings, more numerous still, which remain in manuscript—are vulnerable to any criticism, it is precisely by reason of their *embarras de richesses*.

Yet it would be wrong to see in Elijah Benamozegh only a scholar. He was also in every sense a man of God. Far from wishing to hoard selfishly the constantly accumulating fruits of his understanding, he burned with the passion to share them with others, and saw in them only a means of fulfilling more worthily the obligations of his calling, which he pursued so scrupulously.

It is above all as a Kabbalist that Benamozegh is known; but this epithet, which he always welcomed, has harmed him considerably in the eyes of men as devoted as he to the cause of Judaism, though resolutely hostile toward this school to which he adhered. It is essential, therefore, to point out at once that the Kabbalah—which Benamozegh always considered to be "the most legitimate theology in Judaism"—is in no sense a mere mass of superstitions and puerilities, capable of distorting grievously the very religion which it purports to serve. Rather, it is a philosophical system which has more than one point of contact with Platonism and other systems, and one which a man like Benamozegh could thoroughly reconcile with modern culture. In his opinion, Kabbalism was not even a separate, discrete branch of knowledge. Instead, he readily said of it what Renan said of philosophy in general: "That it is the distillation of all departments of knowledge—the sound, the light, the vibration of that divine essence within each of them."

It is altogether understandable that a timid orthodoxy may be frightened by the unexpected support which the kabbalistic school brings to orthodox doctrines, using new weapons, often forged by its adversaries, and drawing its arguments from sources which orthodoxy has been accustomed to keep at a safe distance. For their part, secularist scholars have some reason to be surprised when they find that ideas which had seemed to them fundamentally destructive to religious belief can be embraced by a mysticism whose legitimacy it would ill beseem them to impugn, as its foundations lie in an area inaccessible to their investigations. In this paradoxical way, Kabbalism uses science to support a religion which independent thinkers had supposed to be as indefensible as all the rest. But the kabbalist is no more upset by the scholar's discomfiture than by the conventionally cautious believer's apprehension. He seeks to reassure the one while confuting the other, by means of the conciliation which he claims to effect (and seeks constantly to enlarge) between science and faith.

This position, which Benamozegh maintained all his life, and which he continually justified in his writings, gave him a unique force. Thanks to the mental discipline which he learned from the masters of Kabbalah, he found seeds for his own thought everywhere he looked. Far from fleeing from objection, he sought it out with obvious relish, analyzed it, inspected every side of it in order to enjoy the profound satisfaction of exposing its defects, and even managed to discover in it arguments in support of orthodoxy. Neither materialism, pantheism, nor atheism itself could frighten him. None of these simplistic systems dear to superficial minds, none of these massive structures of irreligion which some naively suppose to have replaced the ancient edifices of faith, deluded him in the smallest degree with respect to the structural faults which compromise their solidity in the eyes of reflective persons. He had no fear of dealing with them, and he moved along them with self-assurance and ease, taking careful account of error and truth. For him, to deny a certain conception of Divinity is not to deny God, nor is Divine Oneness subverted when God's attributes are perceived in different ways. And he was even so audacious as to show that Kabbalah can establish an inner harmony among the diverse philosophies which conceive of God, each in its own manner—and even between polytheism and absolute monotheism.

Not only do Jewish doctrines thus gain an amplitude and force which antikabbalistic exegesis is powerless to give them, but certain religious practices as well—which some persons, unaware of their authentic content, have come to consider obsolete—are thus justified, and not, in the words of our author, merely as an inheritance from our ancestors but because of their instrinsic value, their universal (even ontological) importance. "Our faith," he would often tell his children, "is clear, simple, and rational in its principles, but mysterious in its worship." But what is mysterious is not therefore absurd.

This esoteric theology, which is to Rabbi Benamozegh the authentic tradition of Jewish religious doctrine, as the Talmud is the repository of authentic Jewish religious *behavior*, thus imparts profound meaning to all Jewish precepts, to all Jewish liturgy. As he wrote to S. D. Luzzatto, "To reduce ritual prescriptions to the condition of mere national observances is to deprive them of three-quarters of their value. It is to lower God to the level of a Lycurgus or a Romulus. It is to bind the destiny of religion, which is eternal, to external contingencies, where nothing is permanent."[4]

Consequently, we see that the philosophical Kabbalism of Benamozegh enabled him to carry his researches with assurance into all corners, and that with the help of Kabbalah his faith revealed itself as spiritual courage, springing resolutely forward with absolute certitude of finding Truth. Nor was anyone able to declare with more authority than he the reconciliation between religion and science: "Grasp each other in fraternal embrace, for you are both children of heaven."

But if this posture offered great advantages, it was not without serious drawbacks as well. The illustrious Rabbi was condemning himself to be misunderstood, and even at times to see the purity of his faith called into question. As we know, his Hebrew commentary on the Torah, *'Em la-Mikra*, was rejected by the rabbis in Palestine as heterodox.[5] Moreover, the intellectual and religious discipline which he owed to Kabbalah, and to which he subordinated all human learning, including the *Wissenschaft des Judentums*, is of so special a kind that he could hardly dream of enjoying an extensive influence outside the circle of his own disciples.

Benamozegh was not a kabbalistic scholar only. Above all, thanks to his manifold knowledge—philosophical, religious, scientific—he developed a most intricate, profound, yet perfectly coordinated system, which permitted him admirably to explain Judaism in all its parts, even those which its apologists find most obscure and problematic. But he was very far from offering this system as the product of his personal intellection. For him it was nothing other than the religious edifice reared by the majestic body of biblical and traditional teachings. Judaism is not a discrete religion to be defended against rival forms of worship, as it declares their errors. It is rather Religion itself. All the others, like so many special religious manifestations answering the needs of the various peoples, gather around it, more or less closely, according as they deviate from the fundamental truths in its keeping or in some measure cleave to them. From the religious perspective, then, all mankind is organized into a very real unity, though inevitably this unity entails many diversities.

Judaism is the touchstone, the focal point of all religion, and the other modes of worship are linked to it, and therefore legitimate, to the degree that they are faithful to its principles. The study of comparative religion seems to us today to be a recent branch of knowledge. It was only in the nineteenth century that scholarship began to investigate ancient mythologies with objectivity and discrimination, and succeeded in finding in them something other than a tissue of coarse, incoherent fables, unworthy of a moment's serious consideration. But long centuries earlier, ancient Judaism had traced in its theology the outlines of that science. May we not say that the Kabbalah, which teaches us to glimpse a spark of truth beneath the name of every pagan divinity, had already given us in essence what modern scholarship has provided in detail?[6]

Is this, however, to say that in these diverse religions there are not errors to correct? Of course not. In its endless fragmentation of the idea of God, paganism—at least in its popular form—completely lost the conception of Divine Oneness, and with it the fundamental basis of human brotherhood and genuine progress. Similarly, in breaking with Israel, the great religions which issued from her have more or less deviated from the universal teachings in her keeping. To reform themselves, therefore, they must return to their origins, for it is in Judaism that may be found the key to tomorrow's religious revival. But however unfaithful they appear, they are still daughters of Judaism, and what has been sundered by ignorance, prejudice, and passion must one day be joined again.

And so, fully confident in the religious destinies of Israel, Elijah Benamozegh labored fervently to prepare the reconciliation of Christianity and Judaism, the supreme object which gave special energy to his activity, and which for all believers and thinkers will remain his best title to glory. He saw in Christianity and Islam not merely religions as such, worthy of respect like any aspiration of the human soul toward the Infinite, but a providential step toward the constitution of that universal religion which the prophets of Israel announced to mankind. So keen, in particular, were his sympathies for the Christian religion that he went so far as to say, and repeat, that if Christianity should consent to reform itself according to the Hebraic ideal, it will always be the true religion of the Gentile peoples. We may point out that the term "Christianity" was for him synonymous with "messianism," the two words having virtually the same meaning, the single difference being that the first reveals all the Hellenic influence experienced by the disciples of Jesus, and the exaggerated importance progressively attributed to this influence, whereas the second brings us back to purely Hebrew thought.

In the last days of his life, Rabbi Benamozegh enjoyed a reclusive retirement in a verdant quarter of Leghorn. When, each morning at dawn, bound in tefillin and wrapped in his ample tallis, he said his prayers, the sound of the bells in a nearby church reached him with a melodious sweetness which gave all of nature a religious voice, and it seemed that as he heard this call of Catholic bells, the great thinker prayed with a more intense fervor.

Through this silver-toned voice, which reminded him of certain lyrical verses of Dante—

> . . . come orologio che ne chiami
> ne l'ora che la sposa di Dio surge
> a mattinar lo sposo perche l'ami[7]

> [. . . like a clock which calls us
> at the hour when the Bride of God rises
> to sing her matins to her Bridegroom, that he may love her]

he felt in spiritual communion not only with all his Jewish brethren in all countries, worshiping at the same hour, but also with all believers, spread all over the surface of the earth, who, in choosing the first hours of the day for prayer, showed themselves without knowing it to be faithful disciples of the ancient masters of Israel.

It is in the Jewish tradition to regard congregational prayer as more agreeable to God than solitary worship. What emotion, therefore, and what joy must our pious master have experienced when he sensed that his own thoughts rose to God in union with those of *all* believing souls!

Nor was he unaware—and he often repeated this to his disciples—that Christian prayers frequently take their inspiration from the thoughts and sentiments of our venerable Psalms: indeed, that most of the time, they are nothing other than a translation of the Psalms themselves. In this he saw accomplished the promise of the Prophets, announcing the conversion of the nations to the true God. What consolation for the grand and venerated Rabbi, and what glory for Israel, to see the ancient Prophets and authors inspired by the Bible become the religious masters of modern peoples![8]

Truth, justice, peace, brotherhood—these are what Rabbi Benamozegh's ears heard proclaimed by each tolling of the Christian bell. The days come, as the Prophets predicted, when the world will be filled with devotion to the Lord, as water covers the sea (Is 11:9).

II

This book occupied Benamozegh for many years. In it he condensed all his religious thought, all that vast system whose chief ideas I have tried to disengage and whose broad outline I have tried to sketch. The interest which has been evoked by this publication is therefore understandable.

Yet the manuscript was very far from being ready for publication. In the state in which Rabbi Benamozegh left it, it resembled rather a vast inclusive mass, for which the author had intended to provide later on a definitive shape. It comprised not less than 1,900 large pages of compact writing, without paragraphing, editing, or division of any kind, the leaves being written on both sides, which indicates clearly that the author never considered giving it to the public in this form. The appearance of this manuscript made one think of some Talmudic tractate, its materials densely mingled, the digressions numerous, the repetitions and detours frequent. The work in this form seemed designed for oral instruction, and was, in any case, unfinished.

It would have been possible, nevertheless, to publish it in this state, correcting the language where this was indispensable and introducing necessary divisions. Alternatively, we could have recast the work entirely, exposing the essential ideas in a more literary and up-to-date form, while suppressing certain materials of secondary importance. Neither of these procedures could have pleased the author's disciples and friends.

Under these conditions, I had no choice but to employ a decidedly more difficult mode of revision, which would combine the other two in the only acceptable way. I have chosen to correct the style and to edit the work as thoroughly as possible, while following exactly the order of the original manuscript, shaping it as the author would probably have done himself had he been able. The interpolations and digressions have been removed; other materials have been shifted to their natural place. Certain passages which were apparently intended to appear later on as amplifications could only be cut out completely, for they would otherwise have extended the work unnecessarily. Nevertheless, I have thought it proper to make these excisions only when they seemed to me absolutely necessary for the orderly progress of the exposition.

The editorial labor which the present work represents is not inconsiderable. Yet it is little enough in comparison with what the subject itself seems to me to deserve. My only claim is to have made possible the publication and reception of Elijah Benamozegh's precious manuscript, which could not conceivably have been issued in the state in which it was left at its author's death.

Aimé Pallière

Introduction

I

*E*veryone agrees that we are in the midst of a great religious crisis. This reveals itself in three ways. The conflict between religion and science is in an acute state, and therefore occupies us the most; but to this must be added the antagonism among religions themselves, and the evolutionary changes which are occurring simultaneously at the heart of each religion.

The contention among religions started with Christianity's affirmation of one God and a single faith for all mankind. Until then, each people had its own special deities but acknowledged the legitimacy of foreign divinities in their own countries. Far indeed from seeking to replace their worship as false and blasphemous, people believed that each nation's duty was to worship the gods which presided over its destinies. But with Christianity—and this is the foundation of its greatest claim to glory—there was now but one religion which could secure salvation, every other form of worship having become sacrilege.

Yet although it is generally agreed that religious unity is desirable, there is no consensus with respect to the authentic religion. Having long ago triumphed over ancient paganism, Christianity has not yet managed to attract all members of the human family. We are not speaking of the great Eastern religions, nor of pagan cults, which continue to exist in other parts of the world. Although the number of their adherents far exceeds that of all the Christian churches together, it is clear that they have long been in decline and that their influence is waning and extremely limited. It is not to these that the future belongs. The religions to be reckoned with are those which have descended from Hebraism—we shall not say, as is ordinarily done, "sprung from the Bible," for they have in fact issued from Hebraism *as a whole*, that is, from the Bible as well as from the Oral Tradition;[1] and their vitality,

39

their current activity, and their future possibilities depend as much upon what they owe to Oral Tradition as upon what they owe to the Bible, perhaps even more. Unhappily, however, these daughters of the same mother are far from agreeing that this is so.

But does peace prevail at least within each of the different confessions? Not at all. Various tendencies work incessantly to disturb the inner harmony of the religions. Wherever there is no outside authority to impose silence on these discordant voices, the differences reveal themselves in broad daylight. Such is the prevailing fragmentation in religious matters that some have even concluded that the only way to solve the problem is to do away with *all* dogmatic belief—that is, to find agreement in rejection: the most conspicuous evidence of disunion and spiritual division.

In those churches where authority confronts the centrifugal impulses, unity is only apparent. One remains silent, resorts to equivocation, or gives in, but in fact the disagreement persists. Sometimes, too, the proclamation of new doctrines drives away men who were but lately among the most devout adherents. These new doctrines themselves are likely to express significant changes, which may indeed be consecrated by supreme authority and offered as mere clarifications, but which actually reveal that profound modifications have arisen in the substance of the faith—with this peculiar circumstance, that the official organs which declare these doctrines are sanctioning innovation at the very moment when they claim to be affirming the immutability of the faith.[2] Thus, the inner crisis of the religions ultimately complicates the other two conflicts.

But at bottom, we are dealing with a single, identical crisis, which is nothing other than the struggle between faith and reason—whether this latter, in trying to evaluate the world and society, finds itself at grips with traditional beliefs, or whether it undertakes to study the contradictory claims of various religions in the light of historical criticism, exegesis, and science, or, finally, whether in penetrating to the core of each religion it induces free scrutiny, and, unable to settle for the old formulas, drives the investigating mind to search for new ones which will allow it to become reconciled with faith.

II

Having noted the existence of the crisis, we may ask what will be its resolution. Will the rupture opened long ago between heaven and earth, between the ideals of religion and the realities of history, be permanent? Are we on the verge of seeing Jewish monotheism proven guilty of impotence in its three forms—Hebrew, Christian, and Islamic—and swept from the earth as polytheism was nineteen centuries ago? If so, what would replace it? Would it be rationalism? Here is not the place to discuss in detail this possibility. Many learned pages have been written on the inadequacy of pure rationalism as a religion. It has been shown persuasively that rationalism could never be the religion of a great number of men, that it is incapable of satisfying the needs of the human heart. But a more careful study would quickly reveal still more serious objections.

One would find, indeed, that Religion—devotion to and worship of the Absolute—cannot simply be a product of the human spirit. Its role being to satisfy the reason, to open to it unknown horizons and to initiate it to a higher life, it must therefore express the *entire* truth, embrace not only the totality of intelligible things but also that mysterious aspect of eternal existence which transcends, and will always transcend, our senses and faculties—which is to say, it must be *revealed*. It is clear that a rationalist religion, which would necessarily be as changeable as the faculty of reason from which it must proceed, is an impossibility. For worship implies the resolute belief that its object is unalterable Truth, without which the worship would be altogether provisional. One can scarcely imagine humanity prostrate before an altar which it knew would be overthrown the next day.

Yet let there be no mistake regarding our meaning: We do not imply that once Revelation has been accepted, the human spirit stops forever in its tracks, that it does not have more and more to investigate, whether it be the necessity of that Revelation, or the meaning and significance to be attributed to it, just as it has also to examine the claims and value of the various other revelations which invite its religious adherence. We assert only that at the heart of a revealed religion, the human spirit believes it is worshiping absolute Truth, whereas it is of the essence of a rationalist religion to avoid any assumption of this kind and to offer its faithful only temporary shelter. Besides, history is there to prove to us that all attempts at purely rational systems of worship have sunk into impotence and absurdity. The necessity of a *revealed* religion derives as much from man's nature as from God's.

Are we, then, to have a new Sinai? Will a new Law come to us from heaven? No one expects the salvation of mankind to arrive thus, for those who believe in ancient revelations obviously cannot look for a new one so long as they remain faithful to the old, and those who regard such things as mere fables would not be able to admit the possibility that *today* there might occur what has been declared impossible in the past.

What then is to be the religious future of mankind? Will man dispense with all religion? And what would be the fate of man if thus spiritually mutilated? What would happen to social institutions? It has been said very rightly that metaphysics is only theology in a short gown. Once religion proper is dismissed for good, it cannot be long till metaphysics too is sent packing. A further deplorable consequence would be the subversion of law, justice, moral beauty, virtue, freedom, heroism, and sacrifice, which are nothing but applied metaphysics, and it is hard to see how such ideas can be preserved when their unique source shall have been stopped up.

It is true of course that everyone does not immediately perceive the necessary implications of a given principle. Society has such inertia that it always requires a certain amount of time for the transformations wrought by the ideas which it accepts to become evident at last in their entire extent; but in the long run, logic always draws the consequences from premises. Already, certain free-thinkers have boldly decided to allow morals to disappear with metaphysics and to cede their place to personal interest as sole rule of conduct. Thus, inevitably, negations are linked up together, hastening men without religion all the way to the brink of an abyss.

One wonders, then, to whom mankind will turn when it has rejected as out-of-date all the traditional religions, while nevertheless it continues to feel the *need* for religion more and more insistently. To resolve this problem, a double quest is necessary, and we bid our readers undertake it now.

III

Have all the religions which free-thought today declares fallen fully revealed their potentialities? Is it, moreover, as universal religions that they have made their mark in history? With respect to Christianity and Islam, there can be no doubt. However, these two religions having presented, so to say, a double version of a single original, Judaism, since both of them claim to have fulfilled the genuine religion of Israel, it seems that *this* religion is, in its turn and de facto, doubly convicted of impotence. Nothing of the sort, however. If Christianity and Islam have given the world all that they were capable of bringing it, one cannot say as much of the Judaism which they have translated in an incomplete and faulty way. Above all, one could not claim that Judaism has ever proven itself as a universal religion. *But is Judaism in fact a universal religion?*

If Judaism had been only a purely national religion, it could not have given birth to two religions with truly universal aspirations. But it is indeed still more absurd to suppose that with its faith in one God, it could be indifferent to the destiny of mankind, so that Jesus and Mohammed were obliged to look elsewhere than in it for the idea of a single religion for all men. For though we may grant that worshipers might at first perceive their god as a tribal deity, and only later, as they see him triumphant over his competitors, perceive him as the universal God, it is absurd to imagine a unique God who would be attached exclusively to a single people and reject irrevocably all others.

But then, one will ask, what precisely is the meaning of that substitution of the Gentile nations for Israel, which was proclaimed by Christianity at the moment when it separated itself decisively from Judaism? Is it not *universal* Christian faith which replaces *national* Jewish faith? No. It is the rupture of the association of two ideas which never ceased to coexist among the Jews, the sacrifice of the second to the first: It is the submergence of Israel, the priestly people, by the Gentiles, who henceforth become, through their belief in Jesus, the sole true people of God.

We were inquiring just now if Judaism is a universal religion, and we answered affirmatively. But here in fact is the way the question should have been posed: *Does Judaism contain* a universal religion? If we formulate the problem in this way, we can find the explanation of the greatest religious phenomenon of antiquity, the key to the disputes of the first centuries of the Christian era, the solution to the crisis which confronts the various faiths at this moment, and, so to say, the last religious hope of mankind. And it is because we understand it thus that we have answered without hesitation that Judaism *is* a universal religion.

With the exception of doctrine and ethics, there is in fact nothing in the Mosaic Law which is suitable to a world religion. Everything there bears the imprint of the most exclusive particularism. One has only to imagine Judaism embraced by everyone and functioning in the completeness of its spirit and institutions to be convinced that it is not a system of worship intended for all peoples, so numerous and conspicuous would then be the practical impossibilities and anomalies. And it is this which has always deceived, and still deceives, so many persons of good faith, to the point that they are able to see in the religion of Israel only a purely national cult. But they can easily turn from their error if they will accept our invitation to inquire, with us, whether Judaism does not *possess the elements* of a universal religion. They will then recognize that it indeed contains at its heart, as the flower conceals the fruit, the religion intended for the entire human race, of which the Mosaic Law, which seems on the surface so incompatible with that high destiny, is but the husk or outer cover.

It is for the preservation and establishment of this universal religion that Judaism has endured, that it has struggled and suffered. It is with and through this universal religion that Judaism is destined to triumph. To study at close range this grand phenomenon, to disclose the connections which link the national religion to the universal in Israel, to show the mutual influence of the one upon the other—such, for the most part, is what this book is about.

IV

Let us first of all point out that the establishment of a universal religion, Judaism's ultimate aim, necessitated an exceptional strictness and severity in the particularities of Jewish religious life. Because its dream was of the *future* of mankind, it was all the more necessary for it to stand apart from mankind's *present* milieu. Glimpsing the realization of its hopes only in a very distant prospect, it was obligated to secure its faithful all the more safely against the hazards, weaknesses, and surprises of a long and arduous journey, so that when the moment should arrive, they might discharge their mission worthily. It had conceived an ideal which everything in the surrounding environment tended to put in jeopardy. It was thus appropriate for Judaism to keep judiciously out of the way of all that could divert it from its desired object.

And it is thus that this most cosmopolitan of peoples, the only one in antiquity which attained the sublime conception of a single God and a single humanity, and which, in every epoch and in every place, was given the task of restoring the family of mankind, has been considered the most selfish, and not only by the ancients, who never understood anything of its principles and institutions, but also by most of those who today study its history. Such, we repeat, is the destiny of the true

INTRODUCTION

friends of man. Their aversion to the crowd is treated as misanthropy, their respect for human dignity is mistaken for pride, and their loathing of all that is base for hate.

If one examines closely that Mosaic code which seems to raise an impassable barrier between Israel and mankind, one soon discovers the reason for those peculiar laws, which were as rigid and narrow as the end toward which they aimed was lofty and remote. The idiosyncratic religion of the Jews was a means of protecting and of realizing the authentic *universal* religion, or Noachism, as the rabbis called it: In this fact lies the explanation of all that otherwise remains incomprehensible in the doctrines, laws, and history of the Jewish people. It is this, too, which enables us to understand the advent of Christianity, that tremendous phenomenon of history, which otherwise would be an effect without a cause—or, more precisely, an effect *contrary to* its cause, since the most universal religion that the world had ever seen would have emerged from that religion which seemed on the surface to be the least universal, the least humanitarian. And to make the enigma still more insoluble, Christianity would have asserted dominion over men's souls and would have achieved its many victories precisely through invoking the beliefs of Israel, appealing to its Prophets, and claiming to be the continuator of its traditions.

But no; all is infinitely more simple. It was that very faith in the universal religion which the Jews believed was contained in its essence in their ancient doctrine, and whose sway they must one day establish, which gave birth to Christian preaching. It is this which gave the disciples of Jesus their conviction that they were the instruments of a universal mission, and the courage to pursue its fulfillment to the ends of the earth. On this point the agreement between Israel and Christianity was unalterable. In the thick of dispute about the nature of God and the Messiah, about the abolition or immutability of the Law, even though quarrels erupted and festered to the point of producing that cleavage which has lasted through the centuries, never were there differences between them with respect to the universal aspirations which they shared, the obligation to evangelize the nations and lead them to the worship of true God. Without that conviction, as fundamental and familiar to Jews as to Christians, all is mystery and contradiction in the history of the first centuries of Christianity.

So why, then, should the matter ever have been in doubt? The historian, certainly, has never questioned this intimate relationship, but has interested himself in Judaism only insofar as it might provide

45

the antecedents of the Christian religion. To be sure, Christianity, during the course of its historical development, has borrowed from foreign sources and been subject to their influence in the formation of its doctrines. But historians are agreed that it is to Judaism that we must look for the very circumstances of its birth. The various Christian orthodoxies are likewise unanimous on this point. For them, as for independent scholars, Christianity is the legitimate heir of the religion of Israel: It is Judaism's ideal which Christianity has done its utmost to attain; Judaism's assurances of the Gentile's religious calling which it has sought to realize; Judaism's Messiah and messianism which it has declared it was bringing to the nations. Here is a fact on which everyone agrees.

Having thus stated our idea precisely, let us see if Judaism, like the religions derived from it, has proven itself—if it has shown itself to be, or to possess, the universal religion. It is not the Mosaic code—that is, the priestly law which is Israel's own—which will occupy us here. No one is likely to contest that *this* religion has indeed justified itself, and in what truly extraordinary circumstances! Its astonishing vitality, its inexhaustible vigor, its capacity for endurance—in the first place, against the Jews themselves, rebellious people that they were, whom it nevertheless managed to bend to its yoke to the point of making them a people of martyrs—then, against the entire world, united through the centuries to destroy it—all this permits us to believe that such a religion has a *raison d'être* and a grand object to attain. Otherwise, it would be senseless still to speak of a philosophy of history. But it is rather to that *universal* religion, preserved by Judaism in sacred trust, that we must here give our particular attention, and inquire whether it has already given the world all that the world was entitled (according to Judaism's own principles) to expect.

V

Except for a very few recent exceptions, what is generally known of Judaism is what Christianity and Islam have said of it. It is these two religions which have presented Judaism to the world, and it is according to their picture of it that Judaism has been judged—now as something admirable, now as something contemptible. We are at liberty to believe in the correctness of this image or we may doubt its fidelity. The fact remains that Judaism has hardly ever come into direct contact with mankind. Except for one quite remarkable period of active proselytism in the century which preceded the appearance of Christianity, it has never had the occasion to disclose itself directly to the world, and to undertake by itself, without a more or less faithful intermediary, the actualization of its authentic ideal.

In fact, however, the accuracy of the image which Christianity and Islam have given of Jewish messianism is anything but definitive, and indeed quite improbable. Let us imagine Judaism at the time of the birth of Christianity, with its Scriptures, its traditions, its numerous and erudite schools of scholarship, and its sages who descend by an uninterrupted chain from the Prophets of the Babylonian captivity, and even, if we may believe their claims, from the very generation of Sinai. For centuries, its learned men have given themselves to study, night and day, in order to spread and apply the doctrines of the Torah. Suddenly a man appears. He is called Jesus. Is he a god? Is he a man? If he is God, all is settled, for he would obviously know more about the nature of true religion than all the sages of all the ages. But even if Jesus were God, can we be sure that the idea of messianism which his church ascribed to his preaching is really that which he himself espoused? To believe this, it would be necessary that the putative infallibility of the founder of Christianity should have been passed on to his immediate successors, and so up to our own days; for these unlearned Jews, strangers to the centers of Jewish learning (as the Apostles and the men of the first Christian generation have been described), could not, without a very special heavenly assistance, preserve the Jewish ideal and interpret it accurately and without deviation. It is logical to assume, as the Roman Catholic Church assumes, that a sacred institution should be protected from all error—that God, besides speaking through it to mankind, must assure the unvarying preservation of His word. But let us consider that if this principle is true, we must start by applying it to Judaism itself. We must believe that the voice from Sinai could not fail to reverberate from age to age, and that God has guaranteed to Judaism that infallibility, that supernatural presence, to which the Roman Church lays claim for itself.

If, however, Jesus was but a man, as is believed by all the other religions and all the rationalists, but also by those Christian churches, so numerous in our day, for whom the divinity of the hero of the Gospels has ceased to be a tenet of faith, is it reasonable to suppose that in evaluating Christianity we must at the same time judge Judaism, and that the Jewish religion has been so perfectly understood and so faithfully represented through the centuries by Christianity that our perspective of the one must be contingent upon our perspective of the other? Indeed, to put the matter a bit differently, can a young man, without the direct intervention of God, arrogate to himself the right to speak in the name of a very ancient people in full possession of its Scriptures and traditions? Even more, can he contradict its most categorical teachings and—despite its solemn protestations—hope to be accepted without qualification? When it is a question of knowing the true nature of Judaism, does common sense allow us to assume that the successors of the young innovator, mostly of pagan origin, should be preferred to the authentic representatives of the ancient religion? And if the world should conclude, rightly or wrongly, that the progress of human intelligence has at certain points passed beyond the Christian ideal, is it fair to include that of Israel in the same judgment? Elementary fairness, simple logic, respect for truth, and the very interest of our religious future alike must reject such a confusion.

So what, then, is in fact that Judaism which had apparently been well understood for centuries? It is only a second-hand Judaism, deposed, torn away from the source of its life, and exposed in the most crude way and without the smallest circumspection to the grossly distorting and deleterious action of the prejudiced, of doctrines and civilizations which had nothing in common with it.

VI

It is in order to make the voice of Israel heard in the present crisis that this book has been written. To achieve our object, a double motive thrusts itself upon us, for we hope our readers will include rationalists as well as messianists, or Christians, of the various churches. To the first, who may be disposed to deny Judaism any trace of universality, we must show that this religion is anything but a particularist or national cult, like those which abounded in antiquity; that, on the contrary, it forms a startling exception, and that its apparent exemption from the laws of history is in itself evidence in favor of Revelation—that is, the transcendent origin of the religion of Israel—and evidence therefore of Judaism's importance and its special role in the destinies of mankind. To Christians, we must explain the Noachide, or universal, Law which Judaism so carefully preserved, and which has been Christianity's point of departure and the dynamic force behind its preaching in the world. We must sketch for them—for Christians—the authentic

INTRODUCTION

Jewish conception of man, of the nations, and of mankind perceived as a harmonious whole.

The religious life of the future must have its foundation in some historically authentic religion invested with the mysterious prestige of antiquity. Of all the ancient religions, Judaism is perhaps the only one which claims to possess a religious ideal for all mankind. Through an exceptional circumstance of history, it has already been privileged to give birth to two great religions which at present dominate much of the civilized world, and which regard the future as theirs. The transformation which we should like to see brought about would thus be all the more easy and natural, because in reality it is a question of the very ideal which Christianity and Islam have sought to advance. Yet their work is but a copy which must be matched with the original. Wherever it may be found unfaithful, wherever it may have gone too far or fallen short—in a word, wherever we may establish that alien, extraneous ideas have succeeded in penetrating it, it will require correction. We are speaking neither of rejection nor of revolution nor of starting afresh. Christianity will always be what it claims to be, messianism; only in its unsound parts will it reform itself.

Everyone who is deeply concerned with the future of mankind dreams of a religious life which fully respects both the needs of faith and the essential principles of modern reason. One understands also the need to link our religion to the past and to uphold everything in the traditional beliefs which is compatible with these same rational principles. "It is natural," says Hartmann, "that these efforts should be connected with traditional religions, whether because it would be a hazardous and impractical undertaking to start afresh, or because the idea of historical continuity has imposed itself upon the modern consciousness as an invaluable good, impossible to replace, for the sake of whose preservation no allowable concession may appear excessive."[3]

Those artificial religious schemes and elaborate syntheses which have been contrived, far from being able to satisfy the needs of mankind, appear rather to be a sign of extreme religious exhaustion. Judaism, however, forms a perfectly homogeneous whole, and displays every desirable affinity with the two existing religions of widest extent (since it is incontestably their mother), and this most ancient religion may become the newest. A salubrious new fountain may yet emerge from the source which has already produced so much fecundating water.

Furthermore, it is clear that any religion, however reasonable, philosophical, or moral it may be, however firmly its foundations rest on reason alone, will nevertheless cut a poor figure if set beside Christianity and Islam—the first above all, with its duration of nineteen centuries, its uninterrupted line of Apostles, Fathers, Doctors, its majestic hierarchy, its claims to divine origin and infallibility. To oppose religions of such antiquity it would be necessary to bring forth another of still more impressive history and lineage. To match their long and venerable tradition and the proofs of supernatural origin which they advance for themselves, one should have to produce another tradition still older and more august, with even more authentic warrants of holiness. Finally, to rival an authority which calls itself infallible and which has existed since the year one of the Christian era, or of the Hegira (thus, in a curious sense, denying or contradicting the very principle to which it appeals), we should have to seek another embodiment of infallibility even more impressive, which, having started with the history of man on the earth, will end only with him. Now we ask once more of all those who are interested in the needs of mankind: Does there exist outside of Judaism—not in its ethnic part but in its universal—a religion which is able to meet these conditions without which nothing solid and durable could be constituted?

VII

And now we turn to the followers of the two great messianisms, Christian and Moslem. It is to Christians in particular that we wish to address a frank and respectful word, and God knows that it is with fear in our heart lest our advances be taken for hypocrisy. No! No impartial and reasonable man can fail to recognize and appreciate, as is appropriate, the exalted worth of these two great religions, more especially of Christianity. There is no Jew worthy of the name who does not rejoice in the great transformation wrought by them in a world formerly defiled. We cannot listen to the noblest and most precious names in Judaism, the echoes of its holy books, the recollection of its great events, its hymns and prophecies, in the mouths of so many millions of former pagans of all races, joined together to worship the God of Israel in churches and mosques, without feeling imbued with a legitimate pride of gratitude and love toward the God who effected such great miracles. As for ourself, we have never had the experience of hearing the Psalms of David on the lips of a priest without feeling such sensations. The reading of certain passages of the Gospels has never left us unresponsive. The simplicity, grandeur, infinite tenderness, which these pages breathe out overwhelms us to the depths of our soul; and we should easily have been won over by the seductiveness of this book if not for a special grace, and if we had not been long familiar with this thrill through the writings of our sages, by the Aggadah above all, of which the Gospel is indeed a chapter.

We can abandon ourselves all the more freely to these agreeable impressions because we are aware of returning, in them, to a realm which is in fact our own, of enjoying our own possession and being thus all the more Jewish as we do justice to Christianity. And we can then say: What does it matter that human passions have conspired, here as everywhere, to accomplish their baneful work! How important need it be that hatred, prejudice, weakness, and crime have cut an abyss of separation between Christians and Jews! The two religions themselves are and will remain sisters. The beliefs and aspirations of the soul do not know these blind repulsions, and if they are fundamentally united and interdependent, no power on earth will be able to separate them permanently. Indeed, to the contrary, they will know at the proper moment how to join their energies of spirit and intelligence, so that in serene contemplation of the truths of history and doctrine, they will recognize their original kinship, and through an appropriate alliance resume their common work for the accomplishment of their great destinies.

Why should this hope not be realized? Why should Judaism and Christianity not unite their efforts with a view to the religious future of mankind? Why should Christianity find it difficult to collaborate with this religion from which it came, whose fundamental truth it recognizes, and which possesses, to a higher degree even than itself, all the qualities of which it is so proud: antiquity, historical continuity, authority, vitality? Let it scorn to stoop to intercourse with the secular spirit of the age, let it make a point of honor not to give way to the seductions of merely human wisdom—that is understandable. But in what way would it be humiliating for it to condescend to candid exchanges with Judaism in the hope of rectifying doctrinal errors and dissipating deadly misunderstandings? Has the Catholic Church not frequently honored the proponents of heterodox ideas by debating with them in its councils? And if from these deliberations with the Jewish mother-religion could emerge a Christianity which preserved its character of divine authority—a Christianity, may we venture to suggest, all the more orthodox as it would have strengthened itself by drawing on an orthodoxy older than itself, but which, as we firmly believe, would satisfy the needs of men better than the present Christian churches can do, and which would be better prepared to provide against the perils of the future—can one imagine a happier portent for mankind, or a more admirable solution to the great religious problems of our day?

We speak particularly of Christianity because it represents a considerable fraction of humanity. Professed by the most civilized nations, it is one of the most learned religions. It was the first to seek to spread the ideals of the Prophets among the Gentiles. Consequently, it is to Christianity that belongs the honor of making the principal attempt to create a universal religion—but upon Christianity must also devolve the responsibility for failure.

VIII

Yet someone is sure to object that Christianity, rather than wishing to acquire strength and light from the ancient Hebrew religion, does not even acknowledge Judaism's right to continued existence. Has it not, from its first centuries, erected the abolition of the Law into a principle? Did it not begin its own historical existence by declaring, before all else, the downfall of Israel? This is unhappily only too true. Here, therefore, is the first point which must be clarified.

Let us recall the first days of Christianity and summarize briefly its history. Owing to causes which it would take too long to set forth, there were at that time two alternative views with respect to the Law. The older of these sought to make the Mosaic Law as obligatory for the Gentiles as for those born Jewish. The other, which finally prevailed, asserted its abolition for all, without distinction. The dominant assumption behind both these positions was that Judaism should give the world the universal religion, whether the special Law of the Jews must apply to all, or whether there should be a new law, common to Jews and Gentiles, extracted from the Mosaic code (though the code itself would be entirely abolished). Both parties agreed that there should be no separation between the old and the new religions—that, in short, Judaism and messianism were a single and identical religion. There was, indeed, between these two extreme positions, a third proposed by Paul as a temporary expedient. This consisted of a temporary, provisional toleration of Jewish rites, though these would henceforth be without any value or effectiveness. But this proposal was so inconsistent, and its duration so brief, that we need not pause over it further.

Of the two major solutions, it was thus the abolition of the Law which won out, despite the justifiable protests which this aroused. To properly appreciate this crucial fact, we must examine it along with its consequences.

To start, let us ask if these two "solutions" were indeed the only possible ones—if without one or the other of them there was no union possible between Judaism and Christianity, between the ethnic worship of the Israelites and the religion intended for the Gentiles, between the Mosaic Law and the Noachide or universal code. Did Hebraic thought not conceive of another kind of normal relation between Mosaism and messianism? Was the first of these supposed to become universal in messianic times, or was it to make way for the Noachide Law, which would henceforth apply to all men, including the Jews themselves? In truth, neither the one nor the other of these Christian solutions, advanced by the two great schools of James and Paul, corresponded to the Jewish ideal. For according to this ideal, the pagans were not to be held to the observance of the Mosaic Law, as James would have wished, and Paul was right to oppose him in this matter. But neither could the Jews abandon their own religion as Paul asked, and James was perfectly right not to exempt them from it. Both James and Paul failed to plumb farther to the genuine Hebraic conception of the messianic kingdom.

What was that conception? We hope that the present work will set it forth fully. For Judaism, the world is like a great family, where the father lives in immediate contact with his children, who are the different peoples of the earth. Among these children there is a firstborn, who, in conformity with ancient institutions, was the priest of the family, charged with executing the father's orders, and with replacing him in his absence. It was this firstborn who administered the sacred things, who officiated, instructed, consecrated. In recognition of these services, he received a double portion of the paternal heritage and the consecration, or laying-on of hands, a kind of religious investiture, which the father sometimes granted to that one of his sons (not necessarily the firstborn) whom he judged most worthy. Such is the Jewish conception of the world. In heaven a single God, father of all men alike; on earth a family of peoples, among whom Israel is the "firstborn," charged with teaching and administering the true religion of mankind, of which he is priest. This "true religion" is the Law of Noah: It is the one which the human race will embrace in the days of the Messiah, and which Israel's mission is to preserve and propagate meanwhile. But as the priestly people, dedicated to the purely religious life, Israel has special duties, peculiar obligations, which are like a kind of monastic law, an ecclesiastical constitution which is Israel's alone by reason of its high duties.

What, then, should have been the position of the first Christians with regard to this double Law? They ought to have held fast to the Jewish conception: the Law of Moses for the Jews, the Noachide Law for the Gentiles. Instead of that, what happened? Either owing to the ignorance of the Apostles (who, it is agreed, were relatively uncultured), or on account of religious fervor, or, finally, because the Noachide code, which had never received general application, was nearly unknown, only the two extreme solutions were advocated—that is, suppression pure and simple of the Mosaic code, or submission of all to that code. Throughout all the religious discussions and disagreements of the time, we can indeed only rarely discern a faint trace of the authentic Jewish system, as for example in two passages of the book of Acts (15:19–20, 21:25).

This is not the place to examine from a theological point of view the question of the general abolition of Mosaism, which preoccupied Christian thought, nor to study the unhappy consequences which resulted for Christianity itself from the suppression of a religion in which the ceremonial or ritual part—that which alone was to be cast aside—was altogether inseparable from the ethical and doctrinal part. The sects which, through their excesses, were not long in scandalizing the church; the glaring errors into which the popular faith fell; the dissensions which rent and bloodied the Christian world on the question of faith and works, on the effectiveness of grace and redemption, on free will and determinism; the obscurities which the doctrines of Christianity exhibit still—all these things are there to bear witness that if men are at liberty to be illogical, the laws of history, at least, have an intrinsic logic, and that biblical ritual, ethics, and doctrine must inevitably stand or fall together.

We address ourselves to Christians and entreat them to ponder seriously whether Judaism has not been right in declining to subscribe to the condemnation brought against it. As a matter of fact, a flagrant contradiction can be seen in the discussions of the first centuries on the rejection of Israel. On the one hand, Christianity is said to be founded on Judaism. All the voices of the church are as one in saying that it is the promises of the Prophets which have been realized in Christianity and through it. But what exactly did the prophecies announce? That Israel, guardian of messianism, would be considered by the converted Gentiles in the messianic age to be priest of mankind, and that Israel's uniqueness as people of God would be all the more assured as the truth of its mission would be generally recognized.

On the other hand, it was maintained that if the pagans entered the church, it was because the sins of the Jews compelled God to reject them and to transfer His fondness to a new Israel, recruited from among the Gentiles. As if the kingdom of God could consist of the substitution of one Israel for another! As if, in fact, the messianic promises had not been indissolubly attached to the recognition of the Israelite priesthood!

Undoubtedly, this error may be explained in a certain measure by the circumstances of the time. Israel's refusal to adhere to the new ideas and to play a role in the newly organized universal religion deprived Jewish messianism of one of its two essential factors, and thus completely altered it. Instead of mankind converted through the voice of a chosen people, there was now perceived to be a new people of God substituted for the old. But Israel's rejection of the Christian advances should at least have demonstrated that the new religion did not fulfill the conditions of true messianism. Could all Jews—with the exception of twelve fishermen, whose lack of learning was a matter of pride—be mistaken in this matter? If such were the case, then the foundations of all Revelation, and thus of Christianity, of Catholicism, would collapse irremediably; for what good is a Revelation if God does not guarantee its preservation by those trustees whom He Himself has chosen?

IX

If we now consider Judaism in its institutional expression, we may still ask whether it was right in persisting to live its own life although it had been declared irrevocably fallen. But does not the very fact of its having remained so long in existence justify its persistence? Religions, like peoples, live only if their existence has a *raison d'être*, and the life of Judaism during these last nineteen centuries has been neither weaker nor less vital nor less fruitful than formerly. How could such a phenomenon be explained, if that religion no longer had a mission to accomplish? Will we accept the explanation that orthodox Christianity occasionally offers, that Israel's continued existence is a punishment inflicted on the Jews for their obduracy? To prolong existence solely to prolong suffering is as unworthy of God as of man.

Will we subscribe to the other, slightly more humane, hypothesis, according to which the Jews have been providentially preserved as witnesses to the truth of Christianity? The evidence would yet be insufficient, for the existence of Israel does not prevent an outspoken critic from questioning the great events of Jewish history which serve as the foundation of the Christian religion. Moreover, one can ask whether the permanent disappearance of the stubborn Israelites would not have better established the putative Christian truths than their dogged opposition through the centuries. The miraculous preservation of Israel, like that of a vigorous tree which the storms have not been able to uproot, and whose life-giving seeds the winds have scattered over the whole surface of the earth, remains, then, an insoluble problem, so long as one persists in declaring its religion exhausted and without a future. But if the religions which have sought to supplant it are far from equal to the aspirations of modern times, is it certain that Judaism itself does not contain something more satisfactory? Is it not clear that it would have been contrary to all the laws of history if that religion, so radically different from paganism, had passed integrally and in all its purity into Christianity, which had replaced polytheism at the heart of the Greco-Roman world? Are men who were born pagan likely to be able not only to completely assimilate the Hebraic ideal but indeed to surpass it? This would have been contrary also to the Law which God, according to the Christian conception, observes in His intercourse with mankind, by which He conforms to the capacity of men and follows a gradual path of Revelation—a Law which, at the very start of Christianity, did not cease to govern the conduct of the Apostles, both in the position which they took vis-à-vis Judaism and in their teaching of the Christian mysteries to converted pagans.

In a word, we have to transpose to the realm of doctrine the same method of inquiry which is generally accepted as useful and reasonable on the historical and critical level: that is, the interpretation of Christianity by means of Judaism.

As for those who tell us that Christianity embodies a new revelation, do they not see that if the Christian mysteries were truly a radical innovation, then the entire system of divine Revelation would be overturned? It could no longer be a question of a unique and

56

perfect Revelation, coming, like the material creation, from the sovereign intelligence of God, but rather a series of fragmentary or partial revelations, successive and consequently capable of improvement, like human institutions and sciences. Christianity, then, to be logical, instead of regarding itself as the definitive religion of mankind, would have to expect to be replaced, in some more or less distant time, by still another. From the moment that one abandons the notion of a *unique* Revelation—with the intention of combating Judaism—there remains only the hypothesis of multiple religions, one superseding the other, by turns, as long as the evolution of humanity will last. To stop this series of revelations at a specific moment in history, on behalf of any religious system whatever, is so inconsistent that it does not deserve serious consideration.

It is sometimes claimed that Christianity has only *perfected* what had previously existed in Judaism. But then it is necessary to give up any theory based on irreducible antagonism between the preceding form and that which succeeds it, though there exists only too much of this antagonism between contemporary Christianity and Judaism. Will one say that this antagonism is due only to the blindness of the Jews, who have not been willing to acknowledge that Christianity was a wholly natural evolution of Judaism, thus obstinately rejecting the legitimate development of their own religion? But it is truly inadmissible that the Jewish people, having consented without the smallest opposition to all the evolutionary developments prior to Christianity, should have shown themselves so completely refractory to this last that only a minute and obscure minority among them accepted it.

In order to avoid disaster, however, Christian apologetics falls into another difficulty. For what does it do when the rationalist critic claims to find the origin of Christian beliefs and practices in the Asiatic religions, in Buddhism, Brahmanism, Zoroastrianism? It insists strongly on the presence in Palestine, at the time of Jesus, of the same doctrines which prevailed afterward in the church, and thus it concludes, with good reason, that it is rather *there*, than everywhere else, that we should seek the first roots of Christianity. Or is it a question, on the other hand, of stressing the value of the Christian religion vis-à-vis Judaism, and so justifying it? In that case, at the risk of contradiction, it is the *differences* between the two which are emphasized, it being well understood that on all points where the two diverge, it is Israel which is in error.

INTRODUCTION

X

We must, therefore, acknowledge that Judaism, providentially preserved through the centuries, has still something to teach mankind. Between the bewilderments of arrogant, vainglorious reason, relying upon itself, and the insatiable yearnings of the human soul groping perpetually in doubt, as if God had not revealed Himself, we believe that there exists a solution, and that only the Hebrew religion is able to furnish it. It is this conviction which has inspired the present work.

Two great lessons will emerge, we hope, from our labor. On the one hand, we shall demonstrate, contrary to the allegations of the rationalist critic, that Judaism, far from being a purely ethnic religion, has a distinctively universalist character, and that it has not ceased to concern itself with mankind and its destinies. On the other hand, we shall show that the ideal which Hebraism has evolved of man and of social organization not only has never been surpassed, but has not even been approached, except from a distance; and that it is in accepting this ideal, in reforming its Christianity on this model, that mankind, without disavowing its dearest principles, will be able to have a reasonable faith in God and in His Revelation.

We shall show that in Judaism, universality as ends and particularism as means have always coexisted, and that particularist Judaism has the very special function of serving as trustee and voice for the universal Judaism, which only a very concrete, practical, and personal religion could do. It will become clear that the greater the obstacles which Israel was obliged to overcome in order to attain the goal to which it aspired, the stronger was its impulse to withdraw into itself, the better to concentrate and focus its powers.

We shall draw freely upon biblical, rabbinical, and even kabbalistic sources. As we believe firmly that only orthodox Judaism can answer the religious needs of mankind, it is to *it* that we address ourselves, to learn if, even as it incontestably favors the yearnings of universal religion, it also possesses the necessary means to realize them. Meanwhile, we shall have recourse to the sources whose legitimacy and antiquity cannot seriously be questioned. Moreover, these ideas are so widespread, so frequently encountered in all the literature of Jewish antiquity, that even if one were disposed to reject some of them as dating from a much more recent epoch, that would not in any way jeopardize the final result at which we aim. As for the different interpretations with which modern exegesis opposes us, we believe we can affirm that none will be neglected, so that truth may dawn despite the thousand difficulties heaped up against her.

We propose, then, in this work, to seek out the universal character of Judaism, in both the speculative and practical domains. Our scheme calls for three principal divisions: God, Man, and Law.

God and Man: These are the mainsprings of Judaism, as of all religion. The means by which relations between God and man shape themselves constitute the revealed Law, in its double identity, Jewish and universal. The *instrument* is Israel; the supreme *object* is the regeneration of mankind, the establishment of the kingdom of God.

I hope that Christians will not forget that what speaks in these pages is the Judaism from which Christianity was born; that the interests of the one and of the other are interdependent; and that, finally, it is Christianity, reformed to be sure on its first model, which will always be the religion of the Gentile peoples.

And this will come about through Judaism itself. The reconciliation dreamt of by the first Christians as a condition of the Parousia, or final advent of Jesus—the return of the Jews to the heart of the church, without which the various Christian denominations agree that the work of redemption must remain incomplete—this return, we say, will occur, not as it has been expected, but in the only serious, logical, and durable way, and above all in the only way which would be advantageous to the human race. This will be the reconciliation of Hebraism and the religions which were born of it. According to the last of the Prophets, as the sages called Malachi:[4] "He shall reconcile parents with children and children with their parents" (Mal 3:24).

PART ONE:
THE GOD OF ISRAEL

1

The Unity of God

*D*id Hebraism, like all the other religions of antiquity, concern itself only with the people who professed it, or, by a unique and marvelous exception, did its religious perspective embrace all mankind?[1] This is the first question which we must ask.

Let us note first of all that even though some historical research into the formation of Jewish doctrine ascribes the notion of a single God—such as exists (and, in our view, has always existed) in Jewish thought—to a relatively recent time, such hypotheses in no way diminish the role of Hebraism in the religious history of mankind. Whatever may have been the moment when it attained its full development, there is no denying that Hebraism gave birth to the religions which are today most conspicuous in the civilized world. It is no less certain that Hebraism remains one of the most important religious doctrines and may properly expect to play a significant role in the future evolution of religious life. But for the sake of this evolution, Hebraism must be accurately understood, and we wonder if this is so, even now. Should Hebraism be perceived as a national religion only, indifferent to the rest of mankind, or can it indeed hold its own in this regard with the religions which sprang from it and which aspire—more avowedly than itself, at least on the surface—to universal influence? This is what we hope will be clarified by a careful investigation of the idea of God in Hebraism.

However remote or recent may be the texts which we shall cite, taken together they reveal such a consistency of perspective and display such lofty ideas of the nature of God and of His relations with the world, that it is difficult not to see in them something more than the normal development of the faculties of the human spirit.

And yet, in addition to the critics who seek to justify their denial of Jewish monotheism by a minute and detailed analysis of the mean-

63

ing, value, and chronology of the Scriptures, we shall also encounter others who oppose us in the name of philosophy or science, but who, without making any systematic investigation, affirm certain principles which they consider beyond dispute—but which, since they ignore experience, must be rejected as arbitrary and contrary to authentic knowledge. What they ask us, in fact, is nothing less than to assume a priori the impossibility of all those extraordinary phenomena which we call (in our view wrongly) the supernatural.[2]

Reasoning from their perspective, it would seem that the Hebrews must necessarily have been polytheists if the other Semites had been such, for there could not (we are told) be fundamental differences among the religious conceptions of peoples sharing a common origin, speaking the same tongue, and inhabiting the same territory. To support this assertion, care is taken to ignore certain undeniable proofs of monotheism among the Gentiles, which historical investigation increasingly encounters. Moreover, these critics neglect another fact hardly less incontestable, the appearance in history of individuals, and even of specially endowed peoples, who have risen so far above the level of their contemporaries that they have in fact outstripped the much slower pace of general progress. We are speaking, of course, of what is for the most part a *relative* superiority; yet it has occasionally seemed almost *absolute*. That is, these exceptionally talented persons or peoples have sometimes attained, in a certain domain, a degree of perfection which mankind in the aggregate reaches only much later if at all. It would therefore seem to be presumptuous to maintain that as regards religious ideas, the law of progress, which calls for a gradual evolution, has never been able to allow a startling exception.

With respect to monotheism, the rationalists have had to agree that there are strong presumptions that it existed in primitive Judaism, since we find traces of it among the peoples with whom the Hebrews had prolonged relations, particularly the Egyptians. "From the most remote times, up to the hermetic books," says Renan, "Egypt affirmed one God, a single living substance, eternally engendering its image, becoming two gods at the same time that it remains one God."[3] It might seem, indeed, that belief in the uniqueness of God ought to be regarded as a Jewish *borrowing*, in view of the Jews' secular contact with the Egyptians. But on that subject, some object that it is inconceivable that the Israelites should have adopted the beliefs of a people by whom they were oppressed.[4] Nevertheless, since we do in fact find monotheism at the same time among the Egyptians and Hebrews, we must choose one of two hypotheses: Either the Israelites produced monotheism by themselves or they borrowed it from the Egyptians.[5]

This last supposition is not so improbable as one might imagine at first sight, for there seems no doubt that the Hebrews endured the Egyptian yoke without too much suffering, and that they did not, therefore, have to be entirely hostile to Egyptian civilization. In fact, we see them more than once in Egypt rebelling against their liberator. The same scene recurred on the shore of the Red Sea, when they burst into reproaches against Moses:

> What have you done to us, taking us out of Egypt? Is this not the very thing we told you in Egypt, saying, "Let us be, and we will serve the Egyptians, for it is better for us to serve the Egyptians than to die in the wilderness"? (Ex 14:11–12)

They are so far from being enemies of slavery that they miss the country of their servitude, because there at least they had everything in abundance (Ex 16:3). Did Moses not say that although they left Egypt voluntarily, Pharoah also chased them away (Ex 11:1)? And Jeremiah saw in the exodus from Egypt proof of Israel's love of its God (Jer 2:2). The Exodus thus seems to have been more an act of obedience to the divine order than an awakening of the spirit of independence.

On the other hand, we see that the Israelites allowed themselves to be led astray to idolatry, following the example of their masters, which shows indeed that they did not escape assimilation. But if they did in fact adopt Egyptian superstitions, it is difficult to deny that they might also have been influenced by the more noble and elevated elements of Egyptian religion. Those of us who consider monotheism as a cultural possession which belonged to Israel in its own right need not deny these borrowings, which seem so probable. We believe that the Hebrews might well have taken from the Egyptians certain fragments of truth—"sparks," in the language of the Kabbalists—perhaps the formulations of science or theology, symbols, esthetic elements, comparable to what Christianity, as we know, later borrowed from Greek philosophy. As for the doctrines themselves which were hidden beneath this symbolism, we must remember that these were not the heritage of all Egyptians but rather the privileged possession of a small number of initiates. There is obviously a very serious difficulty if we persist in seeing these borrowings as something other than assimilations which take place naturally between systems having certain essential affinities, and which have influenced each other, so that it is impossible to determine which doctrine is tributary to the other.

In point of fact, if the Hebrews had actually received from the Egyptians not only some particular truths but monotheism itself, we should have to suppose that Moses himself, unintimidated by the austere rules which would have regulated his putative initiation into the Egyptian mysteries, must have drawn upon Egyptian piety to divulge among his brethren the great doctrine of the uniqueness of God. This doctrine, which among the Egyptians was reserved for a few adepts, would thereby have become the faith of all Israel, and the lowest of these slaves, treated as beasts of burden by the meanest of Pharaoh's subjects, would have known as much of religious truth as the high priest of Isis and Osiris. If rationalists find this hypothesis appealing, we must ask them to admire at least the truly extraordinary aptitude of these Hebraic tribes for appropriating what was most exalted in the Egyptian theology but had remained totally unknown to the immense majority of the people among whom they lived.

We believe, however, that it would be more reasonable to maintain that inasmuch as monotheism was in Egypt the privilege of certain wise men only, its Jewish manifestation should not be regarded as an importation from that country. In teaching it to the Hebrews, Moses was more probably drawing upon the antecedent Patriarchal tradition, which would explain the ease with which he made himself heard.

But let us now address our subject proper: What *was* this God of Israel, whose distinguishing characteristic, by universal consent, is oneness or unity? This oneness should be seen from two perspectives: first, with respect to the divine nature itself (the purely metaphysical aspect); then, by contrast with polytheism (the doctrinal core of a universal religion). In other words, we shall first of all consider the belief in the oneness of God's nature, in God as a unity, and then we shall study the Hebraic belief in God as unique, unlike any other reality.[6]

Spirituality and the Hebrew Conception of the Divine Personality

No one denies that faith in the unity of God exists in modern Judaism. The question is whether this belief was also at the core of early Judaism. In our opinion, there can be no doubt of it. The well-known verse of Deuteronomy, "Hear, O Israel! The Lord is our God, the Lord is one" (Dt 6:4), can, we believe, have no other meaning.[7] The translations "The Eternal is our only God" or "The Eternal is *the* only God," which one sometimes encounters, are contrary to the genius of the Hebrew language. (To express this latter idea, Hebrew regularly uses other expressions.) According to Leone Modena, the verse means that God is, in Himself, an irreducible reality, without multiplicity of any kind, without plurality of substance or attribute.[8]

One could, of course, object that this doctrine is too lofty a metaphysical conception for so early a time. But such a priori judgments have no more place in exegesis than in historical science. It is facts themselves which ought to be drawn from guiding principles. The study of ancient religions shows us, moreover, that they were not unfamiliar with these elevated ideas. The only explanation, in our opinion, which altogether accounts for the existence of pure monotheism among the first Israelites should be sought in the peculiar aptitude of these early ages to lay the true foundations of knowledge, in both the speculative and practical domains. But what we must surely observe is that this special faculty is to be found among the Gentiles only in the most ancient times, whereas it has continued among the Jews throughout all the course of their history. Besides, however exalted may have been certain beliefs of the pagans, they invariably lacked that universality which has always existed and is always best asserted from generation to generation in the doctrines of Israel. Instead of being surprised that the Hebrews were able so early to attain religious conceptions of such purity, we should rather inquire why these conceptions were corrupted and obliterated so rapidly among the Gentiles.

On the other hand, the prohibition of all images, which took root so quickly in the Hebraic religion, must have its *raison d'être* in an unfailingly spiritual conception of God. The idea of the unity of God seems to us inseparable from the belief in His immateriality. Hebraism came also to conceive of a perfect unity, an indivisible monad, as a first principle in *man*, at the base of human life and thought. This is the sense of the word *yehida*, "sole, unique," which is one of the names of the human soul in the rich psychological vocabulary of the Bible. Now it is generally acknowledged that men's ideas of God develop in conjunction with their ideas of man. Is it possible that the Jews could have imagined this perfect oneness in man without finding it at the same time in his Creator?

THE UNITY OF GOD

The last Song of Moses contains a passage which expresses this idea of oneness most explicitly:

See, then, that I, I am He;
There is no god beside Me.
I deal death and give life;
I wounded and I will heal. (Dt 32:39)

This text clearly attributes being to God alone, and admirably paraphrases the Tetragrammaton.[9] A people capable of giving to its God a name of such incomparable metaphysical depth, since it designates Being in Itself, Being first and everlasting, in which the infinite multitude of finite things find their source, their harmony, their final end—such a people would have no trouble grasping this other metaphysical idea of the oneness of God in His essence. And in passing, we ask of the critics who refuse to acknowledge monotheism in early Judaism, if one can reasonably maintain that this God of the Hebrews, whose name excludes in the most categorical way any trace of plurality, and seems in fact to embrace all finite existence in order to declare nothing less than absolute Being, could nevertheless have been regarded as only a local, national divinity, a mere rival of the Baals and Molochs.

In short, the idea of the personality of God necessarily implies that of the unity of substance. Now the critics are so far from denying that Judaism has acknowledged the personality of God as to claim that this doctrine is a Semitic importation unknown to other peoples. Some will object—though vainly, we think—that Christianity, which postulates a trinity of *persons* while maintaining the unity of God's *substance*, demonstrates that unity of *both* divine personality and substance is not inevitable in a religious system. We ask merely if the knowledge that each of these three Persons has of the other two does not necessitate that they merge in a higher unity. If so, it is evident that this name "person" is therefore used very improperly, and that each of them, *separately*, is not God, for the authentic divine personality, the sole true object of worship, remains always a oneness, above this triple modality. But if, to the contrary, one persists in affirming that these three "persons" are perfectly distinct, one cannot at the same time affirm the unity of substance and monotheism. Despite all theological subtleties, we should then find ourselves in the presence of what might best be called *tritheism*.

THE UNITY OF GOD

The Theory of Emanation in Hebraism

The theory of emanation is particularly interesting because it contains a double concept: polymorphism (or the pluralist element in Divinity) and immanence.[10] Let us see if Hebraism does not contain something of the sort, and if the Pentateuch itself does not furnish us with solid foundations for constructing such a system. This at least is what kabbalistic theology affirms; for despite denials from all sides, Kabbalism has the merit of being the first school to declare that the theory of emanation can be found in the Bible.

The first trace which we can discern of it there is in the very word which Genesis uses to designate the act by which God created the world: the verb *bara*. Though some authors have incorrectly seen in this term proof of creation *ex nihilo*, others, principally Ibn Ezra,[11] have pointed out that it conveys precisely the opposite sense: cutting, separating, quarrying, or drawing out from something which is preexistent.[12] Now why do angels, as well as human souls, not appear among the creations of which Genesis makes mention if not because both are supposed to belong to the divine world? In many passages of the Bible, angels are identified with Divinity. The only possible explanation of this is the presence of a doctrine of emanation entailing the progressive, hierarchical descent of beings. Whenever the act of creation is described, it is as a spiritual emission from the Creator. Thus it is with respect to the human soul:

> The Lord God formed man from the dust of the earth. He blew into his nostrils the breath of life, and man became a living being. (Gn 2:7)

Similarly, on a lower level, the animals and plants live only by the breath which God transmits to them, and die when He deprives them of it:

> Take away their breath, they perish and turn again into dust; send back Your breath, they are created, and You renew the face of the earth. (Ps 104:29–30)

The heavens and all that lives there exist only through His mighty breath (Ps 33:6).

As for immanence, a doctrine less abstruse than the preceding, we may expect to find it expressed more clearly still in the Bible. The angels are God's agents in the creation. It is through them that He remains in communication with the universe. It is wrong to say that they are intended to fill a void between the Creator and His visible works, and should be regarded as subordinate instruments to the First Cause, which itself is always unapproachable. To the contrary, the angels appear as the *extension* of Divinity in nature, as His actual presence—or, as the Midrash says, His own members, His own organs.[13]

What could be more striking than the name "life of the worlds" given to God by Hebraism, which in fact constantly ascribes to Him all natural phenomena? Nowhere is God thought of as an isolated being which, having accomplished the work of creation, handed over control of the universe forever to the laws which He had established. These laws are regarded as the expression of an unending intercourse between cause and effect. They constitute the Divine as it exists here, the *Shekhinah*, God inhabiting His creation. Here we are far indeed from that abstract unity without communion with the totality of creation which we have been told is Semitic monotheism.

Whoever takes the trouble to investigate with care the way in which the Bible conceives the relations of God with the world will be struck to see how it is that simple, primitive orthodoxy ultimately finds itself in agreement with the most advanced science. Addressing itself to this question, humanity has gone through three successive phases. At first, it imagined a god or gods doing everything in the manner of men, and everything in nature therefore seemed miraculous. Then it conceived of God separate from the world and controlling it by means of general laws, which—by a kind of final anthropomorphic intervention by the Creator—are occasionally suspended, giving way to miracles. Finally the human spirit perceives God and the universe joined by the bonds of emanation. Nature and miracle, general law and its exception, come together in a higher law. Hebraism, anticipating this advance of human thought, has taught nothing else. For it, the miracle, echo of birth and prelude to renewal (palingenesis), marks the passage from one order of things to another. It is the hyphen which fills any gap in uninterrupted creation. Modern science, in its effort to join the part with the whole, Pan with the monad,[14] is consistent with the fundamental assumptions of Hebraism. This most ancient of religions can thus fairly hope to become universal, precisely because it is able to transcend the alleged philosophical impossibility of linking Greek and Hindu doctrines with biblical monotheism.

THE UNITY OF GOD

We can now see how those who reject the Kabbalah as a foreign importation, under the pretext of defending pure Jewish doctrine, do ill service to their own cause. For ultimately, the Kabbalah alone is capable of restoring harmony between Hebraism and the Gentile world. It is particularly noteworthy that on their common ground, what is everyday doctrine among the Gentiles is esoteric to Jews, while what for them is popular and commonplace is secret instruction for the pagans. For these last, truth has been a thing of mystery, as for Christians it is a matter of faith, and for Jews the subject of learning.

To illustrate this with an example, we may cite the cherubim of the Tabernacle (Ex 25:18–20).[15] In discussing the Hebraic conception of divine spirituality, we mentioned the revulsion against images which is so pervasive. And yet here we find two figures placed in the most august part of the sanctuary. To be sure, these cherubim are carefully hidden by the veil, but nonetheless their wings shield the mysterious "cover" or "throne of mercy." What does this odd anomaly signify? It seems to us that we have here two material symbols from the Kabbalah, one of whose noblest truths they undoubtedly represent. But at the same time, they seem to us to belong, both as idea and as material image, to the popular religion of the Gentiles. This is why such figures were forbidden everywhere else in Israel, while these two, unique exceptions, had to remain shielded from all eyes.

In the development of religious thought, we shall ascribe to the Semites—or rather to the Israelites—the pure monotheist doctrine, free of the philosophical speculation dear to Indo-Europeans; and to these latter peoples we shall attribute the development of symbolism and the mythological element. For the Jews (apart from the Kabbalah) the single, indivisible divine personality is always infinitely above the material creation. The Gentiles, however, feel the need to humanize the gods, to see an embodiment of the Divine even on the lower stages of the scale of being. The Kabbalah allows us to see how these two impulses—the latter embodied in the plural name of Divinity (*Elohim*), the first in the incommunicable name of the one God—are joined in the religious synthesis of Hebraism.

The Influence of Proselytes in Israel

Some consideration of the influence which Gentiles have exercised upon Hebraism is surely appropriate in a book which aims to throw light on the authentic Hebraic conception of God and on the notion of universal religion which proceeds from it. The proselytism which we find in all periods of Israel's history seems to be one of the providential means which have served Israel's universal vocation, and through which the Jewish and Gentile worlds have constantly affected each other.

It is not for nothing that over long centuries, an uninterrupted flow of pagan blood has mixed with Jewish blood, and that each proselyte in becoming converted has contributed his own impulses and personal sentiments to the Israelite heritage. Jewish proselytism could come about only when minds on both sides opened themselves to giving and to receiving. Israel, having lost its political independence, has nevertheless imposed on its conquerors not its own laws but the Eternal Law. Nor has Israel failed to receive in exchange that which its own civilization was capable of welcoming.

It is certain that in the intellectual domain as in the physical world, anyone endowed with a very strong life-force can resist the influence of his milieu. He can then assimilate to his own nature what is strictly suitable to it. This will even become an indispensable condition of his growth. For it is too simple to say merely that environment forms the personality. What happens is that the personality absorbs from the external world what is necessary to its full development. And in this law of assimilation, it is the strongest and noblest personality which transforms into its own substance what is inferior to it, not only for the sake of thus attaining the perfection inherent in its nature, but also in order that the foreign element which serves it, and which it assimilates, may itself be elevated and refined through this same process. Such is the way of all progress, human as well as cosmic. This is what Kabbalism indicates by the beautiful expression "elevation."[16]

Elsewhere in this book we shall investigate the influence exerted by Hebraism on the pagan world. Here, we are concerned with the influence of the Gentile peoples upon Israel. Kabbalism regards the long sojourn of the Hebrews in Egypt as a means used by Divine Providence to *restore* to the religion of Israel—to incorporate in it through a selective process—all that was good and true in Egyptian religion. It points out the resemblance between the words *Mitzraim*, Egypt, and *metzarim*, frontiers or limits, to indicate that Egypt was the nearest country to Palestine, not only geographically but also from a religious perspective. Others have interpreted the gold and silver vessels taken by the Hebrews from the Egyptians (Ex 12:35–36) as a symbol of religious borrowings, or, as we put it at the start, of sparks

72

brought back to their original hearth. The fact that the Roman Senate, when it wished to proscribe oriental religious importations, included in the same condemnation both Egyptian *and* Jewish superstitions demonstrates that the close kinship between these two religions impressed others. Indeed, recent discoveries in Egyptology dealing with religion and social institutions have revealed parallels so surprising that to some, the very uniqueness of Mosaism has seemed to disappear.

But if that kind of Judaism which is crippled by the rejection of crucial elements of its tradition is in an extremely poor position to defend itself against the weapons which modern historical scholarship wields, such is not the case with respect to Jewish orthodoxy as a whole. At a time when the discoveries of science on this point could scarcely have been foreseen, Hebraism had already answered existing objections with its theory of the natural selection of ideas. The resemblances which scholars have discovered between the Jewish and Egyptian religions, far indeed from astonishing us, fully justify what the rabbis said about the reciprocal influence of Egypt and Israel.

Exodus tells us of certain *God-fearing* servants of Pharoah who, believing in the predictions of Moses, arranged for their own servants and cattle to be sheltered against the plague of hail (Ex 9:20). The epithet is all the more remarkable for it recalls the later one which would designate pagans converted to Judaism. We see also that at the time of departure from Egypt, a multitude of people went along with the Hebrews (Ex 12:38). These were no doubt persons who had only recently detached themselves more or less completely from paganism; but their influence on the Hebrews is, in any case, attested by the Bible. The Zohar tells us that this influence persisted a long time after the period of wandering in the desert, and, in fact, that all the religious errors which have haunted Israel for so many centuries come from this source.[17] To be sure, Moses could not have been unaware of the dangers which such contact held for his people, yet he did nothing to spare them these dangers. He did not fear to accept the Egyptian multitude among the Israelites because, presumably, he thought that the advantages which might be expected of them outweighed the possible disadvantages.

What were these advantages? It was not only among the Hebrew masses that the influence of these proselytes made itself felt; it was also among the intellectual elite. From the midst of this multitude of strangers there occasionally arose a distinguished mind, an Egyptian priest or philosopher, who found among his Israelite companions some men capable of understanding him. And what resulted from this union of spirits avid for truth was assuredly a very different thing from the manufacture of a golden calf. Scripture gives us a remarkable example in the relations of Moses with Jethro, his father-in-law. Truly, we must ask ourselves how else to explain—without compromising the very principle of the Mosaic revelation—this influence exercised over Moses by the priest of Midian. A legend from the Midrash teaches us how important was the role the rabbis assigned to Jethro—nearly incredible, in fact, when we remember that he was a pagan.[18] According to this legend, Moses' rod bore the holy name of God engraved in its wood. This rod had been given by Adam to his son Seth, who transmitted it to his own successor; and passing thus from hand to hand over the course of the generations, it fell eventually into the possession of Jethro, who planted it in his garden. It is there that Moses saw it and succeeded in uprooting it from the soil, which no one hitherto been able to do. This fable is sufficiently transparent that we may easily penetrate its inner meaning. The sequence of transmission which brought Moses' rod from Adam to Jethro is that of religious tradition. Since it is from Jethro that Moses received this rod bearing the holy name, symbol of the new revelation, Jethro is therefore one of the founders of Israel. Such is the truth, a little hard perhaps for the national pride, which the Midrash has wrapped beneath the veil of allegory.

Scholarship has detected traces of Tyrian or Phoenician symbolism in the ornamentation of Solomon's Temple, as it has found, in a later time, resemblances between the grandiose visions of Ezekiel and certain Assyrian myths. Neither of these relationships should surprise us. It is made clear in the book of Daniel that during the Babylonian period the flower of Israelite youth were conversant with the science and literature of the Chaldeans (Dn 1:3–4). Later still, in the time of the rabbis, we find some of the most illustrious sages said to be descended from foreigners: Rabbi Akiba from Sisera, Rabbi Meir from Haman. Moreover, we need hardly recall that a number of renowned rabbis were themselves pagans by birth who had converted to Judaism: such men as Shemaiah and Abtalyon, last descendents of Sennacherib, and teachers of Hillel, the glory of the Synagogue; and Onkelos, who translated the books of Moses into Aramaic.[19]

The rabbis tell us about the conversion of distinguished persons, sovereigns and philosophers, even entire populations. Although we are likely to attribute a large part of these claims to exaggeration, there is no doubt that Jewish proselytism penetrated the pagan world deeply, and that by diffusing the great principles of Israel, it produced a spiritual climate which later contributed significantly to the spread of Christianity. But what is no less certain is that Judaism too profited from these relations with the Gentiles, since these same rabbis acknowledge, freely and often, that they in their turn are greatly indebted to pagan scholars and sages for the comprehension of certain texts, and even of questions relating to the most important religious beliefs.[20] And there is a curious but quite understandable contrast here. However reluctant these rabbis may be to listen to the smallest word from heretics, from those who have deserted the faith, whom they carefully distinguish from the pagans, supposing (with good reason) that prejudices and sectarian passions will probably obscure their judgment—just so eager are they preserve an open mind for receiving illumination from Gentile sages, even in matters in which they themselves are past masters. They understood—and, let it be said in passing, this remains equally true in our day—that their religious faith could receive assistance more easily from strangers free of all preoccupation with sectarianism, from wholly independent thinkers, than from Jews, more or less liberal in posture, who strive to reconcile science and religion by means of arbitrary compromises, but succeed only in misrepresenting both of them at once; just as it is less perilous for a ship to reach the high sea than to hug the dangerous coastline, at the risk of splintering on the rocks.

For Kabbalists, it is always the same kind of sorting out, the same selecting that Judaism itself must engage in, whether, through dispersion among the Gentiles, it gathers and incorporates the fragments of truth wherever it finds them scattered, or whether it attracts to itself minds with monotheistic tendencies, and so augments the ranks of Israel by admission of proselytes.

The proselyte remained faithful to the special character of his people in retaining those of his native religious ideas which were compatible with the faith of Israel, while the polytheists remained in error through the corruptions of their system and the exaggerations of their natural dispositions. Similarly, Jewish enemies of Kabbalah sinned through the contrary excess, in substituting a false notion of divine oneness for the authentic doctrine, for the true God is One only if He fills all beings, or, to put it better, if we worship in Him Being itself, just as His universally venerated name indicates.

We must now address a few words to those who might be tempted to object that if Moses had contemplated this kind of comprehensive religious goal, he would have encouraged and not forbidden mixed marriages, since such unions could have done more for the intellectual and moral elevation of the pagan peoples than outright preaching, for which such marriages would have been the best preparation. But who does not see that in such a situation, the small drop of Israelite blood would soon have disappeared in the great arteries of mankind? The breath of Israel would have been smothered, and its mission would not have been accomplished. And so, in order to protect the integrity of Jewish existence, it was determined that scrupulous precautions be taken; and, in fact, a great number of Jewish precepts have had, if not this specific object, at any rate this result. Besides, we must distinguish between the natural disposition, so to say, of a people, and its level of culture. If a propensity toward monotheism is the characteristic trait of the Jewish people, it does not at all follow that the Jews had attained an intellectual level which would permit them to mingle with the other civilized peoples without harming their own originality. This Jewish nation, which had attained the purest monotheism not through philosophical speculation but by virtue of natural instinct, while remaining capable of assimilating complementary principles of culture which came to it from outside, would have yielded place to another people, endowed perhaps with more brilliant qualities, and would have been bereft henceforth of those very qualities which had constituted its ancestral greatness. We should then have seen flourishing in Israel the admirable faculties which produce distinguished scholars and renowned philosophers, but it would have meant the end of the spontaneous impulse which produces apostles, visionaries, and prophets—that is, precisely that genius which was Israel's to give to the human race. The destiny of the Hebraic genius and of faith in the unity of God would thus have been gravely compromised. Shem, with his religion of principles and the absolute, would have disappeared before Japheth, who would have been satisfied with the relative and with devoting himself to analysis.

But the very judicious laws of Moses on proselytes and marriages have preserved the integrity of the Israelite religion, and, as we shall see, they have also saved the religion of mankind. Thanks to these laws, the Jews have been able to keep their double nature, which has made of them a nation truly apart; they have remained a people with a remarkable character, very exclusive indeed, full of pride and passion, but at the same time the exceptional people whose extraordinary vitality finds its justification in the distinguished service which it is called

76

to render to the world, and who, without ever losing sight of what it owes itself, has nevertheless become more and more aware of its universal mission.

Israel and the Pagan Mysteries

The proselytism discussed above makes it clear that Israel had established communication with the rest of mankind, and it shows the extent of this rapprochement. These contacts of Jews with Gentiles continued without interruption during the course of Jewish political existence, and then after the dispersion. If by virtue of the geographical situation of their country and their historical vicissitudes, Jews constantly found themselves in relations with other peoples, the reciprocal work of exchange and assimilation became only more intense, it would seem, after the disappearance of the Jewish nation.

Thus, there have been three successive phases of this mutual penetration of Israel and the Gentile world: the period of political independence of the Jews; the period of foreign domination, which is conspicuous for a greater activity of proselytism, and more numerous conversions; finally, the period of the dispersion of Israel among the nations. In each of these periods, the foreign influence was felt at both extremes of society, among the masses as well as among the elite. We can even say, to better illustrate the point, that this influence manifested itself at the same time in both mythology and theology, each level of the people taking what best suited its nature: the common people, the outer or symbolic shell; the intellectual class, the doctrine concealed beneath the myth. A glance at the pagan mysteries will enable us to understand very clearly the influence of paganism upon the educated class in Israel. Perhaps we shall succeed also in dispelling certain doubts about the possibility of reconciling the duality which we have pointed out in Jewish religion with mankind's oneness of origin and the oneness of Revelation, precious teachings which are the glory and life of the Jewish religion as well as the hope of humanity.

It is demonstrable that in antiquity, wherever Israel pitched its tent, it encountered the pagan mysteries, in Egypt as in Syria, in Babylon and in Persia as in the Greco-Roman world. What precisely were these mysteries? Many hypotheses have been put forward with respect both to their historical sources and to their essential nature. What seems to us most definitely established is that they embodied (in forms suitable to the diversity of time and place which characterized their appearance) religious teachings incomparably more pure and elevated than those of the popular cults. This is a most significant consideration, when we reflect that the Jews, whose own religious beliefs were advanced in all respects, found themselves in touch with pagans who were knowledgeable in the esoteric mysteries, and in whom, therefore, they could not fail to take an interest. The resemblance between the doctrines of each was, indeed, so striking that the question must immediately suggest itself whether one had imitated the other. But perhaps, on the whole, a better explanation is that we have here two versions of a still more ancient belief, like the radiance of a single light which is reflected in different surroundings with varied colors. This original oneness of doctrine corresponds to the original oneness of the human family; the diversity of religious expressions corresponds to the eventual fragmentation and differentiation of peoples.

The most rigorous Jewish orthodoxy cannot fail to recognize the influence of the Egyptian mysteries on the lawgiver of the Hebrews; and these borrowings, in which rationalism has found a decisive objection to the Mosaic revelation, appear, to the contrary, like a ringing confirmation of our principles.

Moses seized what was in the Egyptian religion the sole possession of a hieratic caste and transferred it to Israel, a nation *entirely* priestly. Circumcision, for example, which was a distinguishing sign of initiates, became the common law of the Jews. What had been the privilege of a few adepts was henceforth the heritage of an entire people, who thus became the priests of mankind. Should we, then, be surprised that Judaism has been accused of forming a sort of freemasonry? What is certain is that the theology of freemasonry is quite similar to that of the Kabbalah.[21] On the other hand, a careful study of the rabbinic literature of the first centuries of the Christian era provides numerous proofs that the Aggadah was the popular form of a secret discipline whose initiation methods bore the most striking resemblances to freemasonry.

We are convinced that those who would take the trouble to examine carefully this question of the relation between Judaism and philosophical freemasonry, and the mysteries in general, would be less disposed to hold the Kabbalah in disdain, and would even consider seriously the possible role which kabbalistic theology may have to play in the religious developments of the future. Instead of seeing in it only what the *hasidim*, the miracle-working rabbis of Russia and Poland,[22] have prepared them to recognize, they might better perceive the real value of a teaching whose importance and antiquity are being revealed by the modern study of comparative religions. We shall not tire of repeating that the Kabbalah contains the key to the fundamental problems of modern religion. At the same time, it offers a solution for the difficulties which are encountered by the many mutually hostile Christian sects which share a concern for the reform of Christianity.

The differences pointed out by Burnouf between the Eastern churches, "which have preserved in their metaphysics a strong Alexandrian (and thus pantheist) tendency, and the Church of Rome, nearer to Judaism,"[23] prove that certain churches have been more successful in preserving the *spirit* of the ancient tradition, whereas others have rather formed themselves according to the *letter* of the Scriptures. But even the first of these categories of churches rests upon a confusion, in the sense that the "Judaism" is not authentic Judaism, which, as we have suggested, is connected to a certain extent with the pagan mysteries. The authentic Jewish tradition acknowledges both the immanence and the transcendence of God, and thus links monotheism with the reasonable element in pantheism. Belief in the unity of God, as Israel preserves it, therefore harmonizes the demands of science and the needs of religious faith. One day it will be able also to reconcile the divided churches.

2

The Uniqueness of God

Long before the Alexandrians had synthesized the ancient Olympian divinities in their system of theurgy, and before the Greek philosophers had probed the supernal problems of metaphysics, Israel had already spoken of the unity of God. Long before the early Christians, she chose martyrdom rather than worship idols. We must wonder how it could have been that in times of ignorance, barbarism, and hatred among people, men without any philosophical culture could have risen to conceptions higher than those of Socrates and Plato. Here is a phenomenon which eludes analysis and the laws of historical evolution, a fact which evades the chain of causes and effects, a unique intuition—in a word, what religious thought calls Revelation.

We have only to examine the Israelite conception of Divinity in its various aspects to find there the features of authentic monotheism. Moreover, if, in this connection, we find in all periods of Israel's history ideas of such grandeur and richness that the most advanced theology of later times has not been able to surpass them, the antiquity and originality of this monotheism will then appear to us to have been abundantly demonstrated.

The God of Israel is uncreated. "Before Me no god was formed. . . . I am the first and I am the last" (Is 43:10, 44:6). From Him alone all things derive their existence, and therefore He owes His own existence to no one. His most ancient names—*El, Shaddai*—suggest power, indeed omnipotence; and if the second of these has another meaning as well, it is one still more exalted and metaphysical. He is eternal: the heavens, the earth, and all that they contain grow old, like clothing which inevitably wears out, but He is and remains the same eternally (Ps 102:27–28). He is immeasurable, infinite: "For I fill both heaven and earth, declares the Lord" (Jer 23:24). "The heaven is My throne and the earth is My footstool" (Is 66:1). And, again, in Isaiah:

80

THE UNIQUENESS OF GOD

"Holy, holy, holy! The Lord of hosts! His presence fills all the earth!" (Is 6:3)—or, rather, "All which fills the earth is His presence!"—a more exact translation, perhaps, and more mystical. It can be shown that the name *Makom*, "Place," which the rabbis gave to God, is borrowed from the Bible. What is no less certain is that we find in Scripture the name *Ma'on*, its equivalent.[1] The Psalmist exclaims:

> Where can I escape from Your spirit?
> Where can I flee from Your presence?
> If I ascend to heaven, You are there;
> If I descend to Sheol, You are there too.
> If I take wing with the dawn,
> To come to rest on the western horizon,
> Even there Your hand will be guiding me,
> Your right hand will be holding me fast.
> If I say, "Surely darkness will conceal me,
> Night will provide me with cover,"
> Darkness is not dark for You;
> Night is as light as day;
> Darkness and light are the same. (Ps 139:7–12)

But there is more. The concept of Being in itself, of the necessity of existence, which we might be tempted to consider too abstract a notion for the Bible, is nevertheless found there very clearly expressed. First of all, is it not included in the idea of the creation, which is in effect the potential deriving from the necessary, and also in the concept of emanation, which excludes even the possibility of nothingness? But what shall we say of the Tetragrammaton? It is precisely the idea of Being which is here expressed; and this idea, glossed and confirmed by the paraphrase "I Will Be What I Will Be" (Ex 3:14), of which the Tetragrammaton is but the abridgment, surely implies the necessity of existence.[2] It is abundantly clear that for the Bible, the God of Israel is the Absolute.

Now such a notion precludes polytheism. Two absolutes are, of course, logically incompatible. According to the forceful expression in Exodus, the Absolute is exclusive and jealous: "For I the Lord your God am a jealous God" (Ex 20:5.)[3] The Lord calls Himself jealous, and declares that Jealous is His name (Ex 34:14). We have already observed that the prohibition of all images shows that the God of Moses is infinite. A finite being, even immaterial, could always, if necessary, be represented symbolically under a perceptible form provided that this form indicated the appropriate, recognizable qualities of the being. But how could an image be contrived for the unique Being whose infinite attributes are infinite in number (as Spinoza says), or whose ministers and angels are without number, to use the language of the Bible (which expresses, we believe, the same thought)? The absurd, monstrous idols, the multiple and fantastic images of paganism bear witness to that impossibility. In a well-known passage, Strabo says that Moses forbade the physical representation of God because his god was nothing less than the totality of things, Nature.[4] This text is important because it establishes that the impression made by Mosaism upon cultivated pagans was precisely that which would later be conveyed by the Judaism of the Kabbalah. But Strabo errs in seeing in the Mosaic conception only the *immanent* Divinity, the *Shekhinah*, and not the *transcendent* aspect of God. If the deity of the Hebrews had not been the Infinite but Nature, it would have been capable of represention; for however great and powerful it might be, it would be finite, and there is no reason why something finite may not find an equivalent image in the world of finite things. The fact remains that the God of Israel is unique, whether, like the Greek geographer, we perceive in Him the totality of created things, or whether we worship Him as the Infinite, according to the way of the Jews.

It is important to observe that God's attributes are not deduced from a well-defined theological system; they appear rather as intuitions, resulting from prayer and worship. This very absence of philosophical speculation is an evidence of the religious genius of Israel. A recent author has pointed out an example of this even in Genesis:

The first book of the Bible, in which the creation and early life of mankind are represented by means of ancient traditions and religious and philosophical myths, is like a poetic sketch, an anticipation of rational, empirical cosmogony. For whoever, without pausing over details, can see to the bottom of things, to the mythic form, there appears the idea of evolution from the abstract to the concrete, like the embryonic form of a truth which physics and metaphysics will eventually have to demonstrate. Moreover, if it is compared with the creation myths of other religions, and even with the poetic and religious myths of the Greeks, the biblical Genesis surpasses all in elevation and penetration. This is why Kant,

Goethe, Hegel, and even Haeckel spoke of the Bible only with great veneration.[5]

The divine attributes which the Scriptures reveal to us, like the accounts of events in Genesis and in the teachings of the Kabbalah, do not form part of a definite, harmonious system. As we have said, one must see in them an intuition of the religious soul of Israel. But whether we take each one separately, or bring them together, they all declare the existence of the unique and absolute God.

God as Creator of the Universe and of Mankind

One thesis favored by certain critics recognizes in the religion of Israel a supreme god, but one whose supremacy does not exclude the existence of other, less powerful deities, who preside over the destinies of other peoples. Even if we should be attracted to this theory, that would still not prove that Jewish belief was not ultimately monotheistic. In fact, this conception of a superior God upon whom the lesser divinities are dependent suggests the idea of an articulated structure in which the lower functions are organized under the direction of a sovereign authority.

But apart from this consideration, it is easy to see that if certain secondary powers are regarded in the Bible as, in a sense, Godlike, the elements *themselves* of Divinity, the various perfections of the Absolute, belong only to the sole supreme God. Majesty, wisdom, beauty, goodness, are worshiped only as divine attributes, or rather as emanations of God in the world, as making up the *Shekhinah*. In fact, such an irreducibly divine act as (for example) the creation is never attributed to other than God alone, never to another being of any sort.

In the narratives of Genesis, we can discern a very particular care to avoid anything which might suggest that the entire creation were not the exclusive work of God. Although the Bible affirms the existence of angels who carry out very important missions, and who are, perhaps, for the sacred authors, only the personifications of divine ideas, as Philo asserts, they are never represented as performing demiurgic acts and even their origin, as well as every aspect of their own existence, is passed over in complete silence. It is the same way in the Prophets; and although, indeed, according to some modern critics, what we hear in Genesis is only the echo of the prophetic teachings, the Israelite conception of God is always that of the unique Being, author of all things.

> You alone are the Lord. You made the heavens, the highest heavens, and all their host, the earth and everything upon it, the seas and everything in them. You keep them all alive, and the host of heaven prostrate themselves before You. (Neh 9:6)

And in Isaiah:

> It is I, the Lord, who made everything,
> Who alone stretched out the heavens
> And unaided spread out the earth. (Is 44:24)

This last affirmation has a particular interest by reason of its being addressed to Cyrus, the Zoroastrian, in order to acquaint him with the unique God. Isaiah himself hastens to draw the consequence of this doctrine of the Creation: the oneness of God.

> I am the Lord and there is none else;
> Beside me, there is no god. (Is 45:5)

The words *ein od*, which we translate "there is none else," can actually be translated "nothing else exists." Let us consider also the verses which follow:

> I engird you, though you have not known Me,
> So that they may know, from east to west,
> That there is none but Me.
> I am the Lord and there is none else,
> I form light and create darkness,
> I make weal and create woe—
> I the Lord do all these things. (Is 45:5–7)

The word *efes biladai*, translated here "there is none but Me," can also be rendered "there is nothing outside of Me." The idea of the uniqueness of God could not be more forcibly expressed than in this passage, since the author goes so far as to attribute to God both darkness and the evils which impede worldly happiness, a fundamental challenge to religious dualism.[6]

THE UNIQUENESS OF GOD

And further on:

> Only in You is to be found Divinity,
> There is no other god at all! (Is 45:14)[7]

Then, turning once more to the creation:

> For thus said the Lord,
> The Creator of heaven who alone is God,
> Who formed the earth and made it,
> Who alone established it—
> . . . .
> Was it not I the Lord?
> Then there is no god beside Me,
> No God exists beside Me
> Who foretells truly and grants success.
> Turn to Me and gain success,
> All the ends of the earth!
> For I am God, and there is none else. (Is 45:18, 21, 22)

And finally:

> Bear in mind what happened of old;
> For I am God, and there is none else,
> I am divine, and there is none like Me. (Is 46:9)[8]

But this is not all. In attributing to God alone the act of creation, the Bible sometimes contrasts Him, by way of antithesis, with the local and national deities of paganism. We read in the prayer of Hezekiah:

> O Lord, the God of Israel [national god],
> Enthroned on the Cherubim [obviously local god]!
> You alone are God of all the kingdoms of the earth. (2 Kgs 19:15)[9]

And Jeremiah is perhaps more assertive still when he says:

> Thus shall you say to them: Let the gods, who did not make heaven and earth, perish from the earth and from under these heavens. (Jer 10:11)

Here, then, is the creation put before the Gentiles as proof of the existence of the unique God, for the prophet's use of Aramaic in this passage—the only such instance in the entire book—suggests that he is here addressing the pagan populations of Babylonia.

Nothing could be more natural after this than the name "God of the universe" (*El olam*), which had already been used in connection with Abraham, whom Genesis shows us declaring "the name of the Lord, God of the universe" (Gn 21:33) in the midst of the Philistines.[10] This idea is corroborated when both Abraham and Melchizedek affirm "God Most High, Possessor of heaven and earth" (Gn 14:19, 20).[11] *Konei*, "possessor," is undoubtedly synonymous in this passage with *creator* or *author*, for it is in creating the world that God has made it His. Finally, in a passage of Deuteronomy which has been called uniquely characteristic of this book (though incorrectly, since, as we have just seen, Genesis contains similar texts), we read: "Mark, the heavens to their uttermost reaches belong to the Lord your God, the earth and all that is on it!" (Dt 10:14). The importance of these texts appears greater still when we compare them with pagan beliefs on this subject. To the Gentiles, heaven and earth have different—and often hostile—gods. We know that even in Christianity, earth is constantly in a state of theological alienation from heaven. But for Judaism, the heavens and the earth form a single realm, the domain of the same God.

After describing the creation of the world, the Bible recounts that of man, in terms which leave no doubt about belief in the unique God. At the very start we read of a command given to mankind, which is repeated after the Flood, and is both a promise and a blessing as well: to fill the earth, to subdue it, and to hold sway over all the animals which inhabit it. The God who, for the sake of men, disposes in this way of other beings which He has just created is thus, clearly, their absolute master. The author of Psalm 8 must have had access to the contents of Genesis, or at any rate echoed the same tradition. The grandeur of the creation draws from him a cry of pity for man, who is nevertheless so favored by God that he is only slightly less than the *Elohim*—an allusion, no doubt, either to the words in Genesis 1:27 ("in the image of *Elohim* He created him"), or to those in Genesis 3:5 ("but God knows that as soon as you eat of it [the forbidden fruit] your eyes will be opened and you will be like *Elohim* who know good and bad"); or perhaps to God's words in the same vein after the Fall: "Now that the man has become like one of us, knowing good and bad" (Gn 3:22).

The psalmist is obviously recalling the distinction conferred on Adam in the passage from Genesis just cited: "You have made him master over Your handiwork, laying the world at his feet" (Ps 8:7).

Moreover, the God who created man and directed him also judges and punishes him. To God belongs sovereign power. When Cain feared that he might be slain by those who would encounter him, God gave him a sign to protect him wherever he went, so universal was the obedience that would, it was assumed, be paid to God's will. In the story of the Flood, not only mankind but also the animals and the earth itself are included in the new covenant. Thus, God governs the world at His will, and embraces under His providence all creatures, great and small. And when newly created mankind, still undivided into nations, seeks to settle in a particular place, He intervenes to disperse them, so that the human race may take possession of the entire expanse of its domain. And so the great biblical events, and even their smallest details, reveal that belief in the uniqueness of God is at the heart of Judaism's most ancient traditions.

Monotheism in the Pentateuch

There is a difference between the first four books of the Torah and the fifth, which is so unlike the others that we may even in a sense see there the earliest expression of Oral Tradition. In Genesis through Numbers, the disclosure of the uniqueness of God does not take the form of doctrinal teaching, but is rather deduced as a logical consequence of the narrative and of the laws which are prescribed there. Deuteronomy, however, has a less legislative character and is more moral and theological. But monotheism is not less categorically taught in the first four books than in the fifth, and if these first books of the Sacred Writings seem to proceed in this regard rather by insinuation than by explicit proposition, it is because of an editorial procedure characteristic of ancient times. This way of declaring belief in the unique God as an unquestionable and unquestioned axiom thus appears all the more meaningful.

We may convince ourselves of this by citing a text which at first blush seems by an odd contradiction to be authorizing the most exclusive faith in the national God *at the same time* that it declares His uniqueness. When for the first time Moses tells Israel of its election, he is careful to assert that this is the will of God, who possesses the entire world.

THE UNIQUENESS OF GOD

> Now then, if you will obey Me faithfully and keep My covenant, you shall be My treasured possession among all the peoples. Indeed, all the earth is Mine. (Ex 19:5)

Such a statement, without the smallest qualification, affirms the oneness of God, whether we see in it the benevolence of a universal sovereign, master of all peoples, who chooses his favorite arbitrarily from among them, or whether we recognize in the choice itself the expression of a universal providence. It follows no less certainly from this text that a God whose dominion is universal could never be an exclusively national divinity, as rationalist criticism maintains. Such assertions are utterly demolished by this single verse.

The fourth chapter of Genesis ends with an incidental sentence which has quite properly been regarded as signaling the beginning of polytheism and idolatry: "It was then that men began to invoke the Lord by name" (Gn 4:26). If such is the case, then it is evident that the author takes for granted the previous existence of monotheism, which he regards as having been generally professed up to that time. And in this same book of Genesis we find monotheistic faith again expressed in the form of a prophecy announcing the universal reign of the unique God, the God of the Tetragrammaton. The text to which we refer, Genesis 9:26–27, one of the Bible's first intimations of messianism, predicts that "the Lord, the God of Shem" will one day be acknowledged as the sole true God by Ham as well as by Japheth.[12]

Finally, there is in these books which we are considering an evidence of monotheism which we have already had occasion to point out: the prohibition of image-worship. True, some have tried to evade this evidence by saying that image-worship was forbidden as hostile to that of the national god. But in that case, the prohibition would have been unnecessary, since the divinities represented by images could not have been worshiped anyway. The Pentateuch makes no distinction between the gods and their material embodiments. The history of religion tells us that image-worshipers usually considered the material idol to be inhabited by the spirit of the god, which was essentially identical with the image. Then again, we see that the same prohibition extends to images which might be made of the true God. This, evidently, was not because such images were hostile to the worship of God but because they were worthless and contrary to His spirituality and infinite perfections. Now, as the law was categorical in this matter and always identified a divinity with its perceptible form, we must conclude that the real motive for prohibiting images was that in the view of the Israelite lawmaker, those gods who might be so represented did not exist.

Deuteronomy, which asserts the nonexistence of these gods— "man-made gods of wood and stone, that cannot see or hear or eat or smell" (Dt 4:28)—declares as well, several lines later, that the Lord is a jealous God (Dt 5:9).[13] But this is not contradictory: for though it is true that one cannot be jealous of what does not exist, it is nevertheless possible that the idols in question represented, not gods indeed, but real things and beings. Besides, the sacred author wants to reserve love and adoration for the true God and does not wish to see it shared with anyone, not even with imaginary creatures. If the worthlessness of idols is expressed more explicitly in Deuteronomy than in the earlier books of the Torah, this, we repeat, is only appropriate to the more oratorical form of this last book. One might say that in Deuteronomy, Moses, conversing paternally with his people, gives free reign to the impulses of the heart, whereas in the other books, it is the lawgiver who speaks in order to promulgate his laws.

Certain critics explain the more emphatic character of spirituality which we find in Deuteronomy by attributing the composition of this book to a more recent date. Others refuse to see monotheism even in Deuteronomy. According to them, what we have here is instead *monolatry*, which nevertheless recognizes the superiority of the God of Israel to foreign divinities. But we question whether such an interpretation can be maintained in the presence of texts as explicit as this one, for example: "The Lord [Tetragrammaton] alone is God; there is none beside Him" (Dt 4:35). Or this, in which Moses speaks of Israel's having been seduced by false gods, and exclaims [in God's words],

> They incensed Me with no-gods,
> Vexed Me with their futilities. (Dt 32:21)

How can one still speak of monolatry in Deuteronomy when we see that the word *god* is used there as a synonym for vanity, for pure nothingness, while concern for monotheism is as conspicuous as in the texts of the Prophets, or, among the Apocrypha, of Baruch discoursing on the aberrations of idolatry?[14] Here, moreover, is a passage which cuts short all discussion of the matter. The concept of the special election of Israel, and thus of the national religion, is found expressed at the same time as belief in the unique God. We have here a perfect synthesis of the two notions:

> Mark, the heavens to their uttermost reaches belong to the Lord your God, the earth and all that is on it! Yet it was to your fathers that the Lord was drawn in His love for them, so that He chose you, their lineal descendents, from among all peoples—as is now the case. (Dt 10:14–15)

However we may understand this text, it logically excludes all possibility of polytheism.

But we must agree that there are passages in the Pentateuch where not only is the existence of the gods not denied, but where this existence seems, on the contrary, to be accepted, as in this verse, which follows close upon the ones we have just cited: "For the Lord your God is the God of gods and the Lord of lords, the great, the mighty, and the awesome God" (Dt 10:17).[15] But can we imagine a more effective, forcible way of emphasizing the doctrine of the oneness of God than to affirm that these beings whom men worship as if they were gods are in fact so many creations, subjects, servants of the unique God, who is thus all the more exalted in proportion as these alleged divinities whose sovereign master He is are themselves elevated? Can "gods" who are subordinate to God still claim to be "gods"?

We call the attention of rationalist critics to Deuteronomy 4:35, which we cited above: "It has been clearly demonstrated to you that the Lord alone is God; there is none beside Him." They must acknowledge that it is impossible to be more categorical. The God of the incommunicable name, who, as they would have it, was but the national divinity of the Hebrews, is here explicitly designated the *unique* God. In other words, there can be only a single authentic God, God of the Tetragrammaton, who revealed Himself to Israel through the wonders which He worked.[16] (These are recalled in the verses which precede the one quoted above.) "There is none beside Him." Without straining the sense, our verse could even be translated "Outside of Him there is nothing"—a declaration of uniqueness so absolute that it would surely be puzzling if the scriptural context did not limit and specify its significance.

A bit further on another text expresses the same essential idea: "Know therefore this day and keep in mind that the Lord alone is God in heaven above and on earth below; there is no other" (Dt 4:39). Here we also notice that in Mosaism, God is on earth as well as in heaven—He is both transcendent and immanent—a forceful way of asserting His oneness. We must be struck to find that Moses speaks like Abraham (Gn 14:22), that Deuteronomy in fact uses expressions identical to those in Genesis, and that the two books are in agreement with Exodus, where we read in the Decalogue that nothing in heaven or on earth is worthy of worship except God alone.

And so we read in Deuteronomy:

> See, then, that I, I am He;
> There is no god beside Me.
> I deal death and give life;
> I wounded and I will heal:
> None can deliver from My hand. (Dt 32:39)

But does it not also deny in principle any kind of polytheism? Even dualism (which is not as peculiarly Zoroastrian as one may think) seems to be explicitly refuted by the ascription of both prosperity and misfortune, of death as well as life, to God alone. This is altogether consistent with the spirit of Judaism, which, as Spinoza, among others, observed, does not shrink from acknowledging God to be author of every natural phenomenon whether it be welcome or baneful, and this without any of the embarrassed hedging which modern theodicies bring to the problem of evil. Such indeed was the domination of monotheism over the ancient Jews that it never occurred to them that they could offend the unique God by declaring Him creator of *everything*. The Mosaic ritual expresses this belief symbolically by the sacrifice of the goat for Azazel, which was accomplished in the same sanctuary, by the same high priest, and as part of the same rite as the sacrifice to God Himself, on the most solemn Day of Atonement (Lv 16).

The reader may be surprised that in this survey of texts from Deuteronomy, we have as yet said nothing about the monotheistic verse par excellence, the one which has become Judaism's profession of faith: "Hear, O Israel! The Lord is our God, the Lord is one" (Dt 6:4). There are good reasons to believe that it is the essential unity of God's nature which this passage chiefly affirms.[17] But monotheism can with equal reason be deduced from it. Precisely because God is the indivisible point toward which all converges, the universal monad, the center from which radiates all which has been, is, and will be, He must necessarily be unique, which is to say that there cannot be two centers, two sources, of life. It seems apparent that a religion which has attained the conception of the oneness or unity of God in His nature (as the celebrated verse proclaims) is not likely to tolerate the vulgar conception of polytheism.

Those who, through unwarrantable bias, refuse to see in the religion of the Jews anything more than an unsophisticated monolatry, which, as a result of contact with Greek philosophy, eventually became monotheism, merely confirm us in our conviction by the poverty of their arguments.

The Tetragrammaton and the Uniqueness of God

Now that we have examined certain relevant biblical texts, let us investigate more thoroughly the magisterial proof of monotheism which we find in the Tetragrammaton itself. We have already asserted that this name affirms the oneness or unity of God in His essence, and, consequently, monotheism, since its sublime conception of God as absolute Being precludes any comparison with other divinities. By designating in this way the source of all life, of all power, and of all strength, the Tetragrammaton is more than assertion of divine unity; it is an entire philosophy, and Maimonides was correct in saying that the name which Moses requested of God, and transmitted to Israel, demonstrates unmistakably the necessity of Being.

But there is other evidence that to the Jews, God's name denoted Being itself, the unique God, and by this fundamental affirmation precluded any possibility of polytheism: it is the hatred, often veiled or muted, which the pagan peoples had for them. Israel was regarded as a people absolutely apart, and Israel welcomed being so perceived. This idea goes back to the most remote period of Jewish history, and indeed explains more than one chapter of that history. Why this aversion by the Gentiles? Was it because the Jews worshiped only a single national god, repulsed all foreign divinities, and, in short, professed a rigorous monolatry? But this would not adequately account for the antipathy toward them, for monolatry as such does not deny the existence of other gods, but rather, indeed, implies the recognition of these very gods and of the legitimacy of their authority over the peoples who worship them. It would have been quite different, however, if the religion of Israel was authentic monotheism. In such a case, an abyss would have separated this people from all others. However the pagans might differ among themselves as to which divinities to venerate, they were at one in their acceptance of polytheism per se, and acknowledged the right of every people to have its own gods. But Israel, in denying the existence of these gods, became the natural adversary of all of their worshipers. The name which the Jews gave to God was therefore a profession of faith which in fact cut them off from the Gentile world; and the aversion which that world conceived for them had as cause not the difference of laws and customs but a radical difference in religious conceptions.

Torah law provides evidence of an unmistakable intention to isolate the Jews from all other peoples, no doubt to ensure the preservation of their peculiar identity; but this isolation would make sense only if it were a question of protecting some grand principle which might be compromised by contact with the pagans. The principle could only have been monotheism. It is this which the sacred Tetragrammaton reveals to us; it is this which is at the core of Mosaic Law and animates it.

We find monotheism even in the impulse of national identity. Many rabbinical maxims relate the oneness of God to the oneness of Israel. What could this mean if not that the one seemed like the consequence of the other, in the sense that the laws intended to separate Israel from the other peoples and to maintain its utterly special character had as their ultimate object the preservation of that very monotheism which Israel had in trust? This is how Moses makes Balaam speak with reference to Israel:

> There is a people that dwells apart,
> Not reckoned among the nations. (Nm 23:9)

And in another passage he himself says:

> You have affirmed this day that the Lord [Tetragrammaton] is
> your God. . . . And the Lord has affirmed this day that you
> are, as He promised you, His treasured people. (Dt 26:17, 18)

With respect to the Tetragrammaton, that sublime distillation of faith in the oneness or unity of God, let us venture to recall the services which this doctrine has rendered to human knowledge. Of course, we are not among those who are concerned only with the utilitarian implications of religious doctrine, who think that the only value of such beliefs is in their moral or social effects. If that be Judaism, it is a superficial, merely quantifiable kind of Judaism. But if this practical consequence is neither the unique *raison d'être* nor the ultimate goal of the knowledge of truth, it is nevertheless its natural result. We shall quote the words of a scholar who sees in monotheistic faith a powerful impulse toward the pursuit and veneration of truth, and at the same time does justice to Israel as the guardian of this doctrine:

> The concept of a God who tolerates no other deity beside Himself, who is represented not in the manner of a man-made fiction, surrounded by unworthy legends, but rather as a supreme and absolute Being who claims all human moral aspirations and whose omniscience perceives all transgression in order to punish it—this idea of God, transmitted through the centuries from generation to generation, has ultimately affected knowledge itself and has familiarized the human spirit with the conception of a unique principle of rational order in existence, arousing in man the desire to discover it.[18]

It is proper to point out that the idea of the unity of knowledge is founded on the idea of the unity of God; but we may add that the concept of knowledge itself, and thus of truth, has the same foundation. The irresistible claims of truth and disinterested inquiry—which, from the perspective of the knowledge-seeker, are one and the same—presuppose the ontological absolute, the absolute in itself, which is to say God perceived as unity; for the absolute is unity par excellence and can be nothing else. Polytheism, however, is but relativism in religion, and forms the basis of relativism in the domain of knowledge, which we can therefore regard as a sort of scientific polytheism: a different truth for every mind, a different god for every seeker.

"God of gods"

One of the arguments most often raised against the existence of monotheism in early Judaism is the title "God of gods," *Elohei-ha-Elohim*, which the Bible often gives to the God of Israel, and which, it is claimed, implies a mere primacy among a number of divinities. But in fact, the plural form *Elohim* is frequently used to designate the one God, and if this word used by itself does not have the sense of plurality, why should we feel obliged to give it this meaning when it is part of a compound expression? Moreover, the presence of this expression in

THE UNIQUENESS OF GOD

Deuteronomy, the only book of the Torah that rationalist critics acknowledge to be fundamentally monotheist in inspiration, in itself refutes this objection.

But what, then, is the true meaning of this peculiar plural? Perhaps *Elohei-ha-Elohim* is simply an absolute expression in the form of superlative-comparative; that is, it denotes the One who, in relation to other divinities, is God par excellence. It would follow that if God alone is altogether worthy of the name, the other putative gods are not. Indeed, one of the forms of the Hebrew superlative consists in saying of a thing that it is, with respect to a second, what that is, in its turn, with respect to a third. Thus, for example, there is the expression *Kodesh Kodashim*, "Holy of Holies," to designate what is preeminent in sanctity among other things which are also considered holy. We have, too, the expression *Shmei-ha-Shamaim*, "Heaven of Heavens," by which we mean that what is for us the heaven is but a kind of terrestrial world in relation to the *higher* heaven.

However odd this may seem, such expressions contain an implied negation of the quality in the object of the preposition. Thus, the ones called "gods" are not so at all in conjunction with the One who is *their* God. By virtue of the very fact that they have a God, they cannot themselves be authentic "gods" [though they might be so designated in other contexts]. It is in this frame of reference that we must understand certain words of the Lord to Moses, His prophet, in Exodus: "See, I place you in the role of God to Pharoah, with your brother Aaron as your prophet" (Ex 7:1).

This name *Elohei-ha-Elohim* may also have expressed a pragmatic as well as logical superiority. In the Jewish mind it could refer to the *pagan perception* of God as supreme divinity, and could thus designate "the One whom everybody worships as *supreme* God." We know, indeed, that Jeremiah, Malachi, and the rabbis after them encountered use of the title "supreme God" among the pagans in reference to the God of Israel. The name *Elohei-ha-Elohim* might, therefore, very naturally have been used in this sense.

But we believe that this name can indicate not only a relative superiority, by way of comparison, but also an intrinsic superiority in the theological sense. The God of Israel may have been called "God of gods" in order to emphasize that the idea of divinity, which among the pagans resulted in a fragmentary pantheism through the divinization of various forces, had attained in Judaism an authentic synthetic unity. But let no one misconstrue the meaning of our words. It is far from our

95

intention to introduce vanities and cadavers, as the Bible calls idols (Lv 26:30; Dt 32:21), into the domain of the living God, or to violate transcendent purity and light with corruption and darkness. But if the gods are but expressions of death, this is only insofar as they are separated from the source of life and light. To the contrary, indeed, if they are touched by the luminous energy of God, pure and life-giving, they can then claim a share of both light and life. In making this assertion, we believe we are in no way diminishing our conception of God's dignity but rather enhancing it. Matter, too, is dead if it is not perfected in the organism. It comes alive when it is touched by life, and falls again into death when it is separated from it. We shall presently hear an original thinker call polytheism—very properly—a *putrefaction of truth*. Indeed, when they are separated from the principle of unity, the atoms of truth do not form a living organism, but become a multiplicity (polytheism). But this does not deprive these same inert fragments of their capacity to be organized once again by the unifying principle (monotheism).

If we analyze the elements of this theological conception, we find a twofold principle. The first assumes that a trace of the authentic idea of God survives in the various pagan divinities, mixed with error; the second, its corollary, assumes that the Jewish conception of God was the synthesis of all the partial truths represented by the divinities of paganism—whence the name "God of gods" which we find in the Bible.

Is all this really consistent with Jewish doctrine? It is useful in this connection to recall the way in which Judaism presents the history of mankind and of religion: in the beginning, a common origin and common beliefs, and later, after the fragmentation of peoples and the proliferation of diverse religious ideas, the persistence among all of them of their community of origin. This idea, conformable to perceived reality, is in perfect accord with the teaching of Jewish mysticism. For the Kabbalah, just as imperfection is always mixed with holiness, so truth is perpetually mixed with error. The one is the husk or outer covering, the other the inner reality, the quickening spirit. The way truth objectifies or exteriorizes itself, so to speak, can be an obstacle to, or a medium of, reception, depending on whether the concrete form contains more or less of life. Let us remember that for the Kabbalists, the names of the pagan gods all contain a spark of sanctity. Thus do they reveal in paganism a relative truth.

The Kabbalah candidly teaches that it is truth which gives life to error; that in order to persist, evil, heresy, and idolatry require some particle of truth, without which they could not stay alive; that it is important to free the spirit from the rude prison where it has been suppressed, and, in a word, to kill the devil in order to retrieve the atom of divine life which animated him and to unite it to its source and center. The Kabbalah has distilled all theological error, national or individual, ancient or modern, in this triple formula: excision, disorder, separation (Hebrew *kitsouis, hibbur, peroud*). We may easily recognize here the characteristic mark of polytheism, by which we mean the worship of one or several attributes of God to the exclusion of all the others.

Divine Attributes and Cosmic Forces

That God is the supreme unity, and that the divinities of paganism represent in some sense moments of His existence, is proven likewise by the notion of the *sarim*, angels or spirits appointed by the supreme God for the governance of each people. In the oldest biblical books, this is what we must understand by the *Elohim*, whose God is the Lord. (Thus, the expression *Elohei-ha-Elohim*, "God of gods.") For Hebraic theology, the *sarim* are abstract elements, attributes or partial aspects of the idea of God, who is the synthesis of them all. This doctrine, explicitly taught by the Kabbalah, is contained implicitly in the Bible.

The matter has been very well expressed by an eminent thinker who happens to be totally foreign to our faith: "The hierarchical scale of the gods is only the personification of the hierarchical order of principles, laws, and forces."[19]

Such, in our opinion, is the way we should understand all the biblical passages in which God is represented as presiding over an assembly of superior beings, sometimes called the host of heaven, *tzeva ha-shamaim*, sometimes the seraphim, or the *bnei ha-Elohim*, sons of God. This last name shows God in a functional relation with these beings, and derives precisely from their subordination to the First Cause. It is the divine attributes which are thus represented as "sons of God." Precisely the same name was given many centuries later [by Christianity] to the Logos which was said to be incarnate. Nothing was more natural than to use the name "Father" for the Being itself, as substance, and "sons" for His attributes.

The divine hierarchy depicted in the Bible by the political metaphor of a king accompanied by his subordinates, then by the religious metaphor of a synagogue where God is the minister who officiates, is also represented by the metaphor of an army with its commanding general. Jacob says: "This is God's camp" (Gn 32:3), and in the Song of Moses, God is compared to a valiant warrior (Ex 15:3). Elsewhere, the angel who appears to Joshua says: "I am captain of the Lord's host" (Jos 5:14). The image attains its full development when it represents an organized assembly presided over by the Lord, who has at His right hand and at His left all the multitude of the *tzevaot* or celestial host.

Would it be rash to see in these *tzevaot* (as the Zohar asks us to) the cosmic forces moving harmoniously to the commandment of the Author of all things, and the totality of the laws of attraction and repulsion which govern the celestial and terrestial bodies? The modern scientist has observed in his laboratory that at the heart of the atom the same laws prevail, together with the same motions and relationships, as in interstellar space. To his eyes, matter is simply a conjunction of centers and of forces. John Tyndall[20] appropriates and takes literally the poetical expression of Emerson, "The atoms march in tune,"[21] and another scholar, surely without giving a thought to theology, has said that the supernal idea which rules the world can be compared to that of a commanding general the day of battle. It filters down to the last soldier, who obeys blindly.

In our opinion, this concept unfolds in a way quite contrary to Hegel's teaching. It does not proceed *ex nihilo*, rising to full consciousness. Rather, it detaches itself from the fullness of divine consciousness in order to spread in various degrees as far as the most infinitesimal atoms. According to kabbalistic doctrine, among the four successive planes, the least elevated of which is the visible universe, the physical forces on the lower level (*Asiyah*) correspond to the divine attributes on the higher (*Yetzirah*), the two having the same relation to one another as physical life or force has to soul or thought.

We do not want our readers to have the smallest misapprehension in this matter. Far from conceding any real existence to the pagan divinities, we ascribe them to the supreme Unity which absorbs them even in subordinating them. But in order to preclude any doubt in this regard, we shall show to what level of boldness Jewish theological speculation has risen, and it will then be possible to judge whether Mosaic monotheism really cuts an abyss between a solitary God and the totality of created things, or whether, in the Hebraic conception, an uninterrupted ladder joins all levels of existence, from the most sublime to the most ephemeral.

According to Maimonides, the first article of faith is "to worship no other being than God." The author of the *Sefer ha-Ikkarim*, Joseph Albo, objects that this commandment should not be included among the articles of faith, for

> although this is one of the precepts of the Law, as it is written, "You shall have no other God before me," nevertheless it is not a principle on which all the Law rests. Indeed, one who believed that God, blessed be He, exists, and that His Law is true, and would nonetheless introduce an intermediary between God and himself, would be transgressing the commandment "You shall have no other God before me"; but this does not make it a fundamental principle, with which the entire Law stands or falls.[22]

Rabbi Moses ben Israel Isserles, in his *Torat ha-Olah*, replies that Maimonides is right, not Albo, for

> in my humble view, the entire Law is placed in jeopardy when an intermediary is introduced between God and us, for this provides a pretext for denying God, in saying that the intermediary alone is sufficient, as indeed occurred at the origin of polytheism.[23]

This controversy is most interesting. If Joseph Albo could contest Maimonides' condemnation of the very worship of intermediaries between God and the world, while yet remaining faithful to the entire spirit of Hebraism, what could there be reprehensible in acknowledging, with the Kabbalah, the existence of divine attributes, even in a certain sense personifed, or of consciousness linked to a supreme Consciousness which includes them all—though without, of course, worshiping them? We may note that the most demanding orthodoxy, as represented by Rabbi Isserles, rejects this concept only as a matter of prudence, to avoid the risk of losing sight of the unique and authentic God. The Kabbalah, moreover, forbids us to contemplate in our prayers anything other than the supreme Cause alone, at most clothed in that specific attribute to which we are appealing: that is, God conceived in His entirety, with all of His dimensions. This is the perspective that students of Indian literature find in all the passages of the Vedas where each particular divinity by turns expresses the nature of the supreme God.

But here is another rabbinic doctrine which bears lofty witness to the tolerance and breadth of outlook of the sages of the Synagogue: It is the principle according to which Noachides—that is, all men other than Jews—are not regarded as sinning if they associate any being whatever with God, so long as they acknowledge His unique nature.[24]

However strange this doctrine may seem at first sight, it becomes clear enough once we have a proper comprehension of the *Elohim*, seeing in them the deification by the pagans of cosmic forces corresponding to the various divine attributes. If our theory is sound, then it must follow that a pagan will approach nearer to truth as he succeeds in rising to a more comprehensive synthesis, so that his conception of God thus becomes more nearly authentic. And so the name *Elohei-ha-Elohim* is as fully justified theologically as it is historically. Far from providing evidence against the antiquity of Mosaic monotheism, it rather shows how elevated was the idea of Divinity in early Judaism.

3

The Universality of God

*T*he God of Israel, who is unique and, in His essential being, a unity, is the God of all creation, the universal God. This logical implication of monotheism must be considered more carefully.

The very concept of creation implies belief in the universal God. This has been accurately observed by an author not likely to be suspected of partiality toward Judaism:

> If, when we read the Old Testament, it seems at first glance that the God spoken of by the lawgivers and prophets has the appearance of the national god of the Hebrew people, it is equally true that in so far as He is declared to be Creator of the universe, He is by virtue of that fact regarded as God of all peoples. Here we see the authentically messianic side of the Old Testament, which assuredly confirms it as the book for all times and places.[1]

When Castelli says that the God of Moses and the Prophets seems at first like a national god, we cannot be sure whether he is referring to a stage in the historical development of monotheism in Israel or whether he means to say that this particularism is the aspect of divinity which predominates in Jewish belief. It is nonetheless true that the Bible perceives God as Creator of the universe in using such expressions as "God of heaven and earth," "Lord," "possessor [literally "acquirer"] of heaven and earth," or "God of the universe," particularly in a context of proselytism. An example is Abraham traveling from one country to another, raising altars and proclaiming the Lord "God of the universe," *El olam* (Gn 21:33).[2]

In the Bible, the concept of creation includes not only the material universe but also the human race, so that God the Creator is necessarily the God of all mankind. It is irrelevant for our present purpose whether or not one regards the account in Genesis as acceptable; what is important is the idea of God which Genesis seeks to convey. It is incontestable that for the biblical narrator, Adam was the first man and from him are descended all the families of the earth. This would suffice to establish the universal nature of the biblical God.

And if He is the sovereign Creator, it is to Him that the earliest men must have directed their worship. At what moment does Genesis signal the appearance of polytheism? The rabbis maintain that this was in the time of Enosh. There would thus have been a great extent of time, starting with the Creation, during which the God of Israel was also the God of all mankind, not only by right but also in fact. However, the literal sense of the passage relating to Enosh[3] hardly sustains that interpretation, and if this text is understood otherwise, we must certainly delay still further the origin of polytheism. There is mention indeed of various sins in these remote times, but never that of idolatry. Moral corruption, violence, the pride which leads men to oppose the purposes of the Most High (as the story of the construction of the Tower of Babel shows)—it is for these that the Bible reproaches men, while not a word is said about the worship of false divinities. But even if the Bible were found to limit the acknowledged dominion of God the Creator to a period of short duration, this would sufficiently counter the accusation of particularism and demonstrate that the God of Israel is indeed the God of mankind.

Some will object that the God acknowledged as universal can nevertheless have, according to the faith of His worshipers, a special predilection for a particular people, and that this is seen, for instance, at the core of Hellenism, where Zeus is believed to regard the Greeks as his privileged children. This example has in fact been cited in order to deflate the *Jewish* pretension to being God's chosen people. We are not sure how correct it is to say that the Greeks considered Zeus at once the universal God as well as their own special deity. If that could be established, it would simply show that a certain trace of faith in the unique God persisted among the Gentiles. And those of us, indeed, who even believe that monotheism was explicitly taught among the nations in the form of mysteries would by no means be disturbed. Would this not demonstrate—contrary to rationalist assertions—that mankind at its origins was closer to truth than has been supposed, and would it not also constitute a confirmation of Jewish teachings?

But the question chiefly to be addressed is whether, in the examples cited, monotheism seems to be a fundamental, organic principle, or a pale vestige merely, manifestly contradicted by institutions, customs, and beliefs. There is no doubt that for the Greeks, the monotheistic idea was smothered by the multiplicity of gods in rivalry with Zeus, quite apart from all the foreign divinities whose legitimate worship by *other* peoples was acknowledged by the Greeks—persuasive evidence that Zeus was not for them the universal God. It is true, however, that later, a most remarkable spiritual phenomenon occurred, the result, perhaps, of a distant recollection of true religion: the gods of the various peoples were assimilated and came to be regarded as a single deity, as we can infer from reading Herodotus. But these two conceptions—universal Zeus and Zeus the special divinity of the Greeks—never attained in the popular religion such a synthesis as we find in Judaism, where the God of the human race, who reigns over all men as universal Creator, is believed to have a priestly people, Israel, for whom, by reason of their priesthood, He is also the *special* God.

This phenomenon of a people which declares itself priest of mankind is altogether unique in history, and one of the most startling evidences of the universal character of the biblical God. Jewish particularism exists for the sake of a universal purpose. It has no other ground than faith in the unique God, no other object than the establishment of His sway over all mankind.

Evidences of the Knowledge of God among the Gentiles

After the introduction of polytheism, the knowledge of the true God did not disappear entirely among the Gentiles. The Bible explicitly acknowledges this.

To be sure, the narrow geographical perspectives of these early ages, the prejudices and national antipathies, the pride which Israel's privileged situation could inspire in her, all tended to limit knowledge of the true God to Jews alone, and to instill in them the perception that whereas *they* had access to truth and the light of pure religion, for the Gentiles there was nothing but idolatry or godlessness, accompanied by error and moral darkness. Even if such was not altogether the case, it is certainly true that the idea of universal God formed an integral and inseparable part of Jewish faith. Let us now, however, examine the evidences of the knowledge of God *outside* of Israel, according to the biblical accounts.

We find that Lot, addressing himself to his pagan sons-in-law, speaks of the Lord (Tetragrammaton): "Up, get out of this place, for the Lord is about to destroy the city" (Gn 19:14). God appears in a dream to Abimelech, who calls Him by the name *Adonai:* "O Lord, will You slay people even though innocent?" (Gn 20:4). Even so, Abimelech is so fundamentally polytheistic that Abraham, apostle of monotheism, feels the need to use expressions which seem to negate his own beliefs when he speaks of "the gods" and of "their" treatment of him:

> I thought . . . surely there is no fear of God [*Elohim*, plural form] in this place. . . . So when God [*Elohim*] made [plural verb] me wander from my father's house. . . . (Gn 20:11, 13)

What then is monotheism doing in the mouth of Abimelech, and a kind of polytheism in Abraham's? Have their roles been somehow reversed? What we see is paganism and Hebraism each taking a step toward the other, in order to find a meeting-ground in a conception which we shall find to be that of the larger part of the Gentile world: a supreme God *together with* subordinate gods at His feet. The difference between Jewish belief and that of the pagans lies in this: Israel saw in these subordinate gods only so many divine *attributes*, whereas the pagans lavished their worship on precisely these diverse forms, which they hypostatized and perceived as divinities. Much later, we can observe a difference of the same order between Christianity and the Jewish Kabbalah, from which indeed it is correct to say Christian doctrine came forth, in both senses of the word: first, because the Kabbalah was truly its source, and also because it diverged radically from its kabbalistic origins. Thus, for example, the Christian doctrine of the Trinity transformed into distinct persons what were for the Kabbalists divine attributes.

Jewish monotheism was known to the pagans in the form of a *pan-monotheism*, for the conception of a supreme God together with deified subordinate forces is nothing other than that. This perception of the authentic God, to which the words of Abimelech bear witness, has not escaped the exegetes:

> What, indeed, [asks M. Cahen with surprise] was the religion of this king, who loathes adultery and with whom the true God communicates in a dream? Was the knowledge of God common in Canaan? Is this why God instructed Abraham to go there?[4]

The answer to this last question lies entirely in the fertilization of his monotheistic faith through contact with the Gentiles, as we have already explained.

In another passage of Genesis, a pagan, Laban, says to another pagan, Eliezer: "Come in, O blessed of the Lord [Tetragrammaton], why do you remain outside?" (Gn 24:31). And further on, Laban and Bethuel exclaim together: "The matter was decreed by the Lord; we cannot speak to you bad or good" (Gn 24:50).

The words of Jethro are quite remarkable:

> Blessed be the Lord who delivered you from the Egyptians and from Pharoah. . . . Now I know that the Lord is greater than all gods. (Ex 18:10, 11)

Jethro's profession of faith may no doubt be a consequence of Moses' teachings, or perhaps simply an acknowledgment of the God of the Tetragrammaton as national god of the Hebrews. But when we consider the truly exceptional role which the Bible assigns to this father-in-law of Moses, making him Moses' intimate counselor and the inspirer of his laws, it seems improbable that such importance would be given to a mere idolator, to a priest of false gods. We must likely conclude that Jethro had been led to recognize that the supreme God whom he already worshiped was the God of Israel, and that this people was destined for a distinguished mission in the world.

The fact remains that the two preeminent personalities in Jewish history, Abraham and Moses, found themselves in very close contact with two pagan priests: Abraham in receiving the blessing from Melchizedek, Moses in marrying the daughter of Jethro and accepting spiritual direction from him. In each case, the Gentile world—or, more accurately, mankind—confers priestly investiture upon Israel.

The name of Jethro brings to mind that of Balaam, for according to Oral Tradition, both of them, like Job, lived at the court of Pharoah. The influence of these two Gentiles is therefore connected with Egypt, which, according to the biblical expression, is the "iron furnace" (Dt 4:20) in which Judaism was forged. No one could question that the name of the God of Israel was familiar to Balaam:

> Balaam replied to Balak's officials, "Though Balak were to give me his house full of silver and gold, I could not do

anything, big or little, contrary to the command of the Lord [Tetragrammaton] my God." (Nm 22:18)

Not only does he call the Lord *his* God, but the idea he formulates is so pure and exalted that it has always provided a convincing refutation of those who were tempted to take biblical anthropomorphisms literally.

> God is not man to be capricious,
> Or mortal to change His mind.
> Would He speak and not act,
> Promise and not fulfill? (Nm 23:19)

The divine immutability which Balaam proclaims implies so elevated a conception of God's nature as to exclude all the more rigorously the distinctly human needs and sentiments which the Bible often seems to attribute to God. The very fact that he included the words of Balaam shows that to the sacred writer, these words conveyed an irreproachable doctrine not in the smallest measure inconsistent with the anthropomorphic passages when judiciously interpreted. Besides, the religion of Balaam, which requires seven altars, seven bulls, and seven rams (Nm 23:29), reveals so exact a knowledge of patriarchal and Mosaic observances—or at the very least such conformity with them—that we must surely suppose a common origin.

The worship which Balaam directs to the Lord obliges us to wonder whether the Tetragrammaton was known outside of Israel. We would affirm unhesitatingly that in an abbreviated form, this name is indeed found in a great number of proper Canaanite or Phoenician names. Rashi, in his commentary on the words of the Kaddish "May His great name be blessed," says that if these words are in Aramaic, it is because they refer to the Tetragrammaton, which is itself Aramaic.[5] Scholars have acknowledged this origin, and Babylonian inscriptions have seemed to confirm their deductions. It is certain that the language of the Patriarchs was Aramaic, and that when Hebrew had become the national idiom of the Jews, Isaiah called it the language of Canaan (Is 19:18). The Kabbalists say that just as Bathsheba, before becoming the wife of David, belonged to Uriah the Hittite, so the Hebrew language must have belonged to the least godly of peoples before becoming the sacred tongue. We have here yet another example of the way Israel assimilates borrowings from paganism, and of the ascent which Hebraism sees everywhere, in life and in history, by which things rise from lower levels to the highest spheres.

The rabbis have acutely observed that Pharoah's response to Moses and Aaron—"Who is the Lord [Tetragrammaton] that I should heed Him and let Israel go?" (Ex 5:2)—shows that the God of Israel was known at that time in Egypt only by the name of *Elohim* and not that of the Tetragrammaton. But we find another Egyptian ruler, Necho, distinguishing precisely the special sense of these two names, when having deposed Jehoahaz, king of Judah, he replaced him with his brother Eliakim, whose name he changed to Jehoiakim (2 Chr 36:4).

The Greek authors also know *Iaou* or *Iao*. According to Diodorus Siculus, "*Iao* is the God of the Jews."[6] It is probable that in thus translating the Tetragrammaton, this author was following the custom of the pagans in giving Jewish things names from their own religious vocabulary which corresponded best to the Hebrew words. It is thus that Plutarch, for example, because of a simple ceremonial analogy, called the God of the Jews *Dionysus*.[7] One should not forget, moreover, that the first three letters of the Tetragrammaton form precisely the *Iao* of Diodorus; and if this word does not in fact appear in Scripture as an independent name, it nevertheless enters into the composition of several proper names, such as *Jehoiakim* (which we cited a moment ago), *Jehoahaz*, *Jehonadab*, and so forth.

Finally, one of the most curious texts is that of the oracle of Apollo at Claros, discussed by Macrobius, according to which *Iao* is called the greatest of all the gods, the supreme divinity, the sun god who is imagined to have four faces, which represent the four seasons.[8]

Let us see what evidence the Bible provides of this majestic name among the Gentiles.

Achish, king of Gath, swears an oath to David in terms which a faithful Israelite might use: "As the Lord lives, you are an honest man" (1 Sm 29:6). Later, we see Hiram, king of Tyre, writing in a letter to his friend King Solomon: "Blessed is the Lord, God of Israel, who made the heavens and the earth" (2 Chr 2:11). The God of Israel is here acknowledged to be the universal God, another proof that these two characteristics did not seem incompatible to the pagan who is expressing himself in this way. Whatever may be the degree of authenticity which we care to assign to Chronicles, it is sufficient that this text has enabled us to establish both that the conception of the God of Israel and His relationship with mankind which prevailed in ancient Judaism

clearly possesses the universal character which we have been affirming, and that this idea was not entirely foreign to the Gentiles.

Not only did they have some knowledge of the God of Israel, but
the Bible indicates the existence among them of a legitimate priesthood
of the universal God. It describes Melchizedek as "a priest of God
Most High" (Gn 14:18). The town of Salem, of which this priest was
king, is probably Jerusalem, which is also called Salem in the Psalms.
It must be noted that the kings of the holy city always bore the title of
Melchizedek or Adoni-Zedek; and according to Jeremiah, the king of
the future Jerusalem will be called *Adonai-Tsidkeinu*, "the Lord, our
Justice" (Jer 23:6).[9] Is it not remarkable that the center for worship of
the true God was established at Jerusalem, formerly the site of the
religion of Melchizedek? The choice of that city to be Israel's religious
and political metropolis, the establishment of Jewish monotheism in a
place which had previously been consecrated by the worship of
Gentiles—and that without any resentment on the part of Moses or of
those, whoever they were, who drafted his sacred writings: We have
here a significant argument in favor of Jewish universalism.

And who, then, is this "God Most High" of whom Melchizedek
was priest? Surely it is the very One whom Abraham worshiped, the
One whom Moses worshiped and spoke of. It is the God of Israel who
is designated by this same name in writings of all ages. Moses, indeed,
speaks of Him unmistakably as God of the Gentiles, in this passage of
Deuteronomy:

> When the Most High [Elyon] gave nations their homes
> And set the divisions of man,
> He fixed the boundaries of peoples
> In relation to Israel's numbers. (Dt 32:8)

Similarly, we read in Psalm 82:

> I had taken you for divine beings, sons of the Most High
> [Elyon], all of you. (Ps 82:6)

Melchizedek's distinction is so high and authentic that Abraham,
honored though he is by divine revelations, nevertheless acknowledges
Melchizedek's status and offers him a tithe, receiving Melchizedek's
blessing. As we noted above, the rabbis declared that Abraham even
accepted priestly consecration from him. In thus placing the dignity of

mankind above the glory of his own people, Abraham richly merited the universal priesthood.

Moreover, according to what the Bible tells us of Abimelech, Laban, Pharoah, et al., it seems clear that pagans might receive manifestations of the divine. In speaking of the last days, the seers of Israel described visions and revelations applicable to the entire human race: "After that, I will pour out My spirit on all flesh" (Jl 3:1). This shows that for Hebraism, mankind's destiny is conceived as universally as its origins.

Universalism in the Bible

Was Judaism, in its Scriptures and rabbinical teachings, quite aware that the God it proclaimed was indeed the universal God? We have only to open the Psalms or the Prophets to find many impressive evidences of such awareness.

"From east to west the name of the Lord is praised" (Ps 113:3). And the verse which follows seems unmistakably to allude to "God Most High," the supreme God worshiped by all:

> The Lord is exalted above all nations;
> His glory is above the heavens. (Ps 113:4)

Psalm 8 seems to acknowledge implicitly that in one way or another, the true God is worshiped universally. Compared to the splendors of the firmament, man is scarcely worthy of notice, but nevertheless, in reality, nothing equals his grandeur. All material creation submits to his domination, and even the angels are hardly superior to him, because his is the intelligent voice which declares everywhere on earth the Creator's majesty and sovereign power: "O Lord, our Lord, how majestic is Your name throughout the earth!" (Ps 8:2)

But we now come to the most conclusive evidence that the true God was universally worshiped. We could not ask for a more beautiful or expressive text. In it, the spirit of universalism is such that Israel appears to be consigned to the background in order to allow mankind in its totality to dominate the stage—and, more astonishing still, *pagan* mankind. It is the prophet Malachi who, in a time of general decadence, added in this incomparable passage a precious jewel to Israel's crown. He begins by complaining of the disrespect shown for the modest altar, which, after Zerubbabel, had been erected in place of the old one.[10] It was felt that for so unpretentious a shrine, a sacrifice offering need not be altogether free of blemishes.

> Just offer it to your governor: Will he accept you? Will he show you favor?—said the Lord of Hosts. (Mal 1:8)

This is a bitter allusion to the condition of servitude in which the Persian government then held the Jews. Rather than thus profane the sanctuary of the Lord, let its doors be closed!

> I take no pleasure in you—said the Lord of Hosts—and I will accept no offering from you. (Mal 1:10)

What words will the Prophet now utter in the name of the national God, who, it might have been supposed, having favored Israel, was indifferent to the rest of the world? He expresses Himself in words which themselves would suffice to refute those who speak of Jewish particularism:

> For from where the sun rises to where it sets, My name is honored among the nations, and everywhere incense and pure oblation are offered to My name; for My name is honored among the nations—said the Lord of Hosts. (Mal 1:11)

From the perspective of this Jew, not only is mankind as a whole not excluded from divine concern, but this time it is Israel itself which seems to be so excluded. At least, the possible rejection of the chosen people is suggested so clearly that the Christian Apostles had later only to change into a irrevocable and hateful decree what here is but a conditional threat inspired by wounded love.

In Jeremiah there is a passage which can appropriately be set beside this one from Malachi.

> O Lord, there is none like You!
> You are great and Your name is great in power.
> Who would not revere You, O King of the nations?
> For that is Your due,
> Since among all the wise of the nations
> And among all their royalty
> There is none like You. (Jer 10:6, 7)

Amplification would be required to render the true sense of this passage, which is written in the elliptical style characteristic of Hebrew. Indeed, it seems harder to imagine a meaner conception, one more remote from the voice which the Prophets customarily use in speaking of divine grandeur, than to celebrate the Creator of heaven and earth by saying that He is without equal among the wise men of the nations! But the verses which follow leave us in no doubt about the true meaning of this passage, which we find also in Maimonides as well as in the Zohar.[11] After having acknowledged what is good and true in the pagan religions—the universal worship of God—the Prophet appropriately condemns the error which disfigures this worship: incarnating one's divinity in an idol of wood.

The verse of Zechariah which proclaims the future triumph of monotheism implies that there exists even now a certain knowledge of God among the Gentiles: "And the Lord shall be king over all the earth; in that day there shall be one Lord with one name" (Zec 14:9). This can mean only that the name of God, which is to say His true nature, is at present more or less misapprehended by the peoples who, even so, worship Him, though under false names (which is to say false representations); but God's authentic name and nature will ultimately be recognized by all and universally worshiped.

In support of this interpretation, we shall quote two very remarkable passages from Psalms. The first of these is in Psalm 48, composed on the return of an expedition of Israelites from the land of the Phoenicians:

> The Lord is great and much acclaimed. . . . See, the kings [apparently Solomon and Hiram] joined forces; they advanced together. At the mere sight of it they were stunned. . . . In Your temple, God, we meditate upon Your faithful care. The praise of You, God, like Your name, reaches to the ends of the earth. (Ps 48:2, 5, 6, 10, 11)

The Israelites on their return express their astonishment at having found the name and veneration of the true God even in distant places.

The other text is in Psalm 87:

> I mention Rahab [a poetic equivalent for Egypt] and Babylon among those who acknowledge Me; Philistia, and Tyre, and Cush—each was born there. Indeed, it shall be said of Zion,

"Every man was born there." He, the Most High, will preserve it. The Lord will inscribe in the register of peoples that each was born there. (Ps 87:4–6)

In this last verse, the Psalmist is undoubtedly emphasizing the small number of God-fearing pagans who deserve to be considered as though they themselves were sons of Zion; but he acknowledges with equal certainty that they *do* exist, however few, and thus that true worshipers of God are to be met with among all peoples.

Universalism in Rabbinical Literature

Even if we could point to no other text, Judaism's messianic promises would, we believe, be enough to demonstrate its universal character. Both the Bible and Oral Tradition agree that a time will come when the true God will be worshiped everywhere. On this point the rabbis offer many remarkable examples of their invariable fidelity to the spirit of Scripture.

In tractate Menahot (110a) of the Babylonian Talmud, we find the sages in agreement that the true God was generally known among men, at least as *supreme* God. Others, however, said that a line extending from Tyre to Carthage would divide the earth into two distinct parts with respect to the knowledge of God and the mission of Israel. Were the rabbis who expressed themselves in this way familiar with what was being taught in the philosophical schools of such masters as Porphyry, Macrobius, and Apuleius, and had they submitted in some measure to their influence? We should see in such an encounter of Jewish sage with pagan philosopher a confirmation of our thesis, of the sort we find exemplified in Paul, disciple of Gamaliel, Pharisee and son of a Pharisee (as he calls himself), who in his address to the Areopagus on the unknown god invokes the authority of a pagan author, Aratus of Cilicia.[12]

One could easily produce quotations from Maimonides, Kimchi, or Solomon Ibn Gabirol; but if we are to define the spirit of Judaism, it is preferable to cite the early rabbis.

The data that we seek come to us in an indirect way, through poetic and symbolic exegesis, in several rabbinical texts which we shall pass in review. Giving an allegorical interpretation to the silver basins weighing seventy shekels which were offered by the tribal chiefs at the Tabernacle (Nm 7), the *Yalkut Shimoni* says:

This corresponds to the seventy names of God, to the seventy names of Israel, to the seventy names of the Law, to the seventy names of Jerusalem.[13]

Now according to the rabbis, these seventy names of God represent the seventy nations descended from Adam, each of which in its own way acknowledges God. We find in the same book:

Israel has seventy names which correspond to the seventy names of God, as it is written: "The praise of You, God, like Your name, reaches to the ends of the earth." (Ps 48:11)

This is equivalent to saying that there are as many names of God as there are peoples on the earth, and that it is the same supreme God who is worshiped under these different names. Particularly if we consider that this number of seventy divine names does not correspond to anything else in Judaism, it is clear that no other interpretation is possible.

A rather obscure fact of biblical history is illuminated by this theory. We read in Exodus that Aaron, having taken part in the making of the golden calf, proclaimed for the following day "a festival of the Lord" (Ex 32:5). Without going deeply into the question of precisely what the Hebrews intended to represent by the golden calf, but considering how unlikely they would have been to make it a tangible image of the invisible God, it nevertheless seems certain that by a kind of incarnation of divine glory in a physical form, for the people such as Aaron, the image bore the name of God Himself. So the words of Aaron— "This is your God, O Israel" (Ex 32:8)—not only mean that this was the image of the God of Moses, but also imply the substitution of a *new* divinity in the form of a calf. Aaron's declaration, "Tomorrow shall be a festival of the Lord" (Ex 32:5), shows, then, that the worship of new gods, perhaps as intermediaries, would not preclude the knowledge and worship of a *supreme* God, which, according to the rabbis, was precisely the situation that obtained in paganism.

A number of rabbinic texts hint at least at the idea that beneath the names of the gods of the Gentiles there is an awareness of the unique and true God. Let us note at once that the borrowing of divine names by one religion from another is very natural and quite common. Dante himself did not hesitate to call God *Giove* ("Jupiter"). The school of thought which claims that the Tetragrammaton was not originally Hebraic and that it was only quite late that it applied to the national God of the Hebrews, *El Shaddai*, says in effect the same thing.

The first example we find of such borrowing is the Hebrew name of God *Elohim*, which, like *Adonai* ["my lords"], is plural. These two names undoubtedly reveal a polytheistic origin, but despite the vulnerability to which this adaptation must have exposed the Jews, they used these names for the unique God with a clear conscience. According to the rabbis, when God dictated to Moses the words "Let us make man in our image, after our likeness" (Gn 1:26), Moses had a moment's hesitation and cautioned God, "If You can do this, You will provide heretics with a subject for controversy!" "Keep writing," replied God. "Whoever insists on being misled will manage to be misled."[14]

There is nothing improbable in pagan names for divinity having been adapted just as *Elohim* and *Adonai*. Furthermore, these words should really be thought of as *common* nouns, since their etymology reveals their meaning generally to have been supremacy, rule, king-ship, or power. How much has been written in an effort to explain Azazel![15] The most probable hypothesis is that Moses, with a daring that would have confounded anyone else, adopted and sanctified the name of a pagan deity in order to designate *Absolute Justice*—a kind of personification of one of the divine attributes—because he had encoun-tered this name used by pagans to personify this very aspect of the true God. The instinct of universality led Israel to find its God in all modes of worship, as David discovered His actual presence everywhere in the physical universe.

Certain modern critics, even while acknowledging this fact, use it to assert that the Hebrews were originally polytheistic. They cite, for example, the name *Jerubbaal*, which was given to Gideon, a judge of Israel, to show that the worship of Baal originally prevailed in Israel. For in those early times before the Patriarchs, and even in postpatriarchal times if we think of the ignorant masses, there can be little doubt that this was so. But the presence of pagan *names* among the Hebrews does not in itself prove the persistence of polytheism. To the contrary, it argues in favor of our thesis. We notice, for example, that David gave one of his sons the name *Eliada*, "God knows" (1 Chr 3:8), but this same son is elsewhere called *Beeliada*, "Baal knows" (1 Chr 14:7). *Baal* and *Eil* seem here to be used interchangeably, which suggests that they were regarded as equivalent names. The Hebrew transcription of pagan names provides us with similar instances. Thus in the Jewish name *Putiel*, which corresponds to the Egyptian name *Puthi-phre* or *Poti-phera*, *Eil* is substituted for *Phre*, the name of one of the principal gods of Egypt. Eleazar even gave his son Phinehas (Hebrew *Pinehas*) the name of another Egyptian god (Ex 6:25). And, if finally, we see the name *Bosheth* ("shame, disgrace") replacing *Baal* in certain Jewish names—as in *Ish-bosheth*[16] and *Jerubbesheth*,[17] originally *Ish-baal* and *Jerubbaal*—we have clear evidence that *Baal* was originally the name of the pagan deity; and it would perhaps be rather easy to explain why this name, which seemed to the early monotheists innocent and religious, had a quite different connotation for their descendants.

The best way to summarize what we have been saying about the use of pagan names for divinity would be to recall a principle of the Kabbalists, according to which "all the foreign gods who are referred to in Scripture contain a spark of holiness." The philosophical study of the Hebrew language confirms in its own way this mystical explanation, by showing that the genius of the language is to proceed directly to the fundamental idea without stopping at the verbal form, and that one is perfectly entitled therefore to perceive the expression of divine qualities beneath the polytheistic names.

Besides, it is important to distinguish between the use per se of a name and its inner meanings. This distinction is drawn by Maimonides with respect to a question which Moses asks God:

> When I come to the Israelites and say to them "The God of your fathers has sent me to you," and they ask me, "What is His name?" what shall I say to them? (Ex 3:13)

The true believer is one who possesses the inner meaning of the divine names; for it is clear that if comprehension of their authentic sense is lacking, it is not the true God but a false approximation which is being worshiped.[18] Moreover, the expression "to know the name of God" means in the Bible to possess true religion, and the rabbis used analogously the expression "handing down of names" to denote the teaching of religious doctrine.[19] Among the ancients, theological speculation was not isolated from the practical application of words. This assumption of the sages that the divine names contain Israel's theological knowledge explains why Moses, in God's presence, insists upon knowing His name so that he might be able to provide evidence of the authenticity of his mission. Otherwise, it is hard to see what he could have hoped to gain from the merely verbal possession of a name. We see also why Scripture, urging us to fear and love God, speaks of the fear and love *of His name*. We may now perceive that exalted theological concepts are concealed within the names of God, and in the sacred Tetragrammaton par excellence, whose extraordinary (not to say antigrammatical) form in itself suggests the idea of a mystery.

> In a people which is still in its infancy [says Maury] the idea of a god does not go much beyond the word which designates it. This word contains nearly all of such a people's conception.[20]

But as ideas of God become more complex, people try to compensate for deficiencies in their original conception by adopting new names, each of which represents a particular aspect of the newly amplified idea of divinity. The study of the meaning of each divine name in conjunction with that of other words has therefore led to the development of a general theory of the nature of God arising from the totality of His diverse designations.

The Bible reveals this perspective when it has God say to Moses: "I have singled you out by name" (Ex 33:12)—exactly the opposite of what we mean when we say that we know someone "by name" in order to imply that we do not know him personally. But to Judaism, the name *is* the person, the word contains the essence of the being; and in deriving God's paramount name from the verb *to be*, it generated the most profound theological mystery that any language has ever been able to conceive: the union of two principles which some philosophers consider incompatible, the absolute and the individual.

These considerations may help us understand how the Jewish sages could remain faithful to the spirit of Hebraism at the same time they were seeking that part of the truth which might be concealed in the names of pagan divinities.

Far indeed from regarding monotheism as its exclusive fief, Israel finds its glory in being the heir, the representative, and the guardian of mankind's most essential beliefs, and it has always recognized these beliefs under the countless fables in which their authentic character was corrupted by the Gentiles. It is not only the grand principle of the unity of God which the sages strive to uncover in Gentile culture, but even, here and there, some knowledge of Jewish history and tradition, some observance of Jewish practices. The existence of these affinities between Jew and Gentile has long since been established. Some have used them to attack, though others to defend, Judaism. What concerns our present thesis is that Judaism has been aware of these analogies and has affirmed the very principle of their existence.

4

Divine Providence

We must now inquire into the particular characteristics of Judaism's faith in the universal God. Once again we shall turn to the Psalms in order to show that all mankind is invited to worship the God of Israel, that no people is regarded as alien to the divine concern.

> Let all the earth fear the Lord; let all the inhabitants of the world dread Him. (Ps 33:8)

> Ascribe to the Lord, O families of the peoples, ascribe to the Lord glory and strength. Ascribe to the Lord the glory of His name, bring tribute and enter His courts. Bow down to the Lord majestic in holiness; tremble in His presence, all the earth! Declare among the nations, "The Lord is king!" (Ps 96:7–10)

> Raise a shout for God, all the earth. . . . All the earth bows to You, and sings hymns to You; all sing hymns to Your name. . . . O peoples, bless our God, celebrate His praises. (Ps 66:2, 4, 8)

> Praise the Lord, all you nations; extol Him, all you peoples, for great is His steadfast love toward us; the faithfulness of the Lord endures forever. (Ps 117)

> All kings and peoples of the earth, all princes of the earth and its judges, youths and maidens alike, old and young together. Let them praise the name of the Lord, for His name, His alone, is sublime. (Ps 148:11–13)

DIVINE PROVIDENCE

We may appropriately follow this last text with one from Isaiah:

> None but the Lord shall be
> Exalted in that day.
> As for idols, they shall vanish completely. (Is 2:17–18)

Both texts announce the end of idolatry and the universal triumph of pure monotheism.

The dominion of the God of Israel—the God worshiped by Israel—knows no limit.

> Answer us with victory through awesome deeds, O God, our deliverer, in whom all the ends of the earth and the distant seas put their trust. (Ps 65:6)

> The Lord has established His throne in heaven, and His sovereign rule is over all. (Ps 103:19)

> Let all the ends of the earth pay heed and turn to the Lord, and the peoples of all nations prostrate themselves before You; for kingship is the Lord's and He rules the nations. (Ps 22:28–29)

And this jurisdiction of the true God does not extend over the human species alone; it embraces all of nature, and all created beings are called upon to praise Him:

> Heaven and earth shall extol Him, the seas, and all that moves in them. (Ps 69:35)

Psalm 148 in its entirety expresses the same idea, which is summarized in the very last words of the Psalter:

> Let all that breathes praise the Lord. (Ps 150:6)

By way of striking contrast, the Bible sometimes contrasts the universal dominion of the God of Israel with that of the gods of paganism. We hear the pagans speaking a language similar to that of our modern rationalists, and the Israelites respond in a way that shows clearly how utterly absurd they found the notion of a god whose sway is limited to a single people. Let us have a closer look. We may recall the Assyrian general, "the Rabshakeh," who harangues the Jews in the name of Sennacherib the king, reminding them of the innumerable people who were subjugated by the conqueror's sword without the gods of those peoples being able to rescue them, despite all the confidence that had been reposed in these deities:

> Did any of the gods of other nations save his land from the king of Assyria? Where were the gods of Hamath and Arpad? Where were the gods of Sepharvaim, Hena, and Ivvah? [And] did they save Samaria from me? (2 Kgs 18:33–34)

After these examples, how was Israel to believe in the word of its king, Hezekiah, who tried to persuade the Israelites that *their* God was capable of rescuing them from the Assyrians?

> Which among all the gods of [those] countries saved their countries from me, that the Lord should save Jerusalem from me? (2 Kgs 18:35)

As far as the Assyrian messenger is concerned, the assimilation of the God of the Jews with the gods of the Gentiles is as complete as possible.

What are the Israelites to answer? Their response will, in fact, provide their posterity with an index of their beliefs. The issue is, of course, whether the God of the Jews can logically be compared with other deities, and if, consequently, Judaism were nothing more than a national religion like all the others. Let us hear the admirable prayer which Hezekiah offers at this very moment. The particular importance of its beginning lies in the contrast which it draws between the authentic conception of God and the pagan system of local or national deities:

> O Lord of Hosts, Enthroned on the Cherubim! You alone are God of all the kingdoms of the earth. You made the heavens and the earth. (2 Kgs 19:15)

Then the king of Israel, refuting the errors of Sennacherib (and, by anticipation, those of the rationalist critics), exclaims:

> True, O, Lord, the kings of Assyria have annihilated the nations and their lands, and have committed their gods to the

flames and have destroyed them; for they are not gods, but man's handiwork of wood and stone. But now, O Lord our God, deliver us from his hands, and let all the kingdoms of the earth know that You alone, O Lord, are God. (2 Kgs 19:17–19)

Truly, we could not imagine a more convincing proof that for the ancient Israelites, nothing escaped the sovereign dominion of their God. Let us now see in more detail how they understood that universal Providence.

Universal Providence

It has been pointed out that when Aeschylus saw God's hand in the disasters which strike nations, he inaugurated the philosophy of history. But if it is true that according to the Hebraic conception, God's Providence embraces the entire universe, then the honor cannot belong to Aeschylus. Max Müller acknowledged this when, seeking a definition that would cover all the Semitic religions, he said that these are characterized by the worship of God in history, in contrast to the Indo-European religions, in which God is worshiped in nature.[1]

With respect to paganism, this definition does not seem very precise, for since the Indo-European peoples had national gods, we cannot be sure that they did not possess the conception of Divine Providence at least on the level of these national deities. Nor can one claim that the Semites were unaware of God as He manifests Himself in nature. What is, at any rate, certain is that even before Moses, the God of Israel had been clearly perceived with the characteristic of universal Providence. Thus, the patriarch Abraham intervened on behalf of sinners in the Cities of the Plain: "Shall not the Judge of all the earth deal justly?" (Gn 18:25).

And Isaiah declares:

> The Lord stands up to plead a cause,
> He rises to champion peoples. (Is 3:13)

The prophet's assertion in the verse which follows that the Lord will judge Israel is a specific application of this universal quality of the Lord as judge of all peoples.

Nothing better exemplifies this concept of general providence

121

than the notion of guardian spirits, invisible protectors, which Hebraism associates with each people. In no sense are these spirits to be regarded as deities equal to the God of Israel, as has been claimed; they are merely agents of the unique and sovereign God. Esoterically, they may be regarded as attributes or particular aspects of Absolute Being, which each people appropriates for itself, whether it personifies them as distinct deities—the basic error of polytheism—or subordinates such particularized conceptions of divinity to faith in the divine Unity, which produces the authentic religion for the Gentile world. The Hebrew expression "God of gods" should be understood in this context.

According to the Bible, how does Divine Providence reveal Himself?

> But the Lord abides forever; He has set up His throne for judgment; it is He who judges the world with righteousness, rules the peoples with equity. The Lord is a haven for the oppressed, a haven in times of trouble. Those who know Your name trust You, for You do not abandon those who turn to You, O Lord. (Ps 9:8–11)

> Peoples will praise You, O God; all peoples will praise You.
> Nations will exult and shout for joy, for You rule the peoples with equity, You guide the nations of the earth.
> The peoples will praise You, O God; all peoples will praise You.
> May the earth yield its produce; may God, our God, bless us.
> May God bless us, and be revered to the ends of the earth. (Ps 67:4–8)

Psalm 36 describes Providence, with notable religious and poetic inspiration:

> O Lord, Your faithfulness reaches to heaven; Your steadfastness to the sky. . . . Man and beast you deliver, O Lord. How precious Your faithful care, O God! Mankind shelters in the shadow of Your wings. They feast on the rich fare of Your house; You let them drink at Your refreshing stream. With You is the fountain of life. (Ps 36:6–10)

And Psalm 45 contributes its own inimitable accents:

The Lord supports all who stumble, and makes all who are bent stand straight. The eyes of all look to You expectantly, and You give them their food when it is due. You give it openhandedly, feeding every creature to its heart's content. The Lord is beneficent in all His ways and faithful in all His works. (Ps 145:14–17)

A modern author writes:

Already in the Pentateuch, God's actions are not limited to the chosen people. It is He who sends the Flood and disperses the nations following the construction of the Tower of Babel; it is He who destroys Sodom and Gomorrha. He saves the Egyptians from their famine. He destroys Nineveh, and awards victory to Cyrus.[2]

After the Flood, when God establishes His covenant, it is with all mankind, in the persons of Noah and his family: "I now establish My covenant with you and your offspring to come" (Gn 9:9). And that is not all. In benignant words which are often quoted, St. Francis of Assisi called the animals his "younger brothers." According to the Bible, it is not men only but the animals too who are included in the divine covenant:

This is the sign that I set for the covenant between Me and you, and every living creature with you. . . . I will remember My covenant between Me and you and every living creature among all flesh. (Gn 9:12, 15)

Joseph is not afraid to tell his brothers—these Bedouins of some three thousand years ago—that his going to Egypt was willed by God in a scheme of mercy, "to bring about the present result—the survival of many people" (Gn 50:20). Do we not find here, alongside the idea of universal Providence, a conception even more elevated—that the experiences and trials of the Patriarchs were means employed by God to advance the welfare of the Gentiles? And this text was written after the slavery in Egypt, at the moment when the Mosaic Law imposed upon the Jews a profusion of observances intended to perpetuate its memory! Will we be accused of exaggeration if we conclude finally that from the Jewish perspective, the dispersion of Israel and its worldly misfortunes were willed by God for the salvation of the nations? We have evidence of it here, at the very start of Israelite history, in these words of Joseph which are so generous and so filled with the sentiment of universal charity.

We have seen that in many passages of Scripture, God is called Judge, and that divine justice extends to all peoples. This presupposes a universal law, obligatory for all the human race, and a Providence who applies it without distinction among peoples, everywhere and always.

Divine Justice and the Election of Israel

We may say that the justice of God is the beginning of history. We see it at work in everything the Bible tells us about Adam and Eve, Cain and Abel, in the general condemnation at the time of the Flood, in the partial sanction against the Cities of the Plain. God comes in a dream to Abimelech in order to avenge the honor of Sarah, and Abimelech cries out an eloquent expression of the way in which he perceives this justice: "O Lord, will You slay people even though innocent?" (Gn 20:4)

The expulsion of the inhabitants of Canaan by the Hebrews has always evoked indignant protests from the enemies of biblical inspiration, who consider it to be a massacre blindly decreed by the whim of God for the sake of His chosen people. But in fact it is an expression of impartial justice. According to Moses, God's expulsion of the Canaanites is quite simply on account of their sins:

> For all those abhorrent things were done by the people who were in the land before you, and the land became defiled. So let not the land spew you out for defiling it, as it spewed out that nation that came before you. (Lv 18:27–28)

> So that I will do to you what I planned to do to them. (Nm 33:56)

> If you forget the Lord your God and follow other gods to serve them or bow down to them, I warn you this day that you shall certainly perish; like the nations that the Lord will cause to perish before you, so shall you perish. (Dt 8:19–20)

DIVINE PROVIDENCE

All these declarations are of the first importance. Israel is subject to the same divine Law as all mankind. Sins which rupture the universal harmony entail inevitable consequences for those who commit them, because for the sake of public order, the providential law of cause and effect must prevail consistently. Its inescapable force is nothing less than the expression of divine wisdom.

Not only does the Bible persist in emphasizing the similarity of Israel and the Gentiles with respect to divine justice, but it takes special care to refute the notion that Jewish people could have been chosen by an arbitrary act or even because its merit was found to be greater than that of its enemies.

> Say not to yourselves, "The Lord has enabled us to possess this land because of our virtues"; it is rather because of the wickedness of those nations that the Lord is dispossessing them before you. It is not because of your virtues and your rectitude that you will be able to possess their country; but it is because of their wickedness that the Lord your God is dispossessing those nations before you. (Dt 9:4–5)

Elsewhere, as if to discourage the smallest impulse toward pride, Moses calls Israel "the smallest of peoples":

> It is not because you are the most numerous of peoples that the Lord set His heart on you and chose you—indeed, you are the smallest of peoples. (Dt 7:7)

The great lawgiver provides as reason for the election of Israel God's love for her and His wish to keep the oath He had made to her Patriarchs. And we should not imagine a contradiction between this declaration and the ones cited from Leviticus, for it is clear everywhere that this special love of God's is ultimately nothing other than the consecration of Israel's special aptitudes for becoming guardian and propagator of the Divine Law in the World.

But here is something more remarkable still which adds a final touch to this portrait by Moses of the just and universal Providence. The lawgiver declares to his people that the misfortunes which will fall upon Israel will serve as moral lessons to the Gentiles, even as *their* trials have provided moral instruction to the Israelites:

And later generations will ask—the children who succeed
you, and foreigners who come from distant lands and see the
plagues and diseases that the Lord has inflicted upon that
land . . . all nations will ask, "Why did the Lord do thus to
the land? Wherefore that awful wrath?" They will be told,
"Because they forsook the covenant that the Lord, God of our
fathers, made with them when He freed them from the land
of Egypt; they turned to the service of other gods and worshiped them. . . . So the Lord was incensed at that land. . . .
The Lord uprooted them from their soil in anger, fury, and
great wrath. (Dt 29:21, 23–27)

This text needs no gloss. One could scarcely imagine a more
explicit expression of impartial justice and wise providence. Moreover,
it allows us to regard other expressions of the same order, wherever we
may find them—in Philo, perhaps, or in Josephus—as faithful echoes
of biblical ideas themselves. Before Paul expressed the idea, Philo
declared that belonging to Israel by virtue of birth does not give one
the right to call oneself a worthy son of Abraham.[3] He had only to
recall the emphatic words of Moses:

But if you do not obey the Lord your God . . . the stranger
in your midst shall rise above you higher and higher, while
you sink lower and lower. (Dt 28:15, 43)

But we find such a conspicuously orthodox sect as the Pharisees,
fully in the mainstream of Jewish belief, expressing itself in the same
way—though the Pharisees seemed, indeed, at least on the surface, to
scorn the pagans as warmly as they were scorned by them, and
through their rigorous discipline tended unceasingly to keep Israel as
far as possible from the Gentiles. One can be sure that their teaching is
a faithful statement of authentic Jewish faith, with no concession made
to the surrounding pagans. To the Pharisees, Abraham is the father of
all men—they have no compunction about calling him this—and whoever, abandoning idolatry, professes pure monotheism, may, whatever
his ethnic origin, be called Jew.[4] It is the echo of these Pharisee doctrines that we hear in the mouth of Justin Martyr when he declares that
those who have lived according to the Logos, such as Socrates,
Heraclitus, and others like them, were Christians before the preaching
of the Gospel.[5]

DIVINE PROVIDENCE

Let us recall once more that doctrine of the Pharisees, often cited, according to which all the just, whatever people they belong to, have a share in eternal salvation.[6] Such ideas, which the rabbis received from their religion, are consonant with those which the sane philosophy of the Gentiles suggests to its adepts. Consider, for instance, Eratosthenes of Alexandria, the "second Plato," who, two centuries before the Christian era, was teaching that we should not divide men into Greeks and barbarians but rather distinguish those who do good from those who commit evil.[7]

We find in the Talmud a passage which curiously recalls the reasonable element in Paul's doctrine of the rejection of Israel. It may be useful to cite it in connection with the biblical texts which we have quoted above, in order to show the continuity of Jewish thought on God's justice and Providence:

> The Holy One, blessed be His name, says: "These on one side are My creatures, those on the other are also the work of My hands. How, therefore, can I sacrifice one group for the other?" R. Papa said: "Thus men say, When the ox runs and falls, the horse is put into his stall."[8]

Rashi comments on this passage:

> This is what the Master would never have considered doing before the downfall of the ox, for He very much loved His ox. And when the ox eventually succeeded in recovering from his fall, the Master felt sorrow when he expelled His horse in turn from the stable. Likewise, when the Holy One, blessed be He, saw the fall of Israel, He conferred greatness on the Gentile peoples of the earth; and when Israel returns to God and receives God's mercy, God will suffer from having to depose the nations on account of Israel.[9]

When we read in the Gospels (Mt 3:9) that God can raise up children unto Abraham even from stones, this is no more harsh than what we find in the rabbis themselves. We can well imagine that the authors of the Gospels, all too disposed to sacrifice love of the Jewish heritage to their messianic ideal, made such declarations as a consequence of their hostility toward Judaism; but that the rabbis, faithful Jews and zealous patriots, could pronounce such words—this, surely, is convincing evidence of the austere concept they had of God's sovereign, universal justice.

Divine Providence in the Governance of Peoples

We have up to this point considered God's justice only in general terms. Now, we must ask how the Jews, who were so passionately patriotic, could conceive of God as the judge between all peoples, upholding all of them by His just Providence.

To begin with, we find the God of Israel intervening in the domestic government of the Gentile peoples. On God's order, Elijah anoints Hazael king of Syria (1 Kgs 19:15). Daniel says, as a general principle, that it is God who overthrows and installs kings (Dn 2:21). We recall, too, Isaiah's apostrophes against the tyranny of Sennacherib. Are we witnessing here the origins of international law, which even today is still in process of formation? The establishment of *jus gentium* has been credited to the Romans, but incorrectly, for the Romans regarded their empire as co-extensive with the world. The truth is that historically, Moses was the first to affirm its essential principle, and from a philosophical standpoint, it is clear that the very doctrine of universal Providence contained the germ of *jus gentium;* for if God rules the peoples of the world according to inviolable laws, nothing could be more natural or more just than that the peoples in their mutual relations should themselves be held responsible for the observance of these laws.

With regard to the destruction of the peoples of Canaan, we have seen that the Hebrews were the executors of an act of providential justice. One could point to similar episodes in the history of other peoples. Moses tells us in Deuteronomy 2:20–22 that the Rephaim were destroyed by the Ammonites precisely as the inhabitants of Canaan were later overthrown by the Hebrews. The prophet Isaiah explains that it is the God of Israel who presides over the conquest of nations (Is 45). In the prophecy on the expedition of the Persians against Babylon, God is represented as a commander-in-chief (Is 13:4). It is He who summons the "peoples of the north," together with King Nebuchadrezzar (Jer 25:9); and we see that the "cup of wrath" is given without distinction to Jerusalem and the cities of Judah, to Pharoah of Egypt just as to the kings of the Arabian lands and of the land of the Philistines (Jer 25:18–26). Thus Israel is not differentiated from the multitude of pagan peoples who must receive punishment for their wicked works. This principle of equality of treatment is carried so far that, according to the Bible, it was from God Himself that Sennacherib received the mission to subjugate Israel.

What, according to Judaism, are the manifestations of this "international law" which proceeds logically from faith in a single universal Providence which is guardian of all peoples? In Scripture, God is everywhere represented as the sovereign judge of the nations. In His eyes it is a crime to violate a people's frontiers and to attack its independence. Such is the reproach which Amos addresses to Damascus, Gaza, Tyre, Edom, Ammon, and later to Judah and Israel themselves just as to the Gentiles. So firmly rooted in the spirit of Judaism was respect for the rights of peoples that the Prophets are surprised that God does not always protect the rights of pagans from the violence of their oppressors (Hb 1:13). This is the context in which we should understand those solemn judicial assemblies of which the prophet Joel speaks, to be held in the Valley of Jehoshaphat,[10] where the nations which have enslaved Israel will find themselves called to judgment: Israel is not to be the object of special favor, but will receive divine justice exactly as the other peoples.

Let us note further that a God who is concerned not only with Israel's struggles but also with those of all the nations is truly the God of mankind, whose Providence is universal. It is this kind of situation that Amos addresses in declaring the divine punishment of Moab:

> Because he burned the bones
> Of the king of Edom to lime.
> I will send down fire upon Moab,
> And it shall devour the fortresses of Kerioth.
> And Moab shall die in tumult. (Am 2:1–2)

In the eyes of the Prophet, Israel is on the same level as the Philistines and the Syrians:

> To Me, Israelites, you are
> Just like the Ethiopians—declares the Lord.
> True, I brought Israel up
> From the land of Egypt,
> But also the Philistines from Caphtor
> And the Arameans from Kir. (Am 9:7)

We shall have occasion to see how human, generous, even heroic is the Mosaic principle not to hate the Egyptians (Dt 23:8). This people which had persecuted the Hebrews, and was properly punished for so doing, is in its turn set before us by Ezekiel as the object of divine redemption from the hand of *its* oppressors, just as Israel had earlier been redeemed from Egyptian hands. Divine Providence embraces all, Jews and Gentiles alike, with sovereign equality. The idea of impartial justice is here fully expressed.

The biblical prophecies are full of threats and promises relating to the pagan peoples. In Jeremiah, it is now Egypt which will be conquered by Nebuchadrezzar, now Gaza which will be subdued by a pharoah; or Moab, Ammon, or Elam which in the fullness of time, after severe punishment for their transgressions, will be restored. We read in the same prophet:

> Lo, days are coming—declares the Lord—when I will take note of everyone circumcised in the foreskin: of Egypt, Judah, Edom, the Ammonites, Moab, and all the desert dwellers who have the hair of their temples clipped. For all these nations are uncircumcised, but all the house of Israel are uncircumcised of heart. (Jer 9:24–25)

And a bit further:

> Thus said the Lord: As for My wicked neighbors who encroach on the heritage that I gave to My people Israel–I am going to uproot them from their soil, and I will uproot the House of Judah out of the midst of them. Then, after I have uprooted them, I will take them back into favor, and restore them each to his own inheritance and his own land. (Jer 12:14–15)

It is evident in all of these passages that it is the God of Israel Himself who gives to each people the soil which it should possess as an inheritance. Thus, the Bible mandates for Israel an unqualified respect for the rights of other peoples, for whom God is judge and avenger:

> And charge the people as follows: You will be passing through the territory of your kinsmen, the descendants of Esau, who live in Seir. Though they will be afraid of you, be

very careful not to provoke them. For I will not give you of their land so much as a foot can tread on. (Dt 2:4–5)

We must observe that these words [beginning] "Though they will be afraid of you" are tantamount to saying "If I strongly advise you to respect their rights, it is not because I fear that they will inflict a defeat on you; it is precisely *because* they will be afraid of you that I expressly charge you not to surrender to the temptation of an easy victory." Moab is the object of the same solicitude:

> Do not harass the Moabites or provoke them to war. For I will not give you any of their land as a possession; I have assigned Ar as a possession to the descendants of Lot. (Dt 2:9)

But justice by itself is not enough in international relations; mercy is as important. Peoples must extend help to one another in times of trial. It is precisely because they neglected this obligation with regard to the Israelites in the wilderness after the Exodus that these same Moabites were punished. Isaiah asserts that one should assist a wandering people, and we know how often the Prophets express their compassion for the calamities of the pagan peoples. This pity is even today embodied in the liturgy of Passover, and the credit goes to the early rabbis who commented on the matter:

> Why does the Torah not use the word "joy" in connection with the Feast of Unleavened Bread? It is because of the destruction of the Egyptians. Similarly, we read the entire Hallel during the seven days of Tabernacles, but only on the first evening and day of Passover. And why is this? Because you should not rejoice when your enemy falls.[11]

If, according to the Hebraic conception, God's plan legitimizes the existence of all peoples, if His Providence extends over all of them without distinction—if, in a word, each of them has rights as well as obligations—it goes without saying that the engagements which they contract among themselves must be honored as a religious duty. As a final example of this, we may cite an oath made to a pagan king by a king of Israel but violated by him. Zedekiah, having sworn fidelity to the king of Babylon, goes back on his word and rebels against him (2 Chr 36:16). The Bible and the rabbis are unanimous in regarding this violation of an oath to a foreign sovereign as a criminal act in the eyes of God.

It is clear, therefore, that Judaism recognizes a natural law which is international in scope. For her, a state of peace is the normal condition among peoples. At an early stage in Hebraic development, war was condemned, and aspirations toward universal peace became increasingly unambiguous in Hebrew literature up to the memorable moment when the great Prophets announced with unforgettable eloquence the coming of the messianic age.

Among the Gentiles, however, a state of war among peoples seemed usually to be normative. Hobbes, in his social philosophy, does not hesitate to apply this element of paganism to Christian society.[12] Plato makes Cleinias say:

> What most men call peace is only an empty word, and in reality all states are, in the nature of things, in a condition of continual war among themselves, without this endless war having to be declared.[13]

In order to achieve the concept of a universal providence extending to all peoples and sanctioning the legitimate rights of each, men must cease to believe that the national or ethnic group is all that counts, that mankind has no significant existence apart from the nation or tribe—an illusion similar to the geographical short-sightedness which limited the habitable world to certain small areas. "Narrow horizons beget stunted ideas," as Victor Hugo observed. We should not be surprised that such has not been the case with Hebraism, which teaches that all mankind has the same origin and thus that a single Providence looks over all.

Here, indeed, is an incomparably precious text of Isaiah:

> In that day, there shall be a highway from Egypt to Assyria. The Assyrians shall join with the Egyptians and Egyptians with the Assyrians, and then the Egyptians together with the Assyrians shall serve [the Lord]. In that day, Israel shall be a third partner with Egypt and Assyria as a blessing on earth; for the Lord of Hosts will bless them, saying, "Blessed be My people Egypt, My handiwork Assyria, and My very own Israel." (Is 19:23–25)

Before such words the spirit is abashed. Here, three thousand years ago, is an extraordinarily beautiful and tender confession of unqualified faith in Divine Providence. Unlike Paul, we do not say of this Providence that it knows neither Jews nor Greeks,[14] for that implies an inadmissable leveling of differences, a suppression of all nationality. We affirm, rather, that Providence recognizes equally Jews, Greeks, and Barbarians—in a word, all races and peoples, who ought to be perceived as one though without losing their individual identities. The divine blessing is given to Egypt and Assyria in moving language. Particularly admirable is God's use of the expression "My people" for Egypt. Some may say that these epithets are negated by the one which is conferred on Israel herself, for if Israel is God's "very own," is not the equality subverted? But no: it is *because* the Lord is God of all mankind that He accepts as His special portion a small fraction of the human race, the "firstborn" of the peoples, just as He receives the tithe of the fields and of the cattle, and the firstborn of man and beast.

Here is what the rabbis tell us in this matter:

> The election of Israel can be explained by means of a fable. A king possessed a cloak, which he commended to his servant, saying to him, "Shake it, fold it, take scrupulous care of it." "Lord," said the servant, "of all the cloaks which you possess, why do you give me such instructions about this one only?" The king answered, "It is because this one clings to my body." Likewise, Moses says to the Holy One, Blessed be He, "Master of the universe, among the seventy peoples You possess, You give me commands only for Israel." God answers him, "It is because they cleave to me, as it is written, 'Just as the girdle is attached to the vitals of man, so have I attached you to Me, O house of Israel.' It is because they proclaimed My kingship at the time of the Exodus from Egypt, in saying, 'The Lord reigns for ever.' "[15]

Thus understood, the designation of Israel as God's "very own" seems specifically intended *not* to contradict the idea of equality among peoples, which follows from the same passage. In this text, Isaiah is alluding to the subject which is the keystone both of Israel's history and destiny and of the religious future of the world: the conciliation of priestly Israel with lay mankind in a providential scheme embracing the salvation of the entire human race.

Moreover, we read in Psalm 82:2: "Arise, O God, judge the earth, for all the nations are Your possession."[16] This passage shows that Divine Providence reaches out over all peoples just as over the Jews, and that in each people there exists an "Israel," a portion which is God's own, in the persons of just and pious men.

Finally, no one is likely to dispute that the idea of a universal providence, which is the same for all and rules all peoples, attains its highest perfection in the messianic prophecies, which foretell the conversion of the entire human race to the authentic God worshiped by Israel.

5

The Idea of a National God in Judaism

According to our critics, the Israelites moved from their original polytheism toward pure monotheism by first of all attaining a conception of their own God, the special protector of the Jewish people, as being unlike the other divinities who presided over the destinies of the foreign peoples. This was their first step toward the notion of a unique God.

But as we have already pointed out, it cannot be denied that many texts clearly ascribe a universal nature to the God of Israel. What is necessary first of all, therefore, is to reconcile these passages with those in which the concept of God is said to be exclusively Jewish. It may be claimed that these latter texts are the oldest, and that the doctrine which we find in the others is much later in date; but it is impossible to prove this critically, for the two contrasting conceptions are found simultaneously in the biblical documents of every age and source. In this regard, some have objected that as the textual distinctions are so elusive, there is no reason to favor some texts over others unless to serve the needs of an a priori religious position. But what we have said about polytheism in general is surely relevant here: When the human spirit rises to a certain level in the refinement of its conceptions, it is this higher level that deserves our principal attention. Its less elevated expressions may reasonably be attributed to the inevitable inconsistencies of human thought, which, as it ascends, sometimes draws back in order to advance later: *reculer pour mieux avancer.*

The idea of a national god, let us hasten to say, is absolutely alien to Israel. According to Jewish thought, the God of Abraham, Isaac, and Jacob most assuredly existed before the Patriarchs. But whose God was He then? Is it conceivable that He whom the Scriptures call "Creator of heaven and earth" would for long ages have been God of no man? Let us not forget that according to the Mosaic doctrine, the human race is much older than Israel, and that 2,000 years had elapsed between the creation of man and the time Abraham received his call. It seems apparent that until the revelation at Sinai, or at least up to the time of Abraham, the God whose prophet Moses became was God of all men. How then can we explain this sudden transformation of the universal God into an exclusively national one? A little reflection will help us to avoid this common error of assuming that the God *acknowledged by Israel only* was also the God *of Israel only*. While each of the other peoples made it a point of honor to guard jealously its particular god, to feel no transcendent kinship with foreigners and even to regard all their finite deities as in a state of ceaseless contention, one with the other, Israel persisted in acknowledging no deity other than the One which, according to Jewish belief, must eventually be accepted by all men. It thus showed that unlike the other peoples, it conceived of mankind as one, by virtue of the common origin, nature, and destiny of all men. It is in this sense that we must understand the rabbinical dictum: "It is you, Israelites, who are men; but the pagans do not deserve that name."[1]

A text in 1 Kings juxtaposes with exceptional clarity the universalist conception of the Jews and the pagan notion of local or national gods. The ministers of the king of Aram, after his defeat by the Israelites, say to him, with reference to the God of the victors:

> Their God is a God of mountains; that is why they got the better of us. But if we fight them in the plain, we will surely get the better of them. (1 Kgs 20:23)

Later, the "man of God" who is adviser to the king of Israel, reporting these words of the Arameans to him, says:

> Thus said the Lord: "Because the Arameans have said, 'The Lord is a God of mountains, but He is not a God of lowlands,' I will deliver that great host into your hands; and you shall know that I am the Lord." (1 Kgs 20:28)

But, some will object, is the epithet "God of Israel" which we encounter at every step in the Bible not itself proof of the particularist spirit of the Jews? We have already noted that according to the simplest and most natural explanation, this expression refers to the God who is *worshiped* by Israel. Even after Israel's election, we often hear of the "God of Abraham, Isaac, and Jacob." Are we to assume that this God is somehow different from the God of Israel? In fact, surely, the expression is meant to remind us that Abraham, Isaac, and Jacob passed on their knowledge of God to their posterity. Analogously, "God of Israel" tells us that Israel, which inherited its faith from the Patriarchs, must by reason of its special calling transmit this faith in God to the other peoples—as has in fact been the case in all periods of its history. How grand, therefore, are the implications of this divine epithet with which we are sometimes reproached!

In general, when one made reference in antiquity to the God of a certain individual, the intention was to indicate a concept of deity rather than to provide a definition: to invoke, by association, God as the person in question conceived Him. From this derives the idea, so favored by the Kabbalists, that whenever the Bible speaks of the God of someone in particular, a reference is intended to one of the attributes or dimensions of the Divinity, and that these various qualities together form the *Merkavah* (Chariot),[2] which is to say, in philosophical language, that the complete conception of God is the consequence or totality of all the ideas which holy persons have formed of Him or have embodied in their lives. From the same premise comes also that beautiful conception of the Kabbalists that the union and harmony of spirits in this world is the means of bringing about the descent of Divinity to earth and His establishment here.

Furthermore, if the "God of Israel" has certain names which carry similar implications, He has other names whose character is unquestionably universal. What name could be more suggestive in this regard than *God of heaven and earth* or *God of all flesh*, to whom nothing is impossible, from whom nothing is hidden?

With respect to this name "God of Israel," the *Mekilta*, a rabbinic work older than the Talmud, contains a curious passage which exemplifies the universalist sentiment that prevailed among the rabbis of the Synagogue.[3] In the Torah section *Ki Tissa*, we read: "Three times a year all your males shall appear before the Sovereign Lord, the God of Israel" (Ex 34:23). The rabbis ask:

Why is it said "before the face of the Sovereign Lord, the God of Israel," since elsewhere we read simply "the face of the Lord?" It is because the name of God has been specially associated with Israel.

In the same vein, the *Mekilta* says:

Why do we read "Hear, O Israel! The Lord is our God, the Lord is one"?[4] Because it is we who should most particularly acknowledge His unity.

And elsewhere the *Mekilta* asks:

Why does it say "Thus speaks the Lord, God of Israel"? Is He not also called the God of all flesh? Once more, it is because God has joined His name most emphatically to Israel.

Likewise, it is written:

Pay heed, My people, and I will speak,
O Israel, and I will arraign you.
I am God, your God. (Ps 50:7)

The *Mekilta* comments:

"God" means God of all who come into this world, but despite that I have joined My name only to Israel.

We need not point out the importance of this passage. The *Mekilta* underlines in the various biblical texts both the particularist and the universalist implications, contrasts them, and reconciles them. An exception is made for the second of the passages [i.e., the Shema], in connection with which it is not said that God is here drawing closer to Israel but rather that Israel is attached more closely to God because of its special task of acknowledging His unity. Thus, a universal meaning is drawn from the text where one would expect it the least.

But here is another, hardly less striking, example of proximity between particularist and universalist ideas in Hebraism. On the one hand, we read in the Bible that the heavens are God's throne and the earth His footstool—even more, indeed: that the heavens and the heavens of heavens do not suffice to contain Him and that the earth is full of His glory—but on the other hand, not only does He reside in Zion, but He inhabits the Temple in Jerusalem, and more particularly still, the Holy of Holies, that tiny enclosure between the two cherubim. (From this last comes the biblical epithet "who sits enthroned on the cherubim.") Perhaps this double conception corresponds to the modern ideas of immanence and transcendence.

The matter has not escaped modern critics.

> What also characterizes the Israelite faith is that this exiled God, who embraces the world in His omnipotence and governs the universe itself, is linked to them in an intimate relationship. He is the God of their people, the protecting God who revealed Himself to their fathers and to the Prophets, who manifests Himself in their very midst. This combination of the most general and the most particular is altogether unique.[5]

We shall understand more about this double concept of deity when we consider Israel's role among the other peoples. We shall then discuss its idea of priesthood, which so admirably harmonizes the two Jewish notions of national and universal faith. But without anticipating these important matters, let us recall that there is in Isaiah a verse in which the two conceptions of God are not juxtaposed but combined, like two dimensions of a single idea:

> The Holy One of Israel will redeem you—
> He is called "God of all the Earth." (Is 54:5)

This is the same idea that we find in Moses:

> Now, then, if you will obey Me faithfully and keep My convenant, you shall be My treasured possession among all the peoples. Indeed, all the earth is Mine, but you shall be to Me a kingdom of priests and a holy nation. (Ex 19:5–6)

This passage is of the first importance, for it asserts at once and in the most categorical way the two conceptions. "You shall be My treasured possession"—these are the words of the national God. "But you shall be to Me a kingdom of priests"—now we hear the universal God; for inasmuch as priests are ordained only for the sake of a laity, the priesthood of Jews presupposes a mankind in whose service the Jews have been placed by Providence. We must observe also that the conception of a universal God is found even in the very words which evoke the particularist idea:

> You shall be My treasured possession among all the peoples. *Indeed, all the earth is Mine.*

Let us add, finally, that the election of Israel is offered as a reward:

> Now then, if you will obey Me faithfully and keep My covenant, you shall be My treasured possession among all the peoples.

These cannot be the words of a national God merely, a God who exists only for His people, as this people exists only for Him. Would the Lord not have been God of anyone if Israel had not fulfilled the conditions of election? A God, indeed, who can choose His people of preference is, evidently, the sovereign master of all. Far from being in His essence a national deity, He is clearly universal, since He has sovereignty over the entire world.

It follows from this that Mosaic religion, beyond its inherent aim with respect to Israel, is destined to fulfill a role in the life of all mankind. It has a double identity, national and universal; and Israel calls the Lord *its* God because in worshiping Him it worships the God which it has been called upon to make known to all men.

Incompatibility of the Idea of a National God with Jewish Thought

The Prophets are concerned throughout their writings with what the future holds for the worship of the God of Israel and the religious elevation of the Gentiles. This is all the more remarkable in periods when national feeling was especially strong and might be expected to suppress any universal impulses if the God of the Jews were, as it has been claimed, a purely national God. To the contrary, however, the two conceptions, particularist and universalist, appear side by side in perfect harmony, for the first of these expressed a basic instinct which vibrated through all of Israelite life, public and private, while the second embodied a most authentically Jewish aspiration which engaged all religious souls in Israel.

We cannot emphasize too strongly that the great profusion of texts in which the national idea and the universal conception of faith are linked form decisive evidence that the two doctrines, far from being successive steps in a spiritual evolution which proceeded from a lower concept to a higher, were conceived at the same time and appear to constitute a single, identical conception, which can be apprehended in two different ways.

Though this may surprise our readers, we would say further that the idea of a national god is not even conceivable in Israel. The religion of the God of Israel has no territorial homeland, unless we think of the place where mankind originated. According to its sacred Scriptures, this religion began with the creation of the world and of mankind—a conception which is in itself a decisive argument against any sort of localization. But even if we concern ourselves only with the history of the Jewish people, we see this history begin with a family of nomads whose descendants are enslaved in Egypt. The rabbis have so little sympathy with the notion of a local or national God that they trace Mosaic worship all the way back to the origins of mankind. In regarding Adam, the primal human unity, as the source of all subsequent humanity, the essence of all peoples, and in linking their own religion to this primal man, they intended, in a sense, to show that it was appropriate for the entire human race.

In the system of local divinities, however, god and territory are so indissolubly linked that one cannot exist without the other. The dominant characteristic of all the [other] ancient religions was autochthony, but it would be absurd to speak of territorial religion in connection with a people like the Jews which did not believe themselves autochthonous. Moreover, Mosaic religion, if we are to be precise, does not begin with Moses, and the rabbis' claims on this point are not without foundation. It had a long pre-history, a period of preparation. It seems reasonable to believe that the religion of Moses did not lose the universal character of the one which it replaced. The pre-Mosaic religion, altogether universal as it was, lacked a unifying organizational center. Thus, it was the more vulnerable to corruption and irreparable degeneration. But with Moses, it was provided with a permanent constitution, a center for worship, and formal participants.

Certain critics have satisfied themselves with saying that if the God of Israel was not God of the Jews only, at least He was to His worshipers a special protector, their very own. We believe that we have shown, with respect to Divine Providence, that the Bible proclaims equal justice for all peoples without distinction. If the "special protection" has any foundation in fact, it is, as we shall demonstrate in due course, solely for Israel in its role of priestly people—a role which is in the interest of all mankind. The "special protection" thus becomes, in a sense, perfectly universal.

Particularism and Universalism

But nevertheless, there is a sense in which the God of Israel *can* be called a territorial or local God without contradicting the universal conception at the heart of Hebraism. For a long time the worship of the true God had its seat in Palestine, and according to providential design, this tiny corner of the earth is destined once again to become its center when religious truth will be universally acknowledged. Conviction of this accounts for the unique role of the Holy Land in Mosaic religion, for the repeated declarations concerning the excellence and preeminence of this land, and for all the reiterated scriptural, rabbinical, and liturgical assertions which seem to limit Judaism itself (and, at times, even the dominion of God) to Palestine.

Such was the sanctity attributed to the land of Palestine that men would convey quantities of its holy soil to other lands so that altars might be established there and sacrifices offered. Here we shall cite neither a rabbinic nor a kabbalistic source but the Bible itself. When the Syrian Naaman, cured of his leprosy by Elisha, admits that "there is no God in the whole world except in Israel," and urges the prophet to accept a gift as evidence of his gratitude, Elisha refuses, whereupon Naaman cries out:

> Then at least let your servant be given two mule-loads of earth; for your servant will never again offer up burnt offering or sacrifice to any god, except the Lord. (2 Kgs 5:15, 17)

It has been said, too, that the authentic Mosaic worship was so territorial, so proper for Palestine, that it could not have been transferred elsewhere without losing its original character and form.[6]

It will not be contested that the life of a people is generally linked to the soil which it inhabits. According to the Zohar, the world (*alma*), man (*adam*), and the law (*oraita*) are the three complementary elements of history and of nature—that is, climate, nation, and religion are aspects of a single reality, depending upon whether one considers the land, its inhabitants, or their God.

But just as the overall nature of our planet and its relation to the entire universe underlies the climatic, geographical, and geological diversities of the various countries, so too, besides the particular laws of each place, there are the fundamental, underlying principles which form the common cultural resource of mankind. And likewise, from the religious perspective, beneath the idiosyncratic forms which distinguish or localize a religious ritual, and which, for example, have sometimes seemed to link Mosaic religion exclusively to Palestine, there is the conception of higher, universal ends which know neither political boundaries nor historical limits.

In fact, Mosaic religion is so far from being uniquely Palestinian that Moses' expression "in all your settlements" (Lv 23:31) surely signifies the adaptation of part, at least, of the religion to the diverse lands of Israelite settlement, just as the expression "throughout the ages" (e.g., Lv 3:17) has the object of universalizing it in time. And history has indeed shown that this cosmopolitan character of Judaism has helped it resist all dispersions and maintain its own life in all lands. Although the Holy Land is ever its preferred (though not indispensable) location, Judaism is so little tied to this soil that Moses, foreseeing the dispersion of the Jews over the entire face of the earth, stipulates as a condition of their return to Palestine the faithful fulfillment of the precepts of the Law:

> And [when] you return to the Lord your God, and you and your children heed His command with all your heart and soul, just as I enjoin upon you this day, then the Lord your God will restore your fortunes and take you back in love. He will bring you together again from all the peoples where the Lord your God has scattered you. Even if your outcasts are at the ends of the world, from there the Lord your God will gather you, from there He will fetch you. And the Lord your God will bring you to the land that your fathers possessed, and you shall possess it; and He will make you more prosperous and more numerous than your fathers. (Dt 30:2–5)

This extraordinary aptitude of the Jews for living under all skies and accommodating themselves to all countries—this remarkable and altogether unique instance of a people and a religion adapting to the most diverse cultures and resisting all upheavals, all external vicissitudes—

demonstrates vividly that Israel's calling was not merely national but universal.

But it will doubtlessly be pointed out that the Mosaic religion is clearly ethnic. Whether we study it at the period when it seems attached exclusively to the Palestinian soil, or whether we observe it later when it has survived the ruin of the Israelite homeland, it always presents itself as the religion of a particular people. We will not find in it, we are told, unmistakable signs of real universalism. To this we would answer what we have already said so many times, and must repeat, until justice has been rendered to Judaism: In this religion, particularism and universalism are closely linked, with the first at the service of the second. If there are Mosaic institutions intended exclusively for Jews, there is also the universal Noachide Law, which embraces, preserves, and proclaims the Mosaic religion. The priesthood of the Jews gives meaning to both, and forms a bond between them. Thus, Palestine and Israel are simply the two specific instruments providentially chosen to attain a universal end. The fortunes of this country and its peculiar people are bound up with those of all mankind.

PART TWO:
THE HEBRAIC IDEA
OF MAN

1

The Origin of Mankind

*M*en everywhere, impelled as much by ignorance as by pride, have attempted to trace their ancestry all the way back to our primal parents, while denying other peoples this same distinction of origin. If generous, they may permit these less favored groups to be mentioned in an appendix to their own history, where they themselves appear as the principal race of men. The foreigner or barbarian is thus presented as an inferior being whose nature remains coarse and whose development is incomplete. In refusing him the honor of common origin, we justify fighting with him, despoiling him, even killing him, as soon as our interest requires it. So it was in ancient times; so it is today, even among peoples who nevertheless pride themselves on their civilization.

The ethnology of the Jews rested on more liberal ideas, and their holy books are as interested in the ancestral origins of the other peoples as of Israel itself. To be sure, their Bible is intended especially for Jews, and except for a certain period in the early history of mankind, it neglects the other peoples in order to focus upon Israel. But it is also true that in its first chapters it sketches an outline of human history, before and after the Flood, which is so disinterested that it embraces all the peoples of the earth in a spirit of absolute equality. But even in its various parts which deal with Israelite history it is not unusual to meet with small digressions about some pagan people which show that for the biblical authors, there was no inclination to ascribe a contemptible origin to foreigners. Israel is so far from having been indifferent to the origin of the Gentiles, and to their historical development, that it can be said—with a good deal more reason than Florus had in speaking of the Romans[1]—that in reading through her history, we find not only the story of a single people but that of the entire human species.

147

THE ORIGIN OF MANKIND

In declaring that all mankind shared an original unity, Hebraism's conception of man rose to a lofty height. It put man on the very throne of God. It placed him, at the dawn of creation, on the still formless chaos, as a creative and organizing force, by deriving the soul of the first man from the spirit of God—the propulsive wind which blew on the waters—and from that soul deriving the soul of the earth.

For certain thinkers of our time, man is but the improved descendant of a quadrumane. For Rabbinic Hebraism, however, the monkey is a retrograde man. Thus, Hebraism agrees with science in affirming the relationship of man to all organic being. Perhaps we hear an echo of that tradition in the words of St. Francis of Assisi, when, like Buddha, he calls all the animals his younger brothers. Rabbinic thought makes of man the organizing force of the earth, and thus the germ of all that has life. Such is the meaning of that Aggadah which describes an Adam whose stature reaches from earth to heaven, and whose width extends from one end of the world to the other.[2] And from still another perspective, the Kabbalah sees in Adam the male principle of the world and in Eve the female, both being represented later by the two cherubim of the sanctuary, who were also male and female, born of the Logos (*Tiferet*) and the Cosmos (*Malkhut*).[3]

What boldness and breadth of vision! In its perceptions of the original unity of the human race, Jewish universalism attains improbable proportions. And yet this is far from being a freakish interpretation of the rabbis but is authentically biblical. Without it, the opening chapters of Genesis contain a mass of contradictions, mysteries, and puerilities.

We certainly do not wish to suggest that ours is the only acceptable reading of these first chapters of Genesis, nor that, apart from this nearly cosmogonic conception, the rabbis do not acknowledge a historical Adam, nearer to us and created in our image. We assert rather that one has only to read the biblical narrative in order to discover something more than the literal meaning. If a historical Adam existed, a mass of mythic ideas has nevertheless accumulated around him, apart from what Oral Tradition says of him, to the point of making him unrecognizable. Whatever the case may be, scriptural or not, this imposing conception of Adam is incontestably rabbinic and Hebraic. It should therefore enter into our calculations when we consider the universal tenets of Judaism.

In the light of these ideas, we believe that one should no longer speak of narrow perspectives or nationalist parochialism in connection with a religion which, in surveying its own origins, includes in a comprehensive embrace all men, animals, plants, and indeed the entire creation. Perhaps we should recall a certain rabbinic legend whose beauty has not been properly appreciated. In order to form the body of Adam, God took earth from beneath the future location of the altar in Jerusalem, or as the sages say literally, "from the place of His pardon."[4] How admirable all this is: the merciful love of the Creator; the supernal dignity of Adam, father of mankind, whose body was fashioned at the very altar of God; the gleaming flash of religious universality which illuminates this Judaism that has been considered so scrupulously particularist and this Temple which has been called the stronghold of the most selfish nationalism. We can also glimpse here the bond which in rabbinic thought joins the unity of mankind to the divine Unity. But indeed, once the latter has been accepted, is it not natural to think of the human species as having been created by a single act of that unique and sovereign power? In theory, the national deities might be imagined to have created the particular peoples which each was supposed to rule, but a *universal* God cannot be conceived as initiating so many special creations. Thus, belief in the oneness of human origins provides a new argument in favor of the existence of monotheism among the ancient Hebrews.

According to a distinguished author:

In polytheism, the division of peoples goes back to human origins, and is perpetual, for it derives from the plurality of gods, each of which is the emblem of a distinct people. Moreover, despite the progress of philosophy, the thinkers of Greece and Rome had rather the suspicion than the conviction that all men are brothers. This impediment to the conception of brotherhood does not exist in Mosaism. A single God creates the human race, and as a sign that all men are one in their nature, the Creator arranges for them to be born of a single man. He wishes even that the woman whom He gave to the first man should be drawn from him, so that the two sexes should in fact be one. Thus, the special election of the Jews was transcended by a higher, all-embracing doctrine: the unity of God, the unity of the creation.[5]

The brotherhood of all peoples and the communion of all with Israel, which is the focal point where all religious conceptions must meet—such is the ultimate consequence of mankind's unity of origin, which Hebraism proclaims so forcibly. Unity of origin becomes unity of history. The human race, single in its nature, since it issued from a single primal couple, continues to be single in its evolution, equal and without distinction before God.

There is a well-known rabbinic parable of a royal banquet, which appears also in the Gospels though with significant differences. In Matthew 22:1–14, we hear of a wedding feast prepared for invited guests, who, however, are indifferent to the invitation and refuse to attend, upon which the king changes the affair into a public banquet. In the rabbinic version, the banquet is, at the start, open to everyone, but because most of the guests have not responded, it becomes a private meal for the king's family only.[6] The great organism of human society is formed by a centripetal movement, and the day when there arose a people which took upon itself the mission of possessing and preserving religious truth and teaching it to all—on that day universal religion was born. And from that moment to this, it has not ceased its advance.

Superiority of Biblical Traditions to Pagan Legends

We can discern in pagan culture certain traces of mankind's most ancient legendary traditions. Hercules and Osiris, for example, are cosmopolitan figures. Osiris may well have been only a fiction designed to show that Egypt was the cradle of knowledge and enlightenment, which then spread among other nations; but since we find equivalents of this Egyptian deity nearly everywhere, we may conclude that the essential significance of Osiris is common to all peoples.

These dim, shadowy suggestions of a primal human community seem to us to demonstrate, by virtue of their similarity, and despite their differences from Hebraic traditions (or perhaps thanks to these differences), the truth of such very Jewish traditions. They also permit us to perceive the incontestable superiority of the biblical narratives to the more or less analogous legends which we find in paganism. All the Jewish accounts of the history of mankind apart from the particularisms of race or people, for example, appear radically transformed, with an altogether different character, when they spring, so to say, from pagan soil. The traditions of a common humanity, which are preserved by Israel, always wear, among the pagans, a national or local garb. Events in the Bible which concern the entire human race assume, when they pass into pagan culture, the impress of a particular history, proper to the people who are recounting them. This is a startling phenomenon, which emphasizes the faulty sense of universality among the pagans, and so renders this element of Hebraic culture all the more impressive.

The exceedingly remarkable matter of which we speak has not escaped the attention of scholars whose objectivity could not be suspect. According to M. Burnouf:

> These traditions of Genesis are in fact found in more complete and explicit form in the sacred books of Persia, and even, in part, in the Vedas, where they are presented as belonging to the race which has produced these books, whereas in Genesis, they are most often alien to the Israelite traditions.[7]

We must note this significant fact, that the traditions of Genesis are found in a "more complete and explicit form" in the sacred books of Persia and in the Vedas. Here is striking confirmation that the scriptural writer did not invariably draw his materials from his own mind or from the traditions of his people, but from a common source, richer than his narrative itself, which, with respect to this source, is inevitably fragmentary.

> The particular national character which has clothed each version [says M. Maury] could not contradict the essential singleness of the Flood story, since whenever a mythic tradition is imported into a country where it is foreign, it necessarily takes on the character of this new culture. The comparative study of ancient religions has shown this to be so without a doubt. Every people brings to its culture materials whose original context it does not understand, and imposes a local shape and habitation upon the poetic expression of phenomena which are common to all the earth.[8]

It is not, finally, from the historical point of view only that Genesis affirms Hebraic cosmopolitanism; we can also infer from this cosmopolitanism a program for the future of our species. Mendelssohn, who seems to have been the first to notice this, explains it in these words, which we borrow from his friend Friedenthal:

> It is Mendelssohn who asserted a principle which is indispensable in the study of our holy Law. The entire narrative of Genesis, he says, and everything which Scripture reports of Adam and Eve, Cain and Abel, is true and certain without any doubt. All that is told of these figures actually occurred to them. We find here, however, be it type or symbol, the very pattern of what must happen to all the human species in general. . . . That is why the Bible uses so many details in speaking of these figures.[9]

And let us note that this kind of historical typology has been applied to other scriptural texts as well. The Six Days of Creation have been interpreted as a prophetic paradigm of the entire history of the world. The history of the Patriarchs symbolizes that of their descendants, and the life of Adam is regarded in the Talmud as adumbrating that of Israel.[10]

2

Human Dignity

*I*n no religion or philosophy has respect for human dignity, even for the human form itself, been developed more fully than in Judaism. Human value and holiness have imbued many Jewish doctrines, each more suggestive than the other.

For the rabbis, all souls were comprehended in that of Adam. They even go so far as to introduce the human form into the spiritual world, in their conception of the Celestial Man which is composed of all individual souls.

> Know that there exists on high a substance called "body" (Hebrew *guf*) in which are found all the souls destined for life [as the rabbinical sages have taught]. The son of David will not come before all the souls which are in the *guf* have completed their descent to the earth.[1]

But we hardly need such a curious doctrine if we recall that when the Bible tells of God's revelations, He always manifests Himself in a human form. In Genesis, man is not only the most perfect of created beings, but he is called, in so many words, the image and likeness of God. We are well aware that for some biblical critics, the narratives of the Torah convey mere anthropomorphisms, in which God is imagined by the inspired author to possess a bodily form just like man's, whereas for other exegetes, the resemblance of God and man according to Mosaic thought is purely spiritual. Our own view is that the true meaning of such scriptural accounts should be sought in the Kabbalah, which refuses to separate physical resemblance from spiritual resemblance, any more than it is willing to separate soul from body. Thus, for the Kabbalah, the assertion of Moses that man is created in God's image refers to *both* soul *and* body.

Not, of course, that the Hebraic Kabbalists ever dreamt of ascribing corporeality to God. Indeed, they would sooner deny it even in created life, at least in the sense in which corporeality is commonly understood. But they believe that the body must be made in the image of God in the same sense that they believe it is made in the image of the soul or spirit, which shapes its material manifestation according to its own authentic nature. That is, they do not conceive of any force, function, form, or capacity in the human body which is not a material realization of corresponding aptitudes, forces, or properties in the Holy Being. There is no need to add that it is the same for moral and intellectual faculties; for thought and its manifestations, as well as life and its functions, are modeled on the supreme archetype of all things.

However we may understand the resemblance between man and God which Moses affirmed, the high dignity of man is axiomatic, and the implications of this idea are unalterably precious. But in Hebraic thought, man is not only created in the image of God; he is also regarded as a microcosm, an epitome, of the entire universe. This rabbinic conception seems to us to have its origin in Scripture. Man, the last-created of God's creatures, is by his very nature a synthesis. According to Nachmanides, the words "Let us make man" (Gn 1:26) are addressed to all the forces of the universe.[2] This suggests that the notion is not foreign to the Bible. Moreover, the same conception of man can be found in classical antiquity. One scholar writes:

> This theory of the Stagirite [Aristotle] is profound: considering man to be the highest development of organic creation, it sees in him the natures of all inferior beings joined together, plants (nutrition, vegetative life) as well as animals (sensation, movement, desire, sensory life). What distinguishes him is his rational soul.[3]

Man, then, image of God and epitome of the universe, has according to Judaism an incomparable nobility and grandeur. And when we consider that according to its traditions and sacred writings, these sublime prerogatives belong not to Jews only but to all men equally, pagans as well as barbarians, we wonder with amazement how a four-thousand-year-old religion was able to advance such doctrines, and how it can be possible even now to question its universal aspirations.

HUMAN DIGNITY

Man as Temple of God

Hebraism bestows on man a still more majestic title in making him the temple of God on earth, because, as we have said, he epitomizes all parts of creation and fulfills, in a sense, the necessary organic conditions for receiving and sheltering the Spirit which animates him. (In the same way, the human soul can attain natural life only when attached to the human body.) This is not a kabbalistic idea only, but is professed also by such theologians as Judah Halevi, author of the *Kuzari*, who—without drawing on the Kabbalah—teaches that appropriate form or material organization is a necessary condition for the descent and habitation of Spirit.[4] Yet if we reject the Kabbalah, we shall lose an abundant source of noble and profound doctrine.

To the Kabbalists, the human body and its physical faculties are the embodiment and clothing of spirituality. Created in the image of divine reality, man is its realization in matter. Not only do the rabbis of the Talmud and Midrash agree on this point, but the Bible itself is familiar with it. The notion of the presence of God, the immanence of the *Shekhinah*, appears often in Scripture; and though here it is nature, the totality of created things, which is represented as the temple of God, the ideas are closely related, and the more comprehensive conception of divine presence implies (at least in a certain measure) the other.

Assuredly, the perfect temple is the holy nation itself, pending the time when it will be all of mankind; but the individual, as one of the stones of the edifice, is also a temple, not only by virtue of being a part, but because on his own level and in his limited sphere he too reproduces the holy. For the world, viewed from a spiritual perspective, has this characteristic: Its component materials, which together form man (the higher being), are not merely means; they have their own ends and their own intrinsic value, at the same time that each joins with the others in the composition of the whole. For Hebraism, the universe, mankind, the nation, and man are in reality so many stages through which the Holy reveals Itself and in which It dwells. Consequently, it is reasonable to see in these stages so many parts of the temple of God.

This theory of man as temple of God has appeared elsewhere besides Judaism. When Jesus, questioned about the coming of the kingdom of God, answered: "The kingdom of God is within you" (Lk 17:21), he was undoubtedly repeating what a thousand voices, all around him and before him, had declared. But paganism itself, through the voices of its most illustrious thinkers, sometimes spoke with a keen intuition of this truth. *Deus in viro bono sedet* ("God is found in a good man"): thus Zeno.[5] Demosthenes also uttered this noble sentiment: "The most beautiful and most holy altars are in the very soul of man."[6] Hebraism does not dispute with the sages of Hellenism the glory which is justly theirs. It claims only to have said these things earlier, and to have said all of what they have said fragmentarily.

Nobility of the Human Body

When Hebraism insists that man is the image and temple of God on earth, it refers to the physical as well as spiritual dimensions of man's nature. This is a unique postulate of Jewish thought as was noticed long ago, for among all the peoples and religions of antiquity, Hebraism and the Hebrews were the only ones who redeemed or rehabilitated matter. It has even been asserted that they went so far in this direction as to have repudiated the claims of the spirit itself and to have glorified matter alone; that conceding importance only to the external realm, they, in effect, denied the existence of the spiritual in man. Such a conclusion, though biased and erroneous, at least demonstrates vividly how highly Judaism regards the human body and all that concerns it. Though essentially false, it nevertheless shows that by a broad consensus, Hebraism ascribes an exalted dignity to the human body. Even a hasty survey of biblical, Talmudic, Midrashic, or kabbalistic literature would suffice to convince us of this.

In the ritual legislation of Judaism, the body receives the most minute attention. No physical matter is considered unworthy of religious notice. This kind of constant concern for the body is, however, entirely different from the regimen of penance, of systematic constraint, in which other religions strive to hold it. The premise from which these other religions draw their inspiration, far from being the same as that of Judaism, is in fact radically antipathetic. Between the two there is all the distance that separates esteem from scorn, love from hate, the desire to gradually transform the body and its processes into submissive instruments of spirituality from the fixed determination to overthrow it, even to annihilate it: in a word, all the difference that exists between the body ennobled and the body extinguished in nirvana. Material goods, health, wealth, happiness, longevity are evaluated according to the same touchstone. What one thinks of them depends on the value one places upon the body itself. Here, indeed, is the root of that error which infers from the significance that Judaism attaches to the body (and to material goods generally) a proof that its conception of spirituality is defective. This is, rather, the most unchallengeable evidence of its spirituality, since the form and well-being of the body, life itself and its diverse goods, are indissolubly associated with religion and sanctity, the love and fear of God. Temporal fulfillment is linked to obedience to God's commands. We obtain it as a reward, we lose it as a punishment. We use it for objects always moral and lofty. It is regularly accompanied by spiritual gratitude and submission. It is not, then, that in Judaism spirituality is lacking, but that the material realm is saturated with it. Spirit is not absent simply because it must accompany a body.

There is in this aspect of Jewish ritual and law something analogous to what Judah Halevi points out in Jewish history. He says, quite accurately, that a people which has witnessed in all phases of its public and private existence the direct, nearly visible intervention of God had no need to be talked to about the Spirit, about its authority and influence, since its entire life had constituted an eloquent plea on behalf of the spiritual.[7] It is much the same with respect to the practical precepts of Judaism, so numerous in comparison with the relatively few professions of spiritual faith that we find in the Bible. Material life was itself disciplined by spiritual principles. One tried to shape it in such a way as to make it reproduce in itself the life of the spirit. Just as matter and spirit were not conceived separately, so also (with a logic almost beyond admiration) in the principles and laws concerning man, this creature at once physical and spiritual, material act was not set apart from act of faith, motion from thought, history from conscience, earth from heaven, this world from the kingdom of God. In practice as in principle, all were linked together, and the concerns of the temporal domain inevitably called to mind and implied the life of the spirit.

Human Freedom

According to Moses, is man a free agent? In the view of some, the answer is no, and they have seen the great lawgiver as precursor of that modern school which believes it possible that society as well as individual moral life can exist without freedom. And yet the language of Moses seems to show that he did indeed believe in human freedom. If he had not seriously counted on this great force or powerful lever to raise and sustain the social structure, one could scarcely imagine his mission of religious lawgiver and founder.

His philosophy of penal law surely demonstrates the same point. It may be conceded, no doubt, that he aims at the moral effect of his threatened punishments, at the salutary example which punishment of the guilty ought to have for others; and this can be reconciled with determinism. But what is still more certain is that Moses contemplates an ideal of justice which requires the expiation of the offense and which links the punishment to the crime as effect to cause. The *lex talionis* (law of measured retaliation) itself—which, if we follow the rabbinical tradition, was by no means part of Moses' intention even though it appears in his language and formulations—was, in any case, the most energetic expression of justice which is neither utilitarian nor pragmatic but rather ideal and meaphysical. Now this penal system cannot be sustained without the i   a of freedom. The biblical instances which seem to put human will at the mercy of God, such as the hardening of Pharoah's heart or similar cases, show what human nature becomes when it is left to itself. It is as final punishment that God blinds or hardens. The exception confirms the rule, for one would certainly not speak of divine intervention in such a small number of episodes if all human act, without distinction, were the effect not of free will but of God's decree or a blind fate.

We find another demonstration of Moses' faith in human freedom in the proscription of star-worship. This is a condemnation of determinism, which, for the ancients, depended on the influence of celestial bodies. For the Torah, man is not a slave to the material world but is superior to it. "Look toward heaven and count the stars," says God to Abraham (Gn 15:5). With respect to which the rabbis, commenting upon the word "look" (Hebrew *habbet*), which means to look down from above, say that God raised Abraham above the skies to show that he is superior to them, and that instead of being under the yoke of nature (as he would necessarily be if deprived of freedom), he is master of it, having been called to dominate and subjugate it.[8]

Freedom of moral decision follows so ineluctably from the Torah that it provides, in our opinion, one of the best arguments against the presence of pantheism, which some have claimed to find there. There is no doubt that if pantheism were the basis of Hebraic thought, freedom would not play such a large role in the Bible, for there is nothing more repugnant to pantheism than free will. One might even say that freedom is its chief and perhaps only negation, since it is the most resounding manifestation of the personality of the autonomous individual.

The conception which Hebraism has developed of the dignity of man requires the solemn affirmation of freedom, and it is because he is free that he is also perfectible.

The Imitation of God

Is it possible to imagine a free being who is not capable of moral improvement? Can we imagine a morally perfectible person who is not, at the same time, free to draw nearer and nearer to an ideal of absolute perfection? And what good would it do a man to be free if he did not use his freedom to fill up the gaps in his being, to advance, as it were, his own creation?

Being free, man is therefore necessarily perfectible. Freedom is precisely the means at his disposal to acquire what he lacks. And let no one object that God, being absolutely perfect, is free without being perfectible. It is exactly in this quality of absolute perfection that we call Him free, for freedom in Him is identical with necessity. As He is absolute and infinite Being, and as there is nothing outside Him which can influence Him—as He cannot experience any necessity—freedom for Him consists in acting according to His own nature, which is absolute and perfect. In other words, His freedom necessarily expresses itself in the direction of the Good. Other beings, however, having only a relative perfection, are influenced in their acts because there are causes outside themselves which act upon them, and perfectible beings are free to rise or fall precisely because they are perfectible. Their improvement is contingent upon the good use of their freedom.

Belief in human perfectibility has given birth to a great ethical principle of the Bible and rabbis: the imitation of God. Man, created in God's image, should recognize as a practical rule of conduct the imitation of his Creator, that is, a drawing ever closer to his divine model, an effort ceaselessly increasing to reproduce in himself that image which is the law of his being. From this comes the law of indefinite progress, which is derived on the one hand from the infinite perfection of the model, and on the other from the imperfect nature of the copy. For it would be inadmissible to claim that man is created in the image of God if he were infinitely distant from his model and without at least the capability of drawing ever closer to Him.

It is easy to find in the Torah other proofs of belief in human perfectibility. It is not, indeed, merely by chance that although the account of each day's creation in Genesis ends with the words "And God saw that this was good," nothing of the sort is said after the creation of man. That is because only man is not good *until he perfects himself.*

Also relevant in this connection are the blessings (*berakhot*), of which the Torah offers many examples, along with their effectiveness. They are a religious expression of faith in progress, for every *berakha* implies the idea of a good which we do not yet possess but wish to obtain. And as the blessings are informed by an ethical order, belief in the perfecting of man is implicit in them.

But there are demonstrations still more convincing. Domination of nature is the great promise made to man, and the great duty which is imposed upon him from the moment of his creation. Now that domination, by reason of the nature of the worker and the conditions of the matter on which he works, can only be successive and gradual, so that this grand, imposing promise assumes faith in human progress. As a matter of fact, man will never achieve mastery of nature unless he masters himself, unless he perfects his intelligence and strengthens his will. Morally and intellectually, he must make himself ever more worthy of his mission. He has to achieve interior, subjective progress before he can gain external, material progress. In Mosaism, man is so essentially perfectible that he draws nature with him in his ascent.

To be sure, in Genesis, domination of nature takes the form of dominion exercised over the animal species. But if we reflect upon the particular conditions of human existence which obtained in the first ages of the earth, upon the antediluvian animals whose nature was such as to inspire great terror in men, of the continual struggles which were required against them, we must agree that in humanity's infancy, the divine idea could not have assumed any other form better able to impress the imagination. Among the ancients in general, moral confrontations and (with all the more reason) social and ethnic conflicts easily assume the shape of hand-to-hand struggle with giants or monsters. Even the gods and heroes of paganism had to fight against wild beasts. Nevertheless, this blessing in Genesis has a much more general character, for it extends the domination foretold for man over the entire terrestrial globe: "Fill the earth and master it" (Gn 1:28). The words are as precise as possible and omit nothing from the domination promised to Adam's descendants. It is not merely a question of arable land but of the entire earth. To these words are linked all the triumphs of mankind on the planet we inhabit.

We would be misconstruing the grandeur and fruitfulness in this blessing on the first page of Genesis if we were to limit its importance to the awareness of nature. This awareness, and the polytheism which sprang from it, focused men's attention, in general, on material reality, and induced a kind of fatalistic acceptance of what exists, beautiful or ugly, useful or hurtful, evil or good. To bring about moral changes as well as the wonders which human knowledge can impose upon nature, another factor is needed, which is not and cannot be mere reality, pure and simple; what is needed is faith in the ideal, we might almost say the opposing of the ideal to the real. For it is only when man rebels against nature, which crushes him—when he rises up against the outer world—that he imposes his will upon it and makes even material progress possible.

But to acknowledge the ideal is to recognize that there exists something transcendent, something beyond nature, of which nature is but a pale image; something which shines with a purer luster in the thoughts of men. And the proof that we do not derive this ideal from nature herself is that we perfect nature by means of it.

The name which "human perfectibility" bears in Hebraism suggests ethical, social, intellectual, and at the same time religious progress. It is a road, a way, a journey, a route—all these things are included in the highly expressive word *derekh*, which is strikingly analogous to the Chinese *Tao*. The act of perfecting, all effort, all human progress, is an advance (Hebrew *aliyah*) along this road—which calls to mind once again man's natural disposition to imitate God, for every road necessarily implies a goal toward which one strives. The starting point, the guide, and the goal—or as the Evangelist, whose mind is filled with Hebraic ideas, [quotes Jesus], "the way, and the truth, and the life" (Jn 14:6)—are divine. Hebrew also offers three other significant expressions for the idea of moral perfecting: to walk before God, to walk with God, and to walk behind God. Offense, error, ignorance, evil, rejection by God, are thus either a turning aside or a turning back.[9] With a fine clarity, the Bible says of the wicked that they go backward and not forward. To disobey the law of God is to go backward. The thought here is as profound as the image is striking.

The idea of rising or ascending is often joined in the Bible with that of walking. We read of an ascending path, a mountain to climb, a summit to attain; and in these expressions what is at issue is not always the Temple of Jerusalem. Perhaps the Temple's location gave birth to this figure of speech because people had come to relate the idea of holiness to the idea of height, but the image itself was already an appropriate convention for representing human perfectibility.

This notion of moral perfecting is related to the rabbinical doctrine of metempsychosis or reincarnation. According to the sages, the object of reincarnation is to allow souls to attain the degree of perfection of which they are capable but which they had not been able to realize in their earthly life—this by means of *successive* lives. It seems to us that the theory of reincarnation, like the idea of resurrection—which is surely the most audacious affirmation of progress!—does not belong to the rabbis only but has solid foundations in the Bible itself. But we are considering it here from the philosophical point of view. Just as belief in palingenesis is a declaration of progress in the cosmic order, whereby the successive renewals of the world lead naturally to amelioration, so the doctrine of reincarnation attests to the faith of Hebraism in human perfectibility.

> The ox is called an ox from the time it enters the world [say the rabbis]. And it is so with the other animals. But man becomes a man only when he earns this identity.[10]

And with regard to a phrase in Numbers 15:39, "Observe them" (i.e., "fulfill My precepts")—in Hebrew *va-acitem otam*—the sages note that *otam* can be read in the holy text as if it were *atem*, "you," and the phrase then be read "you will be your own creators."[11]

Finally, we shall cite a curious Midrash.

> One day a philosopher asked Rabbah Hoshaya this question: If circumcision is so precious to God, why was it not ordained for Adam? The sage answered: "Why do you shear part of your hair but allow your beard to grow?" "It is because my hair has grown along with me since my early infancy" [i.e., my hair has been with me since childhood and therefore is of small value]. "If that is the reason," responded the rabbi, "should you not also blind your eyes and cut off your hands, since they too have grown with you since infancy?" The philosopher answered: "Have I come to see you only to receive such answers?" To which the rabbi responded: "Since it is not possible for me to send you away without an explanation, hear this: All that was created during the Six Days requires perfecting, and man too needs to be perfected."[12]

Immortality of the Soul

This is not the place to examine the arguments, as strong as they are numerous, that have been advanced to prove that belief in immortality of the soul exists in biblical Judaism. We ourselves have studied them in detail elsewhere,[13] and we believe that they will convince every man of good faith, however sure he may be that Moses and Scripture are generally silent on this subject. We shall say only that Hebraism's exalted conception of the dignity of man implies this belief, and that its presence in our sacred texts can easily be demonstrated. When Adam is expelled from Paradise, God says:

Now that the man has become like one of us, knowing good and bad, what if he should stretch out his hand and take also from the tree of life and eat, and live forever! (Gn 3:22)

Man is thus capable of immortality. But what in this text is a mere potentiality had previously been an actuality. The sole prohibition he was given in Paradise was eating of the tree of the knowledge of good and evil. All the others, including the tree of life, were therefore permitted to him. We can infer this only indirectly, from the prohibition itself, but directly, from the earlier permission, which even takes the form of an order or injunction:

And the Lord God commanded the man saying, "Of every tree of the garden you are free to eat; but as for the tree of knowledge of good and bad, you must not eat of it." (Gn 2:16–17) [14]

So if Adam had not been immortal by his original nature, he would have become so by eating of the tree of life. It is only on account of his sin that he loses this privilege; but God's original design has not been given to us in vain, and sooner or later it must be fulfilled. Indeed, these chapters of Genesis seem to present an ideal and a program aimed at this very fulfillment. It follows that the destiny of man is to become immortal. And if we recall that the Law is called "tree of life" (Prv 3:18), and that its precepts give man life,[15] we shall not hesitate to see in eternal life the ideal which is offered us. This illuminates, too, in an unexpected way, that promise of life which the Torah repeats so often for those who observe the Law.

It will not be disputed that in these passages and others like them, the idea of national life in Palestine, and even that of individual longevity, are not entirely absent. But the text from Leviticus just cited, in which it is not a question of either of these, shows that Moses understood another life which is neither physical nor individual, nor the political life of the people. What he alludes to here is, surely, analogous to the life with which Adam was endowed, which he lost on account of his transgression, and which he was said to be capable of regaining, even after the Fall, by eating of the tree of life. Immortality, then, is a divine gift which he is destined to recover; for if the role of man is to crush the head of the serpent—that is, to destroy the cause of evil, the principle of his downfall—it is evident that the privileges of his earlier condition will be returned to him.

Such is the psychological constitution of man upon which his intellectual and moral nature are founded. It is this last, both before and after the sin, which particularly interests us. The future of the human race indeed depends upon the moral state of man after the Fall, for it is only insofar as he has preserved his natural disposition to love the good that one can hope to see him realize it on earth. To resolve this question about man's moral condition after the Fall, we are led to ask another, which is both historical and metaphysical: From the perspective of Hebraism, what is the sin of Adam?

However we address this question, we can assert that for Judaism, the consequences of Adam's sin are not so deadly that the nature of man is irreparably corrupted by it nor human existence and destiny poisoned by its influence forever. According to Hartmann:

> Mosaism expresses most clearly a faith in the possibility of realizing individual felicity here on earth. It does this both through the expectations which it fosters and through the optimism of certain of its general conceptions about the world, in which there is no transcendent element.[16]

Reasoning in this way, however, is to address only one side of the issue. Moses does not have faith only in progress. He has faith also in human nature, which is the principle agent of progress and which, if it were irremediably corrupt, could accomplish no good. Original sin, it must be repeated, is not at all for Hebraism what it later became for Christianity. The moral corruption which Christianity derives from it is foreign to Jewish thought.

Just as in theology immanence does not preclude divine transcendence, so too in contemporary thought matter and spirit are like the two dimensions of a single subject. Similarly, for Hebraism, this world is not separated from the other. To the contrary, they are joined, as inside and outside complement one another in the dimension of space, or as present and future in the dimension of time: a twofold continuity to which Hebraism bears witness, first through belief in metempsychosis or reincarnation, second through faith in resurrection and palingenesis. Both are realizable on the same stage where the life of our world enacts itself.

Here then are the privileges which Hebraism ascribes to man. They are summed up in a title which Scripture freely gives him: Man is the creature of glory, nobility, honor, dignity. "Man is in honor and understands it not" (Ps 49:21).[17] And in a slightly different way: "Man is in glory and does not remain there" (Ps 49:13).[18] The psalm which emphasizes the greatness of man says that he has been adorned with glory and majesty (Ps 8:6). Such a being can be destined only for immortality. The Bible, which certain critics find so materialistic, gives the human soul a name to which there is nothing comparable in any other language nor in any other spiritual system: *kavod*, glory. When, therefore, the rabbis call Adam the glory of the earth, they are only borrowing the language and ideas of the Bible.

For Hebraism, there is nothing more glorious than man: and man as such, not the Israelite only.

3

The Jewish Idea of Progress

*J*udaism's approach to history is shaped by the fact that unlike other
religions, it locates perfection not at the beginning but at the end of
history. This, surely, is the meaning of its commitment to the coming
of a messianic era, which we may define as faith in a future perfection
of the human race—religious, moral, social, material—which must be
achieved in the last days.

We know that rationalist criticism divides the development of the
messianic doctrine into successive stages, according to which the complete idea dates only from a relatively recent time. It would be point-
less to enter here into a debate on the antiquity of messianism. Whenever it first appeared, sooner or later Hebraism acquired it, and, most
importantly, placed the realization of its hopes at the end of history.
This feature of the Jewish faith is so characteristic, so essential, that
although Christianity considers itself the realization of messianism, it
has never ceased, as heir of Israel—and despite the contradiction between this idea and the body of its doctrines—to appoint the end of
history for the accomplishment of its own promises of resurrection and
rebirth.

Ecclesiastes is echoing traditional Israelite thought when it says:
"The end of a matter is better than the beginning of it" (Eccl 7:8). And
to show that it is no good being impatient, and that we must know how
to await the course of events, it adds:

> Better a patient spirit than a haughty spirit. Don't let your
> spirit be quickly vexed, for vexation abides in the breasts of
> fools. (Eccl 7:8–9)

One might claim that such a statement trivializes thought, that such trite wisdom is far removed from the principles of human progress. Admittedly, what we have here is a narrowly conceived application, but one which implies the general principle; and this is indeed formulated by the author immediately after in terms which embrace all history, and is offered as an answer to all those who prefer antiquity to modern times:

> Don't say, "How has it happened that former times were better than these?" For it is not wise of you to ask that question. (Eccl 7:10)

If we now leave Scripture to seek the opinion of the Talmudic rabbis, or those of Midrash or Kabbalah, who are equally representative of the Hebraic tradition, we shall find agreement with Ecclesiastes, that what comes after is better than what has come before. Applying this touchstone to family status, we have already noted that the Bible seems to give preference to younger brothers over their elders. Cain, Ishmael, and Esau are rejected in favor of brothers born after them. This is what the mystics understand by the expression "the peel comes before the fruit," or "the dross must leave the crucible before the pure gold." Sometimes, too, a name which is in itself distinguished, to which usage has attached lofty associations—for example, *b'chor*, firstborn—designates the imperfection or incompleteness of a thing, its crude or defective beginning.[1] These contradictory meanings or usages are explicable when one considers the two cycles which form the overall development of beings: the one by which they descend from God, and the other by which they rise again to Him. In the first of these cycles, the rank and title of *b'chor*, firstborn, is a high distinction, since it expresses a nearer proximity to the source of being. In the second, however, the word expresses only the chief aspiration of finite being, its initial movement toward the perfection from which all proceeds, an effort necessarily incomplete, as it is but the initial passage from the state of potentiality to that of actuality.

According to the sages, after Adam sinned, the *Shekhinah* (the divine in the world) withdrew ten degrees from the earth, but eventually, thanks to the accomplishment of the Patriarchs, it returned the same distance.[2] This is a poetic way of saying that the movement of regeneration begins as soon as sin has been consummated and proceeds

167

throughout history by means of the deeds of godly men. We thus see that in the historical conception of the Bible, the Fall and its accompanying moral degradation are the work of an instant; they are something literally prehistoric, outside time. But the work of redress, restoration, and perfecting begins with history, is coextensive with it, and must ultimately occupy it entirely. The serpent which introduced evil into the world is destined constantly to have its head bruised by the descendants of man, even as these descendants will be bitten in the heel (Gn 3:15).

Beneath the childish image of the serpent is hidden a profound thought, and this narrative of Genesis has a very important significance. It seems certain that in the unceasing conflict between man and reptile, it must be man who will have the victory, since the foot which receives the bite can always bruise the serpent which bites it. What is at issue is nothing less than the perpetual struggle between good and evil, in which good must have the advantage. This symbolic story of the Adam of the first days thus becomes the story of the laborious regeneration of mankind, and the plan for its future evolution.

We know that the Talmud says that the world will last for 6,000 years in all, which it divides into three periods of 2,000 years each. The first belongs to chaos, the second to law, and the third to the messianic era.[3] In this outline of a philosophy of history, what is most remarkable is the conception of progress, to which Hebraism has become so devoted that it has raised it to the eminence of a theory. For Judaism, history is not a succession of events without connection, but rather an organism which develops, a world which acquires form, which has at its start, chaos (the *tohu va-vohu* of Genesis), and at its end, Shabbat (the name given to palingenesis, or cyclical rebirth, in imitation of the Shabbat which followed the six days of creation).

Intellectual and Religious Progress

The concept of intellectual progress is of great relevance to religion, which has, however, a decided tendency to regard ancient times as intellectually superior to the present, and thus to reject the idea. But if Judaism professes belief in progressive perfectibility, we have an impressive proof that the principle of progress has indeed penetrated deeply into Hebrew thought.

Going back in time, let us first see what has been said on the subject by theologians and Kabbalists. Everywhere in their works, we meet the idea that the explanation of life's mysteries will be given only progressively, and that complete knowledge—that, at least, which human nature is capable of acquiring—will be reserved until the last days, the messianic era. The importance of this doctrine for our understanding of the origins of Christianity should be obvious to all. There is no idea which recurs more often in the Gospels. Jesus asserts that he has come into this world to declare aloud—according to Luke 12:3, to preach "upon the housetops"—what before him had been taught secretly. As he believed himself to be the Messiah, and his disciples believed the messianic era to have begun, they thought that they were henceforth excused from all caution; and so the esoteric theology of the Pharisees was exposed in broad daylight and revealed to a throng which could scarcely comprehend its least word. Here is not the place to consider the result of this disclosure, but what we must point out is that this aspect of early Christianity ought to be pondered by those who would claim that the Israelite principle of secret teaching was thought up subsequently so as to mask the novelty of certain doctrines which had actually been unknown to early Judaism, and to give them, despite their recent importation, the prestige of antiquity. What happened, however, at the time of the spread of the Gospels gives the lie to this explanation.

Religious progress can be seen even before Moses. Men grew morally: Abraham is superior to Noah, and Moses is greater than Abraham. In an ingenious parable, the rabbis compare the pre-Mosaic revelations to flasks which the master of the house offers his guests; the revelation at Sinai, however, is like a cask whose contents are received through an ample opening. In this regard, Moses has words which are startling in their boldness and daring; only the habitual reading of them makes them seem natural to us. With his own advent, the Patriarchs had been surpassed and a more complete knowledge of God granted. A name, if not new at least newly revealed, came to take the place of the old divine names, or, rather, was henceforth preferred to them:

> I appeared to Abraham, Isaac, and Jacob as El Shaddai, but I did not make myself known to them by My name JHWH. (Ex 6:3)

It is always the same mode of development; esoterism disappears, and what was once hidden may now be seen, whether by special design or by natural inevitability, as the flower brings forth the fruit.

THE JEWISH IDEA OF PROGRESS

After Moses, the same principle continues to govern the development of religious understanding. We can see in glancing over the Bible
that there is a difference in the way religion is conceived between early
and later times. This is evident, and there seem to be only two plausi-
ble explanations. Either we must agree with the rationalist critics that
new books, doctrines, and rites had been introduced, or we must
accept the metaphor of religion as an organism, developing through all
its phases from the seed to the fruit, always changing, but—like everything that lives—always identical in substance.

Indeed, the rabbis adopted this hypothesis of religious evolution.
The accusation made against them in the Gospel, that they elevated
human traditions above the word of God, is enough to show that they
were scarcely disposed to regard religion as unchanging. The assevera-
tions of the Sadducees, and indeed the very existence of that party,
bear out the reproaches in the Gospels. Today, even the historical critic
recognizes that the Pharisees represented change and religious progress
at the very heart of Judaism. Yet we must not confuse the natural
growth of an institution, its organic evolution, with changes which
may be imposed in order to adapt the institution to new times and
places. The first kind of change is proper, legitimate, in a word orthodox, whereas the second is false and injurious to the idea which it
claims to serve.

But what is significant is that the Pharisees, with a surprisingly
clear conscience, do nothing to refute the accusation that they are
friendly to innovation. Unhesitatingly, they elevate Rabbi Akiba above
Moses—Akiba, the preeminent representative of Oral Tradition, both
applied and doctrinal; the only man, according to the Talmud, who
could devote himself without danger to the study of the Merkavah
(Mysteries of the Chariot).[4] In another passage, it is said that when
Moses ascended Sinai to receive the Law, God enabled him to see all
the generations of his successors. On the remotest level, he saw Rabbi
Akiba, who was preaching volumes of doctrines about every word of
the Torah. Not understanding what Akiba said, Moses felt acute grief,
but was reassured when he heard Rabbi Akiba conclude, "All these
doctrines come to us from Moses, who received them on Sinai."[5] This
stupendous passage would constitute the most subtle disparagement of
the Written Law, if in fact it were not that Law's most profound
vindication. This image of Moses, who does not understand what is
said in his name, who feels heartened only when he hears the most up-
to-date Pharisee theories attached to his own teaching on Sinai, is a

masterpiece of truth and profundity. Distilled here in a few words, we have an entire system of concordance between the Written and Oral Laws, between immutability and progress. Can we say that if the seed were endowed with intelligence, it would recognize itself in the plant? Does the child know himself in the man? No, because the difference is too great and there is no consciousness or memory to testify to the continuity, the sameness of existence. But the plant knows itself in the seed, the man in the child, because once the evolution has become an established fact, all the moments of existence are linked together and form an uninterrupted chain which allows the being to affirm its own identity.

There is thus no reason to be amazed that the Zohar places Rabbi Shimon ben Yohai above Moses. Commenting on Genesis 1:3, "God said, 'Let there be light'; and there was light," the Midrash Rabbah says: " 'Let there be light' refers to Moses; 'and there was light' refers to Rabbi Shimon ben Yohai."[6]

Nothing could be more elegant, expressive, or original than this commentary. It is the potentiality and the actuality set forth together, the preparation and the execution, the plan and its fulfillment joined together like the beginning and the end. Who, in fact, can say—and in our view this is more than merely conjectural—if Jesus, declaring "Think not that I am come to destroy the law, or the prophets: I am not come to destroy, but to fulfill" (Mt 5:17), did not mean to speak of a fulfillment of the kind we have just considered? This is the only explanation which allows us to reconcile the role of reformer, which he had assumed, with his role of revealer of doctrines until then kept secret. Yet it is not for the branch to impart the potency of growth to the entire tree; that is the function of the trunk, of the roots—that is, of the entire people, or better still, its peculiar genius, that nameless but pervasive force which encompasses its past, present, and future.

The Pharisees even accomplished the miracle of lending respectability to a word which in any other religion is synonymous with heterodoxy: *hiddush*, change or innovation. For them, change is legitimate. Innovation is praiseworthy and seems to be one of the indispensable elements of religious life. Together with respect for Oral Tradition, it forms the regular rhythm of the history of religion. Consequently, they asserted that all *hiddush*, all that the student of Torah can say that is new, was revealed to Moses on Sinai. How could this be? Evidently in the same way that the teaching of Rabbi Akiba could be attached to that of Moses. Elsewhere, the nail and the branch, the one a symbol of fixity, of unchangeableness, the other an emblem of growth and development, are made to signify these complementary properties of the Law.

> The sayings of the wise are like goads, like nails fixed in prodding sticks. They were given by one Shepherd. (Eccl 12:11)

The commentators ask: Are the words of the wise therefore unstable, like a goad? No, since they are also compared to nails. Are they therefore as barren and sterile as nails, which neither increase nor multiply? No, since it is said that these nails are embedded in branches or sticks.[7]

We must add only this general truth, which we hope to demonstrate more fully on a later page: For Hebraism, it may be said that the Bible and Oral Tradition, the Written and Oral Laws, are identical with the divine Logos, the Creative Wisdom, and thus with the law of life or being, the law of the entire universe—that is, with the cosmic law itself. In this grand conception of the Divine Law, how would it be possible to deny that if we are to conceive of the very possibility that a finite intelligence should be able to acquire any knowledge of such a Law, progress must be postulated as a necessary condition? The Law is the Logos, the totality of the divine knowledge, which finite man can, consequently, never completely possess. Thus, the rabbis speak of fifty gates through which men can pass to reach divine knowledge, but even Moses was able to achieve only forty-nine of these, the fiftieth being reserved for God alone.[8]

Another rabbi tells us that the reason it is written that Moses *received* the Law at Sinai,[9] and not that God *gave* the Law to him there, is that Moses was incapable of receiving all of it. To say that Moses *received* it means that he received as much of it as he had the faculty to understand.[10] Moreover, the text does not say *ha-Torah*, the Law, but *Torah*, Law, nor does it say that Moses received it "from God" but "from Sinai." Why? So as not to attribute to God an imperfection.

Finally, the rabbis explain why Jews who are called to the Reading of the Law in the Synagogue do not say, in the blessing which precedes the reading, "Blessed art Thou, O Lord, who *gave* the Law," but "who *gives* the Law." The Law was not given once, nor ten nor a thousand times, once and for all, but it is given continually. It is a fountain whose flow is never extinguished.[11]

If, among all the Jewish sects, the Pharisees were the only one which professed this principle of progressive revelation, it does not mean that in so doing they were unfaithful to the Bible. Scripture is full of the promise that religious knowledge must increase, that it will attain its highest level in the last age, and that the divine spirit will then spread over all men without distinction of age, sex, or condition.

> After that [declares Joel], I will pour out My spirit on all flesh;
> Your sons and daughters shall prophesy;
> Your old men shall dream dreams,
> And your young men shall see visions. (Jl 3:1)

And according to Jeremiah:

> No longer will they need to teach one another and say to one another, "Heed the Lord"; for all of them, from the least of them to the greatest, shall heed Me—declares the Lord. (Jer 31:34)

And Habakkuk:

> For the earth shall be filled
> With awe for the glory of the Lord
> As water covers the sea. (Hb 2:14)

The earliest Christians believed all these texts to have been fulfilled, and from all sides there arose prophets and visionaries, for it was believed that the messianic era had opened.

We find significant words also in Daniel: "Many will range far and wide and knowledge will increase" (Dn 12:4). That is, religious progress will occur not only quantitatively but qualitatively as well. This is why the author also writes:

> And the knowledgeable will be radiant like the bright expanse of sky, and those who lead the many to righteousness will be like the stars forever and ever. (Dn 12:3)

Now that we have recalled these noble prophecies, it seems hardly necessary to mention that the same principle was applied to matters of ritual and legislation, whose practical nature, however, made the principle more readily accessible to less speculative minds. We refer to the Talmudic rule according to which in matters of religious authority, the most recent of the sages must be preferred to their predecessors.[12] The reasoning, no doubt, is that the most recent, being in possession of all that the earlier sages had taught, are thus in a better position to advance still another step toward knowledge. Here we can clearly see the principle of progress authenticated by the most august authority. Admittedly, one could easily find passages which seem to contradict this principle by elevating the ancient sages far above the more recent ones. But it seems to us that the contradiction disappears as soon as we distinguish between the individual and the mass. Great personalities were more numerous and remarkable in ancient times than in modern, and this difference may be deplored. But what has risen is the general level, thanks to a greater diffusion of knowledge, facilitated by the wonderful techniques of writing and printing. In this connection, it would be appropriate to point out certain remarkable coincidences at the heart of Judaism. The Torah appeared virtually at the moment when alphabetical writing was invented. The Oral Tradition or Law began to be written down when the use of manuscripts became general in Western civilization. Finally, it was at the time of the invention of printing that esoteric learning was brought within the reach of all those who could profit from it.

But does the myth of Adam not contradict the doctrine of progress? (According to the Adamic conception, perfection was originally to have been man's portion, but since the primal sin, which brought moral and physical sickness into the world, mankind has found itself not advancing but rather fallen.) We have already answered this objection in part, with reference to human perfectibility. Let us note once more that in the myth we speak of, Adam is presented as both more perfect and less perfect than historical man. According to Hebraism's idea of the golden age, the first men were better endowed by nature with certain faculties, especially spontaneity or inventiveness. The truth of experience is that in a man's early years, not only is his human organism more active, but his ethical faculty is more intense, than later.

> Just as physical development is never more keen than in infancy [observes Reynaud], so too there is no period in life in which there is more motivation than then.[13]

We should, therefore, not be surprised that men experience a sensation of decline as they grow older and find their faculties growing weaker.

But is Adam's perfection itself an historical phenomenon? One could indeed defend the notion that when the Bible tells us about

Adam's felicity, it has no other object than to depict the ideal of perfection which man can and should achieve. The idea of primitive perfection that was developed by certain other peoples is radically different from that of Hebraism. When and if these peoples conceived of progress, it remained implicit and unconscious, whereas in Judaism, progress was a clear, well-established and articulated doctrine, at least as luminous as the doctrine of original perfection; for although this idea is found only in Genesis, and, surprisingly, recurs here and there in the Bible only as a feeble and uncertain echo, altogether out of proportion to the importance of the Eden narrative, the conception of progress permeates the entires Scriptures.

Between the approach of Greek mythology, which locates perfection at the beginning, in the golden age, and that of modern thinkers, who defer it completely to the distant future, what is the position of Hebraism? It espouses an intermediate doctrine, by affirming final perfection as a result of progressive development. For Judaism, progress is a road (which assumes a point of departure), a journey, and a goal. This being granted, to those who ask if, from the Jewish point of view, man has advanced or retreated, we answer: "Man has *grown*." Thus, he has lost in spontaneity and natural instinct, but gained as a free, self-conscious, and moral being. The first men were superior to us in instinct, like the animals; but we surpass them in thought.

It is in this sense that the rabbis, comparing the prophet and the sage (or learned man), formulated the great maxim that the sage is superior to the prophet.[14] This does not mean that human wisdom or learning is superior to inspiration. No doubt the prophet has a more lavishly endowed spirit, but his individuality is less asserted, for he lacks awareness of all he possesses. To a certain degree, the sage has created himself through his persevering efforts, and his consciousness is stronger, though its contents are less. The prophet is superior in capacity, the sage in intensity.

The Messianic Hope

An eminent author whom we have cited several times, M. Laurent, asserts that antiquity lacked faith in progress:

The philosophers, even those we regard as utopians, poets, prophets of the future, did not conceive of a better world where violence had given way to law, where brotherhood prevailed instead of hostile divisions among peoples. They had no faith in perfectibility, which moves and consoles us. They believed that the great historical events were phenomena without purpose or moral meaning, that men revolved always in the same circle, that the same evils were always awaiting them. One ancient doctrine applies this desolate idea to all of creation. The conception of the Great Year is the negation of progress and perfectibility. After a certain number of years, everything must start its same existence all over again.[15]

It is easy to show that the Hebraic conception is precisely the antithesis of these pagan ideas. All the voices of Judaism agree in predicting this future perfection which the philosophers of paganism could not even imagine. Moreover, the doctrine of Divine Providence, which for Israel is the pivot of history, is just the opposite of the pagan principle of a history without moral meaning. To be sure, the Great Year of the pagans bears an apparent resemblance to those seven-year cosmic cycles which the Kabbalah calls *Shemittot*, or the fifty-year cycles called *Yobelim* (Jubilees).[16] The idea of these cycles is, of course, found in the Bible itself. But there is this essential difference: In the pagan cycles, there is merely a repetition of what had come before, whereas in the Hebraic, the recurrence brings improvement.

The author whom we have just quoted adds this important acknowledgement:

> In the opposition of the Jews to Jesus Christ, and in their belief in another Messiah, there is a keen sense of the real needs of mankind, needs which must find satisfaction in this world. For Christians, the messianic moment is purely mystical; Christianity has never dreamt of realizing on this earth the brotherhood, equality, and peace which it promises to believers. All these hopes are for Heaven! The protest of the Jews against this mysticism was a kind of call to the future. The call has been heard. Christian ideas are beginning to penetrate into civil society, but this is occurring, in a sense, despite Christianity, despite at least the Church which is its voice. For it to occur has required the influence of forces hostile to Christian religion. This shows that in certain re-

spects the Jews were right not to embrace the Gospel. Even in this conflict, they have remained faithful to their prophetic mission.[17]

The doctrine of progress formed so important a part of the Israelite heritage, and it was so abundantly clear to all that instead of evil disappearing forever, as had been hoped, it continued in all its forms to afflict mankind, that in spite of the new beliefs, messianic hope did not disappear completely. Biblical and rabbinical traditions which deferred the messianic epoch to the last days lived on among those very people who believed they no longer needed them, and we see Jesus himself appealing to the future Paraclete,[18] who "will bear witness to me" (Jn 15:26).

We may cite millenarianism as an unmistakable example of the survival of messianic hopes. This formed part of the faith of early Christianity, and like faith in the resurrection, attests in the clearest way to belief in universal progress. The millenarian ideas and what we may call the apocalypticism which, according to Renan, flourished in Iran from a very early time are found once more today in certain Protestant sects. These Christians believe that they are thus being more faithful to the thought of Jesus. In any case, they demonstrate the vitality of the Jewish ideal in religions deriving from Hebraism but unfortunately separated from it.

Catholic and Protestant theologians have explained millenarianism as the return of the Jews to Palestine, their conversion to Christianity, and the rebuilding of the Temple of Jerusalem, where all peoples will go to worship God.[19] In the Middle Ages, Thomas Aquinas declared progress to be the universal law of things, and especially of human knowledge: If the Gospel contains all of divine revelation, there is still unceasing and limitless progress to be made in understanding it. The Montanists, and later Amalric, Joachim of Flora, and John of Parma, divided universal history into three great periods: that of the Old Testament, which forms the reign of the Father; that of the New Testament, or the reign of the Son; and finally that of the Eternal Gospel, or the reign of the Spirit. Dante, Paracelsus, Campanella, and Lessing accepted more or less this division.[20] Finally, what all Christians call the glorious advent of Jesus Christ, his second coming, has no other source or explanation than the persistence of messianic expectations.

Independent writers fully share our perspective, and perceive Islam in the same light. According to one of them, "Christianity with its glorious advent and Islam with its *madhe*[21] attest that messianism has not yet started."[22]

Progress in the Scheme of Creation

For traditional Judaism, man, or the human race as a whole, stands in the same relation to the terrestrial as soul to body. According to Hebraic tradition, it is as if Adam formed the Cosmos, though it could also be said that the Cosmos formed Adam—or, to be more exact, gave him his body, precisely as the soul of each of us devises its own physical abode, which then serves it as medium and voice for its various functions.

The common opinion, of course, is that Adam was called by this name because he was taken from the earth, *adama*. But the Bible says nothing of this, and if we recall the analogy of the Hebrew words *ish*, *isha* (man, woman), and their close connection with the earth (Gn 2:7), it may not require excessive daring to see in the names *Adam, adama*, the implication that the earth has man for its husband. It is he who is called to subdue it and to dominate all the other creatures who inhabit it. To man has been given the complete task of transformation, or, to be more exact, of appropriation, so that the earth may be a docile instrument of his will. We have already cited the rabbinic legends which show us an Adam of such stature that he reaches the sky and encompasses the world from one end to the other.[23] In a sense, this Adam is portrayed as an earth in human form. The rabbis tell us, in this connection, that everything that exists in man has its equivalent in the earth.[24] This is what has been called the doctrine of macrocosm, by contrast to that of microcosm, which is man, and following logically from it; for if man is the world *en petit*, the world must be man *en grand*.

Moreover, the story of Adam shows more that one analogy with that of the earth. Our world fell with him, and so with him it must again rise. And there is a logical relation between these ideas: Since man took the earth with him in his Fall, is it not reasonable to believe that the earth will take part in his regeneration?

When we shall turn to the law of man, we shall see that for Hebraism, the creative law of the universe, the *universal* Logos, the Wisdom of the book of Proverbs, is identical with the *human* Logos, or to use the language of the fourth Gospel, "the true light that enlightens every man" (Jn 1:9). And as the Logos is complete only in mankind as a whole, it is thus that mankind, or Adam (who represents and epitomizes it), is the *soul of the world.*

> Can the human body really be what we ordinarily call by that name? We think, rather, that this body is but the nucleus of another that is far more vast. In this sense the entire universe can be regarded as our body.[25]

It is an Italian philosopher, M. Fornari, who writes this, expressing in scientific language certain ideas which are found in a number of mythologies. These ideas are simply the amplification of a short Midrashic formula which presents as clearly as possible the theory of Adam as soul of the world.

> When God began to create heaven and earth—the earth being unformed and void, with darkness over the surface of the deep and a wind from [*or* the spirit of] God sweeping over the water. . . . (Gn 1:1–2)

This wind or spirit, say the rabbis, is the soul or spirit of the first Adam.[26] In such a small rabbinic commentary we have ample evidence of what Hebraism postulates of the relation between man and the earth. A Midrash says:

> We learn that the Holy One, blessed be He, created worlds and destroyed them. And He said, "I am satisfied with some of these, but those others do not please me."[27]

There is thus a tendency toward progressive improvement in creation, as worlds become more nearly perfect. But even if we limit ourselves to the biblical text, we find a categorical commitment to the idea of progress. Each new creation in the work of the Six Days marks a step forward, an advance beyond the preceding creation. After inanimate being comes life, and among the manifestations of animal life, there is a progression leading to the appearance of man, the last and most nearly perfect of beings. To us, then, the Hexaemeron, the six-day period of creation in Genesis, seems, in its relation to God, the creative force, to be a chronological representation of the progressive character of creation. And after the creative period of six days comes the Shabbat, which corresponds to the cosmic period.

179

In any event, the perception in Genesis of the creation of life as a progression from lower to higher forms has always attracted attention. It is a remarkable anticipation of what science would establish much later. Anaximander has sometimes been called a precursor of Darwinian theories, but in fact he has only a vague idea of this progression. According to him, the effect of the sun on the earth, which was then covered by the waters, generated particles, which produced imperfect organisms, somewhat like the protoplasm of modern science, and when these organisms developed gradually, they gave birth to all the species now existing.[28] The ancestors of man were thus aquatic animals not unlike fish. We have only to reread the first page of the Pentateuch to be convinced of the superiority of biblical conceptions to the theories of the Ionian philosopher.

Just as the present order of things represents an advance beyond what has come before, so too, that which will follow will surpass what is. In the history of the earth, each period thus forms a palingenesis, a renewal or rebirth, with respect to the preceding ones, while it is a birth or beginning with respect to those which will follow. The succession of worlds and their increasing perfection, whether in the past or in the future, are of indefinite extent. There is an evolution governed by the laws represented in the Kaballah by the various *Sefirot*, aeons, hypostases, or emanations.[29] This is but a vast application of what Scripture teaches us about the various ages of mankind, in each of which God is worshiped by a different name: *Elohim, Shaddai,* and finally the Tetragrammaton. Human rationality gives us a philosophical expression of this doctrine. "The idea of progress," says Hartmann, "appears above all in the philosophy of Hegel, for whom the life of the universe is only the progressive and spontaneous evolution of the idea."[30] And a Catholic, M. Fornari, says: "This very hierarchy [of divine ideas], transferred from space into time, and from substance to event, is called progress."[31]

It is important to note that the cycles established by the civil law in the land of Israel followed the model of these cosmic periods. Each world, or cosmos, corresponds to a *shemitta*, or week of years; and seven cosmic periods represent a *yobel*, jubilee. The universe thus develops by intervals of sevens. This is the system of the Kabbalists, but we meet something of it at least in the Talmud, namely, the cosmic cycle of seven. We read in Sanhedrin 97a: "It is only after 7,000 years that God will renew the earth." In another passage, we find this proposition: "There existed an order of time before Genesis."[32] Finally, in Genesis Rabbah, Rav Hiyya says:

> *In the beginning God created*—here is the creation. *The earth was unformed and void*—here is the destruction of the world. *And God said, "Let there be light!"*—here is the rebuilding.[33]

The Jewish *shemittot* and *yobelim* are surely quite different from the pagan conception of historical change. The pagans assimilated the history of the world to that of the individual, or of heaven, or of nature. The Jews, however, related it to the history of mankind as a whole, and more specifically, to the thread of progressive improvement in human history. The civil institutions of *shemitta* and *yobel*, the connection which the Prophets continually made between social and terrestrial renewal, together show that from the Jewish perspective, the world and mankind, those two great collective entities—if indeed they are two and not one only—share a common destiny.

In our tradition, the future is always portrayed as an improvement upon the present, and there is no reason to think that this refers to a single period, or to our planet only. We have already observed that according to Rabbi Abbahu, God invariably said to each world that He created before ours, "This one pleases me, though the others did not!"[34] One could hardly imagine a more unaffected way of suggesting the idea of progressive improvement in creation.

A number of critics believe that the Bible itself, as well as the rabbis, accepts the idea of a sequence of worlds. They find it in the *tohu va-vohu* of the first page of Genesis. To them, these words seem—properly, we think—to point to the debris of an old world, from which God created the new, thus accomplishing in the creation of our world Isaiah's prophecy for its future *renewal:*

> For behold! I am creating
> A new heaven and a new earth. (Is 65:17)

Can we imagine such a succession of worlds without also imagining a single law to which they are all subject?

A commentator upon Joseph Albo adds that the *tehom*, abyss, and the waters, *mayim*, of which the second verse of the Torah speaks, are nothing other than the debris of the preceding creation.[35] Several Jewish theologians share that opinion, and Judah Halevi declares that from the religious point of view, the Israelite who believes in this succession of worlds is blameless.

It has been very properly noted that the etymology of *tohu va-vohu* suggests the overthrow of a preexisting order rather than the confusion and formlessness of a creation *ex nihilo*. This theory is confirmed by an analysis of three other biblical texts in which the expression appears. Isaiah says, with respect to the ruins of a one-flourishing earth:

> He shall measure it with a line of chaos [*kai tohu*]
> And with weights of emptiness [*va-avnei vohu*]. (Is 34:11)

Elsewhere the same prophet uses the word *tohu* in opposition to the idea of terrestrial order and settlement:

> For thus said the Lord,
> The Creator of heaven who alone is God,
> Who formed the earth and made it,
> Who alone established it—
> He did not create it a waste [*tohu*],
> But formed it for habitation. (Is 45:18)

And Jeremiah, after saying

> I look at the earth,
> It is unformed and void [*tohu va-vohu*];
> At the skies,
> And their light is gone

amplifies his own words in this way:

> I look at the mountains,
> They are quaking;
> And all the hills are rocking.
> I look: no man is left,
> And all the birds of the sky have fled. (Jer 4:23–25)

But this particular expression from Genesis is not our only intimation of the existence of earlier worlds. Its entire scriptural context can be understood in this sense. The heaven and earth of the first verse may indicate these vanished worlds, and their destruction may be the subject of the second verse, where we read

the earth being unformed and void,

[*tohu va-vohu*—the first words of this verse may quite accurately be translated "Now, the earth became . . ."]

with darkness over the surface of the deep and the spirit of God[36] sweeping over the water

[i.e., in order to form a new world]. (Gn 1:2).

A passage from Job supports this interpretation. Extolling the wonders of God, it says:

He it is who stretched out Zaphon [i.e., heaven] over chaos [*tohu*],
Who suspended earth over emptiness. (Jb 26:7)

The Psalms, too, endorse this conception of the succession of worlds:

Of old You established the earth; the heavens are the work of Your hands.
They shall perish, but You shall endure; they shall all wear out like a garment; You change them like clothing and they pass away. But You are the same, and Your years never end. (Ps 102:26–28)

If the notion of cosmic progress, or of the plurality of creations in general, is not expressly indicated in this text, it can be deduced from the images which appear here, for that of the clothing which wears out and is replaced embodies quite clearly the idea of the succession of worlds.

The prayer of Moses begins with these words: "O Lord, You have been our refuge in every generation." It then rises to a more general conception, where it is no longer a question of Israel alone but of the entire universe:

Before the mountains came into being, before You brought forth the earth and the world, from eternity to eternity You are God. You return man to dust; You decreed, "Return you mortals!" For in Your sight a thousand years are like yesterday that is past, like a watch in the night. (Ps 90:1–4)

And in another psalm we read:

> Blessed is the Lord, God of Israel,
> From world to world.[37] (Ps 106:48)

And again:

Your kingship is a kingship of all worlds;[38] Your dominion is for all generations. (Ps 145:13)

—thus embracing both past and future.

For the Bible, then, as for other expressions of Hebraic tradition, not only did worlds exist before this one, but others will exist after it, and the grand principle of advance to a higher state is a law which governs the birth, development, end, and rebirth of all the successive universes.

Before leaving this question of the Jewish conception of cosmic progress, let us consider for a moment the myth of the Garden of Eden, or earthly paradise, in Genesis. The Garden of Eden is the anticipation of the world to come. Just as Adam is the archetype of mankind, so Eden is the image of the world which he is to inhabit.

That this state of felicity must, according to Judaism, be realized some day (even though one were to grant that it already existed at the beginning) cannot be doubted, when we see that it is represented in the Bible as the normative condition wished by the Creator, who cannot fail to achieve the end which He has conceived. If the story of Adam yields an argument for [personal] resurrection, by the same token it yields an argument for palingenesis, the resurrection or renewal of the earth.

But can this palingenesis be inferred with certainty from the Bible? We may recall the controversy on this subject between Maimonides and other theologians,[39] the first preferring a metaphorical reading of the passages which seem to predict new heavens and a new earth, the others interpreting them in their literal sense. What appears not to have been noticed in any quarter is that there is a higher consideration which subsumes both approaches. Even if it were to be shown that these passages were allegorical, we should have to acknowledge that the scriptural authors would never have dreamt of using such images if these images were not founded in some way on popular ideas. An image or metaphor which is entirely without perceived reality would only impede the communication of truth rather than advance it. Why should the figure of the resurrection of the dead have been used to depict the political restoration of Israel, and the figure of new earths and heavens to announce universal peace in the days of the Messiah, if these two kinds of events, resurrection and cosmic palingenesis, had not been regarded as future realities, still far off but indubitable? If the two concepts had been totally foreign to established belief, instead of strengthening faith in the messianic regeneration and national revival, they would have subverted it.

As the Talmud bears witness, the ancient sages never doubted the literal truth of these texts. The only question which divided them was whether the renewal of the earth would be different from the messianic era (in which all would remain as formerly except for the deliverance of Israel), or whether the two eras would be identical, with the advent of the Messiah representing both national restoration and terrestrial regeneration, as the first Christians in particular believed.

Sabbath and the Philosophy of History

Hebraism affirms progress not only in cosmic evolution as a whole but also in the history of each of the worlds, and especially ours. The rabbis saw the biblical account of creation as a paradigm of the historical evolution of mankind. Each day of the creation represented for them a period of history, and Israel, the people which preeminently epitomizes history, has of course its own particular place in the historical development. The day of the creation cycle which corresponds to Israel's role in the world is the Sabbath, the day consecrated to God, even as Israel is specially consecrated to Him from among all the nations.

Coming at the end of the week, the Sabbath gives it structure and order. It is the center upon which all the other days converge. The uncompleted creations which are the weekdays find their completion and consummation in the Sabbath repose, the fulfillment and crown of all creation, which thus attains in the Sabbath its unity. With the appearance of Israel in history, religion enters the world to bind all together, to form the center where the diverse elements of human civilization may be rejoined and the confused crowd of man and races may become *mankind.*

This connection between Israel and the Sabbath is expressed by the rabbis in many ways. According the the Kabbalists, the soul of the world bears the double name of *Sabbath* and *Keneset Yisrael,* Congregation of Israel, which is in keeping with an expression in the Talmud: "Let the Congregation of Israel be thy companion!"[40] Israel, like the Sabbath, is separate, apart, and the Jewish liturgy tells the faithful:

> Blessed art Thou, O Lord, who separates the holy from the profane, the day from the night, Israel from the other peoples, and the seventh day from the other days!

On the text "He brings everything to pass precisely at its time" (Eccl 3:11), the rabbis embellished the parable of the field and its master, intended to show that only the master knows how to adapt the planting of seed and the labor of husbandry to the specific requirements of his lands and the cycles of seasons. They also compared God, who returns souls into this world by means of incarnation so as to allow them to improve and perfect themselves, to a gardener who sees that a plant or tree may not be flourishing in a particular spot and so transplants it to another.

Perhaps all these images from the Midrash and Kabbalah are distilled into that comprehensive image by which the entire creation is compared to a garden of pleasures, whether in Genesis (if the meaning we have found in Eden is correct), or in the mystical tradition which gives the name *Gan Eden,* Garden of Eden, to the *Malkhut,* the immanent God, the Divine in the world, or perhaps in a group of Midrashic parables in which Eden is seen as an image of the universe, the creation, and human knowledge of the creation.

We shall conclude this discussion of cosmic evolution as leading to the Sabbath—which is like a sketch of the philosophy of history according to Judaism—by citing certain distinguished authors whose authority gives them claim to our attention. According to M. Haag:

> The Jews believed firmly that after a period of 6,000 years from the creation of the world, there would occur the Great Sabbath, which would last 1,000 years. They based their calculations on the story of the six-day creation in Genesis, in

conjunction with this verse in Psalms: "For in Your sight a thousand years are like yesterday that has past." (Ps 90:4)[41]

Renan could not be more affirmative: "The philosophy of history is a Jewish creation, being in a sense the last manifestation of the Prophetic spirit."[42] M. Laurent writes that Aeschylus inaugurated the philosophy of history when he showed the hand of God in the calamities which strike all peoples.[43] We do not know if there are other ancient peoples who can also lay claim to this honor, but what is certain is that no other people has such good reason for doing so as the Jewish people. The doctrine of Providence so characteristic of the religion of Israel is all the more synonymous with an ideal order in history in that it has as its goal perfectibility and general progress, for the goal of justice itself, whether divine or human, is the moral improvement of the sinner. Ritter offers a similar definition, in which Providence and the philosophy of history seem to be interchangeable:

It is the expression of the conviction that every action is guided by universal law, and has a role in the accomplishment of that law.[44]

Or as Proverbs has it: "The Lord made everything for a purpose" (Prv 16:4). And a few chapters later:

Many designs are in a man's mind,
But it is the Lord's plan that is accomplished. (Prv 19:21)

We find the idea also in Isaiah:

All who are linked to My name,
Whom I have created,
Formed, and made for My glory. . . . (Is 43:7)

Finally, M. Mamiani writes:

Do we not read in the Zend-Avesta that the ever-renewed struggle between good and evil will diminish little by little until the final and glorious triumph of Ahura-Mazda? Did the same expectation not warm the heart of the Prophets of Israel, and did one of them not describe that joyful time when rivers of milk would flow and serpents would lose their venom?[45]

When the same author afterward discusses Christianity and its pleas for the coming of God's reign, it is impossible not to hear in the Gospel an echo of beliefs which are the authentic patrimony of Israel.

Progress on the Plane of Created Things

The word *aliyah* (literally "ascent" or "rising"), with which Hebraism designates progress in the created world itself, is very characteristic of Jewish doctrine, for it brings together the two ideas of change and elevation. This is something more than "evolution," the term which is in common use today but does not denote the second element, though that is so precious. The *aliyah*, however, is an ascent.

This word belongs to Hebraic mysticism precisely in the sense which we have given it, but the concept itself, and the doctrine which proceeds from it, are found only among the Kabbalists. It is the heritage of all rabbinic Judaism; or, to be more precise, the Kabbalah, here as in so many instances, is a faithful exponent of rabbinic thought. An eminent thinker who is also a great writer conveys the essence of *aliyah* admirably when he writes:

> Enamoured of beauty, nature soars toward her with an unceasing impulse, and approaches closer and closer to her in its forms. The universe is thus an immense being which rises relentlessly towards a higher end which it has prepared through all its previous efforts, proving at once its enormous desire for the good and its marvelous ingenuity.[46]

According to the Kabbalah's conception of physical reality, what is mineral changes into vegetable, vegetable into animal, and animal into man. In man himself, what is at first physical becomes intellectual through the ingestion of food. This is why nourishment has such great importance in Kabbalism, for it is regarded as transforming the corporeal into the spiritual, as acting as intermediary between the one and the other, so that when it is governed by religion, it is considered as if it were as holy and as meritorious as the very act of sacrifice.

We may ask what it is that man himself changes into. We are told that he is the substance from which a superior being emerges. This act bears the noble name and holy form of a sacrifice. According to the rabbis, "Michael, the celestial high priest, celebrates the sacrifice of the souls of Israel."[47] A passage in Leviticus offers essentially the same idea. With respect to the death of Aaron's two sons, it is said: "And fire came forth from the Lord and consumed them" (Lv 10:2), on which the rabbis comment that their bodies remained intact for it was their souls which the divine fire consumed.[48] The death of the just is consummated in a kiss by which two spirits unite.[49] For the Kabbalah, the supreme object of all Jewish worship is the *Yihud*, the unification of the real with the ideal, of immanent God (*Shekhinah*) with transcendent God (*Tiferet*), through the agency of man, his soul, and his works.

> In nature as in us [writes our eminent thinker], what is less precious is the *sine qua non* of what is more precious. What exists is the substance of what will be, of what must be. If we consider the succession of beings in time, or their co-existence in space, we see always the same principle observed: the lower prepares for the higher, and as soon as it has appeared, is sacrificed to it.

Perhaps it would be more exact to say that this sacrifice is the very condition of its appearance. And the same author, after noting that nature always behaves consistently, in a continuous flow, without interruptions or repetitions, concludes: "[Nature] brings higher life to birth out of life itself; it makes the ideal flourish in the soil of reality."[50]

It will certainly not have escaped the reader that this law of progress in created being, of continuous advance to a higher state, is strikingly analogous to that principle which (as we believe) determines the assimilation by Hebraic monotheism of the scattered truths in paganism.

At root, these are one and the same law. Far from destroying the identity of the being, it hallows it. The foundation of property rights has, reasonably, been detected in our ability (both by effusion and by infusion, as it were) to make things become a part of ourselves. It is this which justifies the rabbis in having sometimes placed the same value on property as on life, in judging outrages against the one as severely as against the other; for the natural tendency of the "I" is to absorb in order to grow.

4

Man in Partnership with God

A mong the capabilities which Judaism assigns to man, from the very first pages of the Torah none is more essential than his domination over nature. This sway extends not only over creatures but over the earth itself. Human beings, by multiplying, must fill it and subjugate it—which shows that their dispersion over the entire surface of the globe at the time of the Tower of Babel was but God's execution of His original design, against which the earliest tribes had rebelled by refusing to disperse.

The Psalmist no doubt had in mind the account in Genesis when he wrote: "You have made him master over Your handiwork, laying the world at his feet" (Ps 8:7). If the promise of universal dominion inspired the preceding words, then the memory of man's creation in the image and semblance of God obviously evoked the following: "You have made him little less than divine, and adorned him with glory and majesty" (Ps 8:6). We must notice, however, that the text does not subordinate the *entire universe* to earth. The sacred poet, exalting the heavens above man (who, in comparison with them, seems so lowly a creature), conceives of their immensity not in the way of the ancients but as we ourselves might conceive it today. The anthropocentric cosmology, universal in the Psalmist's time, which appeared then so natural, is totally excluded from this passage. Thus the dominion ascribed to man, if it is more modest and is limited to this world alone, is also more authentic and legitimate.

This dominion enters Genesis with Adam's assigning of names to all the animals. It is as though a sovereign is taking possession of his subjects. But another idea is hidden in the biblical narrative: the knowledge which man is called upon to acquire of the creatures. For in order to name them, he must know them.

190

Man's rule over all living beings is solemnly confirmed once more to Noah, after the Flood:

> The fear and the dread of you shall be upon all the beasts of
> the earth. . . . They are given into your hand. (Gn 9:2)

This purely physical supremacy, moreover, is not separate from the earlier one, which knowledge reserved for civilized humanity. The diversity of means employed corresponds to the diversity of moral conditions among mankind. The rationalist can see only a myth in this domination which, according to the Scriptures, an individual would have possessed over nature even in those remote times; but he cannot deny that the myth was conceived as if it were a reality.

A trace of this primeval condition remains in the fascination which men exercise over animals. On the other hand, degraded men—those in whom the divine image is distorted—become slaves. They are themselves dominated by physical and animal nature. This is why Cain, after his crime, says: "Anyone who meets me may kill me!" (Gn 4:14). And the Talmud declares that animals succeed in dominating man only when he appears to them in the form of a beast.[1]

In order to dominate nature, man must act upon it; and for Hebraism, this domination is a cooperation with God. In imitating his Model, man reigns over the creatures and over earth itself, in order to perfect them in the very act of subduing them.

The Kabbalists have represented this domination as both a *victory* of man over God and a *collaboration* of man with God: a victory over God as perceived in His works, that is, as Creator; a collaboration with God perceived as Ideal, as Redeemer. The triumph is in reality His, man being only an instrument in His hands. Therefore, in commenting upon this verse—

> He who rules men justly,
> He who rules in awe of God (2 Sm 23:3)

—the Kabbalists understood the Lord to say, "Then who reigns over Me? The just."[2]

There is no questioning the influence of man upon nature; but as he is endowed with free will, his action can be beneficial or baneful.

He has the duty of participating in the divine plan: that is, to improve the works of God instead of allowing them to degenerate. We see in the biblical myth of Adam that the effect of the primal man's sin made itself felt over the earth generally: "Cursed be the ground because of you" (Gn 3:17). Before the Fall, man's influence was necessarily beneficial. Adam was placed in the Garden of Eden in order to cultivate and protect it. Now the Garden of Eden represents the state of the earth before sin and after future redemption. In God's curse which followed the disobedience, there is something else besides the statement of fact or the simple assertion of the inescapable consequences of human behavior. There is also the proclamation of a duty, the sacred duty of work which will complete the promise of terrestrial dominion which had already been made to Adam. If Eden has disappeared on account of man, then man is responsible for its reestablishment by means of his activity in conformity with the Creator's purposes. Consequently, Hebraism, through the instrument of its Prophets and rabbis, has unceasingly extolled the noble and sacred character of labor.

When we observe in the Bible the results of men's evil behavior while in a state of rebellion against God, we see that in the days of Noah,

> The earth became corrupt before God; the earth was filled with lawlessness. When God saw how corrupt the earth was, for all flesh had corrupted its ways on earth. . . . (Gn 6:11–12)

Likewise, in the time of Moses, the Israelites were warned not to imitate the guilty conduct of the peoples whom they had vanquished and whom the earth had spewed out before them:

> So let not the land spew you out for defiling it, as it spewed out the nation that came before you. (Lv 18:28)

It is, then, through obedience to the laws of the Sovereign Master that man will exercise his legitimate dominion here on earth. It has been said that man is called upon to compete with nature by imitating her. But a moment's reflection will enable us to see that it is impossible to compete with nature through mere imitation. Such rivalry or emulation requires that man first of all conceive of the Ideal, which nature herself has imitated. Then, modeling his intention on the *divine* intention, he will labor on its behalf and for its ends.

Man as Priest and as Apex of Creation

For Hebraism, man is not only the king of creation; he is also its high priest. The first token of man's priesthood appears in the blessings which God confers upon him. The Bible contains numerous symbols of priestly investiture, such as that of Melchizedek to Abraham, or that of Isaac to Jacob. But the idea appears most clearly in the writings of the rabbis. "Adam," we are told, "is the glory of the world, and when he approached to offer sacrifice, he put on the garments of the high priest."[3]

In rabbinical literature, the priesthood is said to have passed from father to son, down to Shem, son of Noah. What is most interesting here is the bond which joins the priesthood of mankind with the priesthood of Israel; for Shem, according to the rabbis, is none other than Melchizedek, the representative of the priesthood of mankind, who transmitted this dignity to Abraham, who in turn attached it to his family and descendants. The sages express themselves clearly on this matter of the transmission of priesthood from Melchizedek to Abraham:

> We read in the Scriptures, "Now Melchizedek, king of Salem, offered bread and wine." This means that he transmitted to Abraham the rules of the high priesthood: the bread represented meal-offerings, the wine drink-offerings.[4]

These traditions are confirmed in the Kabbalah. According to Rabbi Isaac Luria, Kabbalah teaches that the high priest Aaron was a kind of reincarnation or reembodiment of the nature of Adam.[5] This teaching not only assumes that Adam was a priest, but also acknowledges explicitly the bond between the Israelite priesthood and that of mankind. Moreover, we see here a manifest demonstration that Hebraism accepted the presence of a legitimate priesthood among the Gentiles, at least to the time of Moses. In assigning to the first man the double role of king and priest, it recognized implicitly that these prerogatives had passed to his posterity, that is, to mankind as a whole. From the Jewish point of view, then, man is autonomous, both politically and religiously. But just as in particular societies, political and religious functions are delegated to certain men who—in the name of the entire community—exercise them as representatives of all, so also when it is a question of mankind *in toto:* The religious ministry must be specifically allotted to a people chosen from among

193

the rest, which by reason of the particular conditions of its existence, historical and psychological, happens to be most suitable to fill it in the name of all.

Man, high priest of creation, is thus its culmination, so far as earth is concerned, and this high dignity, which leads him to cooperate with God in the accomplishment of the designs of Sovereign Wisdom, links up in him the terrestrial creation with the rest of the universe.

Joined directly to God through his spirit, man contributes toward joining God with nature in first of all binding the earth to the universe, so that it may ultimately be linked to its First Cause. Thus there occurs *Yihud*, unification, which, according to orthodox Judaism, every faithful Jew ought to have in view as the object of all his acts:

> So as to join the Holy One, blessed be He [the transcendent God], and His *Shekhinah* [immanent God, the Divine in the world].[6]

No doubt the unity of nature exists in itself, independently of the human spirit which can only glimpse and reflect it. This unity is in the *Shekhinah*, in the divine immanence, which Christianity has transformed into the conception of a man-god, thus opening a chasm between the world and *transcendent* God, who remains outside the world.

But man cooperates in the unity of nature, and through it in the union of all things with God, which thus becomes the universal and absolute end. According to Isaiah, everything that exists was created, formed, and achieved for God's glory. The Kabbalists understand this to refer to all forms of the finite, the sum total of beings. King and priest, man is both the culmination of terrestrial creation and the means by which our world is joined with the totality of the universe. In this double role, his function is summed up in cooperating with God, in elevating nature to Him and uniting it with its Creator.

The Doctrine of Human Cooperation

What is the metaphysical basis for this concept of the cooperation of man with God? Let us recall that in Hebraism, man is endowed with free will and therefore has the power to promote or oppose the Creator's designs. When man acts conformably to God's plan, he is cooperating with God.

Beneath this truth lies the kabbalistic principle that man exerts influence on the entire universe, both consciously and unconsciously. It could not be otherwise, since, from the theological point of view, freedom, the will, the soul itself, seem to us in their origin and substance to be divine—like a ray, a part, but also a limitation, of the omnipotence of God. Being in so intimate a relation to the Universal, the Eternal, it is impossible that what the soul wishes and does should be inconsequential for the totality of creation. If human thought has its sole source in an unending communion with the Absolute, it is inconceivable that this cause and continuous intercourse should not vastly enlarge the sphere in which man's action has significance. We have spoken elsewhere of concentric rings of consciousness, one inside the other, extending all the way to divine Consciousness, which embraces all.[7] If that is true, we can surmise how high the influence of man can rise—man, who, as some theologians have suggestively called him, is a thought in the mind of God—free to cooperate with the universal order or to contend with it.

But we must not be accused of absorbing human nature into divine nature, following the example of the Gnostics, of philosophers of the school of Alexandria, of extravagant mystics. To be sure, man is a thought in the mind of God, but an active thought, that is, a thought capable of acting for itself. A writer who is assuredly not a mystic, M. Havet, has said, as we should happily have said ourselves: "When we seek God, it is God who seeks Himself in us."[8]

This conception of the influence of man upon creation, beneficent or baneful, may be found, we think, in the beliefs of the Parsees. Inspired by them, Michelet has written a lyrical celebration of the nobility of a head of a family who—in the middle of the night, when wife and children are sleeping—performs the ritual of his religion and intones before the fire certain words which he believes will give life to the universe itself:

> How keen will be the holiness of a man who considers himself so necessary to the existence of the worlds! In the silence of midnight, alone, he feels himself in harmony with all the tribes of the pure who, at this very hour, are also saying the very same words of life.[9]

And here is how a philosopher, Fichte, whose austerity of thought is as impressive as the vitality of his poetry, expresses himself:

I conceive that it is sufficient that any will should simply exist *qua* will (even though the matter may remain hidden in the mystery of my intelligence) . . . for it to become in this world the cause and common center of a multitude of intellectual modifications which, starting from this point, spread out in waves to the last limits of intelligible space, just as in our visible world, the slightest movement of the smallest portion of matter generates other movements of various sorts, which also radiate through all the immensity of the material universe. . . . The law of duty is the point where the invisible and visible worlds touch. It is the bond between them. It is the sense, the organ by means of which man can act in the sphere which is veiled from his terrestrial eyes.[10]

We should ponder this passage of Fichte, and if so, we shall surely notice how consistent it is with the ideas which we have been developing. However, we would wish to qualify his conclusion:

It is only by complying with duty that the wills of finite beings are able to attain a relationship with infinite will; otherwise, from the perspective of infinite will, they are as if they had never existed.[11]

We should like to point out that it is impossible to know how the action of finite will, in accord with duty, can affect infinite will, unless it is sensitive to infinite will even when it is in contradiction to duty. It is not, therefore, on the universe only that free will acts, but on God Himself (if we may speak in this way), in advancing or impeding the accomplishment of His design.

This doctrine is entirely in accord with the divine nature and origin of the human spirit. All that man, who is created in the image and resemblance of God, may do, he does in order to assist and complete the action of God in the world. It also explains the effect which man can have upon what Fichte calls the infinite will—what the Kabbalah calls the *Shekhinah*, the divine in the world. When the human will rebels, it is the part revolting against the whole; it is the kingdom divided against itself (Mt 12:25), for in the Kabbalah, the *Shekhinah* is also called *Malkhut*, kingdom. Here, then, is how we can render intelligible what we read in the Bible and in the writings of the rabbis about the influence of man on the divine world, about the grief which human actions may inspire in Divinity—in a word, anthropopathy. We can also reconcile certain contradictory biblical texts, for some acknowledge and others deny that human deeds influence God; but the first must refer to the *Shekhinah*, the Soul of the World, or divine immanence, whereas the others are concerned with transcendent God, the Ideal which is inaccessible to vicissitudes of creation.

There is another truth implied by the doctrine of human cooperation with God: It is that the law of God and the law of man are single and identical, for cooperation is possible only if both parties take inspiration from the same thought, if they follow a single rule. We see that sometimes it is man who is asked to imitate God, sometimes God Himself who executes what man is obliged to do. We have here two different ways of expressing this idea of the unity of the Law. The first is dominant in the Bible, whereas the writings of the rabbis ascribe an equal authority to both of them. We need not at this point speak further about the imitation of God as man's duty. But we shall point out, with regard to the other expression of this truth, the general principle from which the sages derived so many applications: that God Himself observes the Law.[12] The rabbis tell us that the Law served as plan or model for the creation.[13] And this suggests another doctrine: that human souls cooperated in the work of the six days, man's law having started out by being that of God and of the universe.

Voltaire, followed by later critics, said that if God made man in His image, man has surely returned the favor.[14] Others too have maintained, in a more serious manner but with the same meaning, that theology is at bottom only anthropology. However, some have said that it is really the other way round: Anthropology is theology, in the sense that the subjective conception which man forms of God would not exist if the Absolute had not provided it for him, had not inspired in him the intuition of Himself—in a word, if there had not been an *objective* God. This is approximately the argument of Descartes, and it is no doubt perfectly legitimate in its place. It will suffice for us to point out what modern knowledge increasingly demonstrates: that the law which governs the universe in all its parts constitutes (despite the diversity of its applications) a plan, a unique model. According to Hebraism, there is a unity of design which, starting from God, extends to the farthest rank of created things. In the same vein, we could reverse the terms of the proposition, as atheists wish, and assert that theology derives from anthropology. It is really immaterial whether we start from one side or the other, since the Voice which pronounced the fiat of creation from the highest heavens reverberates from step to step over the entire ladder of being. To borrow the language of the Kabbalists, the ten supreme *Sefirot* (emanations) recur in all life even down to the most minute creatures.

This unity of design which governs all creation becomes in man a consciously perceived, rational law, and cooperation, to which he is called by reason of his nature, leads to a veritable continuation of the creative work, what the Italian philosopher Gioberti has very happily called "co-creation."[15] And the work of man has characteristics which makes it superior even to nature, for nature is a simple, direct effect of God's creative act, whereas human action is the continuation, completion, and in a sense *perfecting* of this act itself. The creative principle in free, self-conscious man proceeds with the work of Genesis, and it must exult in precisely this human freedom, which is true freedom only because it interrupts the chain of natural causes and effects, breaking its continuity. It is a permanent miracle, which we must accept unless we are to deny freedom itself. (As for that which is usually called miraculous, it is nothing other than the occasional return to the act of creation, an echo of Genesis, which came before, and prelude to what must follow. It binds together and establishes unity among the worlds.)

Man is the redeemer of nature. Laboring under the inspiration of the Word, of the Logos incarnate in the Divine Law, he identifies himself with his spiritual part and becomes, in the only acceptable sense, the man-god.

Rabbinic Doctrines and Pagan Ideas

The rabbis have taught us as explicitly as possible the doctrine of the cooperation of man with God. They call just men *partners* of holy God. We read in the Talmud that whoever renders a judgment in conformity with the truth becomes the partner of God in the work of creating heaven and earth.[16] We are told in another passage:

> God said to Abraham, "Since you have shown hospitality toward strangers, I shall credit it to your account as if you were My partner in the creation of the world." This is the meaning of these words: "Blessed be Abram of God Most High, Creator of heaven and earth!" (Gn 14:19)[17]

198

And finally, just as it is said that God meditates upon the Law in preserving the world through His Providence, so too, according to the sages, man contributes to the creation and preservation of the universe when he gives himself to the study of Divine Law.[18]

We do not have to seek far to find an echo of these ideas in contemporary philosophy. Giuseppe Allievo writes:

> The school of absolute idealism started by postulating as a fundamental premise the identity of being with thought, and ended, through logical necessity, by confusing intelligence with the operation of the will, or, if you like, man's speculative life with his active life. . . . From this comes the maxim of modern idealists that to philosophize about the universe is equivalent to creating it.[19]

This rabbinical concept is distinctly different from pagan ideas, some of which the rabbis themselves most remarkably provide for us in their own writings. Elsewhere, they tell us that in paganism all things depend on fate or necessity, which allows human freedom only a very secondary role. We can imagine that the philosophers in question were the Stoics, who more than the other schools resemble the Pharisees, and whose ethic had as its supreme principle the obligation to comply in all things with nature. (The Epicureans, less influential than the Stoics, upheld the claims of moral freedom, which they considered a higher principle than physical necessity.[20])

Epictetus said:

> Just as in all his creative activities, intelligent man submits to moderation or just measure, so also the good man must submit to the legitimate order of the universe. The whole is better than the part; the city is better than the citizen. Since you are a part of the whole, you ought to put yourself in harmony with it. If the good man could understand the future, he would accept even his own illness, mutilation, or death, with tranquillity and satisfaction, knowing that the order of the universe wishes it thus.[21]

And according to Marcus Aurelius:

Religious thought favors the idea that we ought to encourage the natural course of things. It would be reckless and evil to interfere with the ways of Providence, even if we could.[22]

However that may be, here is what Tinneius Rufus raised as an objection to Rabbi Akiba: "If your God loves the poor, why does He not feed them?" To which the rabbi answered that it is in order to allow their fellow-men the merit of doing so; and that, far from reproaching them for having acted contrary to His decrees by aiding the poor, He will be grateful to them for it. If a king, added Akiba, finds himself obliged to punish his own son on account of his faults, would he not be grateful to the man who secretly passed assistance to the son? Such generosity, however, he would not tolerate if it were a question not of his son but of a slave.[23]

This entire passage is most remarkable. First of all, there is the idea that God loves the poor, which is indeed authentically Jewish and not exclusively Christian, as is often claimed. Then there is the important distinction between slaves and children, which throws a clear light on the relation which Judaism postulates between God and men—or, to put it better, the ideal which it places before our eyes as an object to attain. But what most particularly interests us here is the contrast which is offered between the Roman theory, with its deference to reality and its altogether practical morality, prescribing simple obedience to nature, and, on the other hand, the role which Judaism attributes to man with an eye to correcting and improving nature itself. At bottom, this idea is at the very heart of Akiba's argument. It is equally crucial in another passage from rabbinical literature, where once again there is a controversy with pagan sages: "Some philosophers asked of a rabbi, 'If God does not approve of polytheism, why does He not abolish it?' " (The polytheism in question, as the context makes clear, is the adoration of nature at her most magnificent.) Once more, the rabbi's response sets up an opposition between the worship of material fact, or natural reality, and the worship of the Ideal, which is the sole worship worthy of man.[24]

Later sages, too, among others Rabbi Elghazi, have also seen the matter in its true light, in pointing to a preliminary question which is asked in the Talmud: Which of the two parts of creation is superior, heaven and earth or man? The pagans decided in favor of nature, but the rabbis chose man and his works. "The deeds of the just," they assert, "surpass the creation of heaven and earth." It is not without reason that this wonderful maxim has been called "the noblest thing that has ever been said on the subject of human nature."[25]

It remains to compare the conceptions of oriental paganism with Hebraic doctrine. The most characteristic such conceptions are those which come from India. We know what almost superhuman perfection the holy persons of that country can attain; we know how heroic are their virtues, how prodigious their asceticism; we know the respect, even fear, which they come to inspire in the gods themselves. In India we find a sort of religious faith so unusual that people have attempted to distinguish it precisely from Semitic religion.

> According to Semitic ideas [we are told], great personalities can certainly achieve marvels, but their power depends entirely on the Eternal, from whom they are separated by an abyss, and who, if He draws His hand away from them, can precipitate them into annihilation. In India, however, heaven is not inaccessible.[26]

There is good reason to inquire whether this description of the holy or righteous Jew is accurate, and whether the domination of nature which Buddhist mystics achieve can truly be likened to that which biblical and rabbinical Judaism promises man.

For us, the answer to both questions lies in the distinction between God and the gods. (This is a legitimate and necessary distinction even in pantheism, though here, perhaps, we should substitute for the word "God" an expression such as "the One" or "the Great All.") If we allow this, all becomes perfectly intelligible. It is indeed true that among the Semites, the saintly person is nothing if God chooses to abandon him. But why is this? Precisely because the Semite is a monist, and for him nothing created can count for anything in opposition to the Absolute Unity. But as soon as the Semite encounters the universe, nature, the multiplicity of created things, with the realm of *finite* forces, angels, celestial powers—or, in a word, "gods"—then his own greatness appears at once. The just person, whom the Talmud proclaims to be greater than the heaven and earth, and the saint, whom the rabbis call the partner of God, are superior not only to nature but also to the angels and the gods.

We agree that in the eyes of Buddhist saints, nature is very small, since we often see them treating their gods as equals—gods which are

201

but natural forces exalted and called divine. But we can readily see the difference between this perspective and that of Judaism. The Hindu saint is only a thaumaturge, or miracle-worker; the Jewish saint *can be* a thaumaturge, but he is above all a man. The goal of the first is not to improve or perfect nature, much less to use it, and he masters it without subduing or disciplining it. The second, however, is not a capricious magician who seeks only to display his powers; what he has in view is above all the moral, social, humanitarian order. In him, the supernatural is in harmony with nature. He does not wish to destroy nature but to improve it.

Man as Creator

We have already pointed out the close rapport between the doctrine of the cooperation of man with God and that of the unity of divine and human Law: they are in fact a single doctrine. The rabbinical conception of divine kinship puts the seal on this teaching. As we have seen, the sages are lavish in their praise of the upright person, giving him the extremely eloquent title "partner of God." But in addition, they call him "friend," "companion," and even "brother" of the Lord. This last designation makes us instinctively think of the name which Christianity gives its faithful, of whom Jesus was called "elder brother." It is by reason of their common humanity that the individual Christian is called the brother of Jesus. But we should remember that the Christian Incarnation is but an imitation of the Hebraic *Shekhinah*, or divine immanence, of the *Malkhut* of the Kabbalah—though with an essential difference. According to Christianity, the descent of God into the finite is accomplished in the bosom of mankind alone, or rather in a single man; but for the Kabbalah, the incarnation exists in and through the very fact of the entire creation, although man occupies the central focus, loving Him who brings him there and upholds him.

Finally, we encounter in the rabbis a doctrine which stuns us by its grandeur and gives us the measure of the elevation which the spirit of the Pharisees could reach. According to them, man exerts a certain influence on the universe; he has the power to disturb or advance, to assist or oppose the divine order. This influence extends up to God Himself, at least to the *Shekhinah*, the divine in the world, and it is in this idea that we must seek the explanation of all the biblical and rabbinical passages in which we see divinity feeling the effect of good or bad human actions. We shall not be surprised, then, to find this very conception in the Kabbalah. On this point as on all others, its doctrine is in perfect accord with the doctrines of exoteric Judaism. We see once more that there is nothing more erroneous than to persist in pointing to Kabbalism as a later importation, something foreign to Hebraism.

Christianity struck out a path toward those modern philosophers who present this teaching more intelligibly and justify it in their own way. There is a passage by Paul which is concise and extremely significant:

> For we know that the whole creation groaneth and travaileth in pain together until now. And not only they, but ourselves also, which have the first-fruits of the Spirit, even we ourselves groan within ourselves, waiting for the adoption, to wit, the redemption of our body. (Rom 8:22–23)

If we are not greatly mistaken, this verse from the Epistle to the Romans contains visible traces of gnostic-kabbalistic doctrines which Paul had learned in the Palestinian schools. Nature's condition of suffering, her sighs and groans of which we hear so much in the *Aggadot*—this is the *Galut ha-Shekhinah* of the Kabbalists, the scattering of the holy through the world. In this context, the idea of messianic deliverance, *g'ulah*, exchanges its political significance for a mysterious metaphysical meaning, and the work of redemption is assigned not to a single individual, even a man-god, but to all mankind.

Other great intellects have likewise glimpsed this principle—or, rather, this great fact.

> It is important to know [says Fichte] that everything is linked together in each of the possible worlds. The Universe, whatever it may be, is made all of a piece, like an ocean. The smallest motion has an effect which is felt at the greatest possible distance, although this effect becomes less perceptible as the distance becomes greater, so that God has ordered everything in advance and once for all, having anticipated the prayers of the virtuous and the wicked deeds of the rest. And each thing has made its contribution, ideally before its own existence, to what has been determined with respect to the existence of everything.[27]

This last thought is found almost exactly in the rabbis. John Stuart Mill is still more precise when he declares that "the virtuous man seeks to assist God."[28] This is virtually what the Talmud says. And the rabbis comment significantly on this verse from Deuteronomy:

> O Jeshurun, there is none like God,
> Riding through the heavens to help you,
> Through the skies in His majesty. (Dt 33:26)

Instead of reading "to help you," they suggest that we should understand the words to mean "to be helped by you."[29]

Here, finally, is a passage from Spinoza, which is about the way freedom works:

> The proper end of a being can serve at the same time a higher end, without the being's having knowledge of this. This is how the bee in making honey also works for the interests of man. In the same way, even while man believes he works only for his own interests, he serves at the same time the ends of nature in general, which uses him as an instrument. Thus, man's moral laws, even though they are brought into being by the idea of humanity's welfare, are at the same time serving the aims of the Universe.[30]

5

The Idea of Nationality in Judaism

The peoples of mankind are bonded together historically in Adam, psychologically in the *Shekhinah*, the Divine in the world, center or focus of all souls, and ideally in the Word or Logos, which is the Intelligible World.

Many profound consequences arise from this. Every people finds its *raison d'être* in the particular idea which it represents. Thus is its very existence legitimized, its laws rendered inviolable. Moreover, its achievement is part of the cosmic order and an expression therefore of providential design. But the ultimate goal toward which nationalities are directed seems to be their organization into a unity or consummating harmony, an evolution which can be found elsewhere in various parts of nature. The perfection of the whole indeed increases in proportion to that of the parts. The book of Genesis, in representing all mankind as members of the same original family, and the Prophets, in predicting the eventual unity of the human race, reveal to us the existence of that universal consciousness which was later expressed by Hebrew mysticism, according to which the body of Adam contained in its different parts all individuals and all peoples, both in their diversity (with each responding to the individuation of its own nature) but also in their ideal unity (symbolized by the material unity of the first man's body). We know that the Zohar compares Israel to the heart of mankind, while the other peoples represent the other parts of its body. For the Kabbalah, it is not only Adam's body but also his soul which embraces all of future mankind. The totality of humanity, so to say, ideally merges into a single consciousness.

The Kabbalah images all this in an *ilan*, or genealogical tree, which graphically represents the *Sefirot*, to each of which is linked one of the great peoples of history: Egypt, Babylon, the Persians, the Medes, Greece, Rome, Christian Rome, and Islam.[1] It is like a condensation of the entire philosophy of history.

The Hebraic Conception of International Law

For Hebraism, the notion of nationality is a simple philosophical or theological conception, a feeling whose intensity does not have to be demonstrated here. To the contrary, it is so conspicuous and intense that rival religions, as well as independent critics, have often taken their turns in accusing Hebraic nationalism of being excessive and exclusive. What has not been sufficiently acknowledged, however, is that for Jews, national feeling is never separated from their commitment to mankind.

The very fact that Judaism, if not indeed a nationality in itself, has provided at least the foundation, organization, and *raison d'être* of a people shows how important this sentiment must have been in its eyes. Its most treasured beliefs acknowledge the sacred rights of peoples. It affirms that Divine Providence extends without distinction over all of mankind, that God is the universal judge of nations as well as of individuals, that they perish only on account of their own transgressions, that an identical justice rules Israel and all the other peoples. It declares that every violation of national independence is a crime which the sovereign Judge punishes, for if He is the redeemer of Israel, He glories also in being the savior of every oppressed people; and if He defends His people against the attacks of its enemies, He also ordains that they must respect the frontiers of other states. In all these doctrines we can undoubtedly detect the foundation and endorsement of international law.

It is surprising to find the basic conception of nationality, as well as the conditions of its realization, in one of the oldest strata of Genesis. After enumerating the descendants of Noah, the Bible adds, with an obvious emphasis on Japheth:

> From these, the maritime nations branched out. [These are the descendants of Japheth] by their lands—each with its language—their clans and their nations. (Gn 10:5)

And then, turning to Ham and Shem:

These are the descendants of Ham, according to their clans and languages, by their lands, according to their nations. . . . These are the descendants of Shem, according to their clans and languages, by their lands, according to their nations. (Gn 10:20, 31)

And let us cite once more this passage from the Song of Moses:

When the Most High gave nations their homes
And set the divisions of man,
He fixed the boundaries of peoples. (Dt 32:8)

Rashi says of this verse:

When God divided the earth among the peoples, He gave every nation specific boundaries, so that each people might retain its particular identity.

It seems to us that this text implies quite clearly that the separation and dispersion of peoples had as its object the formation of nationalities. Thus, when God said to the first man, "Be fertile and increase, fill the earth and master it" (Gn 1:28), the separate identity of peoples was already a part of the Creator's original plan. Indeed, this distinction among the peoples was a necessary consequence of man's fulfilling the divine command, and of God's granting man the promised mastery over the earth, since climatic differences and the diversity of living conditions could not fail to produce variations among men. In his discourse to the Athenians, Paul echoes the doctrines of Hebraism when he says:

And [God] hath made of one blood all nations of men for to dwell on all the face of the earth, and hath determined the times before appointed, and the bounds of their habitation. (Acts 17:26)

The Family of Mankind and the Brotherhood of Peoples

According to Hebraism, there exists a definitive number of nationalities: seventy. This number, which we often encounter in the rabbis, is of biblical origin. The list of nations which descend from Noah, enumerated in Genesis, comes to seventy. This is also the number implied by the complete passage from the Song of Moses quoted in part above:

> He fixed the boundaries of peoples
> In relation to Israel's numbers. (Dt 32:8)

This text alludes to the seventy children of Jacob who, with their father, went down into Egypt. The implication is that the sons of Israel are, on the religious plane, representative of the other peoples, these seventy Israelite family chieftains becoming then the religious representatives of the seventy nationalities of the earth. This is undoubtedly why the number remained constant in Judaism. The first supreme council instituted by Moses in Israel, as later the Sanhedrin, were each composed of seventy members. A verse of Balaam's prophecy seems to allude at once to the number of nations, their relationship, and the special place reserved for Israel:

> As I see them from the mountaintops,
> Gaze on them from the heights,
> There is a people that dwells apart,
> Not reckoned among the nations. (Nm 23:9)

These peoples, whose number was fixed by Divine Providence, are interdependent, each one responsible for all the others in the large scheme of mankind, as all their members are on the level of individual existence.

Each people has its own special character and embodies a particular idea, and so has an appropriate field of activity in which its genius must develop and express itself. All of them are bound together by common goals and obligations, and strive cooperatively toward the flourishing and perfection of life on our globe, and toward the formation of that ideal mankind of which they are the necessary and providentially ordained elements. Despite the ethnic differences intended by God from the beginning, all peoples participate in a single plan, and according to the spirit of Judaism, this interdependence assumes a form which perfectly expresses the idea of humanity as a single organism. Indeed, for Hebraism, the world of peoples, who divide the earth among them, corresponds in structure to the human family.

This analogy probably goes back to distant antiquity, when man was led to think of the invisible cause of his being as his father, and the nature which nourished him as his mother. God, nature, and Adam form an authentic family, a holy family which is the reflection of two others: the transcendent God, the Ideal or Logos, and the *Shekhinah* or divine immanence; and more exalted still, at the very heart of divinity, the Intelligent, Intelligence, and the Intelligible.

Finally, if God and mankind constitute a family, it follows that the abode of this family is the world, where God lives alongside His children. Numerous texts might be cited to support this conception.

> Thus said the Lord [cries the prophet Isaiah]:
> The heaven is My throne
> And the earth is My footstool:
> Where could you build a house for Me,
> What place could serve as My abode? (Is 66:1)

It is probably in this sense that we must understand the Temple, or *Heikhal*, of which Isaiah speaks in the famous vision of the sixth chapter. (The house of the Lord in Jerusalem is but the smaller embodiment of this "Temple.") The same conception is found in God's own words when He extols the superior inspiration of Moses over that of all the other prophets:

> Not so with My servant Moses; he is trusted throughout My household. With him I speak mouth to mouth, plainly and not in riddles, and he beholds the likeness of the Lord. (Nm 12:7–8)

According to Maimonides, this house is the entire creation, the universe, the totality of existing things.[2] In Proverbs, the word appears with the same meaning:

> Wisdom has built her house,
> She has hewn her seven pillars. (Prv 9:1)

The same metaphor occurs in a number of other scriptural passages as well, to denote society, state, or kingdom.

The notion, then, that the conception of God as Father appears for the first time in Christian writings is quite erroneous. In this matter, as so often, the Gospel is echoing the ancient voice of the Prophets and sages of Israel. In the house of God, which is the universe, the Lord is Father on earth as in heaven. He is the Father of men as well as of angels (who are called His children, sons of God). To show us how we should venerate God, the prophet speaks of the respect which an infant owes his father:

> A son should honor his father, and a slave his master. Now if I am a father, where is the honor due Me? And if I am a master, where is the reverence due Me?—said the Lord of Hosts to you. (Mal 1:6)

David calls God "father of orphans" (Ps 68:6). Elsewhere, God's love for those who fear Him is compared to a father's love for his children:

> For whom the Lord loves, He rebukes,
> As a father the son whom he favors. (Prv 3:12)

"But now, O Lord," exclaims Isaiah, "You are our Father." And so that no one might suppose that he is referring to Israel alone, he adds:

> We are the clay, and You are the Potter,
> We are all the work of Your hands. (Is 64:7)

The metaphor sometimes carries accents of tenderness hardly known even in Christianity, for God is not only a father but also a mother.

> Like an eagle who rouses his nestlings,
> Gliding down to its young,
> So did He spread His wings and take him,
> Bear him along on His pinions;
> The Lord alone did guide him. (Dt 32:11–12)

Isaiah, imitating this language, says:

> Like the birds that fly, even so will the Lord of Hosts shield Jerusalem, shielding and saving, protecting and rescuing. (Is 31:5)

And further on:

> Zion says,
> "The Lord has forsaken me,
> My Lord has forgotten me."
> Can a woman forget her baby,
> Or disown the child of her womb?
> Though she might forget,
> I could never forget you. (Is 49:14–15)

And the same prophet later gives us these words of surpassing tenderness:

> You shall be carried on shoulders
> And dandled upon knees.
> As a mother comforts her son
> So will I comfort you;
> You shall find comfort in Jerusalem. (Is 66:12–13)

Judaism regards all men as children of God. It has been noted, with respect to the title "son of God" which was given to Jesus, that it was in the Hebraic tradition to bestow this honorific upon the most eminent men. Thus it is said of Solomon: "I will be a father to him, and he shall be a son to Me" (2 Sm 7:14).

Peoples are similarly called sons of God. And if the first examples which we are going to cite refer to Israel specifically, in others this affectionate appellation extends to all peoples, including the pagans. In Deuteronomy: "You are the children of the Lord your God" (Dt 14:1).

> None other than the Lord your God, who goes before you, will fight for you, just as He did in Egypt before your very eyes, and in the wilderness, where you saw how the Lord your God carried you, as a man carries his son, all the way that you traveled until you came to this place. (Dt 1:30–31)

In his last song, Moses exclaims to the Israelites: "Is not He the Father who created you, fashioned you, and made you endure!" (Dt 32:6). And Isaiah says:

THE IDEA OF NATIONALITY IN JUDAISM

> Surely You are our Father:
> Though Abraham regard us not,
> You, O Lord, are our Father;
> From of old, Your name is "Our Redeemer." (Is 63:16)

This last text is particularly remarkable, for the prophet seems to acknowledge only God as true Father of Israel, to the exclusion of the Patriarchs, thus seeing Israel as one among the other "nations" with respect to the common paternity of God.

But there is a very striking passage in Jeremiah, in which all peoples without exception are called the children of God:

> But I said: "How would I put thee among the children,
> And give thee a pleasant land,
> The goodliest heritage of the nations!" (Jer 3:19)[3]

The designation of Israel as the firstborn among peoples (Ex 4:22) is the crowning confirmation of this belief in the universal fatherhood of God, for the notion of a firstborn assumes the existence of other peoples who are also children of God. The idea evoked is precisely that of the family; and we must recall that in the Israelite family, as in ancient society generally, the firstborn was the family priest, charged with priestly duties on behalf of his brothers. The special place accorded Israel, then, is not a selfish privilege, as has too often been claimed in a spirit of reproach. It is instead a necessary religious expression of the concept of mankind as a great human family. Another important consequence follows from this conception: that all peoples are brothers. If this idea has triumphed in Judaism, it has been in spite of a thousand hostile influences, which amply attests to the doctrine's power.

Consider how Moses instructs the messengers he sends to the king of Edom: "Thus says your brother Israel" (Nm 20:14). Elsewhere, he appeals to the Hebrews in the same spirit: "You shall not abhor an Edomite, for he is your kinsman [lit. 'brother']" (Dt 23:8). It may be objected that what is recalled here is the bond of brotherhood between Jacob and Esau, from whom Edom is descended. But Ezekiel calls Sodom the *sister* of Israel (Ez 16:46). Is this simply because, both having sinned, they deserve to be linked in a common censure? If so, what are we to say of Amos, who calls *all* the pagan peoples brothers, and reproves those who commit injustices against others for having

212

forgot the fraternal bond which joins them (Am 1, 2, 9)? There is even a psalm in which we find these memorable words: "Then will I proclaim Your fame to my brethren, praise You in the congregation" (Ps 22:23). Who are these brothers? Other peoples, for we read several verses later:

> Let all the ends of the earth pay heed and turn to the Lord, and the peoples of all nations prostrate themselves before You; for kingship is the Lord's and He rules the nations. (Ps 22:28–29)

And the same psalm ends with the promise that the mission of Israel, to which allusion has just been made, will be crowned with success:

> The Lord's fame shall be proclaimed to the generation to come; they shall tell of His beneficence to people yet to be born, for He has acted. (Ps 22:31–32)[4]

Relations between Israel and the Gentiles

Let us now consider the ideas about relations among peoples which follow from this conception of the all-embracing human family. For Judaism, God is the Creator and Father of all peoples. He demands respect for the rights of each of them. In a world of peoples who together form a great family, Israel is, as it were, the heart and soul of mankind, with a very special function, and the glorious mission of working for the future unity of the entire human race. What, then, is the behavior which has been prescribed for the Jews in their dealings with the Gentiles? Let us try to extract some relevant principles from among the Mosaic imperatives regarding certain peoples who were unfriendly to Israel.

The descendants of Esau had inherited the hostility of their ancestor toward Jacob with such intensity that the king of Edom refused the Hebrews simple passage through his country. Nevertheless, Moses instructed his people not to hate the Edomites, for they are *our brethren.* And in order to make clear that this injunction is not due to the kinship between Esau and Jacob, he amplifies it in the same verse: "You shall not abhor an Egyptian, for you were a stranger in his land" (Dt 23:8). Why is this said? Could it be claimed that Egypt lavished a benevolence upon Israel beyond what she received from other peoples? To the contrary, indeed, the Jews were so ill treated there that they had all the more reason to be grateful to the other nations. If the text, then, invokes the memory of Egyptian hospitality, it must be an acknowledgement that the generous reception which Israel was initially granted in that country ought to be more remembered than the severe suffering which came later.

To be sure, we find also in the Torah special statutes concerning Amalek, Ammon, Moab, and the Canaanite tribes. But these exceptional laws, authorizing the conquest of certain territories and the subjugation of their peoples, were deemed necessary precisely because in general Israel was required to conduct its relations with the Gentile peoples in an altogether different way. Let us observe, moreover, that these *ad hoc* condemnations carry a moral significance which rises well above the material interests of the Jews. The censure which is addressed to these particular peoples is motivated by the depravity of their conduct, as Moses is quick to point out for the sake of his own people's moral education. The Amalekites, for example, at the moment of Israel's departure from Egypt, threw themselves upon a poor folk who were dragging themselves painfully along, exhausted with fatigue; and in so doing, they showed that they were "undeterred by fear of God" (Dt 25:18). If the pagan were to learn fear of God, he would become as worthy of respect as a brother. As for the Canaanites, Moses leaves us in no doubt that if they are detested, it is not on account of the injuries they have inflicted upon the Jews but because of their corruption and immorality. Israel's role is only to serve as the instrument of divine justice in avenging the honor of outraged mankind.

But there are episodes of Israelite history which are more conclusive still. Thus, we know that Solomon made an alliance with Hiram, king of Tyre, who assists in the holiest of projects, the erection of the Temple. But this was an honor denied to debased Israelites like the Samaritans, who, in fact, even in the time of Esdras, were not allowed to join in the restoration of the sanctuary.

The Hebrews observe this attitude of sympathetic respect not only toward foreign sovereigns but toward their peoples as well. We may recall the fidelity with which Joshua and the elders of Israel kept their oath with the Gibeonites, even though it had been obtained by fraud (Jos 9). This engagement is regarded as so inviolable that we find it fully in force up to the time of Saul; and when famine afflicts the land during the reign of King David, it is still thought to be a punishment for violation of good faith among peoples. David speaks finely with regard to Hanun, son of the king of Ammon: "I will keep faith with Hanun son of Nahash, just as his father kept faith with me" (2 Sm 10:2). An ancient Karaite author commenting on this verse concludes "that we must behave well, following the example of David, even to the unbelievers from whom we have received benefits."[5]

Israel's conduct toward the pagan peoples was such that they called its monarchs godly kings and trusted their generosity without hesitation. We read that when Israel defeated the Arameans, their king Ben-hadad took refuge in the town of Aphek.

> His ministers said to him, "We have heard that the kings of the House of Israel are magnanimous kings. Let us put sackcloth on our loins and ropes on our heads, and surrender to the king of Israel; perhaps he will spare your life." So they girded sackcloth on their loins and wound ropes around their heads, and came to the king of Israel and said, "Your servant Ben-hadad says, 'I beg you, spare my life.'"

Ahab did not belie his good name: "Is he still alive? He is my brother" (1 Kgs 20:31–32).

It was in this sensitive way that King Ahab avoided the humiliating epithet of servant which his defeated enemy had assumed, thus for the first time teaching sovereigns to regard each other as brothers. When, later, the soldiers of this same king of Aram, once again at war with Israel, were led unwittingly into Samaria by a contrivance of Elisha's, this man of God in his turn counselled the king of Israel to treat them magnanimously.

> When the king of Israel saw them, he said to Elisha, "Father, shall I strike them down?" "No, do not," he replied. "Did you take them captive with your sword and bow that you would strike them down? Rather, set food and drink before them, and let them eat and drink and return to their master." (2 Kgs 6:21–22)

PART THREE:
THE LAW

1

Unity and Universality of the Law

*I*s the notion that the law of man is identical to the law of the
universe an authentically Hebraic doctrine? To be sure, this identity is one of the characteristic themes of the Kabbalah. But is the
Kabbalah in this matter consistent with the other sources of Hebraic
belief? We shall show clearly that it is, and this conformity of doctrine
will demonstrate once again the legitimacy and antiquity of the Kabbalah. What is at issue here is not merely an accidental agreement on a
particular point, however important; the concept we are concerned
with goes to the very heart of Kabbalah, in its transcendent perception
of the Law and of the creative Word or Logos which the Law entails, in
its assertion that those who observe the Law are thus participating in
the universal order, and, finally, in the importance—not only ethical or
social, nor even religious, but in some sense cosmic and ontological—
which it accords to the precepts of the Torah. If all of Hebraism's
cornerstones bear the impress of this doctrine, we have ample proof
that Hebraism is profoundly permeated by Kabbalah.

Before returning to the Bible, let us consider what the rabbis teach
us on this subject. Their reflections will give added strength to our
argument. For them, the Torah is not only the civil and religious law. It
has a much larger importance: It is the Logos, the intelligible world, the
pattern or archetype of the creation. This theory of the Torah-Logos
could not be formulated more clearly than Genesis Rabbah has done:

> Just as an architect constructs a building only by consulting
> his plans, calculations, and drawings, so also, in order to
> create the world, the Holy One, blessed be He, meditated
> upon the Torah.[1]

219

Furthermore, say the rabbis, the Torah is the very instrument by which God exercised His creativity; it is the principle by virtue of which the world was created; it is, in fact, one of the seven things which are older than the world itself.[2] Elsewhere, the rabbis put in the serpent's mouth these significant words: "God ate of this tree of knowledge, and it was thus that He created the world."[3] Now the tree of life and the tree of the knowledge of good and evil represent the two faces of the Law, the first that of the perfect man, the other that of fallen man. Philosophically, they symbolize the Ideal and the Real—Philo's *Logos endeithitos* and *Logos prophoricos*.[4]

This profound idea that the world and man were both created on the model of the Torah appears in the Zohar. The law of the world and the law of man are thus identical. But the rabbis go further still in asserting that God Himself observes the Law. This concept has provided the excuse for innumerable protests against the alleged absurdities and blasphemies of the Pharisees; but in order to gauge the true value of a doctrine judiciously, it is necessary to see what its most enlightened partisans think of it. This notion of a God observing the Law, a kabbalistic idea, is found in Talmudic Pharisaism, where not only is the principle expressly stated but it is indeed furnished with details of such a kind as to scandalize our modern conceptions of deity, for apart from the fact the God here fulfills all the obligations of religious ethics, He is said to wear *tefilin* or phylacteries, and to address prayers to Himself.[5] But beneath these metaphors is a ground-breaking philosophical theory.

Let us recall what we have said previously about the doctrine of collaboration between man and God. For man to collaborate with God means that they share the same Law. The epithets of partner, brother, companion of God, which the rabbis bestow on man, may just as properly be linked to the idea of the unity of the Law as to that of human collaboration with God. It has justly been said that the rational person who subjects himself to the Law, freely and with full understanding, is actually fulfilling his own will rather than another's. This thought is found in the Talmud, which says expressly that the Law becomes the law of man as soon as he learns it, though originally it belongs to God and is called the law of God. Since, in the philosophical sense, the Law is natural to man, as it is to the universe of which man is part, and since it embodies an ideal which has not yet been fulfilled in the universe, it is evident that there must be a certain parity between the Law and the man who observes (and so fulfills) it. Moreover, we find the rabbis giving to the human soul, and perhaps to man as a whole, the name *Sefer Torah*, Book of the Law, and stating that religious prohibitions must be set aside when they put human life at risk[6]—clear proof that they acknowledge something more important than the letter of the Law.

Finally, the unity of the Law follows inevitably from the rabbinical doctrine that mankind has the same relation to the earth as the soul has to the body, as indeed it follows from the idea that man's spirit returns to the spirit of the universe, which we encounter in the dying words of Plotinus, and which Giordano Bruno echoed at the moment of his own death at the stake: "I am trying to restore what is divine in me to what is divine in the universe."[7]

We find this concept of the unity of the Law reflected, first of all, in the idea that man should follow the path of his Creator, that his calling quite simply is to imitate God: a notion which is found often in the Scriptures, though it does not usually receive the attention it deserves. If the path is the same, then the Law must be identical as well. They are but two names for a single thing.

The Bible shows us God practicing all that He enjoins man to observe: justice, charity, holiness, forgiveness, moral perfection. Abraham asks: "Shall not the Judge of all the earth deal justly?" (Gn 18:25). Will He who sustains the world through justice be the only one not to observe it Himself? The words of Leviticus express the matter as clearly as possible: "You shall be holy, for I, the Lord your God, am holy" (Lv 19:2).

No doubt God's observance of the Law is a necessary expression of His divine nature. The moral laws themselves cannot, therefore, be understood by God as they are understood and practiced by man, and it is in this sense that Maimonides and other commentators have interpreted these verses of Isaiah:

> For My plans are not your plans,
> Nor are My ways your ways—
> declares the Lord.
> But as the heavens are high above the earth,
> So are My ways high above your ways,
> And My plans above your plans. (Is 55:8–9)

But the difference is in degree, not essence. The Law is one, and its oneness is all the more definitive precisely because it assumes all forms in adapting itself to all the different expressions of being, from the nature of God to that of a grain of sand.

But it will certainly be objected that however reasonable deductive logic may be, it is not the same as textual evidence, and it will be asked if the Bible really contains examples of God observing the Law. Now the Sabbath was observed by God before it was by man, and it is in fact precisely because God observed it that He commanded man to observe it as well. Is this an isolated instance, or is it part of a perfectly consistent biblical system?

We must also observe that the Prophets habitually merge stellar, cosmic, geological changes with political upheavals, the fall and rebirth of empires, into a single conception—that is, they link human and social life with universal life, or, to use their own language, the new heavens and new earths with transformed humanity. Both linkages are closely related to the idea of the unity of the Law; and for the Prophets, this unity is to find future embodiment in the simultaneous renewal of the earth—palingenesis—and renewal of the human race—resurrection.

The principle of the unity of the Law has also been expressed by Judaism in another form, which goes back to Moses: The conception of a heavenly Jerusalem and Temple. In several passages of Exodus, we read that God showed Moses a model of the Tabernacle and of all it would contain: "Note well, and follow the patterns for them that are being shown to you on the mountain" (Ex 25:40)—that is, in the place where dwelt the glory of the Lord. One could cite many other biblical allusions equally suggestive.

There are two psalms which are difficult to understand unless we recognize in them this transposition of terrestrial things into the celestial domain.

> Lord, who may dwell in Your tent, who may dwell on Your holy mountain? (Ps 15:1)

There follows a long survey of the necessary moral qualities. The other psalm starts in a similar way:

> Who may ascend the mountain of the Lord?
> Who may stand in His holy place?—
> He who has clean hands and a pure heart, who has not taken a false oath by My life or sworn deceitfully. (Ps 24:3–4)

222

This tent, this mountain of the Lord and holy place, can scarcely refer either to Jerusalem or to the Tabernacle or Temple. What is evoked here must therefore be their heavenly counterparts.

Another important scriptural text is the account of Jacob's dream (Gn 28:10–19). The stairway between heaven and earth, the angels going up and down, the very name "gateway to heaven" which Jacob gives to the holy place—all these details are clearly significant. To illuminate the matter, we can set beside this last passage the words of the Psalmist when he is absorbed in trying to understand the mystery of why the wicked prosper:

> So I applied myself to understand this, but it seemed a hopeless task till I entered God's sanctuary and reflected on their fate. (Ps 73:16–17)

If the Law preexists in heaven, it is natural that this verse should have been applied to Moses:

> You went up to the heights, having taken captives, having received tribute of men, even of those who rebel against the Lord God's abiding there. (Ps 68:19)

And in the magnificent panegyric on the Divine Law which is Psalm 119, we likewise read:

> The Lord exists forever;
> Your word stands firm in heaven. (Ps 119:89)

But here we must note a fact of considerable interest. This conception of a celestial sanctuary on the model of the Temple at Jerusalem is by no means isolated. Indeed, it forms part of a larger pattern according to which the terrestrial sites of the holy land are regarded as representations of moral states, or spiritual realities in the other life, so that the idea that divine and human Law are one occurs even in the most trifling forms and details. Thus, a discerning author writes with regard to the Valley of Jehoshaphat:

> This valley mentioned by Joel is not the same as the valley between Jerusalem and the Mount of Olives [which bears its name]. Its symbolic name signifies, rather, the place where

the Lord must judge and punish the enemies of His people, and the proof of this is that in Joel 4:14, the Valley of Jehoshaphat is called Valley of Decision, that is, the place where these wicked will have to be severely punished.[8]

We do not deny, of course, the existence of a "Valley of Jehoshaphat" at Jerusalem, which served as a symbol of God's judgment between the Gentiles and Israel. Nevertheless, we have here an example of a geographical location believed to represent a moral condition.

Here is another. *Topheth* was a real locality in the neighborhood of Jerusalem, in the Valley of Hinnom, where children were burnt in honor of Moloch. However, the name was used by Isaiah to denote the place where the enemies of God are punished, whether in this world or (as seems more probable) in the abode of the dead, so that the name *Gehinnom*, Valley of Hinnom (from which we derive *Gehenna*), which was given by the rabbis to hell, is the same as Topheth in the prophecy of Isaiah 30:33.

Let us now consider the texts in which the unity of the Law is addressed directly. These texts are three, and they clarify and corroborate one another. The first is a well-known passage in Proverbs, in which the personification of holy Wisdom in represented as existing before the creation of the world:

> In the distant past I was fashioned,
> At the beginning, at the origin of the earth. (Prv 8:23)

The text adds that Wisdom was at work beside the Lord and that every day He delighted in her.

But where, indeed, can we discern an identity between this Creative Wisdom, present at the world's formation (no doubt to animate and inspire it), and the religious Law of man, Israel's Torah? In an earlier chapter of Proverbs, the author had written:

> The Lord founded the earth by wisdom;
> He established the heavens by understanding;
> By His knowledge the depths burst apart,
> And the skies distilled dew. (Prv 3:19–20)

And he added at once:

> My son, do not lose sight of them;
> Hold on to resourcefulness and foresight.
> They will give life to your spirit
> And grace to your throat. (Prv 3:21–22)

Thus, the Wisdom which created the world is also the Wisdom to whom man ought to listen in order truly to possess the life for which he is intended by his nature. But here is the allegory which conveys the same teaching with exceptional clarity:

> Wisdom has built her house,
> She has hewn her seven pillars.
> She has prepared the feast,
> Mixed the wine,
> And also set the table.
> She has sent out her maids to announce
> On the heights of the town,
> "Let the simple enter here";
> To those devoid of sense she says,
> "Come, eat my food
> And drink the wine that I have mixed;
> Give up simpleness and live,
> Walk in the way of understanding." (Prv 9:1–6)[9]

And a few verses further, we read this declaration:

> The beginning of Wisdom is fear of the Lord,
> And knowledge of the Holy One is understanding. (Prv 9:10)

This house which Wisdom has built and the provisions which she has prepared are obviously the dwelling-place of man furnished with the nourishment which she reserves for those who choose to follow her counsels. She erects "her house" as the life-force fashions the material body, as the silk-worm creates from its own substance the dwelling it requires for its marvellous transformations. For man whom she instructs, she has indeed created the world. She is at once cosmic wisdom and human wisdom, filling in turn the complementary roles of creator and lawgiver. And as if to confirm the sameness of the two laws, it is said that the fear of the Lord—that is, the law of man—is the beginning of Wisdom. Far from being (as some have claimed) simply

225

morality, religion, or human prudence, this Wisdom of the book of
Proverbs is presented as the architect of the world; and even in her
religious implications, she does not lose her preeminent characteristic
of Creative Intelligence, which we may call Logos.

The second text to which we have alluded is in the twenty-eighth
chapter of Job. God, after having created the world through Wisdom,
contemplates her, and then makes her accessible to man:

> Then He saw it [i.e., Wisdom] and declared[10] it;
> He measured it and probed it. (Jb 28:27)

That is, the Inner Word which is revealed only through divine works
becomes exterior as it becomes Articulated Word. The verse which
follows expresses the unity of divine and human Law with unmistakable explicitness:

> He said to man,
> "See! Fear of the Lord is wisdom;
> To shun evil is understanding." (Jb 28:28)

Thus, the law of man is the Inner Word exteriorized: the fear of God,
the abhorrence of evil. The sameness of the two laws could hardly be
expressed with more clarity or solemnity. It is not that the eternal
Wisdom, the Law of the universe, is made to shrink to the proportions
of human wisdom, but the other way round: The law of man is elevated to the law of creation, for Hebraism does not confine itself to
knowledge which is immediately useful to man, which helps in the
discipline of his will, but devotes itself also to metaphysical knowledge, to the law of Being and Understanding. The many biblical passages which declare that the true knowledge of God is moral knowledge, the fear of the Lord, thus become clear in the light of this text
from Job. Practical morality or ethics is thus raised to the level of
divine knowledge. The law of man and the law of God are but a single
and identical Law.

Finally, we may set beside these texts from Proverbs and Job a
third passage, this from Jeremiah, which allows us to glimpse the same
doctrine:

> Thus said the Lord: If you could break My covenant with the
> day and My covenant with the night, so that day and night

should not come at their proper time, only then could My covenant with My servant David be broken. (Jer 33:20–21)

Here, the laws which govern the sequence of day and night are called *berit*, "covenant," the very name which the Bible customarily uses to designate the revealed Law.

Let us say in conclusion that the harmony which we have just shown to exist between the doctrine of the rabbis and that of the Bible can be confirmed, if we wish, in the apocryphal books. In Ecclesiasticus (the Wisdom of the Son of Sirach), we find in fact that the personification of Creative Wisdom is identified with the Torah, which not only was created before the world and will never cease to exist, which extends over the earth, reaches the heavens, penetrates into the unfathomable depths, and reigns over the entire universe, but which has been commanded by God to dwell in Zion: This is, quite simply, the Law of Moses.

Thus science and religion, the law of the universe and the law of man, Wisdom and Torah, are declared identical. We may be permitted to point out a consequence of this idea, while leaving to the reader the task of determining its importance: It is that all knowledge becomes religious knowledge, all understanding is sanctified, and the intellectual act is preeminently a moral act.

Abraham, Apostle to the Gentiles

If, at the exalted level to which we have been raised by Hebraism, the Torah embraces the totality of creation, the entirety of being, God Himself, this Torah must inevitably contract itself when it becomes the law of man, though without losing universality, since its realm extends all the way to the most distant human limits which the conception of mankind allows.

This is what Philo says in his *Life of Moses* when he contrasts the Mosaic Law with the laws of the Gentiles:

Our law is quite different. It exhorts everyone to behave in prescribed ways: barbarians as well as Greeks, inhabitants of the mainland as well as island-dwellers, men of the East and men of the West, Europeans and Asiatics—in a word, inhabitants of all the earth even to its farthest extremities.[11]

It is obvious that what Philo has in view here is not the Law of Moses as a special code for the Jews, but rather the universal religion which Judaism possesses, of which the Mosaic code is but one expression. In keeping with the doctrines which we find in the Holy Land, he believes that this universal religion is the common patrimony of all men and that all are consequently called upon to observe it. It is in this sense too that, elsewhere, he follows the Palestinian rabbis in declaring that when philosophy teaches monotheism, it is teaching Judaism. Indeed, the sages said that "whoever rejects polytheism merits the name of Jew," that "he who abjures idolatry is thereby acknowledging all of the Law."[12]

Up to this point we have been considering the universality of the Law (from the Jewish point of view) in abstract terms. Let us now examine its specific applications.

First of all, we find in it the dual nature of God's revelation of Himself, which, according to Judaism, is both primeval and Adamic, and thus universal in time as well as in space. That it is primeval cannot be doubted. Genesis tells us that God communicated with the first man, while adding a detail which has not been sufficiently appreciated: The first intellectual act to which the first man was called seems to have been a revelation from the Creator:

> And God created man in His image, in the image of God He created him; male and female He created them. God blessed them and God said to them, "Be fertile and increase, fill the earth and master it." (Gn 1:27–28)

Moreover, the revelation is Adamic, it is addressed to the primal parents of mankind, for it is mankind itself which is destined to populate the whole earth.

There exists an entire group of *Aggadot* whose dominant idea, expressed in various ways, is that Adam ought to have been what Israel later became. It is to him, the rabbis add, that the Law had to be given. The obligation imposed upon him in the earthly paradise consisted of the observance of all the positive and negative precepts of the Torah.[13] It seems indeed that all distinction between Israel and mankind is here being obliterated in order to show more distinctly that the divine Revelation belongs to all the children of Adam and not only to the sons of Abraham.

The great Jewish patriarch himself is proof that it is not only at the origin, but also through the course of history, that the revelation of the Divine Law possesses this characteristic of universality. Indeed he appears, according to both the Bible and the Oral Tradition, as the apostle to the Gentiles. The Bible says on a number of occasions, with reference to the altars which he set up in places where he pitched his tents, that Abraham proclaimed the name of the Lord:

> From there he moved on to the hill country east of Bethel and pitched his tent, with Bethel on the west and Ai on the east; and he built there an altar to the Lord and invoked the Lord by name. (Gn 12:8)

Genesis Rabbah interprets this to mean that he tried earnestly to attract converts. "He made every creature call upon the name of the Holy One, blessed be He!"[14] Nachmanides has no doubt about the meaning of the verse: "Most probably this means that he proclaimed aloud the name of God before the altar, and spread knowledge of his God."[15] Maimonides, too, accepts this interpretation.

But what is more important than any philological discussion is the other scriptural testimony in favor of Abraham's proselytizing mission. The text of Genesis dealing with the departure from Haran can be translated literally as follows: "Abram took his wife Sarai and his brother's son Lot, and all the wealth that they had amassed, and the persons [Hebrew 'souls'] that they had acquired in Haran" (Gn 12:5). This has been understood by the sages to mean that Abraham and Lot led away with them all the proselytes that they had made during their stay.[16]

In another passage from the same book, God says to Abimelech: "Therefore, restore the man's wife—since he is a prophet [*nabi*], he will intercede for you—to save your life" (Gn 20:7). Abraham was thus known to the pagans as a prophet. Moreover, it was only for them that he could be a *nabi* at all. To whom would he have addressed his preaching if not to the Gentiles? For this was precisely the role of the *nabi*.

Genesis provides us with another indication of the proselytizing mission of the Hebrew patriarch. We read that the Hittites gave him, as a sign of their respect, the title "Prince of God," *Nasi Elohim*, which may mean religious chieftain: "Hear us, my lord: you are the elect [or 'prince'] of God among us" (Gn 23:6). What can be the reason for this esteem and veneration for a man who, professing the most uncompromising monotheism, must in fact have appeared to pagans as an enemy of their local divinities, if not the success which had rewarded his efforts to draw them to his faith?

We know, too, that God changed the name of Abram to Abraham because he was to be the father of a multitude of nations.

> And you shall no longer be called Abram, but your name shall be Abraham, for I make you the father of a multitude of nations. (Gn 17:5)

This verse cannot refer simply to the families or tribes who would compose Israel, or to the Ishmaelites or Edomites to whom the patriarch would give birth. The promise is too weighty and solemn for that. When Ishmael is at issue, the expression is in fact quite different: "He shall be the father of twelve chieftains, and I will make of him a great nation" (Gn 17:20).

What then is the meaning of this posterity which God promises Abraham? According to Maimonides, it signifies that he has taught the true faith to the Gentiles, or even that all peoples are destined to gather beneath his banner, thus to become members of his spiritual family, his children by adoption.[17] The ancient rabbis understood the matter in the same way. We read in the Talmud that when the proselyte carries the first fruits of his field to the Temple, he will say, like the native Israelite:

> Look down, O God, from the height of your heavenly abode, and bless Your people of Israel and the earth which You have given us, as You swore to our fathers.

The Talmud adds that the proselyte will therefore call Abraham his own father, for God has called Abraham the father of a multitude of nations, or even, as the Midrash says, of all nations.[18]

We cannot fail to recognize the close similarity between this promise to Abraham and that other blessing which God bestows upon him, and which has given rise to so many controversies:

> All the families of the earth
> Shall bless themselves by you. (Gn 12:3)

However we may understand this text, it demonstrates at any rate that the scriptural author's thought—Hebraic thought—already embraced the entire spectrum of mankind. Consequently, there can be no question of narrowing the signification of Abraham's posterity. In that promise there is something even more than the idea—itself so encompassing—of a spiritual fatherhood extending to all peoples; we find there the notion of a human brotherhood, a community, with Israel at its center.

The Bible shows us in another place how Abraham understood the blessing he received. What other meaning could be ascribed to his intercession on behalf of Sodom? Rather than limiting himself to asking that Lot and his family be saved, he does all in his power to obtain grace for the entire guilty country (Gn 18–19).

There is a psalm which can serve as commentary upon Abraham's calling. Psalm 110 begins: "The Lord said to my lord, 'Sit at My right hand while I make your enemies your footstool.' " The meaning which Christian exegetes have found in this verse is well known. Others have seen here the glorification of David's kingship. Yet a few lines later there follows a verse which does not lend itself to any such interpretation: "The Lord has sworn and will not relent, 'You are a priest forever, after the manner of Melchizedek' " (Ps 110:4).

This last name transfixes one's attention. It cannot be a matter of comparing David and Melchizedek, nor is the idea of priesthood applicable to the Jewish king. Moreover, the Psalmist would not give himself the title of "lord," whereas the word would come naturally to David's tongue if he were speaking of Abraham. As for Melchizedek, this must be the king of Salem whose life intersected with Hebraism only through Abraham, and the role of priest, *kohen*, which the psalm ascribes to him is precisely that with which Scripture characterizes this king-priest. His priestly dignity is passed legitimately to Abraham, for as soon as God makes him father of a people who are to be summoned to fulfill the priestly function for all mankind, the authentic priesthood which had been the possession of the Gentiles before the election of Israel is transmitted to this first Jewish patriarch. If the biblical conception of Abraham is that of a priest, does it not follow that this calling brings with it the role and mission of instructing and converting the Gentiles?

Abraham's vocation with respect to the Gentiles leads us to the larger subject of Jewish proselytism, for if this really existed at certain periods in the history of Israel, it is evidence of the universal character which the Jews attributed to the Law.

It will suffice to quote a passage from Zechariah:

> Thus said the Lord of Hosts: In those days, ten men from
> nations of every tongue will take hold—they will take hold of
> every Jew by a corner of his cloak and say, "Let us go with
> you, for we have heard that God is with you." (Zec 8:23)

The faith of Israel is therefore meant for all the peoples, and the
Hebrew patriarch is the first apostle to be sent to them.

Finally, we wish to call attention to a text which, if properly
interpreted, proves that the proselytism of the Patriarchs, and especially of Abraham, is an anticipation and a confirmation of the priestly
mission to mankind with which their descendants were to be invested.
Thus we can understand why God utters this sublime monologue,
whose every word is weighted with significance:

> For I have singled him [Abraham] out, that he may instruct
> his children and his posterity to keep the way of the Lord by
> doing what is just and right, in order that the Lord may bring
> about for Abraham what He has promised him. (Gn 18:19)

God, then, chose Abraham so that the true religion might become
established in him, and that through him there might be fulfilled the
divine promise of a people which should be a source of blessing for all
the earth.

Divine Revelations to the Gentiles

The universality of the Law emerges with equal clarity in the
direct revelations of the God of Israel to the pagan world, which have
been regular and continuous, at least until the election of the Jewish
people. It is enough to recall some matters which we have already had
occasion to mention: the character and role of Melchizedek, the favors
shown to Abimelech, Laban, and Pharoah, which prove not only (as
we have said) the universality of the God of Israel but also of the Law
by which He governs humans.

Outdoing the Bible, the rabbis tell us that "God raised up Prophets for the Gentiles as He did for Israel," and they even name some of
them of whom the Bible is unaware, at least as such. The rabbis must
indeed have been thoroughly familiar with the idea of universal religion to have recognized pagan names which even Scripture does not
mention. Shem, like his ancestor Eber, is for them a Gentile preacher.

232

Eliphaz the Temanite, Bildad the Shuhite, Zophar the Naamathite, Elihu ben Barachel the Buzite, Job from the land of Uz—and, last of them, Balaam—are all mentioned as prophets.[19] According to Rabbi Abraham Abulafia,

> Our Sages of blessed memory have said, "The Torah has been given to the heads of every generation," which means that the ancients were also endowed with wisdom and intelligence and possessed understanding of the truth.[20]

Here is another, equally definitive rabbinic text:

> Rabbi Isaac says: "As long as the Tabernacle in the desert had not been erected, inspiration existed among the Gentiles. It ceased after the construction of the Tabernacle."[21]

At first revelation is general, and the Gentiles received it directly. Then it becomes particularized, and mankind as a whole obtains it indirectly, from a representative group. It is as in civil society, where at first everybody does all things for himself alone, but later devotes himself to a particular activity for everyone.

According to Plutarch's well-known legend, a voice from the bottom of the sea was heard declaring, "Great Pan is dead!"—and at this very instant the oracles became dumb.[22] Christianity, accepting this account, interpreted it to refer to the disappearance of paganism upon the triumph of Jesus. The rabbinic tradition has tried to express something similar by making the end of revelation among the Gentiles coincide with the construction of the Tabernacle.[23]

The figure of Balaam must now arrest our attention for a few moments. It belongs to both periods, that during which divine inspiration was to be found still in Gentile life, and that which followed its disappearance. Balaam marks the separation, beginning as prophet and ending as wizard.[24] But his original status as an authentic prophet cannot be doubted. It impressed the Jews themselves so forcibly that when they tried to explain these favors of God toward other peoples, their national pride suggested the comparison with a clandestine love affair which hides itself in darkness:

> The Holy Spirit visited Balaam only at night. So it is with all the Gentile prophets, such as Laban, of whom it is written:

"God appeared at night, in a dream, to Laban, the Aramean." So it is with a man who hides in order to be unfaithful to his wife.[25]

Nevertheless, Balaam's prophetic inspiration is extolled by the commentators far more than by Scripture itself. The *Sifrei*, with obvious approval, surveys the ways in which Balaam before his downfall was superior to Moses. It notes first of all that the Torah does not declare categorically that there has never been in the world a prophet superior to Moses, only that such a prophet has not existed in Israel.[26] And the rabbis draw from this an inference which would certainly startle every other orthodoxy than their own: namely, that some such superior prophets *have* appeared among the Gentiles—for example, Balaam, who surpassed Moses in several ways. Moses did not know what God would say to him, whereas Balaam did. Moses was unaware when God would speak to him, although Balaam was so informed. Moses received messages from God only when he was standing, while Balaam was so favored when he was lying down.[27]

How can we reconcile this hypothetical superiority of Balaam with the mission of Moses and the excellence of his doctrine? The rabbis in this legend are concerned simply with the *form* of revelation, independent of its content. From another perspective, however, Balaam might be thought to have occupied a subordinate level of prophecy, where he could have apprehended things which prophets of a loftier spiritual rank could ignore. This is what seems to emerge from the comparison with which this *aggadah* on Balaam ends:

Thus it is with him who has charge of the king's provisioning; he can say exactly what the king spends every day.[28]

As for the equality between Moses and Balaam which these sages seem to have in mind, this can be understood quite reasonably, as certain commentators have done: Balaam fulfilled among the Gentiles the role which Moses fulfilled in Israel.

We find the following thoughts in a volume of ancient rabbinic literature:

Seven prophets have arisen among the Gentiles, who will bear witness to their condemnation.

And elsewhere:

> I call upon heaven and earth to witness that the Holy Spirit
> will rest on each according to his good works, whether he be
> man or woman, free or slave, Jew or Gentile.[29]

This belief in the preaching of the Divine Law among the pagans
as well as among the Israelites has, like so many other things, passed
from Judaism into Christianity. We know what Paul said to the Gentiles on the subject, and what providential role he attributed to the
pagan philosophers.[30] After him, Clement of Alexandria tells us in his
Stromateis:

> Just as God wished to obtain the salvation of the Jews in
> giving them Prophets, so he selected from among the most
> distinguished of the Greeks and separated them from the
> common people to the extent that they were capable of under-
> standing divine beneficence. Thus Greeks and Jews have
> been taught, by their different Testaments, about the very
> same Lord.[31]

What is curious in this bringing together of the two traditions, Jewish
and Christian, is that the rabbis have also given the designation of
philosophers to the pagan prophets. Thus, for example, they put in the
same category Oenomaus of Gadara, a pagan philosopher of the second
century, and Balaam, whom they call *nabi* and furnish with a mission
to the Gentiles.[32]

The reason for this confusion among the sages is evidently the
common tradition of preaching among the Gentiles, which is both proof
and consequence of the unity of the Law which the sages acknowledge.
The almost religious character which the Stoics gave themselves, in
assuming not only the language but the practices and appearance of
authentically religious teachers, helped considerably to persuade many
that the philosophers played a role analogous to that of the Hebrew
prophets: a providential mission. In this way we can explain those many
passages in the rabbinical writings which speak of the pagan philosophers in the same terms as those used for the seers of Israel.

We could hardly conceive of a better way to conclude this discussion of the parallel between the Prophets and the philosophers as evi-

dence of the universality of the Divine Law than by quoting these words of M. Rémusat:

> We hear much about the opposition between knowledge and faith. For myself, I would readily believe that the earliest faith came from the earliest knowledge. The insight of one man enlightened the apathy of the many. The Prophets were the philosophers of their time.[3]

2

The Two Aspects of the
Universal Law: Mosaism and
Noachism

*I*f we look at the Mosaic revelation as an historical phenomenon, it seems intended specially for Israel. But our quest must not be satisfied with outer appearances; it must also consider the entire sphere which Mosaism embraces, its entire range of implications. In other words, since Jewish belief in a unique God is incontestable (whenever this belief may have attained its definitive form), and Jews therefore have not had a number of divine codes, particularized and ethnic in character, but rather a single supreme and universal Law, we must ask whether the Mosaic revelation, obviously addressed to Israel, implies the rejection of the Gentiles, their abandonment to a sort of outlaw status.

There are, however, innumerable scriptural texts following the election of Israel which portray God speaking and acting as the God of all mankind, watching over the destinies of every people. They amply refute such a supposition, which, moreover, would subvert the most essential characteristics of a unique God. Such a radical forsaking by God of virtually the entire human race in order to attach Himself exclusively to a tiny people is a hypothesis as monstrous as it is improbable.

If, then, the divine plan aspires toward the oneness or unity of mankind, there are only two solutions to the problem of its realization: Either all peoples must subject themselves to the Mosaic Law, or there must be a law—or, to be more exact, a special expression of the Law—for the Gentiles. In the first hypothesis, we would have an apparently universal religion, but one whose very constitution would tend to preclude Jewish individuality. In the second, we would assuredly have a religion of truly universal character, for it would embrace all of mankind, even while preserving Jewish individuality; nor would this be an Israel to whom all the other peoples were subordinated, but rather an Israel in the service of mankind, which would be altogether in keeping with its vocation of priest-people. But in such a case, what kind of code to embrace Gentiles would Judaism ascribe to Providence?

The Two Parts of the Religion of Israel

The Mosaic Law in its essence must categorically reject the notion that all peoples should submit themselves to it, for the most salient features of Mosaism all bear the stamp of Jewish particularism. It is the individual Jewish life which breathes in it. In Mosaism are reflected the history, the interests, the hopes of Israel. Not, indeed, that this particular life is not linked to the universal life of mankind. To the contrary, it is in this link that the grandeur and noblest aspirations of Judaism can be found. But mankind, at all events, is not destined to be absorbed into it, any more than the life of Israel must dissolve into that of mankind at large. The most intimate union must exist between the two, though without either's being submerged in the other.

This separateness, the preservation of the distinct ethnic identity of Mosaism, is no doubt compatible with the limited affiliation of a small number of proselytes, but it is firmly opposed to the mass conversion of the entire human race. The history of Christianity shows this clearly. Because they lacked understanding (or, at any rate, suitable appreciation) of the *dual* religion which Judaism presupposes—the lay, or Noachide religion of mankind, and the priestly religion of Israel—the founders of Christianity, desiring in spite of everything to fulfill the promises of universal religion which fill the Sacred Books, at first hesitated for some time between the two extreme courses: imposing Mosaism upon everyone, or abolishing it even for Israel. But the first of these possible schemes must inevitable have miscarried, and after ascertaining their failure on that score, there remained to the Christians only the alternative of declaring the abolition of Judaism and expunging it, as it were, from history.

If one reflects carefully on the matter, one notices an intrinsic contradiction in this program of abolition: It is Hebraism denying Hebraism. For such a paradox to have been possible, the name "Hebraism" must be understood to denote what was in fact a dualism, the two elements of which, particularism and universalism, the religion of Israel and that of the Gentiles, which had hitherto been united, now splitting apart so decisively that the second was able to repudiate the first. But the bond which connected the two religious conceptions in Judaism was not perceived by the first Christians, any more than Christian theologians or rationalist critics understand it today. This bond is the hierarchical organization of the human race into priests and layman. It is not a question of merging but of *harmonizing* the two distinct entities.

It is occasionally claimed that the Jews were incapable of conceiving universal religion in the form of a grand human brotherhood, that in fact for them universal religion was nothing other than a dominion which they would exercise over the entire world. But such a conception is alien to Judaism. To be sure, at certain periods Jews have indeed nourished chimerical hopes of universal domination, but Judaism is not responsible for these patriotic dreams. Rather, it is the dreams which imply the existence of a more reasonable doctrine, one so elevated that it was bound to degenerate, among the less refined spirits, into something more flattering to the national pride.

This coexistence of two different expressions of a single code—or, if one prefers, two forms of a single religion—has as precedent a religious phenomenon earlier than Mosaism, which historians have found in many places. Then, too, there was a dual law: one law for the generality of men, another for the elite, the priests, the most wise and pious men among the Gentiles. Now just as this latter law reminds us of what would later be Mosaism, to which it is in a sense the prelude, so the other law differs significantly from Mosaism.

The very existence of a dual religious code among the Gentiles is itself quite instructive. The differences between the two laws are no less than the differences between Mosaism and Noachism, and seem to demonstrate firmly that there is a tendency in human culture for lay law and priestly law to exist sumultaneously. Even in Mosaism itself, alongside the common law of the Israelites there is another, which is especially for the tribe of Levi and the family of Aaron; and even in this priestly law there is still another, more particularized yet, for the high priest, which sets him apart from the other priests of Israel just as the entire Mosaic Law sets off the Jews as priests of mankind. So symmetrical and harmonious a structure can scarcely be the result of chance. From the Jewish perspective there must be an inner force which systematically regulates the entire religious edifice, from its base to its summit. Mosaism is a particular expression of authentic religion. It is no more intended for all of mankind than the priestly code of Israel was intended for all Israelites, or that of the high priest for the entire tribe of Levi.

Ethnic and Parochial Dimensions of Mosaism

The ethnic and parochial character of Mosaism is evident. Some of its laws depend upon the climate and geographical situation of Palestine. The date of Passover, for example, is linked to the Palestinian spring. It could not be otherwise, with each man regulating the celebration of the holy day for himself according to the particular conditions of his place of residence; for this would be contrary to the supreme Law established by Moses, which entails uniformity of religious observance.

We shall not recount in detail the many precepts which are related to the territory of the Holy Land. One has only to open the Talmud, or the later rabbinical writings, to find an exhaustive discussion of them. But the assertions of Moses himself constitute decisive testimony. What is the meaning of the often-repeated promise that God would establish His dwelling-place in the Holy Land, in the midst of Israel? How, indeed, are we to understand the sanctity which was attributed to the soil of Palestine, the reverence in which it was held (which even death could not cancel, since Jews aspired to be buried there), if not by reference to the conviction that the religion of Israel was made for the land of Israel, for Jerusalem, and that Jerusalem and Israel were made for that religion? In the Midrash, the sages even declared that to fulfill various *mitzvot* of the Torah while in exile is to recall and commemorate the past, or to anticipate the future—a way of remembering how to obey these divine commandments and of being prepared to resume the ancient practices in the ancestral land on the day that God will choose. This notion may seem extravagant, but the doctrine behind it is surely true, and excludes the possibility that Jews should nourish, as a religious ideal, the conversion of non-Jews to the Mosaic Law—a law which, in the view of its observant, loses its full efficacy (though not necessarily its authority) outside the borders of the land of Israel.

But here is an equally remarkable fact. If there were no way to salvation available to Gentiles outside the Mosaic Law, we should certainly expect to see in Judaism a much more pronounced tendency toward proselytism, and not only a peaceful proselytism which exhorts much more by means of the word than by act, and still more by example than by word, but also an ardent proselytism of conquest, which would never tire of promising eternal damnation to all who fail to convert to the only true religion. What we find, however, is something radically different. The cautious reserve with which Israel addresses the Gentiles is incompatible with the conviction that it alone possesses the means of salvation. Its respect for other beliefs may seem even to verge on indifference, and some superficial observers have not hesitated to conclude from this that the Jews know nothing of proselytism. This local, ethnic quality of Mosaism and its nearly total absence of organized proselytism are ample proof that the religion of Israel is not destined to become the universal religion. Yet Israel insists on declaring that certain general principles are obligatory for every human creature, a code of laws which cannot be evaded with impunity, whose observance is required by divine justice. Can we doubt that Israel believes itself in possession of a religion which is universal in a way that Mosaism is not, a religion whose basic substance appears even in its Scriptures? Can there be any doubt that here indeed is that other aspect of the Law, which addresses all men and all epochs?

The Jewish Attitude with Respect to Conversion

Let us start by recalling the rules which are prescribed for the Israelite armies when they overcome pagan peoples. Here, surely, we may see how Jews are expected to behave with regard to conversion of Gentiles, and how they understand the matter. In these particular circumstances we shall find the expression of their true feelings. The customary relations of victors and vanquished—the example of other profoundly monotheistic peoples, such as the Arabs, who carried the Koran everywhere on the tip of their sword—remind us how decisively important such circumstances are for our present purpose. Deuteronomy is illuminating here, in regulating the treatment of conquered peoples and instructing Israel how to deal with them (Dt 20–21). Oddly enough, the religious question is passed over in silence. If the conquered people surrenders and accepts a subordinate status, it will be allowed to live in peace.

The Mosaic Law is not at all concerned about the religion of the vanquished. It does not propose to regulate anything other than the political relation. What does this silence mean? Is it indifference, tolerance, or merely oversight? None of these hypotheses seems admissible. A monotheistic religion, and one so conspicuously ethical, which traces itself back to Adam, father of mankind, and which teaches that Providence is the same for all—if such a religion found itself in confrontation with pagan cults which were as ungodly as they were immoral, it would never have been able to push tolerance so far as to extend its protection of conquered peoples to the point of giving sanction to the revolting excesses in which they had indulged. Even the most liberal laws of modern nations, despite our basic principles of freedom of worship and of conscience, could never authorize religious practices which—like most of these polytheistic cults—would be an affront to morality and public safety, to justice and to charity. However little our contemporary states may be interested in the value of religious doctrines, public order and the instinct of self-preservation oblige them to impose restrictions on religious liberty. Is this not proof, if one were needed, that secular society will never be able to be entirely indifferent to the religious question, because there will never be a religion which does not exert either a good or a bad influence on the life of society?

If, therefore, the Pentateuch is silent on the subject which occupies us, it is because its role consists in regulating the *external* relations, civil and political, of peoples and individuals. On all other matters, it is to the Oral Tradition that we must turn.

Rabbi Elijah Mizrahi examines this question at length and in detail. Taking into account all the scriptural and rabbinical materials, he says: "We must distinguish between the Canaanite peoples and the others, between the obligatory wars and those which are optional."[1] In these last, surrender is all that Israel has the right to exact of the vanquished. Even if their religion is the most crass kind of polytheism, it must be respected, and its adherents put under no obligation of any sort. As for the obligatory wars—that is, those which Israel was commanded by God to wage against the Canaanites—this people, so proud of its Mosaic Law, imbued with its own grandeur, was in fact satisfied with very little, with what modern civilization indeed would not hesitate to demand of a barbarous tribe: the fulfillment of the Noachide Law, the minimal code of religion and morality which any society requires in order to survive.

Why this exceptional policy with respect to Canaan? According to Moses: "Lest they lead you into doing all the abhorrent things that they have done for their gods and you stand guilty before the Lord your God" (Dt 20:18). These words are straightforward enough, and Rashi's interpretation of them is equally clear: "We can deduce from this that if the Canaanites do penance, they will be accepted."[2] Let us note that Rashi speaks of penance, not conversion. What is needed is for these peoples to return to the religion which they ought never to have abandoned, that is, Noachism, as Nachmanides asserts.

Here, then, in our opinion, is the only way to reconcile the apparent indifference which Israel professes with respect to the religion of the Gentiles, with its intense concern in the case of the Canaanites. The indifference has to do with conversion to Judaism; the concern is for Gentile observance of the ancient religion of Noah, the only religion which is incumbent on all who are not Israelites. Without this essential distinction, Jewish beliefs, laws, and history are beset with inconsistencies and contradictions. Thus Friedenthal was echoing the tradition of Judaism when he said:

> We do not press the Gentile to enter the community of Abraham our father, but our sublime mission, inherited from the first patriarch, is to convert Gentiles to the religion of the "proselyte of the gate," which consists of abjuring polytheism and observing the seven *mitzvot* of Noah.[3]

And he relies on a passage in the Talmud which says the same thing: "The Gentile will be obliged to observe the seven commandments of Noah."[4]

Because he failed to understand this distinction between the two aspect of the Law, Mosaism and Noachism, Renan was able to write of the apostle James that he did not approve of the conversion of proselytes. Strictly observant Jews could only have applauded any conversion which would lead Gentiles to their *Noachide* Law. But when Christianity claimed to reduce Mosaism itself to the religion of Noah, to suppress all differences between priest and laity, between Israel and the Gentile, and not only to embrace all mankind in a single church but in this church itself to abolish the priestly ministry of Israel, with its very special duties—then and then only, the entrance of pagans into the newborn church must appear a danger to the Judaized Christians.

In fact, these latter found themselves confronting neo-Israelites who not only lacked any feeling of commitment to observe the Law of Moses, but rather considered themselves entitled to bring about its abolition even for the native Jews, substituting for both Mosaism and Noachism a new religion which was neither, not even pure Noachism, since it was in the name of Israel that the Christian Church claimed to have replaced *ancient* Israel. The great misapprehension which so regrettably distorted the development of apostolic, and above all Pauline, Christianity is epitomized in the church's appropriation of the name of Israel. Here indeed, in this demand for a mankind become totally Israelite, while the priestly people itself is deprived of all its functions and merged with the other peoples, we see the negation of the two concepts required by the providential order; and what is more, the denial of one by the other. Thus it is not surprising that those Jews who, while believing in Jesus, still did not intend to give up the Law for him, were alarmed by the conversion of that mass of pagans who, in their ever-increasing numbers, threatened to destroy Mosaism with the rallying cry of the new Christianity: "The Law is abolished!"

The Jewish Christians like James did not wish to abandon this Law, but, faithful to its spirit, neither did they intend to impose it upon the Gentiles. In all periods, in fact, the sages never ceased declaring that the Mosaic Law is intended for Israel, that it constitutes not a privilege but a responsibility. Recall what Maimonides says on this matter, summing up the teaching of the Oral Tradition:

> Moses our teacher conveyed the Law and commandments to Israel, as it is said, "the heritage of the congregation of Jacob" (Dt 33:4), and those of other nations who are willing to be converted, as it is said, "The same ritual and the same rule shall apply to you and to the stranger who resides among you" (Nm 15:16). But no coercion to accept the Law and commandments is practiced on those who are unwilling to do so. However, Moses our teacher was commanded by God to compel all human beings to accept the commandments enjoined upon the descendants of Noah. Anyone who does not accept them is put to death.[5]

To understand these last words, we should remember that the Noachide Laws are essential to the existence of human society, and therefore that whoever violates them thereby puts himself in revolt against his fellow men.

A passage from Psalms can serve as commentary on the words of Moses which Maimonides has quoted, and it confirms his interpretation of them:

He issued His commands to Jacob, His statutes and rules to
Israel. He did not do so for any other nation; of such rules
they know nothing. (Ps 147:19–20)

If we find, nevertheless, an effort to communicate the Law to the
pagans—as, for example, in the command to engrave it on stones
which will be accessible to all eyes (and, according to the rabbis, in
several tongues to facilitate its comprehension)—this, say the sages, is
because in the Law itself, the legal part, Israel's exclusive inheritance,
must be carefully distinguished from the historical, theological, and
ethical materials, which form the patrimony of all mankind.

There are in the Torah such things as the account of creation
and that of the Exodus, the history of the Patriarchs and of
the Israelites in the desert, which we are not only allowed but
obliged to teach to all men, for all are subject to the law of
Noah and ought to know about the oneness of God, Divine
Providence, the rewards and punishments of the other life,
for the sake of preserving human society. Here is why the law
of Moses has emphasized this obligation, insistently and un-
equivocally. But as for the great cycle of *mitzvot*, the other
peoples have no share in them. This is why Scripture reveals
them summarily and with reserve, imparting them in their
fullness of detail to Israel only, by way of the Oral Tradition.[6]

A people's tradition is that special aptitude which makes it more
capable than any other of understanding its own particular task. For
the Jews, this faculty is put at the service of another aptitude, more
directly practical, which completes the theoretical understanding of
their religion.

Mosaic Religion Optional for Gentiles

When Mosaism is born, Noachism forms the first step of a ladder
which the Israelite must climb before attaining the Mosaic Law. Thus,
when Israel went out of Egypt, it was first of all introduced to the
Noachide Law, and only after this preliminary initiation did it receive
the law of Moses. "Moses went and repeated to the people all the
commands [*divrei*] of the Lord and all the rules [*mishpatim*]." (Ex 24:3)

245

Of this verse, the sages say:

> The *commands* of the Lord are the ordinances relating to the
> proper behavior which the people had to observe while wait-
> ing at the foot of Sinai; the *rules* are the seven precepts of the
> sons of Noah.[7]

This sequential conception of the relation between Noachism and
Mosaism is quite different from the relation which developed between
Judaism and Christianity. We can hardly imagine the Christian bishops
introducing pagans to Jewish practices and beliefs before accepting
them into the church by baptism.

In the Jewish doctrine relating to sacrifices, we find an implicit
statement on the subject of the Noachides. It is the principle that
sacrifices offered in the Temple by Gentiles ought to be accepted,
whereas those brought by apostate Israelites must be refused. This
obviously assumes that the *mitzvot* of the Mosaic Law are not binding
upon Gentiles, for no special authorization would be needed for a
practice which was not only a right but an obligation. When a Gentile
offers such a sacrifice, he is observing part of the Law voluntarily.

Maimonides expresses this same idea when he declares that if the
Noachide, while observing his own code, wishes to fulfill some of the
precepts of Judaism, he should not be prevented.[8] Thus, Judaism is
clearly not conceived to be the single religion intended for everyone, as
its practices are optional for all who are not Jewish by birth.

How could one suppose for an instant that the sages believed
Mosaism to be obligatory for all, in view of the rites which they
established for the conversion of Gentiles? It was the story of Ruth
which suggested to them the procedures which became the norm for
conversion. Among the questions and instructions which were to be
addressed to the aspirant, we find this cautionary assertion:

> As long as you do not accept Mosaism, you are not liable for
> punishment if you eat forbidden foods; likewise, if you vio-
> late the Sabbath, you incur no punishment.[9]

The same thing is said with respect to all the other *mitzvot*. The meaning
of course is that so long as the Gentile does not submit freely to the
obligations of Mosaic Law, he is in no way required to observe them.

The ancient rabbis are explicit on this point, the later sages no less so. According to the author of the *Kuzari*, "Moses invited only his people and those of his own tongue to accept his law."[10] Maimonides is equally categorical.

How little Mosaism was thought of as a universal religion may be seen in the way its strictness, even on a matter of altogether fundamental importance, may relax when it is a question of mankind in general. Although Judaism abhors any dilution of its monotheism, it nevertheless declares that Noachides do not commit blasphemy if in their worship they associate other beings, forces, or divinities with God, the Sovereign Creator; for according to the Jewish formula which we cited earlier in speaking of Jewish monotheism, "The Noachide has not been forbidden to link other 'gods' to the worship of the One God."[11]

Therefore, not only are the prescribed observances of the Mosaic Law optional for the Gentile, but in matters of faith as well, he enjoys a flexibility which is denied to the Jew.

The Supernatural Element in the Religion of Israel

Although the common ground of all religions may be found in the Law of Israel, we must not infer from this that Judaism is nothing more than the common residuum which is left after the peculiar features of all the others are set aside.

We must expect to find in the religion of Israel not only what is common to all peoples but also a justifiable, even indispensable element which is supernatural or suprarational. This element is meant to help bring into being the religion of the future. We see, then, that what makes the Jew most qualified among men to become the priest of mankind is precisely his obligation, on behalf of all mankind, to fulfill duties relating to the supernatural.

To be sure, in the perspective of human civilization, all peoples contribute in one way or another to the work of transforming the universe, and to each of these roles there clings, in the present state of our understanding, a certain mystery. Indeed, the most eminent and authoritative representatives of every art and science acknowledge that in the last analysis, there is always something that escapes rational calculation. This is because all things, by virtue of their very existence, participate in the infinite and it is not within the power of a limited, finite intelligence to grasp all their implications. Therefore, every people, in its own particular domain, will exercise a kind of priesthood, the right to which is conferred by its unique aptitude for seeing and feeling, in its particular sphere, things that other peoples are unable to apprehend so completely and profoundly. But because religion, which is the particular domain of the Jew, embodies the divine and the infinite, it is religion, more than any other branch of human culture, which is meant to link the various parts of the finite and the different phrases of universal evolution. Religion is the province of what goes beyond our comprehension, that which (in the present state of our understanding) we call supernatural. Hence the altogether special nature of Judaism, which distinguishes it from the multitude of religious forms which the universal law of mankind is capable of generating. This is the rationale and justification of our dualism—Israel and mankind—which, as we see, in no way contradicts the fundamental unity of the Divine Law.

Let us add a final thought, which seems to us of great importance. Rationalist critics would like every religion to distinguish between that part of its doctrine which is universal and common to all religions, and that which is peculiar to itself; but such critics doubt that a religion can do this without damaging the faith of its followers. Hebraism, however, has done this, by its affirmation of the Noachide Law, the universal code of mankind, alongside the special Law of the Jews, which is Mosaism.

3

Noachides

The Mosaic Law accepts as legitimate the presence in the land of Israel of foreigners who do not adhere to the Mosaic religion. Such a "proselyte of the gate" or resident stranger (*ger-toshav*), fellow-citizen though not co-religionist, is to be distinguished from the "proselyte of the law" (*ger-tsedek*), who has completely converted to Judaism. Not only are proselytes of the gate exempt from the dietary prohibitions in the Law, but Israelites, who cannot eat the flesh of an animal which has not been ritually slaughtered, are urged to give it to them rather than sell it to an ordinary stranger (Dt 14:21).[1] This statute is valuable to us for two reasons: the charitable motive which inspires it, and its clear recognition of a legitimate though non-Mosaic category of religion.

The authentic spirit of Judaism appears unambiguously when we find it affirming that there exist just men among the Gentiles, men loved by God, whose merits are responsible for the prosperity of the nations. Job is not the only such figure whom the sages cite as a just man par excellence. The Bible provides many other examples. Here, for instance, is a remarkable passage in Isaiah about virtuous pagans:

> Let not the foreigner say,
> Who has attached himself to the Lord,
> "The Lord will keep me apart from His people."
> . . . As for the foreigners who attach themselves to the Lord,
> To be His servants—
> All who keep the Sabbath and do not profane it,
> And who hold fast to My covenant—
> I will bring them to My sacred mount
> And let them rejoice in My house of prayer.
> Their burnt offerings and sacrifices

Shall be welcome on My altar;
For My house shall be called
A house of prayer for all peoples. (Is 56:3, 6–7)

Are the "foreigners" in this passage those who have converted
entirely to Judaism? The name given to them here, even *after* their
conversion—*b'nei ha-nechar*, literally "sons of the stranger"—strongly
suggests otherwise. Moreover, the language attributed to them makes
the supposition not less improbable. Would they be likely, even after
their affiliation with Judaism, to say that the Lord keeps them apart
from their people? And the final verse of the passage proves amply that
it is a question of *other* peoples and all races without distinction. As for
the reference to the Sabbath, we must recall that the Noachide has the
option to observe one or more of the Mosaic *mitzvot* as he chooses,
including the Sabbath. But we must add that rabbinic tradition prescribes a half-rest for the ordinary proselyte of the gate, the true
Noachide, on the seventh day. This principle seems consistent with the
text just quoted, and with two other passages in the same book.

Happy is the man who does this,
The man who holds fast to it:
Who keeps the Sabbath and does not profane it,
And stays his hand from doing any evil. (Is 56:2)

In the second passage, the Sabbath is joined by the New Moon (first
day of the month)—both of them days which close one period and
open a new one—as future festivals for the entire human race:

And New Moon after New Moon,
And Sabbath after Sabbath,
All flesh shall come to worship Me—said the Lord. (Is 66:23)

The compatibility of Sabbath observance with the legal position
of the Noachide is revealed not only by rabbinic legislation but also by
history. It is truly a curious spectacle: pagans who have not become
Jews nevertheless observing certain Jewish religious practices, and especially the Sabbath! Historical critics have pointed this out though they
have not explained it.

Many of those who were attracted to Mosaism [says Renan
simply] limited themselves to the observance of the Sabbath.

A similar purity of life and abhorrence of polytheism were what these small groups of pious men had in common, while shallow pagans merely said of them, "They lead the Jewish life!"[2]

Horace speaks in one of his satires of the "thirtieth sabbath" (*tricesima sabbata*),[3] which seems to suggest that it was the custom among the pagans to number their sabbaths. The observers of this custom were apparently numerous, since the poet, who mocks it, presents himself as a free-thinker, unimpeded by such scruples. Seneca, too, in his book against superstitions, jeers at the Jewish Sabbath, which had attracted not only the Judaizing Romans but even the larger mass of people.[4] Philo, speaking of the efforts of the Jews to convert barbarians and Greeks, exclaims:

Where then is the Sabbath not observed? Where indeed is it not celebrated as religiously as the annual ritual of the great fast?[5]

M. Havet, who quotes these words, adds:

The poetry of Horace, that of Ovid, and other texts as well, prove that Philo has told nothing more than the truth. . . . The acceptance of the Sabbath has been Judaism's chief victory, its most striking and lasting success, since the Sabbath is still observed today by all Christianity and all Islam.[6]

We must note that alone of all the Jewish holy days, the Sabbath has a universal meaning and scope. It is not, indeed, a matter of commemorating the exodus from Egypt, nor the beginning of the year (like the Rosh ha-Shanah holy day of Remembrance); it is not an agricultural festival, nor a fast-day of Atonement for transgression of the Law. Instead, it is an assertion of faith in the creation of the world—or, better, in the divine origin of things. We can thus see why, in view of its universal significance, the Sabbath has been more or less rigorously prescribed for the ordinary Noachide. Because it answers a human need and speaks to man's moral nature, the weekly day of rest has quite naturally been adopted by men everywhere.

There is another reason for the popularity of the Sabbath in the Roman Empire: it was probably not without precedent in pagan antiquity itself. Though the seven-day week was originally unknown at Rome, it now seems clear that it existed among the Babylonians, which would explain the probably Chaldean origin of the word *sabbath*. In the poetry of Hesiod and Linus we read:

> The seventh day is a holy day; in it all things were completed. The seventh day is fair, it is the origin of all things, it is the first and the last, it is perfect and fulfilled.[7]

To be sure, these verses are regarded as an interpolation of Hellenized Jews; but even if they are, at least they take for granted a mental climate in the pagan world which would be sympathetic to them.

Circumcision was another of the *mitzvot* of the Mosaic Law which was often accepted by the proselytes of the gate. Some of the sages have considered it to be obligatory for them, but this is questionable. Maimonides is very explicit on the matter. He asserts in so many words that the Noachide, or proselyte of the gate, was not required to observe circumcision, and he defines him in this way: "A Gentile who has accepted the seven precepts of Noah, but [is not obliged to undergo] circumcision or immersion."[8]

These words, with which Maimonides summarizes the ancient Jewish Oral Tradition, are of prime importance for the history and understanding of the origins of Christianity. They show that the Jewish doctrine here surpasses in religious tolerance the Christian form of Noachism, which *does* require baptism.

Renan emphasizes the existence of the authentic Jewish doctrine when he writes:

> The law prescribed by the early Church for new converts from paganism was nearly identical with the code of Noachic precepts . . . which were prescribed for all proselytes. A man who wrote at about the same time (under the borrowed name of the well-known Greek moralist Phocylides) a small work on Jewish natural ethics, simplified for the use of non-Jews, comes to a similar conclusion.[9]

The "God-fearers"

The passage from Isaiah which we quoted above, on the Noachide Gentiles or proselytes of the gate who observe the Sabbath, is not unique in the Bible. There is a considerable number of other texts in which mention is made of "God-fearers," Gentiles whose religious position is (from the Jewish point of view) legitimate.

This name seems to refer to all those who—without either belonging to the Jewish community or practicing the Jewish religion—yet conscientiously and with sincere intent observe the Noachide Law, whether they dwell amidst the Jews in the land of Israel or among the followers of other religions in whatever land it may be. And we must note at once that this term *God-fearers* is used in Scripture whenever it is a question of the conversion of Gentiles. "May God bless us, and be feared[10] to the ends of the earth" (Ps 67:8). "The nations will fear the name of the Lord, all the kings of the earth, Your glory" (Ps 102:16).

When Exodus wishes to indicate those Egyptians who believed in the predictions of Moses and brought their slaves and livestock in from the fields to shelter, it also calls them "those . . . who feared the Lord's word" (Ex 9:20). And what proves that it is not merely a question of some fleeting attraction to the prophetic utterance of Moses but rather a kind of basic Judaism without constraint of law is the substantial multitude of Egyptians who left the country with Israel.

The expression "men who fear God" is found in the other biblical books in the same sense as in the Torah. In two passages which forcefully extol the universal religion, the Psalms reserve a special place alongside Israel and the priestly tribe of Levi for those Gentiles who, though not adhering to Judaism, are converted to the God of Israel:

> Let Israel declare, "His steadfast love is eternal." Let the house of Aaron declare, "His steadfast love is eternal." Let those who fear the Lord declare, "His steadfast love is eternal." (Ps 118:2–4)

> O house of Israel, bless the Lord; O house of Aaron, bless the Lord; O house of Levi, bless the Lord; you who fear the Lord, bless the Lord. (Ps 135:19–20)

The last reference is surely not to the "proselytes of the law," who were no longer distinguishable from other Jews, but to those, whatever their people or land, who have no connection with Judaism yet worship God. Although such persons have no obligation whatever to obey the Mosaic Law, their worship of the one authentic God gave them the right to be considered as belonging, along with Israel, to the true religion, whose rituals were celebrated by the priestly family of Aaron on behalf of all.

There is a most relevant passage in Psalm 22:

> You who fear the Lord, praise Him!
> All you offspring of Jacob, honor Him!
> Be in dread of Him, all you offspring of Israel! (Ps 22:24)

Commenting on these words, Ibn Ezra says that the first sentence applies to the Noachides, or pious Gentiles. This interpretation is confirmed by the context, for in the preceding verse, Israel declares, "Then will I proclaim Your fame to my brethren," referring to other peoples.

It is known that the Rechabites led an independent existence in the midst of Israel.[11] What was their religion? It is not likely to have been Mosaism, for then we should not be able to account for the famous passage of Jeremiah in which God sets forth, as an example to the Israelites, the obedience of the Rechabites to the commands of Jonadab, son of Rechab. If they had been Israelites, they would have been lauded for their fidelity to the law of Moses.

Besides the Rechabites, we find another enclave of Gentiles in the midst of Israel, the Gibeonites.[12] They were respected by the Jews without being in any way committed to the practice of Mosaism.

When Solomon ordered a census of the foreigners or Noachides living in the land of Israel, their numbers came to 153,600, and they were chosen to work on the construction of the Temple (2 Chr 2:16–17). They also had a role in the music of the Temple. All this was animated by the same spirit as we find in Moses' attitude toward his proselytes, in Joshua's treatment of the Gibeonites, and in Isaiah's prophecies.

If we turn to the Greco-Roman period, it is easier still to discern the existence of Noachides. The evidence is abundant. For our purposes, a single quotation should suffice. M. Havet writes:

> It is clear that Jews and Judaism exercised a considerable influence in Rome. They had long been scattered across the Greek lands of Asia and Europe. There were Jews everywhere, Jews by birth or by circumcision, and surrounding them, worshippers of God, or Judaizers, who, though not

circumcised nor observant of all the Mosaic practices, read the Holy Books and sent their money and tribute to the Temple in Jerusalem.[13]

According to some historical critics, the *proseukes* were meeting-centers in places where there were no regular synagogues; but these *proseukes* may well have been Noachide synagogues. Perhaps indeed they were not separate buildings but only that part of each Jewish synagogue intended for the use of proselytes of the gate. It seems, in fact, rather likely that when the Israelites erected their houses of prayer, they tried more or less to imitate the layout of the Temple in Jerusalem, whose outer part was open to the Gentiles. Thus, in the Christian churches of the first centuries, a special place was reserved near the entrance for catechumens. For the Christians, however, this was an altogether temporary situation, meant for those awaiting baptism and complete initiation into the sacraments, whereas in Judaism this religious role for the Gentiles was perfectly legal and permanent.

Wherever the influence of Judaism was felt in the entire Greco-Roman world, a constantly growing number of pagans, influenced by Israelite teaching, maintained close relations with the synagogues. Noachide groups were formed and meeting-places established where Gentiles who rejected the old errors of polytheism practiced a religion different from Mosaism but corresponding exactly to what the sages describe as the only religion binding upon non-Jews: Noachism.

There is extensive evidence that the Jews did not regard their own religion as the single mode of worship suitable for the pagans.

> The Jews disposed toward proselytism [writes M. Renan] have always felt that the part of their religion appropriate for mankind as a whole is its essential monotheism, and that all the rest—Mosaic institutions, messianic concepts, and the like—constitutes a second level of faith which is the special prerogative of the children of Israel, a kind of family inheritance which cannot be passed on to others.[14]

This is accurate, except with respect to messianism, which, far from being the exclusive heritage of Israel, has in fact a basically universal character, inasmuch as its most conspicuous feature is its concern for the religious development of mankind. Renan adds:

The Pharisees did not believe that the Law applied to the entire human race. What in their eyes was most important was that there should always be a holy tribe to observe it and to form a living actualization of the revealed Ideal.[15]

The "Catholicism" of Israel

It is worthwhile noting how diverse are the eminent thinkers who have understood both the particularist character of Mosaism and the universal religion of which Mosaism is the form appropriate to the Jews.

Spinoza tells us that the laws which God revealed to Moses are for the Jews alone and not binding upon any other people.

I have asked myself [he adds] why the Jews have been called God's chosen. Now believing as I do that this means only that God chose them to occupy a particular territory where they might live comfortably and safely, I deduced from this that the laws which God revealed to Moses are nothing more than the particular code of the Jewish people.

The philosopher's explanation of the election of Israel seems at first sight rather curious, but essentially we find in it the biblical and rabbinical idea that the land of Israel, like Israel itself, belongs in a very special way to the God of Israel. What is most remarkable in this passage from Spinoza is that when he turns from the special religion of the Jews to the idea of Noachism, he calls the latter the true universal religion:

Then I wished to know if the universal religion—I mean the Divine Law revealed by the prophets and the apostles to the entire human race—is different from that law which the natural light of reason reveals to us.[16]

There is no doubt that Spinoza's thought here conforms to the ideas which we are attempting to put before the reader. Alongside Mosaism, the national code of the Jews, there is a universal law, a catholicism, of which the catholicism of the Christian apostles has been but an imperfect realization.

As for Philo, we have seen that he interprets Judaism faithfully when he teaches that the light of reason alone would be enough to lead all men to monotheism, which is at the heart of authentic Judaism, and the rabbis have declared in theological terms: "Whoever renounces idolatry is a true Jew," and "Whoever renounces polytheism thereby affirms the entire Law."[17]

No one has better formulated this conception of the catholicism of Israel than Josephus, writing for the pagans.

> The object of all his works is the same [says Renan]. He preaches theism to the idolator, and the precepts called Noachic, that is, a Judaism simplified for their use, reduced practically to the proportions of the natural law. It required the observance of only two or three prohibitions, which even the most liberal Jews regarded as virtually part of natural law.[18]

The same author adds that this basic Judaism differed from Christianity only in the importance which the latter ascribed to the role of Jesus, and that Josephus distilled it to a kind of theism, while acknowledging that circumcision and other peculiarly Jewish practices were proper for ethnic Jews, and that every man's religion, to be authentic, must be freely adopted.

> On every page, Josephus' amiable philosophy speaks forth, sympathetic to virtue wherever it may appear, regarding the ritual precepts of the law binding only for Israelites, declaring straight-forwardly that every just man has the essential capacity to become a son of Abraham.[19]

But where the eminent Renan errs is in representing as a special conception of Josephus this Judaism which is within the reach of all; for in fact it is nothing other than Noachism, the religion of the Gentiles, as perceived by the Pharisees and by all Jews who understood Hebraic tradition.

This conception of Judaism may be found even among the Fathers of the Christian Church. Eusebius, in his *Preparation for the Gospel*, characterizes the Mosaic religion very judiciously, and asserts that it has authority only over Israel. According to him, Moses changed none of the doctrines of the Patriarchs:

> He [Moses] was able to lay the foundations of a system of law
> and a political constitution only by staying in harmony with
> the way of life of the men who surrounded him.[20]

But Moses left unchanged not only Jewish doctrine but also Noachism, which remained for him and his successors, as for those who had gone before, the sole religious obligation of the Gentile. And we must add that the legislation which Moses gave Israel (and which was for Israel alone) addresses the particular needs of Israel's priestly calling.

Equality among Men

Generally speaking, Hebraism has preached and practiced civil and political equality among men, whether Israelites, proselytes, or ordinary Gentiles. It has been noted, quite accurately, that whereas the doctrine of force as its own justification prevailed everywhere in paganism, Judea was the first nation to exhibit respect for the rights of man.

> In the vastness of the Roman Empire, on the one hand, we
> find selfishness and supreme faith in strength; on the other, in
> a tiny, little-known land, belief in the dignity of man, who
> knows no other master than God: such is the vivid contrast
> we find in the early years of our era.[21]

And M. Laurent records in this connection that Christianity, unlike Judaism, preaches equality only on the religious plane, but has not been concerned with introducing its principles into the civil and political order, and that therefore, on this point, Mosaism goes further than Christian doctrine.

But if we wish to gain an accurate understanding of Judaism's conception of mankind, it is not enough to examine the Law, which is only its external aspect; we must also take account of ethics, which is an equally important expression of Jewish thought. We find that universalist tendencies are much more evident in the principles of ethical behavior developed by the sages of the Synagogue than in the Written Law. Here is perhaps not the place to undertake a detailed study of this matter. (See the author's *Morale juive et morale chrétienne*.[22]) It is a field where the crop is so bountiful that one has only to glean in order to gather voluminous sheaves. We shall limit ourselves to a few precepts which illuminate the Jewish attitude toward the Gentile.

We are enjoined not to seek to gain his confidence by deceptive protestations of friendship, which the Talmud calls "stealing the mind of our fellow-men."[23] That is not all. We must in fact behave in a kindly way toward him. The stranger must be allowed, just like Jewish widows and orphans, to gather up what falls from the reaper's hand, and to share with them the unharvested remains and the produce of that corner of the field reserved for the poor. We are commanded in general to look after the Gentile poor, to care for their sick, and to bury their dead, just as if they were Jews, for the sake of peace and good will.[24]

These injunctions are not merely expressions of political or social expediency, rather than moral obligation, as might perhaps be imagined. The precepts are given without any consideration of time or place, and the examples which are cited in support of them are drawn from periods when Israel enjoyed complete national independence. It is the dead multitude of Gog who must be given honorable interment (Ez 39:11). It is David who buries his enemies and sends messages of condolence to Hanun, son of Nahash, king of Ammon, on the death of his father (2 Sm 10; 1 Chr 19:2). It is Rabbi Meir[25] who behaves in the same way toward Avnimos ha-Gardi (who is probably Oenomaus of Gadara, the neopythagorean philosopher[26]). What ultimately reveals the sages' true intention in offering these precepts is the very reason which they put forward, the cause of peace; for this is the motive which they often invoke when it is a question of relations among Jews themselves, and even in connection with rules governing religious ritual.[27]

In any case, we believe we have demonstrated, in our survey of the laws regarding proselytes as well as the precepts governing relations between Jews and Gentiles without distinction of religion, that despite the rigidly ethnic and national character of its worship, Judaism is concerned with the other peoples as well, that its doctrines embrace all of mankind—in sum, that the Revelation which it has in its keeping is truly universal.

4

Noachide Law

*T*his Noachide, or universal, code to which all mankind is subject must, in the nature of things, be more rational than the Mosaic code, more accessible to intellectual perception. Rationality is, in fact, its principal characteristic, even its principal component. The most cursory study of the subject will amply demonstrate this.

Acknowledging the Noachide Law's rationality, Maimonides also introduces another consideration when he writes:

> Whoever accepts the seven commandments and observes them with care is considered a pious Gentile, and has a share in the eternal life; but this is on condition that he receive and fulfill these precepts because God has prescribed them in His Law, and revealed to us through Moses our teacher that these are the rules of life given originally to the sons of Noah. But if he observes them only because reason seems to endorse them, he may not be regarded as a proselyte of the gate, or fellow citizen, or as a pious man or sage among the Gentiles.[1]

With respect to its nobility and holiness, the Law of Noah need not fear comparison with the Law of Moses itself; for it was not only the Law of Adam, of Noah, and of all the patriarchs before Abraham, but also of Abraham, of Isaac and Jacob, of all their children and descendants, and of Moses himself before the revelation at Sinai.

What was the procedure which signaled a man's passage from polytheism to Noachism? A text tells us that the Gentile who wished to be converted must present himself before three *haverim* (brothers, companions), a name which was given on certain occasions to the sages of Israel. In their presence he must declare his intention of adhering henceforth to the Noachide religion.

It is quite probable (though the ancient sages are silent on this point) that a ritual of baptism or absolution accompanied the conversion of a pagan to Noachism, just as it was part of the conversion ceremony to Mosaism itself. In fact, such a ritual was practiced not only by the Gentile entering Judaism[2] but also by the pagan slave entering the service of a Jew,[3] and by an apostate Jew returning to the communion of Israel.[4] It also marked the passage to a higher level of holiness, as for the high priest on the Day of Atonement, and formed one of the essential conditions for purifying oneself from all manner of defilement. We see that Elisha prescribes it also for the Syrian general Naaman (2 Kgs 5:10, 14, 15), who makes no mistake about the religious meaning of the ritual. It would therefore have been most surprising if a ceremonial ablution had not been required for the pagan who was converting to Noachism. What is certain is that Christianity grasped its significance, for it made the practice obligatory for the converted pagan, and later, if not at the same time, for the Jew also.

In any event, whatever may have been the manner in which the new Noachide was received at the moment of his conversion, our present concern is to examine the law which he took upon himself. We have alluded often to its seven precepts; we must now address each of these seven—which certain sages have considerably augmented—and try to determine its meaning. But before launching into this detailed analysis, let us first consider the overall contents of the Noachide Law.

Whatever may be the true number of Noachide precepts, it is clear that each of them represents not a single commandment but rather an entire group of related obligations. It was indeed natural to organize the entire Law of Noah into general categories, by analogy with the Law of Moses, in which each precept—and they are vastly more specialized—includes a larger or smaller number of particular provisions.[5]

We know, moreover, that the Jewish law-courts were sometimes entrusted with applying the Noachide code, and it was therefore necessary that their decisions be based not on the arbitrary or ephemeral opinion of some judge but on a set of principles which would delineate the profile of the laws in a lasting way. The Talmud addresses this question explicitly. It discusses the "sanctification of the name of God" (*Kiddush ha-Shem*), that is, the Jew's obligation to accept martyrdom rather than deny true religion. Is the Noachide held to this *mitzvah*? The objection is made that if he were, the number of Noachide precepts would rise to eight, whereas the Oral Tradition speaks of seven

261

only. The answer given is that these seven precepts embrace all related issues.[6]

We have already mentioned an important Talmudic principle which we may recall here: that the Noachide, apart from his universal law, may also observe whatever Mosaic precepts he chooses.

> If he wishes to fulfill one of the other *mitzvot* of the Law [says Maimonides], he should not be prevented from doing so just because his own laws does not require it.[7]

Thus, the entire Law of Moses is available to the Noachide. He can take from it what he wants, so that his own personal code, which consists of a small number of obligations which cannot be set aside for any reason, can, if he desires, be augmented with such Mosaic observances as he wishes to practice as well.

The compatibility of all these legal provisions is admirable. The situation of the Noachide *since* the promulgation of the Law of Moses is exactly the same as that of the Patriarchs of Israel *before* Sinai. In point of fact, according to Scripture and Oral Tradition, the Patriarchs freely committed themselves to certain observances which are part of modern Judaism but were optional in their time, having become obligatory only with the appearance of the Mosaic Law. What were originally precepts of perfection for a small number of pious men are today the religion of an entire people, but these precepts retain their voluntary character for all those who do not adhere to this religion by virtue of birth or free conversion.

Here is another Talmudic assertion which, without specifying the number of Noachide commandments, nevertheless helps clarify the question. The sages say that all seven of the basic Noachide *mitzvot* are conceived as negative precepts, the positive ones remaining outside this inclusive enumeration (though presumably some of these are implied in and may be deduced from the negative formulas).[8]

The Seven Commandments

Let us now examine what we may call the nucleus of each Noachide precept. These nuclei have often been mistaken for the laws themselves, whereas in reality they form only the chief principles of the Code of Mankind.

The oldest *baraita* enumerates them in this way:

Our sages have said that seven commandments have been prescribed for the Sons of Noah: the first requires them to have judges; the other six forbid sacrilege, idolatry, incest, homicide, theft, and the consumption of a limb taken from a living animal.[9]

Another *baraita* substitutes for the first precept the prohibition of castration, and for the second the prohibition of the cross-breeding of different species and of the grafting of trees.[10] At first sight, one is surprised to find this second text ignoring the necessity of a judiciary, and thus seeming to allow the possibility of a human society without courts charged with the administration of justice. But we must repeat that this list of commandments offers nothing more than a method of classification. If it omits justice, this is because it regards justice as the purely instrumental aspect of the Noachide code, and as an inevitable result of the very existence of this code.

The idea of a unique God, which implies the worship of Him alone and obedience only to His will, follows from the very revelation of God and of His commandments. The story of the creation of woman and of the institution of marriage, presented with such solemnity (Gn 2:22–24), constitutes a quite solid foundation for the prohibition of forbidden relationships by the fourth Noachide law, and the rabbis did not fail to deduce from it the proscription of adultery and unnatural vices.[11] The account of the punishment of Cain, Abel's murderer, is clear evidence near the beginning of Genesis that homicide is a punishable crime. The law which condemns him is later formulated most explicitly in the covenant established with Noah (Gn 9:5). The prohibition of theft exists in embryo in the distinction made by God as sovereign master of the earthly paradise between what Adam may take and what is forbidden to him (Gn 2:16–17). As for the Noachide commandment relating to the consumption of a living animal, we find this in full in the laws given to Noah after the Flood.

Since we have just touched on God's covenant with Noah, here might be the appropriate place to consider the specific precepts which it contains and its relation to the code which would later be called Noachide.

First of all we find the duty of procreation (Gn 9:1). This is omitted from the list of seven commandments, perhaps because this list is conceived in terms of negative rather than positive injunction. It is also possible that God's call to "increase, and fill the earth" is here interpreted, following the opinion of some commentators, as a blessing rather than a command. If, however, the undeniably positive precept of justice is included, it may perhaps be because justice is a *sine qua non* for punishing any transgressions whatever.

In addition to the obligation of procreation, we find in Genesis 9 the law relating to food, which we mentioned above. This law, contrary to the instructions originally given to Adam (Gn 1:29), permits renewed mankind to eat any animal at all (Gn 9:3). The difference seems to be intentionally stressed by the biblical language itself, for after saying "Every creature that lives shall be yours to eat," the text adds, "as with the green grasses, I give you all these." This means, evidently, that just as all possible vegetable foods had once been granted to Adam, so now Noah is to be given, in addition, all of the world's animal life to use as food.

The very liberal conditions of this concession, and the solemnity of its statement, remind one of the famous vision of Peter, in which the apostle "saw heaven opened, and a certain vessel descending unto him, as it had been a great sheet knit at the four corners" (Acts 10:11), this vessel containing all the quadrupeds, reptiles, and birds—while a voice said to him:

> Rise, Peter; kill, and eat. . . .
> What God hath cleansed, that call not thou common. (Acts 10:13, 15)

We know that the first Christians claimed that they were acting on the authority of Peter's dream in abolishing the distinction between pure and impure animals in the Mosaic Law. But the Jews, for their part, had no need to abolish any such ritual distinction with respect to mankind at large, for none had ever been imposed. The freedom allowed to Noachides in this matter is as complete as the restrictions placed upon Israel are explicit. The coexistence of two separate laws shows that it would be as absurd to try to subject all men to such ritual prohibitions of diet as to claim that it would be an improvement if the Jews' special dietary laws were abolished. The single obligation for the Gentile—that he must not eat the flesh of a living animal (Gn 9:4)—is enough to give legal sanction to the freedom which he enjoys otherwise.

The verse which follows, according to which God holds man responsible if he takes human life (Gn 9:6), may be interpreted so comprehensively that the Talmud, properly, sees here the condemnation of suicide.[12] Proof of the accuracy of this interpretation can be seen in the following principle: A criminal who has incurred capital punishment, and thus becomes the indirect cause of his own death, is declared responsible for the loss of his own life, and is obliged to account for this before God. We can infer this from the laying-on of hands to which he was subjected before being led to his execution.

The concluding sentence of this ancient Noachide Law, a truly precious document, also deserves our attention:

> Whoever sheds the blood of man,
> By man shall his blood be shed;
> For in His image
> Did God make man. (Gn 9:6)

Must we see in these last words only a kind of justification of the capital punishment imposed on the homicide who by his crime has offended the image of God? Perhaps there is also a consecration or authentication of human law, of man's acting on behalf of God in order to exercise a jurisdiction over his fellow men, by virtue of his resemblance to the Divinity, which gives him an intuition of moral truth, an understanding of what is right and true. If to this text in Genesis we add the many others in which justice is called a divine thing, which show God as seated in the midst of those who administer it, and even *in them*, according to the literal meaning (cf. Ps 82)—if we recall that the condemned man is thought of as consecrated to God, even perhaps as a sacrifice—we shall not hesitate to recognize that the second interpretation is highly probable.

Such is the relation between the terms of God's covenant with Noah and his descendants, and the "Noachide Law" whose various principles we must now consider in some detail.

Prohibition of Polytheism

The second Noachide precept forbids polytheism and requires the Gentile, like the Jew, to acknowledge only one God.

Let us hasten to add, however, that the Noachide religion is far more permissive in this matter than Judaism itself. Whereas Israel must observe the oneness of God with uncompromising rigor, without any trace of reference to other divine beings, at least in worship, the Gentile is thought not to sin if in his religion he relates other divinities to the authentic God, provided that he acknowledge and worship only a single supreme God.[13] Is the difference a result of the Gentile's special situation, or rather an allowance which is required by his habits and prejudices? We do not know. All the same, the fact is certain, and it far surpasses all that Christianity has believed to be most tolerant in its proselytizing approach to pagans.

This concession is surely not due to any pagan influence, nor does it imply an attitude of religious condescension on the part of Jew toward Gentile. With this single exception—of the highest significance, to be sure—there is complete equality between Jew and non-Jew regarding monotheistic worship and doctrine. Acts punishable by death in Jewish courts are also forbidden to the Noachide; those which do not entail capital punishment for Jews are permitted the Gentiles. This is the Talmudic principle.[14]

Inevitably, the Talmud asks if the non-Jew has the obligation of submitting to martyrdom rather than betray his commitment to monotheism. The question is not even raised with respect to the Israelite, and history attests to the incomparable heroism with which Israel has always accepted this duty. But the sages have raised a doubt with regard to the Noachide, and their very controversies on the matter prove how carefully they considered all aspects of universal religion, and with what generous tolerance they regarded the Gentiles who were drawn to the doctrines of Judaism. Moreover, these considerations absolve the Pharisees of the reproach, made in the Gospels, that they wanted to impose on pagan converts a more onerous yoke than the one they accepted upon themselves (Mt 23:4).

Here is the relevant Talmudic passage:

> It was asked of R. Ammi:[15] Is a Noachide bound to sanctify the Divine Name [i.e., through martyrdom] or not?—Abbaye[16] said: Come and hear. The Noachides were commanded to keep seven precepts. Now, if they were commanded to sanctify the Divine Name, there are eight. Rava said to him: Them, and all pertaining thereto [i.e., the seven precepts as well as all their implications must be observed]. What is the decision?—The disciples of Rav[17] said: It is written, "But may the Lord pardon your servant for this: When my master enters the temple of Rimmon to bow low in worship there, and he is leaning on my arm so that I must bow low in the temple of Rimmon—when I bow low in the tem-

ple of Rimmon, may the Lord pardon your servant in this. And he [i.e., Elisha] said to him [i.e., Naaman, a Noachide]: Go in peace" (2 Kgs 5:18–19). Now, if it be so that a Noachide [such as Naaman] is bidden to sanctify the Divine Name, he should not have said this?—The one is private, the other public. [That is, if Naaman were obliged to sanctify the Divine Name, Elisha would have explained to him the distinction between a *public* act of worship, which is forbidden, and a private act, which is allowed when life is in danger.][18]

What is interesting is the doctrine which has been drawn from this passage of the Talmud. On this point as on so many others, opinion is divided. According to Rashi, the problem has not been resolved. According to the Tosafot, however, the question has indeed been decided: Gentiles are exempt from the obligation to sanctify the Divine Name. Maimonides, R. Jonah,[19] and R. Nissim agree with the Tosafot. Yet Nachmanides, addressing the matter, declares explicitly that when it is a question of public worship, Noachides, like Jews, are required, whatever the consequence, to sanctify the name of God—that is, to accept martyrdom, if necessary.[20]

Sacrilege

What is the source of the prohibition of sacrilege, which forms one of the seven Noachide commandments? The Talmud derives it from this text in Leviticus which deals with the punishment imposed on the half-Israelite, half-Egyptian man who blasphemed God's name:[21]

> Anyone [Heb. *ish ish*] who blasphemes his God shall bear his guilt; if he also pronounces the name Lord [i.e., Tetragrammaton], he shall be put to death. (Lv 24:15–16)

Hebraic tradition infers from the scriptural doubling of *ish,* "man," in this text that sacrilege is forbidden to non-Jews as well as to Israelites.

Jewish monotheism stems from the universal monotheism which prevailed in the earliest times; and we know that the religious fragmentation which appeared was engendered by the diverse names used to address the one God. By degrees this variety of names replaced the original religious unity with multiplicity, as men were persuaded to believe that these words, which at first expressed only the various

267

attributes of a single God, rather represented—each of them—distinct and independent personalities, as occurred later in Christianity, when the church councils defined the Trinity of persons. In asserting that all the versions of God's name have a legitimacy,[22] Jewish doctrine brings mankind back to its starting point. Beneath the religious differences— which it respects, but among which it banishes all antagonisms— Judaism affirms the fundamental unity. Nothing could express this doctrine more characteristically than the Noachide law on blasphemy, which forbids the Gentile to blaspheme not only the names of the God of Israel but also those of the various divinities of paganism, in which Judaism teaches their adherents to discover the scattered fragments of divine Truth.

Murder

Like the other Noachide commandments, the precept against homicide has been understood by the sages in a much amplified way.

With respect to the words "Of man, too, will I require a reckoning for human life, of every man for that of his fellow man" (Gn 9:5), the Talmud[23] concludes that an act of homicide has been committed even though one pay an intermediary to perform it. R. Hanina adds that a single witness, a single judge, and proof that someone had been commissioned to execute the murder are all that is needed for the Noachide's condemnation. This last doctrine is based on the text

Whoever sheds the blood of man,
By man shall his blood be shed. (Gn 9:6)

Instead of interpreting the second clause to refer exclusively to the right conferred on courts of justice to impose capital punishment, the rabbis also linked "by man" to the first clause: "Whoever sheds the blood of man *by man*. . . ."

It is important to point out that Jewish Law differs significantly from Noachide Law on this question of homicide committed indirectly by a third party: In Jewish Law, only the person actually performing the murder is guilty of it. "Every authorization to commit an offense is regarded as nonexistent." This is the accepted rule, founded on the principle that when there is a contradiction between two orders, one of which comes from the master (i.e., God), the other from the disciple (i.e., a man who asks another to sin), it is the first which must be obeyed.[24]

This is by no means the only difference between the two codes on the subject. Contrary to Mosaism, the Noachide Law declares abortion to be a homicide also punishable by death. The Talmud justifies this determination by the expression *ba'adam*, "by man," in Genesis 9:6, cited above; for *ba'adam* can also mean "in man," thus yielding the reading "Whoever sheds the blood of man *in man*. . . ." The rabbis see here an allusion to the child in its mother's womb. Pagan antiquity's tolerance of abortion is well known; Aristotle and Juvenal attest to the prevalence of this infamous custom.

Among the other acts which Noachide Law considers to be murder and punishes as such are terminating the life of an incurably sick man, leaving a man to die of hunger, and binding a prisoner so that he is defenseless and may be devoured by a wild beast. Maimonides, echoing the Talmudic doctrine already cited, even asserts that a man who, while defending himself legitimately, kills his aggressor when merely wounding him would have saved his own life, is guilty of homicide and should be appropriately punished.[25]

With respect to involuntary homicide, we find that the rabbis quite logically apply the principle which governs the entire Noachide code: Ignorance of the law is no justification, and the Noachide is punished for not having learned what he ought to have learned.

This principle differs essentially from the Mosaic code, according to which, for there to be a misdemeanor, the law has to have been brought to the attention of the guilty party, before his culpable act, by the witnesses for the prosecution.

This difference follows naturally from the essential character of the two codes. The Noachide Law is intrinsically rational. Not so the Mosaic Law, however, for this is the priestly law, decreed not only for this world but for heaven as well. That is, in philosophical language, Mosaism expresses the relation between the earth and the material and spiritual universe. Noachism addresses the observance of what is true and right to the degree that the interests of the individual and of society require; in Judaism, however, this observance acquires all the amplitude which the universal order itself calls for. Necessarily, therefore, the Mosaic code eludes man's present understanding, which comprehends only a more limited sphere, and its precepts have a significance far more vast, extending to the universe itself. This universe thrusts itself upon *man*'s consciousness in the form of revelation, as it speaks to *animal* life in the form of instinct. We can say that Revelation is but instinct of a higher order, which puts man in harmony with the universal order, and, by means of Israel, links mankind with the entire world. Thus, the Israelite is presumed to be ignorant of the Law as long as he has not been expressly instructed in it; but this excuse cannot do for the Noachide, whose conspicuously (indeed, exclusively) rational code is accessible to the human conscience.

This fundamentally rational quality of Noachism has a consequence which at first sight is surprising but which actually proceeds from it very naturally. The rabbis, who are often accused of slavishness and narrowness of spirit, ask a question as unexpected as it is important—a question which has perhaps not been asked in the criminal law of any other people. If ignorance is not acceptable as a legitimate excuse for the Noachide, what about rejection or denial of the law by a man who acknowledges neither its authority nor its justice, whose *reason* refuses to accept its commands? Is he to be considered guilty or innocent? We read in the Talmud:

> He who believes in his heart that homicide is an allowable thing, that its prohibition has never been binding, is [nevertheless] considered by Raba to be very like a murderer.[26]

Maimonides shares this opinion.[27] But what will astonish those who fail to recognize the spiritual elevation of the disparaged Pharisees is that two sages of the Talmud, Hisda[28] and Abbaye,[29] are of a contrary mind on this issue. "He who believes that homicide is a permissible thing," they say in so many words, "is victim of a force outside his control."[30] Here indeed is a modern idea, very radical even, which is surprising in so remote an epoch and in the Talmudic milieu.

The Laws of Marriage

According to the rabbis, God Himself established marriage when He created woman, and the inviolability of the marital union for Noachides is confirmed by this verse in Genesis: "Hence a man leaves his father and mother and clings to his wife, so that they become one flesh" (Gn 2:24). The sages say: "It is written that he will cling to his wife, not the wife of his neighbor."[31]

What exactly is marriage in the universal Noachide religion? It is simply the fact of belonging to each other exclusively. But it is natural to suppose that since the establishment of courts is one of the Noachide precepts, this exclusive pairing of spouses must be established by public authority, if only to make possible the prosecution of adultery and the devolution of inheritances. A text of Maimonides, drawn from the Talmud, clearly demonstrates that such is the character of marriage:

> If a Noachide, after having promised a female slave to a male slave, then permits himself intercourse with her, he will be punished by death.[32]

This example expresses a spirit of fairness truly astonishing for its time. Master and slave are both pagans, but the latter, according to Jewish thought, nevertheless enjoys his inviolable rights as a husband, and in this is equal to his master, who faces capital punishment if he dares violate these rights of his *fellow-man:* Such indeed is the eloquent term (*havero*) which the rabbis use in this context to designate the slave.

Let man not sunder what God has joined together—that of course is the basic issue; but the question is to know what God has joined, or, to use the rabbinic expression, what the man can properly consider as *his half.* If the woman he married were certain to be such a one, we should have to say that dissolution of the marriage would be counter to the divine will. But inasmuch as it is not necessarily thus, and couples are not always well mated, one can maintain that on occasion it is indispensable to dissolve a conjugal union precisely in order to facilitate the joining of "what God has joined"; and thus man's sundering may actually serve the cause of God's joining.

As for the marital union itself, no one has understood it more perfectly than the rabbis, and especially the Kabbalists, who see it as a joining not only of bodies but of souls as well. In their view the complete human soul embodies the nature of both sexes. They have even asserted in the Talmud that man without woman is not truly man. Moreover, if we recall the role that children play in biblical and traditional Judaism, we shall welcome the description of marriage which comes, according to Michelet, from the laws of Manu:

> The essence of marriage—and no society in the future will find a truer formulation of it—is this: man is man only so far as he is triple, which is to say man, woman, and child.[33]

Mysticism has sanctified this doctrine by introducing the concept of the "holy family" into its symbolism, and it is quite probable that here is the original form of the Trinity: man (Father), son (Logos), and mother (Holy Spirit).[34]

But despite the elevated concept of marriage which the sages formed, we must repeat that divorce was not therefore impossible: only (according to the unanimous opinion of the commentators) that Noachides are not held to the formalities of divorce required by the law of Israel. Just as the marriage itself is contracted by the simple consent of the spouses, so it can be dissolved by their mutual consent. Such is the doctrine which Maimonides affirms. We find in the Palestinian Talmud a text which, owing to its terseness, is less transparent, but is no less instructive:

> Does divorce exist for the Noachides? R. Yehuda answers: "Either it does not exist at all, or the right of divorce is allowed to the woman as well as to the man."[35]

To our knowledge, the Noachide code contains no special provision concerning polygamy. Nevertheless, there is no lack of arguments to suggest strongly that although there was no explicit prohibition of polygamy in Israel, it was monogamy which was at least favored by the law and by its most eminent spokesmen. This makes it probable, we believe, that Noachism of the same period shared the Jewish bias toward monogamy. The most important texts in favor of monogamy, and the most notable examples, come to us, indeed, from the pre-Mosaic period, which is to say that they express Noachide life in its full flowering. The creation story, among other texts, is surely significant for the conception of marriage which it contains. From the biblical point of view, it is manifestly appropriate to man's nature to have but a single wife: Adam had only one, who was created from his own flesh, and we might thus even venture to say that there existed at the beginning of humankind only a single human being, at once male and female—an androgynous Adam, according to the rabbis,[36] who were being more faithful to the sacred text in this matter than one might have imagined. In contrast to Lamech, who had two wives, we have the far more significant instances of Noah and his sons, each of whom had but one. Abraham also would have been monogamous if Sarah had not urged him to take her maidservant Hagar. Isaac had a single spouse; Jacob had four, but only because of Laban's trickery, in the first instance, and afterward, the expressed wish of Rachel and Leah. The mother of Moses had no rival, and as for Moses himself, even if the Ethiopian woman about whom Miriam and Aaron complained at Hazeroth was not the same as his wife Zipporah, it has not been proven that he took her while his spouse was alive. For his part, Aaron had, so far as we know, only one wife, Elisheba, daughter of Amminadab.

We thus come to the threshold of Mosaism with an abundance of evidence that monogamy was already the norm. Did matters change under the Mosaic code? The verse prohibiting a man from taking at the same time a woman and her sister was interpreted by the Sadducees as a categorical proscription of polygamy. In the Oral Tradition, however, the prohibition applies only to the marrying of two sisters simultaneously, and is not regarded as excluding polygamy, but in fact is held to take polygamy for granted. This is a sound exegesis. Without pursuing the matter further, however, we may suggest that the interpretation of the Sadducees should not be ignored. Exaggerated though it may be, it at least testifies to the dominant spirit in Judaism. By contrast, the Pharisees preferred not to extend a text's meaning beyond its plain sense. To be sure, they laid increasing emphasis on the importance of monogamy, but without categorically prohibiting polygamy. In their writings, we are always encountering the distinction between law and ethics, a distinction which they carefully respected at all times, and which is the key to our understanding of exactly what many of their institutions and precepts signify.

For example, whenever the Law asserts the obligation of marriage, it is not polygamy which the Oral Tradition specifies—manifest proof that although polygamy is tolerated as an expression of individual freedom, it is never prescribed, no doubt because it was not thought to be the most perfect state. In this spirit, a man was required to marry his sister-in-law when his deceased brother had left no child; but if the brother happened to be survived by two or three wives, the survivor could in no case marry more than one of them.

Not only does the Law refuse to endorse the polygamous state, but there are instances where it prohibits it, and the circumstances in which it then imposes monogamy lend a special value to the prohibition. The high priest who officiated on the Day of Atonement had to be married, for the Law says: "Aaron is to offer his own bull of sin offering, to make expiation for himself and for his household [lit. 'house']" (Lv 16:6). Because the word *house* is in the singular, the Oral Tradition deduced from this text that the high priest, at least on this occasion, could have but a single wife.[37] The eloquent implication of such a law for all Jews of the time is abundantly clear. If the man occupying the most august position in the priestly hierarchy, performing the most exalted functions of his ministry on the holiest day of the year, was obliged to have only one wife, it is obvious that monogamy was felt to be the higher state.

Perhaps it will be objected that if this were indeed the law's meaning, true perfection for the priest who was called to these lofty functions would consist not in having only a single wife but in having none at all. It cannot be denied that Judaism, even Mosaic Judaism, contains the germ of such asceticism, and that the ideas of the Hasidim, the Essenes, and the Kabbalists in this regard embody an authentically Jewish principle, but one which appears among these groups in an exaggerated form, divorced from contrary Jewish principles which must moderate and correct it. However, the asceticism of total renunciation does not inform this law governing the conjugal state of the high priest who officiates on the Day of Atonement. As he represents in his solemn role all the family heads, the entire Jewish people, he too must have his "house": that is, he must be married, in the manner considered most worthy, the one which was probably the most common.

What were the conjugal unions forbidden by the Noachide code? There are two kinds of incest proscribed by the Mosaic Law which the sages discuss in connection with the Noachides. However shocking the matter may seem to us, we must not ignore the evidence of history, which shows that mankind, in all ages and in all places, has been unanimous in prohibiting certain kinds of marriages. On this subject, Montesquieu said all that could be known in his time.[38] Modern studies of the various races at all stages of civilization have increasingly confirmed that although the moral distinction between good and evil is found everywhere, the way in which each is conceived differs considerably from one people to another. (Thus, mankind's need for a superior norm to which all are subject.)

We may recall that among the Tartars, a father might marry his own daughter. According to Priscus, "Attila married his daughter Exa, a marriage allowed by the laws of the Scythians."[39] Unions between brothers and sisters were extremely common in antiquity.

The primitive peoples [writes M. Houzeaux] were not horrified by these marriages, as are modern civilized peoples. To the contrary, Inca princes married *only* their sisters, in order to perpetuate the royal line.[40]

Language, that faithful mirror of ancient customs, has preserved memories of such marriages; this is why the Hebrew sometimes uses "sister" to mean "wife" (cf. 1 Chr 7:15). The rabbis interpreted the word *bat*, "daughter," in the second chapter of Esther, in the sense of "wife,"[41] and it is perhaps owing to this synonymy that the Decalogue does not speak of "wife" but only of "daughter," which must in this case refer to any woman in a subordinate relationship.[42]

Apart from illicit unions, the Noachide code forbade marriage with the uterine sister, mother-in-law, and mother (even after the father's death). Sexual relationships contrary to nature are also forbidden. In the face of the widespread depravity which defaced the entire pagan world, it is an admirable spectacle offered by this small people, rising proudly in its moral superiority, with serene impartiality, to declare this authentically catholic Noachide Law binding upon all men without distinction, a law which none dares transgress without degrading himself lamentably.

Condemnation of Theft

It is curious to see how the rabbis account for the prohibition of theft in the Noachide code. They trace it all the way back to Eden, where Adam was, of course, given permission to eat of all the trees except the tree of the knowledge of good and evil.[43] The contents of Eden as a whole were not, therefore, his property, since he required divine permission to use them legitimately.

Theft itself, however, is not the only form of culpable appropriation which is forbidden to the Noachide. It goes without saying that any kind of pillage or armed robbery constitutes an aggravated form of theft; but so also does the kidnapping of a captive woman. The master who refuses to pay his servant's wages, the laborer who (while resting in the vineyard) eats the owner's grapes—these too are guilty of theft.[44] Trading in slaves is also included in the prohibition of theft. We need hardly add how gratifying it is to find this explicit condemnation of slavery in such an age and such an environment.

As Judaism perceives it, the Noachide code imposes an exceedingly rigorous penalty on theft in all its forms, even as severe as death.

If we need to persuade ourselves that this sanction is perfectly justified, it is enough to invoke the evidence of history. We find peoples whose conditions of existence were such that the greatest severity with regard to theft seemed like a necessity. According to Montesquieu, "Where the rights of property are violated, there can be reasons for imposing capital punishment."[45] It has been said, quite rightly, that accidental crime is many times more worthy of leniency than crime which is premeditated, and that, all things considered, it is the latter which causes the more injury to society.

This is perhaps the place to recall Judaism's conception of property. For the Oral Tradition as for the Bible, the notion of acquisition is linked to that of labor. It is by work that property is created, and the transformation of an object is the title to its possession.

The right to landed property, therefore, cannot be absolute, as is an individual's right to the product of his own labor. Considerations of common interest can alone justify an individual's exclusive possession of the soil. When private ownership of the land does not profit the commonweal, it is unjust. In the light of these basic axioms, we can understand the profound difference which Jewish law established between personal property and real estate, the first belonging without reversion to the individual, the other reverting after a certain period of time to the community. It would be superfluous to add that this distinction, calling for the inalienability of land, is not an isolated phenomenon in history. Certain ancient law codes forbade the sale of land. The notion that land is owned collectively by the tribe, which may still be found in some countries, is said by scholars to be a stage of civilization through which all peoples have passed.

Dietary Laws

Here is the biblical text which is the basis of the dietary prohibition in the Noachide code:

> Every creature that lives shall be yours to eat; as with the green grasses, I give you all these. You must not, however, eat flesh with its life-blood in it. (Gn 9:3–4)

Contrary to the opinion of certain commentators, who see in this passage only the prohibition of eating flesh torn from the body of a living animal, and accordingly maintain that the Noachide is permitted to eat the blood by itself, R. Hanania ben Gamaliel believes that this is a double prohibition: of blood, and of flesh thus cut.[46] This opinion surely seems consistent with sound exegesis. It is the proscription of blood which in fact seems to be the single object of this precept, for it logically implies proscription of the flesh of the living animal. We know, moreover, that in another passage, blood is called the "life" of the animal:

> But make sure that you do not partake of the blood; for the blood is the life, and you must not consume the life with the flesh. (Dt 12:23)

The matter has a very special importance in the early history of Christianity. This rabbinic discussion is closely related to those which occurred in the early church relating to the prohibition of blood, or of the flesh of suffocated animals. In connection particularly with the prohibition of blood, it is surely as a final homage to the Noachide code that this interdiction was preserved for the Gentiles by early Christianity. In doing so, the church would have been a faithful interpreter of Judaism, if not for its untenable pretension to have supplanted it in reducing (even for Jews) the number of laws to those which it chose to maintain.

Finally, we may summarize the difference between the Mosaic and Noachide codes with respect to the consumption of animal flesh. For the Noachide, it is enough that the animal should have ceased to live, whatever the manner in which it had been killed. For the Israelite, however, the animal must have been killed by jugulation in order to be fit for consumption.

Additions to the Noachide Code

The rabbis devote much attention to possible additions to the Noachide code. R. Hanania ben Gamaliel (as we have seen) adds the prohibition of eating blood from a living animal. R. Hidka prohibits castration. R. Shimon bans witchcraft, and R. Yose extends this interdiction to all related practices covered by the relevant section of the Mosaic Law, including human sacrifice, divination, auguries, oracles, and summoning the spirits of the dead.[47] In the text of the Pentateuch which treats these matters (Dt 18:9–12), the Canaanite tribes, whom the Jews are to expel from the land in punishment for their gross superstitions, are in fact blamed for all these practices specifically. It is clear, therefore, that these prohibitions are (as R. Yose affirms) part of the Noachide code, whose precepts, as we see once again, are in fact categories. Thus, a number of related offences are gathered under the rubric of witchcraft or sorcery. The number seven, then, which Oral Tradition has attached to the Noachide precepts, is very far indeed from accounting for the entire Noachide code, since Scripture itself prescribes others, as the instance just noted reveals.

R. Eleazar forbids Noachides to cross-breed two different species of trees or animals,[48] and Maimonides, at the same time that he accepts in principle the concept of seven precepts, endorses the prohibition. And certain rabbis add the obligations of procreation and circumcision. One of them, however, appends the important qualification that these two positive commandments were imposed on the Gentiles only until Sinai, but since then have been obligatory only for Israel.[49] There were no doubt weighty reasons why the Talmudic sages were reluctant to include these two *mitzvot* in the Noachide code; but this does not mean that the first of them, at least, does not have universal import, unless we understand the words of Scripture "Be fertile, then, and increase" (Gn 9:7) not as a command but as a blessing which expresses God's will, so that it will always be a virtue in man to comply with it.

Friedenthal adds the Sabbath to the seven precepts, because it is written:

> You shall not do any work—you, your son or daughter, your male or female slave, or your cattle, or the stranger who is within your settlements. (Ex 20:10)

He includes also the prohibition of work on the Day of Atonement, citing Leviticus:

> And you shall do no manner of work, neither the citizen nor the alien who resides among you. (Lv 16:29)

Additionally, Friedenthal includes the prohibition of eating blood (discussed above), and of forming those incestuous relationships which, the Torah tells us, led to the expulsion of the Canaanites.[50]

Let us add, finally, a few observations on some of these rabbinical amplifications of the Noachide code.

The proscription of castration which was added by R. Hidka[51] seems to be based on a deduction. Scripture says:

> Nor shall you accept such [mutilated animals] from a for-eigner for offering as food for your God [i.e., as sacrifice], for they are mutilated, they have a defect; they shall not be accepted in your favor. (Lv 22:25)

Perhaps it was inferred that since the animals in question could not serve as sacrificial offerings from the Gentiles, then the practice of castration would also be prohibited to them.

R. Shimon believed that the Noachides were not permitted to practice magic; R. Yose added the proscription of sacrificing children to Molech. In point of fact, the text in Deuteronomy which forbids these practices to Israel includes this significant assertion:

> For anyone who does such things is abhorrent to the Lord,
> and it is because of these abhorrent things that the Lord your
> God is dispossessing them before you. (Dt 18:12)

The sages who did not reason with Shimon and Yose in these matters surely assumed that the Noachide code's provision against homicide included the sacrifice of children, and that magic was included in the injunction against all idolatry.

Ethical Laws of Noachism

Finally, we must consider two classes of practical precepts which have not formed part of the scheme outlined above. These are the principles of ethics and of politics, which could not, at least in their essence, have been left to individual discretion.

As regards ethics: It is certain that when Scripture speaks of human behavior, it addresses mankind in general, and that its precepts embrace all humanity. And this is so not only in the Prophetic books and in the books of the Writings, such as Proverbs, but even in the Torah, which also affirms that the moral life is indispensable to the dignity of all men without distinction, as the sages acutely observed in connection with the immoralities of the pagans.[52] Moses says: "For all those abhorrent things were done by the people who were in the land before you, and the land became defiled" (Lv 18:27), suggesting that ethical laws are universal, applying to Gentiles as well as Jews. This text is but a single example, among many others, in which we see God approving or condemning, rewarding or punishing the Gentiles—appraising their conduct, whether as Lawgiver or Judge, and doing this with reference to a higher law to which they are held as responsible as the Israelites, which is in fact the same for all men. This universal moral standard is invoked not only in the pagan's relation to God but also in his relation to Israel, and in a general way in the relations of all men with one another. It is this standard which obliges Israel to treat even idolators, their religious (and, very often, political) enemies, with justice and charity. Perhaps this uniformity of mankind's moral code explains why the Mosaic Law is so substantially dominated by national, political precepts rather than ethical. Moral values are perhaps assumed to be generally known, whether by a natural instinct of mankind or through a tradition common to all peoples. In human culture, as a rule, the most fundamental beliefs tend to be taken for granted and not formally spelled out.

As for social precepts, which are of course extremely important, these must also form part of the Noachide Law. To be sure, we shall not find there a complete system of government nor an actual political code, but rather general truths, germs of future progress, essential principles of common law. From a philosophical point of view, politics merges with ethics; and if ethics is part of the universal Noachide code, then politics, which derives in large part from it, must be represented there as well.

We know that a celebrated political philosophy has been conceived according to biblical principles; and though we are by no means able to accept all of Bossuet's interpretations of the divine Word, it is obvious that for him to have attempted such a project at all, he must have found its substance in the Bible.[53] It would, however, be very useful to examine Bossuet's study from a critical and Jewish point of view. In the modern conflict between church and state (or, if one prefers, between religion and secular culture), a work of this kind would have considerable value. But for our present purposes, it will be sufficient to demonstrate that Judaism possesses not only a religion and an ethics which embrace all mankind, but a universal political philosophy as well.

5

Religion and the State

*I*t is still widely believed that the government of the Jews was a theocracy, like that of Egypt or India, which it to say that the supreme power, the principal public offices, and even the larger part of the territory and of the public wealth belonged to the priests [observes M. Franck].[1] But M. Salvador[2] easily demonstrates that nothing could be more contrary to the texts of the Scriptures and to the history of the Jewish people. In Israel, the priest's only mission was to conduct the sacrifices and to preserve in its integrity the text of the Torah. As for property, he had none. He lived only from the tithe and the sacrificial animals. In other matters, he was, as we should say today, subject to the common law, and he had the same obligations as his countrymen. He was judged by the same courts and he paid the same taxes, including the tax of blood.[3]

Who, then, was the priest in Israel? To answer this question, we must go back to the origins of the institution. It is beyond doubt that up to a certain time after the exodus from Egypt, priestly functions were entrusted to the firstborn of each family. According to some sages, it was thus until the erection of the Tabernacle. The Mishnah is of this opinion;[4] but other rabbis believe that Aaron and his sons assumed the priesthood at the time of Sinai.[5]

This transformation of the priesthood is analogous to the transformation of families into a federation of tribes. As long as Israel consisted only of families, the role of priest belonged to the firstborn. Even among the sons of Jacob, it is to Reuben and his sons that this dignity would have fallen if their sin had not made them unworthy of it. Another tribe—Levi—took Reuben's place, and became in the great family of all Israelites what the firstborn of each house had been before there was a nation: the portion of Israel specially consecrated to God, dedicated to the divine service—in effect, the representative

281

before the Lord of the entire group, as well as of every family. Analogously, the firstborn of the animals was offered up as a sacrifice to God, like the firstfruits of field and tree, and like the tithe set apart from the produce of the land. This harmonious correspondence of all phases of Israel's historical evolution, of Mosaism itself, is found also in Israel's relation to mankind. In a famous passage in Jeremiah, the chosen people is actually called the *terumah*, or consecrated part, of mankind:

> Israel was holy to the Lord,
> The firstfruits of His harvest. (Jer 2:3)

Thus, we can see that the Jewish priesthood embodies a most significant feature, which protects Israel from the danger of theocracy: The priest, rather than being God's representative to the people, is the people's representative before God.

The functional, representative role of the Levites, by Moses' authorization, was to take the place of the firstborn in the ritual of worship. No one ever claimed that the firstborn son was God's representative in the family, rather than the member who was consecrated by the family to the worship of God. He who offered up the sacrifice was also himself a sacrifice: the two roles are inseparable. Some historical critics have even suggested that this consecration of the firstborn represents what at one time was a genuine sacrifice.

But, some will ask, if the Levites took over the role of the firstborn with respect to religious ritual, did they assume his other functions as well? For the eldest son exercised temporal as well as spiritual authority in the family. However, we must keep in mind a circumstance which characterizes every kind of evolution, social or otherwise: I mean what we call today the division of labor. In Israelite society as in every other, functions and powers which were once concentrated in the same persons tend later to be divided and separated. The priesthood and the monarchy are instances of this. In the ancient family, these two roles were joined in the same individual, as they were in the person of Moses at the dawn of Israelite nationality. Until the formation of the priesthood, Moses was unquestionably both spiritual and temporal leader of the Hebrews.

After this period of change, the two powers were clearly separated. And if this "division of labor" came to Israel by virtue of an evolutionary principle whose effects can be seen in many societies, Israel's religious superiority lies simply in its having achieved the separation sooner than the others. For every people, there is some expression of civilization in which it attains this position of primacy with respect to its brethren. Israel's primacy has been attained in the religious life and everything related to it.

In its origin, its place, and its characteristics, the Israelite priesthood comes nearer to the modern ideal than to the prevailing conception in antiquity. An analysis of its functions shows that it is closer to Western than to Oriental values. These functions consisted in serving the needs of Temple ritual and of public worship. There was no priestly power or authority outside these special duties; and we should not lose sight of the fact that the priestly functions themselves were performed by a sort of delegation of authority from the firstborn of each family. Nor should we forget that by reason, perhaps, of this ancient authority of the eldest sons, even after the Aaronides were given their national role, the ordinary Israelite continued to retain a part of his former influence in ritual matters.

These apparent encroachments on the prerogatives of the priesthood by lay Israelites may be seen as a periodic return of hieratic rights to their primitive source, when justified by some urgent necessity. This was, as it were, a temporary return to the entire nation of those powers which it had delegated. Ordinary Jews, chosen by roster to represent the entire people, participated in the regular or special sacrifices which were offered in the nation's name at the Temple.[6] This procedure is surely not inconsistent with the priesthood's official role, sketched above, as representative of all Israel. As a matter of fact, it was a general rule for all ritual precepts that even when their execution was entrusted to some authorized representative, he should not be alone as he performed the ritual, particularly the laying of hands on the head of the sacrificial animal.

Was the instruction of laymen one of the priest's duties, as a number of texts seem to suggest?[7] Certain distinctions are necessary here. In the first place, we know that the study of the Law is incumbent upon every Israelite as one of his chief obligations, and that the father is commanded to instruct his children, and the Bible reminds us on nearly every page.[8] Moreover, there were always sages and scholars in Israel, not only during the last centuries of nationhood but even in earlier times, as the oldest parts of Scripture demonstrate.[9]

The Prophets themselves were sages of the Law,[10] whose faithful observance they never ceased to urge.[11] What teaching function, then, was there for the priests to perform, and how should we understand those biblical passages which seem to attribute such an official function to them?

It is not religious instruction in general which the priests were assigned but rather a particular branch, dealing with worship, religious rites, the distinction between pure and impure, between holy and profane; laws of diet, rituals, we may say even hygiene, if indeed this term is applicable to the rules which regulate the everyday contact of certain persons or things with society. It is quite possible, to be sure, that the Levites were more able, indeed more inclined than Israelites of the other tribes, to study the Law. Free of the obligation to provide for their own subsistence, they had more leisure than the others. Care of the Torah was their special responsibility, and religious duties formed their regular occupation. Thus, they would have been especially predisposed toward such study. It is to this state of things that the biblical story bears witness: and as, in Judaism, teaching is inseparable from study, we can readily believe that the Levites devoted themselves to this as well, and that as a consequence of their natural disposition and actual superiority in the field of learning, they must have exercised among Jews the influence which everywhere belongs to the most educated class. Yet their rank brought them no legal privilege, no special duties, let alone any monopoly, even de facto, for such privileges would have been precluded by the categorical duty to study the Law to which every Israelite was subject. We have in fact numerous examples of ordinary individuals, and even entire tribes, who received notice for their thorough knowledge of the national literature and religion: the tribes of Judah,[12] Manasseh,[13] Zebulon,[14] and Issachar.[15] The only part of the Torah in which the priests received a special legal authority was the Levitical legislation, represented in the Pentateuch by a special book (Leviticus) and called from the earliest times *Torat Kohanim*, or Priestly Law.

What role did the priest play in exercising the supreme power of national public office? Deuteronomy speaks of priests and judges in a general way (Dt 17:8–9) and wholly confirms the rabbinical tradition on this subject. It describes the precise role which the priesthood should play in the Sanhedrin, the highest political body, declaring that priests, Levites, and ordinary Israelites should all be represented. This seems the only way to understand the relevant text:

[You shall] appear before the levitical priests, or the magistrate in charge at the time, and present your problem. When they have announced to you the verdict in the case, you shall carry out the verdict that is announced to you. (Dt 17:9–10)

In this sketch of the Jewish priest which we have just traced, we thus find nothing at all to justify the accusation that ancient Israel was a theocracy.

Priests, Prophets, and Kings

What indeed were the relations between the priesthood, on the one hand, and the prophets and monarchy on the other? Monarchy and priesthood were formal institutions, and therefore had fixed, authorized statuses with respect to one another. Prophecy, however, was not precisely institutionalized, and in this fact lay its distinctive character and its strength. It was the loftiest expression of the national life, so exalted that it escaped all constraint or regulation. It was superior indeed to all institutions, at least since the Prophets were empowered to suspend any of them, excepting only monotheism. Between prophet and priest, then, the only conceivable relations would have been of a moral or ethical sort.

What were they? It has been asserted that the priesthood represented stability, the preservation of tradition, whereas the Prophets represented progress. This is the opinion of M. Salvador,[16] and of the rationalists in general, and quite acceptable to us, provided that we understand by "progress" those natural developments which flowed from Revelation, in whose basic ideas they virtually existed in embryo. It was the function of the priest to deal with matters of a practical kind, whereas the prophet concerned himself with religious idealism. This division is also consistent with the picture we find of each in the Torah. The priest is trustee of the Written Law. He receives it from the hands of Moses himself; he is commanded to furnish a copy to the king; he is charged with preserving it and studying it unceasingly. But the prophet, as successor to Moses, is dedicated to Israel, not indeed to legislate, like him, but to interpret and cultivate his work. The role which we are attributing to the prophet is authenticated by the very corruption which is foreseen and condemned in the Mosaic text, namely, the incitement to polytheism and idolatry. Moses's solemn warning clearly indicates the sphere in which the prophet's activity would be practiced, and the limits within which he would function.

R. Judah Halevi in his *Kuzari* addresses these ideas in a remarkable way. According to him, it is to the priests that the *Written* Law is entrusted, whereas the Prophets have charge of the *Oral* Law.[17] If we reflect on this last assertion in the context of Hebraic thought, we shall see that the conception of prophecy as instrument of progress is already anticipated in the doctrine of this celebrated medieval rabbi.

In a passage of his *Études d'histoire religieuses*, Renan contests this notion of prophecy. He writes:

> In general, the political views of the Prophets appear narrow and hostile to progress. It was the kings who represented a more liberal way of thinking, and several of them whom we read of as wicked were perhaps in fact reasonable princes, tolerant, advocates of useful alliances with foreign powers, responsive to the needs of their time and to a certain inclination toward luxury and trade.[18]

There are, we think, several errors of fact and interpretation here. Far from opposing any friendly relations or even alliances with foreigners, the Prophets often encouraged them. Differences between the Prophets and the prevailing policy arose only over questions of choice, of prudence, of opportunity. There were Prophets in the time of Solomon, who was allied to King Hiram of Tyre, and they do not seem to have shown dissatisfaction with this relationship.[19] Prophets such as Elisha attended the Syrian kings (2 Kgs 8:7–15). Jeremiah preaches obedience to the king of Babylon (Jer 29:4–7), which is something quite different from an alliance. And Israel is mentioned along with Egypt and Assyria in Isaiah's benediction (Is 19:24–25). Patriarchal history provides, moreover, instances of alliances with Gentiles. Abraham, for example, contracted one with Abimelech; Aner, Eshkol, and Mamre are also called his allies (Gn 14:13).

Prophetic invective against foreign alliances was intended solely to preserve the national spirit from lapses which would have compromised the purity of Israelite morals and faith, as well as the reliance which Israel must have in God, and thus Israel's status as the chosen. The distinguished author whom we just quoted was surely as aware as anyone of the superiority of Jewish civilization to that of its neighboring peoples, and thus was unjust in calling men like the Prophets enemies of progress—men who labored with all their might, even at the risk of being misunderstood by their fellow countrymen, in order to safeguard the Jewish spirit from dangers of all sorts which threatened it. For those who are in advance of their contemporaries, progress does not consist in lowering themselves to the level of the mass, but rather in retaining their relative position, despite all the difficulties which doing so may offer. Far from being more narrow in outlook than the advocates of foreign alliances, the Prophets looked higher and farther. It was mankind of the future which they beheld; and even when, in their grand vision, they might sometimes have jeopardized the present political interests of their people, they were only subordinating the transitory Israel of mortal existence to the ideal and spiritual Israel which occupied the larger place in their thoughts. If they were guilty of overstatement, it was in connection with their all-embracing universality. Luxury and trade might perhaps have suffered, but they knew that there are some things in this world so precious that they must take precedence over all else.

From a slightly different perspective, one could say that the priesthood stands for Israelite particularism, while prophecy represents Israel's cosmopolitan inclination, that is, progress not only in time but also in space. In this sense, the priesthood, monarchy, and public administration are all expressions of Israelite particularism: the priesthood as administrator of that part of the religion which is Israel's particular heritage, the suprarational element; the monarchy as protector of Israel's [political] interests; the public officials as upholders of the legal foundations of Israelite society. Prophecy, however, is the very life of Israel itself. It too addresses these peculiarly Israelite matters, but passes beyond them. It extends to all of mankind, embraces the future, and rises above merely national interests and everyday contingencies all the way to God.

With regard to the relation between priesthood and monarchy, Judaism was careful to distinguish between their respective functions and even to separate them. The king was not allowed to encroach on the prerogatives of the priests. However, the executive administration had jurisdiction over the priests (including the high priest himself), and they were likewise under the political authority of the king, with respect to whom they were hierarchically subordinate. And in no case could a priest aspire to the crown. This subordination of the priest appeared even in the posture which was to be observed during prayer. The principle was that the higher one's rank, the more conspicuously

287

must one's posture give evidence of obedience to God. Thus, the ordinary Israelite was to bow his head only at the first three and last two benedictions of the Shemoneh Esreh; the high priest was obliged to bow at the beginning and end of each of them; but the king might not raise his head from the beginning to the end of the entire prayer.[20]

Authority in Israel

The study of Israelite political institutions and legislation will enlarge our grasp of the Noachide code, as of many other matters. We have no intention of trying to survey exhaustively all that the Gentile world can learn on this subject from Israelite institutions. But in view of the current struggle between religion and modern society, it seems to us important to emphasize the Jewish concept of the state and of political authority.

Analysis of this concept may cast significant light on the compatibility of the biblical ideal with the political institutions which Europe now considers essential to its legal fabric.

In order to grasp the central idea of Israelite doctrine on this crucial matter quickly and accurately, let us proceed by a process of elimination and determine first of all what that doctrine categorically rejects. Where is supreme authority to be found in Israel? Does it reside in a man or in a family invested with supreme power? The very idea of a Revelation which embraces all of life, public as well as private, precludes any such possibility. A Revelation so total cannot speak through any single entity whatever, whether priest or monarch. We have already indicated the reason. Neither the king nor the priest can possess unlimited authority, for each moves in a well-defined sphere and his function is circumscribed by impassable limits.

Nor is supreme authority vested in a privileged class, an oligarchy or an aristocracy. The provisions of the Law, the history and conception of Revelation itself, prove, if proof be needed, that there can be no such class. Neither is it to be located in the totality of Israelites, at least not in the sense of an absolute power residing in the people as a whole, which would legitimize all that the people might decree. As for the authorized interpreters of the Revelation, however, the people convey their sovereignty in this matter to those whose place in the hierarchy renders them qualified, according to established rule. This role of the community is the only one which is logically possible in a state faithful to a Revelation.

If, then, according to Judaism, supreme authority adheres neither to the high priest, nor to the king, nor to an elite, nor even to the entire people as a collectivity, where is it to be found? In God alone; which is to say, using modern categories, in absolute reason and justice. God is the only legislator, and the people His only interpreter on earth. Such is the Jewish ideal. It matters little if some choose to call this system a theocracy. In the sense of government by priests, which is what the word is usually taken to mean, there could be nothing more remote from Israelite thought. But if we understand "theocracy" in its etymological meaning, government of God, then it is altogether certain, as Josephus observed, that the government of Israel was a true theocracy, perhaps (as we believe) the only one which has ever existed.

To have an authentic theocracy, according to the Israelite conception, under that name or another, there must be acknowledgement of something higher than the human will alone; despotism in all its forms must be rejected; there must be belief in the sovereign authority of the absolute principles of justice and morality, independent of any whim or special interest, whether individual or collective. It is not necessary that these principles be related to an historical, objective revelation. It does not even matter whether or not we attribute them to a divine source. Men's ideas about things do not affect their intrinsic nature. We have two choices: to reject any absolute principle of justice and morality and to base our political system upon convenience or pleasure, with the will of a man or the whim of the masses the sole criterion; or to recognize that it is the Absolute—that is, God—who reigns, even though He may not always govern.

With regard to the exercise of the Law, there is no doubt that this is by the people itself as manifest in its hierarchical organization and its authorized bodies, which, by virtue of the way they are formed and the persons who compose them, represent the people as an aggregate—all the better, indeed, since the obligation imposed on every Israelite to educate himself in the various parts of the Law inevitably gave to society an influence and a role similar to those of public opinion today. *God is God and King, and the people is His prophet:* Such is the true Jewish theocracy. It is to the Lord that supreme authority belongs and not to the priests, and it is exercised by the people, whose representatives are the public officials of all ranks, together with the priests and the king himself. Everyone could aspire to the high positions of the state. (The most notable example is the Sanhedrin, which was open to all citizens.) The various offices, even the monarchy, are occupied only by public servants. Every functionary must serve the nation, which is indeed the only sovereign authority, as expressed in the person of its representatives.

The theory which we are sketching here is said by some commentators to be that of Moses himself, who formulated it this way in his last benediction:

> Then He became King in Jeshurun,
> When the heads of the people assembled,
> The tribes of Israel together. (Dt 33:5)

This text is remarkable, for not only does it establish the principle which we are setting forth, but it also clarifies a passage in Genesis which rationalist critics have considered an interpolation: "These are the kings who reigned in the land of Edom before any king reigned over the Israelites" (Gn 36:31). The king of Israel referred to here is indeed nothing other than political authority itself, or the essence of Jewish nationality in the time of Moses. It is as though the text said "These are the kings who reigned in the land of Edom before Israel was formed into a state."

The words *shofet* (judge), *nasi* (prince), and *melekh* (king), which are often taken to be synonyms, show what we have already seen. They all represent, fundamentally, the supreme authority, which assumes different forms and bears different names but is in fact always the same. The concrete here replaces the abstract. Let us quote, from among many other sources, the conclusion of a learned Italian author:

> The basis of the constitution which governed the Semitic race was the notion of representation. At certain periods, the Jewish monarchy became absolute, but these were exceptions. The axis of Hebraic institutions is an assembly, and as a consequence of the dispersion of the Jewish people, it was the Synagogue which became heir to the representative forms and preserved their traditions.[21]

The characteristic delegation of power appears not only in the principles of Israelite law but also in the choosing of kings, in which the people played a more or less considerable role. This is apparent in the very name given to the sovereign, *melekh*, which is so similar to *malakh* (representative, messenger, delegate). That this title *melekh* can also refer to an absolute monarch, and has in fact sometimes done so, will not be contested; but we must observe that it was also applied to the supreme head of the army and even to subordinate officers. Thus, the lieutenants of Ben-hadad, king of Syria, are called "kings," *melakhim* (1 Kgs 20:16); and the governor sent to Edom by the kings of Judah serves the function of a king (1 Kgs 22:48).

With regard to Samuel's famous depiction to the Israelites of their future monarch,[22] the prophet is merely reflecting the legal conventions governing monarchy at the time. We are much mistaken if we seek for the ideal of Judaism in his words. In fact, if we examine the context, we shall see that it is not only the corruption of monarchy but monarchy itself which is at issue, and which Samuel repudiates. All the more reason, then, for not assuming that he ascribes any legitimacy to this unlimited power which he depicts. His clearly exaggerated expressions and highly charged description in fact persuade us of the contrary. In a word, if this text does not offer satire, it contains a threat, or we might say a picture which calls to mind the sociopolitical pattern of the Orient, which he feared to see copied in Israel, and which has in it absolutely nothing that is authentically Jewish.

But does the Law of Moses not prescribe—or at any rate permit—the choosing of a king? Let us see, however, what kind of king this is. The very text which anticipates monarchical government describes most explicitly the nature of the monarchy. There is no authority above the Law, which must govern the king as well as the humblest citizen, and its continual study will constitute the monarch's first duty. He will always have a copy of the Torah with him, in order, says Moses, to meditate on it all the days of his life and not to deviate from it, either to the right or to the left—in order, too, that his heart should not rise above his brethren, for Judaism affirms the equality of all before the Law. It is on these conditions that Scripture promises the king a peaceful reign for himself and his descendants.

We must note also that the law concerning monarchy comes immediately after the one providing for the Sanhedrin, the supreme body of the state, which is the court of last resort, whose decisions must be scrupulously obeyed by all. The king has no comparable power, but is himself subject to the Sanhedrin's authority like all his people.

In the most ancient Jewish law, there was, to be sure, a confusion of executive power with judicial; but when the disadvantages of this arrangement became clear, the original system gave way to a separation

291

of powers. No longer was the king judge, nor was he liable to trial in a court of justice, and his role in the state anticipated the principle of nonaccountability embodied in modern monarchies. Here is additional evidence that with respect to form of government, as for all other matters of civil and political law, the people remained entirely free to choose the constitution which best suited them. Such a monarchy is consistent with the conception of supreme authority which we have attributed to Judaism, and is in fact its most eloquent confirmation. The Oriental idea of a single man's having absolute power is here rejected; the sovereign whom Moses seems to expect is rather one who is public servant and executor of the Law: in effect, a constitutional monarch.

We know of course that Samuel, despite his initial opposition, finally complied with the will of the people. In shouldering the responsibility of installing a king and extending to him the protection of his own authority, Samuel show that the monarchical wishes of his fellow-citizens were reconcilable with the Law of Israel. But in this case, why was he so unenthusiastic when the first overtures were made to him on the subject? Above all, perhaps, it was because Moses seems to make the introduction of monarchy contingent upon the solemn expression of the popular will, thus introducing a drastic distinction between this manifestation of the sociopolitical order and the other commandments, which are never subject to such conditions. The text in the Torah dealing with monarchy can be interpreted not as a command at all but as a prediction, and it implies acknowledgement of complete freedom of choice with respect to form of government. Keeping in his mind this obligation of freedom, as affirmed by the Mosaic Law, Samuel did his best to educate the people to their high responsibilities.

Another reason for the prophet's opposition to monarchy was the way in which the popular will expressed itself in the matter. The king-judge whom the people craved, the sovereign who would enjoy unlimited power, is not the political leader foreseen by Moses. If his authority were indeed to extend over legislation, even though this might be limited to civil law, it must inevitably, sooner or later, encroach upon the domain of conscience, and in any case it would interfere with the dignity and interests of the citizens. When Moses speaks of the future king, he makes no reference to judicial functions, whereas the Israelites appear to be demanding precisely this authority for their monarch, which would lead to the exercise of legislative power itself. The biblical text is unambiguous on this point: "Samuel was displeased that they said 'Give us a king to judge us' " (1 Sm 8:6).[23] This emphasis is obviously significant, as is God's response to the prophet:

Heed the demand of the people in everything they say to you. For it is not you that they have rejected; it is Me they have rejected as their king. (1 Sm 8:7)

God alone is the lawgiver of Israel, but it is a kind of rival to God whom the people call for so rashly. The Jews wish to abdicate their grandest privileges. It is this ill-considered desire that Samuel protests with such indignation.

Political Ideals and Realities

But if, according to the ideal Jewish conception, God is the only authentic sovereign of Israel, why do the Jewish kings, historically, seem free of all constraint? In point of fact, they often speak and act as if they were absolute masters of their people, and they display little concern to accommodate their conduct to the prescriptions of the To- rah. Why, moreover, does there appear so little check upon the royal power by a supreme body designed to serve as a counterweight to the king, if indeed, as we have asserted, the Israelite constitution provides for this very body?

Let us note, first of all, that we must not put undue emphasis upon the specific events related in the Bible. It is most regrettable that rationalist criticism chooses to evaluate Jewish law by reference to the behavior of kings, priests, generals, or even less exalted person- ages, while neglecting the content of the laws themselves, or contest- ing their authenticity on the grounds that they are contradicted by the historical accounts which are interspersed with them in Scripture. The comprehensive moral level of any people must fall short of the ideals set forth in its laws. Legislation can never be other than a more or less imperfect reflection of the philosophical values of a particular epoch. Hence, it should not surprise us that what is in theory the noblest of monarchies should in practice be flawed. Nor can we justly ignore the fact that events which seem openly in violation of the Law may nevertheless acknowledge it, though indirectly. Can one imagine a more outrageous violation of human rights than the plundering of Naboth's vineyard (1 Kgs 21)? And yet we see the royal hypocrisy carrying solicitude for legal forms even to the point of arranging a trial with false witnesses, in order to give the expropriation at least the appearance of legality.

Jewish Conception of Societal Life

According to M. Maury:

> The ancient philosophers believed that the object of political institutions was not so much to govern and protect the interests of citizens as to lead them toward virtue. . . . If one regards government as nothing more than a regulator of interests, it is natural for it to invoke all concerned parties, either directly or through representatives; but as soon as government is thought of as a means of education, an absolute or aristocratic system must prevail. Then, as Socrates said, only the good can take part in the direction of affairs. Plato, therefore, maintains that government should be entrusted to a small number of men, and in some cases to one only.[24]

For Aristotle, supreme political authority resides by nature in the family or individual who surpasses the others in virtue, and so in a way is superior to all law. This man or family possesses a kind of divine nature though living among men. This is what Scripture seeks to convey in honoring judges, great men, and holy men almost as if they were gods,[25] and what the rabbis say in so many words with respect to the superiority of learned and saintly men to the common people,[26] a distinction for which they have been severely reproached.

Virtue and the protection of interest, then, seem to be the two principal objects of government, the first of these in antiquity, the second in modern times. How does Judaism address this important question? Two of its defining characteristics will provide the answer. On the one hand, Judaism is notable for the high moral or ethical level of its adherents. It places strong and constant emphasis upon morality, and from this perspective, we might properly consider it a true theocracy. Spiritual perfection—religious, if one prefers—is surely the *raison d'être* of its institutions, as well as its ultimate object.[27] But on the other hand, as if by a curious contradiction, there is nothing in Judaism—at least in its political concepts—which turns away from this world and focuses on something other than material, even individual interests. Long life and abundant issue, riches, power, a good name—these are the principal rewards, perhaps the only ones, which it promises its faithful. A merely superficial inspection of its doctrines might suggest that these are the objects toward which all its resources are directed, including even the spiritual perfection which it preaches unceasingly. It would seem then as if Judaism's yearnings extended no farther than these, as it were, tangible assets. But is this really so, and does this subordination (one might even say bondage) of spiritual elements to material interests do justice to the profundity of its thought? What is hidden beneath this glaring contradiction? A simple but essential truth: That in political society, the good—moral perfection—should be embodied in law only to the degree that it contributes to the well-being of the community. Society's aim cannot reach beyond this world, precisely because society, unlike the human soul in its destined consummation, has no existence other than the mundane. Thus, the state should patronize virtue with its legal sanctions only to the extent that these are necessary for the preservation of society. Of course, preserving society has its own ulterior object, which is to provide the individual with the most effective means of attaining his own perfection.

Then again, perfection of the individual has its own effect upon the condition of society, strengthening its powers and capabilities, so that, by reciprocal influence, society and the individual engage in a relationship of unceasing cooperation. The individual is useful to society by virtue of his morality; society profits the individual by offering him security. It goes without saying that we are speaking here in very general terms, and that we do not wish to deny that society can influence the morality of its members, nor that individuals can contribute to the well-being of society. The two great foundations of government, virtue and protection of interest, play, each in turn, the double role of means and end: Virtue, which is an end from the perspective of the individual, is to society a means, while protection of interest, which is the end of society, is for the individual a means only. Thus we see how the two dimensions of Judaism, which seem so incompatible, the most spiritually elevated and what may seem the most grossly materialistic, are but the two parts of a single system, the two perspectives from which we can contemplate the life of society, protection of interest constituting the object and guideline of political activity, while virtue is the rule of conduct and the goal of the individual. *Interest by way of virtue and virtue by way of interest:* This is the teleological formula of society.

Perhaps we may be allowed to dream of a still higher synthesis, which would convert this duality into a unity. If we consider virtue from a certain perspective, we shall see that it is itself an interest—of a lofty kind, no doubt, but a genuine interest nevertheless; and that interest in the comprehensive sense, which is the satisfying of a legitimate human need, is but the fulfillment of an obligation toward ourself, a refinement of our nature, which is still a virtue, though of a lower order. Finally, if we abandon the sphere of these two controlling ideas for a perspective still higher, we shall see that the two principles are themselves grounded in a third, which embraces both, or, if we prefer, serves them both as a final end: The order of the universe, from the standpoint of which even virtue is a means, or at any rate, the subjective aspect or perception of the matter.

But here we verge upon the most sublime doctrines of Jewish mysticism, which direct us toward the ultimate, authentic end of human activity in the domain of the holy within this world, in the order of the universe itself: perpetually linking the Ideal with the Real, the Logos with the Cosmos, the Creator with His creation—or according to the kabbalistic expression, "the Holy One, blessed be His name, with His *Shekhinah*."

This universal order, of which man's political order is only a reflection and a partial realization, comes into being not solely through civil and political institutions (like human society) but by virtue of the entire range of human activity, moral, religious, liturgical, even ascetic, as well as through the life of society, through science and art—through reason as well as faith, the one taking us up to the elusive, remote borders of human understanding, the other impelling us beyond the furthermost boundaries of our imagination to the very heart of the unknowable.

Judaism, then, has precious guidance for mankind with respect to the principles which should govern the relations between religion and the state. Some may conclude, with us, that in the struggle between church and secular society which currently stirs the West, both parties might discover it to be in their interest to set aside old prejudices and return to the very source of their civilization and faith in seeking out the solution long ago proposed by Hebraism to the grave questions of today.

6

Universalism in Mosaic Judaism

The Pharisees, those sages upon whom such scorn has been heaped, take infinite pains to find signs of a universal design in the account of the revelation at Sinai. What language, they ask, did God use for speaking to His people? Although the Decalogue is composed entirely of Hebrew words, the rabbis nevertheless exercise their ingenuity in discerning there the echoes of other languages, and in deriving from this a concept which is relevant to our present study. According to them, when the Lord gave His Law to Israel on Sinai, He spoke not only in Hebrew but in other tongues as well—in certain languages, in fact, which play a preponderant role in the ancient history of mankind: Arabic, Latin, and Aramaic. Thus they interpret Deuteronomy 33:2:

> He [i.e., Moses] said:
> The Lord came from Sinai;
> He shone upon them from Seir;
> He appeared from Mount Paran,
> And approached from Riberoth-kodesh.

"Came" (*ba*) is Hebrew, but "shone" (*zarach*) suggests Latin, "appeared" (*hofia*) Arabic, and "approached" (*v'atha*) Aramaic.[1]

What is interesting in all this is obviously not the doubtful etymologies so much as the cosmopolitan spirit which inspired them. Neither national pride, nor religious convictions, nor the most legitimate resentments could suppress this idealism, and over the ruins of prejudice and parochialism we see arise the majestic structure of universal law, given to mankind through Israel. For these four languages which the rabbis acknowledge scarcely express the breadth of their vision, which encompasses an infinitely vaster horizon. According to them, the voice from Sinai addresses all humanity. Thus, R. Jochanan asserts that the text

"The Lord spoke those words—those and no more—to your whole congregation at the mountain, with a mighty voice" (Dt 5:19) refers in fact to a multiplicity of voices; the sound of the holy voice divided itself into seventy voices so that all the nations might hear it.[2]

Equally significant is that the Jews put both of their own languages, Aramaic and Hebrew, at the service of religion. We leave to the philologist the task of clarifying the role of Hebrew as a vernacular in the time of Moses. It seems likely that Aramaic, the original tongue inherited from the Patriarchs and brought from Mesopotamia, was then generally in use; but the Jews were already in possession of Hebrew at that time, as we can infer from certain quite persuasive evidence, such as proper names. But even if we conclude that Hebrew was the ancestral language, either because it was a dialect of Aramaic or because the Israelites had adopted it since their settlement in Canaan, and that Aramaic persisted among them as a recollection of Mesopotamia or as a language which they learned through contact with the Phoenicians and Canaanites, the fact remains that both tongues continued to be used in Israel. Thus did Judaism demonstrate that the truths which it declared, the sacred Law which it had received, were not to be kept only for a small number of initiates, like the teachings of the Egyptian mysteries, nor indeed were these truths the exclusive patrimony of Israel, but they were meant to illuminate all of mankind.

Translations of the Torah

We find further evidence that the Mosaic revelation was intended to spread beyond Israel's frontiers in the impressive conception of translation which developed. The first biblical translations, as we have seen, were attributed to God Himself, who, on Sinai, translated the Law into all the languages of the nations.

It is true, however, that the sages of the Synagogue were of two minds with respect to the Greek version of the Seventy. Some praised its merit, but others disparaged it. To account for this negative view of the Septuagint, it has been pointed out, with reason, that when Hellenized Judaism gave birth to Christianity, it was natural for those who remained Jews to deplore a work which seemed to have led to such a result. Yet it is also true that the rabbis spoke eloquently about the role played by the Greek language in propagating Hebraic ideas in the world. We read in the Talmud that R. Shimon ben Gamaliel says:

"The books [of the Bible] are permitted to be written [i.e., translated] only in Greek."[3]

R. Shimon's true intention appears in his choice of text to support his opinion:

> R. Jochanan asked, "On what does R. Shimon ben Gamaliel base his judgement? On this verse: 'May God enlarge Japheth, and let him dwell in the tents of Shem' (Gn 9:27). This means: Let the words of Japheth be heard in the tents of Shem. And it is to prevent the objection that the languages of Gomer and of Magog must also be included that it is written, 'Yafte Elokim l'Yefet,' that is, 'Let the most holy of the languages of Japheth be welcomed in the tents of Shem.' "[4]

(Gomer and Magog were sons of Japheth, as was Javan, father of the Greeks, according to the Bible.) The text from Genesis predates the reception of the Law. It is uttered by Noah, father of all men, and is addressed to all mankind. The most precious language of the Gentiles, we thus learn, is also intended to serve as a holy tongue beneath the tents of Shem (which stand for the synagogues).

Revelation and the Gentile Peoples

The sages go so far as to say that before He gave the Law to Israel, the Lord offered it to all the other peoples of the earth, but they declined to accept it.[5]

This idea appears in the Talmud as well as in the Pesikta. One rabbi offers this significant explanation: It was because the Holy One, blessed be He, does not behave arbitrarily with His creatures. If the text of the Mosaic benediction quoted above (Dt 33:2) links only Seir and Paran with Sinai, the commentators say that this is because these two names stand for all of mankind, for they represent the two great powers which at that time contended for domination of Judea: the Arabs and the Romans, the East and the West.[6] The Pesikta, moreover, invokes this passage from Psalms:[7]

> All the kings of the earth shall praise You, O Lord, for they have heard the words You spoke. They shall sing of the ways of the Lord, "Great is the majesty of the Lord!" (Ps 138:4–5)

The notion of God offering His Law to the Gentiles at the very moment of His appearance on Sinai has a dramatic beauty which accentuates the philosophical and historical importance of this rabbinical idea. The rabbis assert the same point in a more rational way:

> Know and understand that from the day when God created the world up to the moment when Israel departed from Egypt, God visited all the nations of the world, in turn, to offer them His law, but they did not wish to accept it. Know too that in every generation, [Gentile] witnesses appear to attest this fact. These are Eliphaz the Temanite, Bildad the Shuhite, Zophar of Naama,[8] Job of the land of Uz, and last of all, Balaam son of Beor.[9]

Thus, what is otherwise presented as part of the revelation at Sinai is here perceived as nothing less than a continuous motif of history from the start. The Law was offered to all peoples in succession, and they refused it. But what is most extraordinary about this *aggadah* is its assertion that witnesses to the divine impartiality have arisen among the Gentiles in every epoch, in the person of the Gentile prophets themselves. This text is strikingly reminiscent of the well-known words of the apostle Paul telling the pagans that the thinkers and philosophers whom God has in every age sent among them, to recall them to the sacred truth, will one day be their reproof.[10] Paul's affirmation, together with the Midrashic text, exemplifies the universalist beliefs which flourished in this Pharisaical milieu where Saul of Tarsus received his inspirations.

According to the rabbis, the universalism implicit in the giving of the Mosaic law can be seen not only in the plurality of languages used by God but also in the very content of Revelation. At the same time that it addresses each people in its own tongue, the Law makes itself accessible to every individual by adapting itself to the particular quality of his mind. Religious truth thus has many voices in order to speak to various levels of intelligence.

Every man, like every people, has a natural disposition to receive truth in one way rather than another, to contemplate it from a particular perspective. So it is, as we have said, with the very idea of God. These diverse conceptions of God are hypostatized by the various peoples into their own particular divinities, but when joined together in a higher synthesis, they become, with respect to human worship and human understanding as a whole, the authentic God. This is how the unity of mankind is the necessary condition—and, subjectively, the agent or instrument—of the oneness of God. The many-sidedness of the Divine Law (if we may describe it so), its multiplicity of voices, is but the result of this principle extended to all of religion. Just as each people takes from the idea of God that which it is capable of apprehending, so each people takes from religion that which best suits its temper and mentality. For some, it is metaphysics, with the exalted symbols and rites which come from it: these are the people whom Jesus called "children of light."[11] For others, anthropomorphism, with its imagery of sacred animals, its allegories and incarnations. Some peoples are drawn to profound speculations and mysteries, others to superstitions and barbaric cults.

We notice every day that if two related ideas are presented simultaneously to several minds, these minds will not perceive the same relationships between the ideas. And just as a city may look different according to the side from which one views it, and so, in a sense, is multiplied by these diverse perspectives, so too, says Leibniz,

> it happens that by reason of the infinite multitude of simple substances, it seems as if there were many different universes, though these are only multiple perspectives, from the point of view of each monad, of a single, identical universe.[12]

In fact, we find Catholic philosophers acknowledging the justness of this principle, even in the religious order.

> Faith in a spiritual truth [writes Mariano] presupposes differences, even asserts and engenders them. Out of diversity, unity acquires strength, solidity, truth. A unity which is indistinct, indifferent, or inert, is manifest evidence that faith, spirit, and truth are faint or diseased.[13]

Such are the rational or metaphysical grounds of the multiplicity of the revelation at Sinai. Let us now see it in its rabbinical formulations. According to the rabbinical sages,

> the text of the Torah is composed of 600,000 letters, corresponding to the number of Israelites in the time of Moses, which was also 600,000. This is to say that every Israelite

301

lays hold of the Law and attaches himself to it by one of its letters.[14]

Elsewhere, we read these suggestive words:

> Fifty gates of understanding have been created in the world, and when God taught the Law to Moses, He showed him on each point forty-nine different implications of permission or legal purity, and forty-nine other implications of legal impurity or prohibition.[15]

Regard for different opinions seems to be taken even to the point of paradox. We read in the Talmud:

> Seeing that some prohibit and others allow, you may say, "How can I learn what the Law is?" The truth is that although this is the case, all these opinions are utterances of the living God. A single God has pronounced them all, a single Shepherd has declared them all, in the name of the Lord of all things, blessed be His name.[16]

We encounter the same ideas in a variety of other forms. It is said, for instance, that God's face assumed many expressions at Sinai, each appropriate to that part of the Law which He was communicating to Moses. God adapts His language and manner to His "auditors," according to whether they be old or young, men or women or children, adjusting His teaching to the intellectual capacity of each.[17]

Furthermore, the various tongues which (according to the sages) transmitted Revelation to the Gentiles also presuppose a diversity of interpretations.[18] Indeed, each language has a unique capacity to communicate ideas from a particular perspective rather than from another.

Symbolism of the Temple

It is a very ancient Hebraic idea that the House of the Lord in the holy city was a reflection, as it were an epitome, of the entire universe. A careful study of its architecture and its various rites clearly reveals its highly symbolic character. Indeed, archeology finds this kind of symbolism in all ancient cults.

According to M. Fornari, a Catholic author:

> The Tabernacle was an epitome of the creation, a reflection of the world which had been established by the divine architect. The entrance opening to the east gave access to a vast enclosure in which were the place of ablutions and the altar for sacrifices. . . . Thus was represented the separation between mankind as a whole and the priestly people. . . . The holy place—i.e., the middle enclosure—did not represent humanity in general but Israel particularly. The parvis [outer court] represented all the rest of the family of Adam, and the entire edifice represented the universe itself.[19]

Many other authors have interpreted the design of the Temple this way, following in the tradition of rabbinical sources which assert that the Temple was modeled on the universe, reproducing its various parts. An eminent naturalist, Dr. Nank, has called the attention of the learned world to the anatomical knowledge embodied in the structure of the Temple;[20] and a Jewish author who quotes his work observes accurately: "These discoveries of a celebrated contemporary scholar were taught centuries ago by many of our sages, and especially by the great Kabbalists."[21]

We shall not consider in detail the abundant testimony on this subject in the writings of the post-Talmudic rabbis. Ibn Ezra, Nachmanides, Maimonides, R. Levi ben Gershom, and many others—not to mention Philo and Josephus, who were also influenced by the national traditions—all corroborate the conception of universal religion which we find in Mosaic worship, and especially in the form of its Temple. We shall limit ourselves to quoting certain rabbinic ideas, which, though they do not focus on the design of the Temple, provide convincing evidence of Jewish universalism. The Palestinian Talmud teaches that the particles of earth which God used in creating man were taken from the site where one day the altar in Jerusalem would be erected.

> R. Judah ben Pazi said: "A handful of earth was drawn by God from the site of the Altar, and He created from it the first man, saying, 'It is in order that man, made from the earth of the Altar, may survive.' "[22]

And elsewhere we find these moving words, to which we have already referred: "Man was created in the place where he would one day find forgiveness."

According to a rather strange legend, found also in Moslem traditions, the head of Adam was found at the very spot where David raised the Altar, and it appears that this circumstance, far from impeding his choice of the region of Aravna, or Mount Moriah, as the designated location for the future Temple, rather encouraged it. We find always the same theme: the linking of all mankind with Mosaic worship.

Equally revealing is the history of the construction itself—first of the Tabernacle, then of Solomon's Temple, and finally of the Second Temple. Let us note first of all a very remarkable provision, which emphasizes the spirit of peace and humanitarianism that profoundly characterizes these Houses of God. The Torah prescribed that no iron be used for the cutting of stones, at least for the sacred enclosure: "For by wielding your tool upon them you have profaned them" (Ex 20:22). According to the insightful rabbinic interpretation, this means "that it would be improper for the sword which cuts down human life to serve the erection of the Altar, which is intended to prolong it."[23] If we recall that the Prophets' prayers call for the day when swords will be turned into ploughshares and spears into pruning-hooks, when war will be banished from the face of the earth (Is 2:4), and that David was denied the glory of constructing the Temple, though he had assembled materials for the purpose, because he had undertaken great wars and caused much blood to flow (1 Chr 22:8)—all this without Scripture's making any distinction between the blood of Gentiles and that of Israelites, then we shall not doubt for a moment that the exclusion of iron from the construction of the Sanctuary has indeed the significance suggested by the rabbis.

Here is another relevant passage from the Torah:

> And in the open, anyone who touches a person who was killed [lit. "slain by the sword"] or who died naturally, or human bone, or a grave, shall be unclean seven days. (Nm 19:16)

The rabbinical sages say that contact with a sword, like contact with a corpse itself, causes impurity and debars a man from touching the holy things or even entering the Temple enclosure.[24]

Let us now consider the role played by Gentiles in the erection of the Sanctuary. We have already recalled that the precious materials to be used for this purpose all originated in Egypt (Ex 3:22). The Aramaic paraphrase (*Targum*) seems to indicate that these included amulets and other objects having a religious character. (The expression used to designate these objects is *k'dishei d'dahava*, "holy things of gold.") They had probably been taken as trophies of the victory of the God of Israel over the gods of the Egyptians, and were therefore used later for the construction of His Sanctuary. On the other hand, we know that in Egypt and in the desert, many proselytes committed themselves more or less fully to the religion of Israel, and it is reasonable to assume that they volunteered their assistance in constructing the Sanctuary. We even find Moses and Aaron asking Pharaoh expressly for sacrifices which they would have offered to the God of Israel in his name.

Moreover, it stands to reason that the workers, designers, artists of all kinds who were employed in various tasks connected with the Sanctuary, had acquired and perfected their skills in Egypt. It is true, of course, that the Bible speaks of God imparting to them their special talents, but it is equally certain that these artists had already been trained and had become expert in the exercise of their crafts. If we consider the remarkable similarities which modern archeology has established between the Egyptian sanctuaries and religious objects and the Tabernacle and sacred implements described in Exodus, it is impossible to doubt it. This partnership with the Gentiles is characteristic of the dominant spirit of the Bible, from one end to the other, which consists in distinguishing between truth and falsehood in the various religions of mankind, and in preserving all that is good and lawful in them.

The history of the first Temple seems to repeat that of the Tabernacle. Tyre and its king, Hiram, take the place of Egypt and Pharaoh. It is Hiram, indeed, who complies with Solomon's request that he furnish materials and craftsmen for the construction of the Temple in Jerusalem. Equally important are King Hiram's declarations of monotheistic faith, which accompany his assistance. Solomon had sent him this message:

> See, I intend to build a House for the name of the Lord my God. . . . The House that I intend to build will be great, inasmuch as our God is greater than all gods. Who indeed is capable of building a House for Him! Even the heavens to their uttermost reaches cannot contain Him, and who am I that should build Him a House—except as a place for making

burnt offerings to Him? Now send me a craftsman to work in gold, silver, bronze, and iron, and in purple, crimson, and blue yarn, and who knows how to engrave. (2 Chr 2:3–6)

In response, Hiram addresses a letter to the king of Israel in which he expresses himself as a Jew would have done in his place:

Because the Lord loved His people, He made you king over them. . . . Blessed is the Lord, God of Israel, who made the heavens and the earth, who gave King David a wise son, endowed with intelligence and understanding, to build a House for the Lord and a royal palace for himself. (2 Chr 2:10–11)

King Hiram was a skillful artist, and Scripture takes care to identify him as the son of a Jewish mother and a Tyrian father, as if to suggest that in him Israel and the Gentile world joined together to accomplish the sacred task.

In a passage from Ezekiel, the prophet harks back with satisfaction to Hiram's merits, while regretting that his heart had been corrupted by pride:

Thus said the Lord God:
You were the seal of perfection,
Full of wisdom and flawless in beauty.
You were in Eden, the garden of God. . . . I created you as a
    cherub
With outstretched shielding wings;
And you resided on God's holy mountain. (Ez 28:12–14)

The allusion to the Garden of Eden probably represents Jerusalem and its Sanctuary. The comparison of Hiram to a cherub is a particularly striking evocation of the Temple.

When the Second Temple was constructed, there was a virtual repetition of the circumstances surrounding the Temple of Solomon. We recall the important role played by Cyrus:

But in the first year of King Cyrus of Babylon, King Cyrus issued an order to rebuild this House of God. Also the silver and gold vessels of the House of God that Nebuchadnezzar had taken away from the temple in Jerusalem and brought to the temple in Babylon—King Cyrus released them from the temple in Babylon to be given to the one called Sheshbazzar whom he had appointed governor. He said to him: "Take these vessels, go, deposit them in the temple in Jerusalem, and let the House of God be rebuilt on its original site." (Ezr 5:13–15)

And some lines further we read:

In the first year of King Cyrus, King Cyrus issued an order concerning the House of God in Jerusalem: "Let the house be rebuilt, a place for offering sacrifices, with a base built up high." (Ezr 6:3)

This memorandum was found by King Darius in a scroll filed in the archives at Babylon; and he proceeded to issue a similar edict on his own behalf:

Allow the work of this House of God to go on; let the governor of the Jews and the elders of the Jews rebuild this House of God on its site. . . . They are to be given daily, without fail, whatever they need of young bulls, rams, or lambs as burnt offerings for the God of Heaven, and wheat, salt, wine, and oil, at the order of the priests in Jerusalem, so that they may offer pleasing sacrifices to the God of Heaven and pray for the life of the king and his sons. . . . And may the God who established His name there cause the downfall of any king or nation that undertakes to alter or damage that House of God in Jerusalem. (Ezr 6:7, 9–10, 12)

King Cyrus was the instrument or agent of the Temple's reconstruction, but it was the God of Israel who commanded him in the matter, as He commanded him to resettle the Israelites in their own land. It is this which gives that period of Jewish history a very special importance with respect to the relations between Jew and Gentile. Isaiah gives us God's words on this subject:

[I] am the same who says of Cyrus, "He is My shepherd; He shall fulfill all My purposes!

He shall say of Jerusalem, 'She shall be rebuilt,'
And to the Temple, 'You shall be founded again.' "
Thus said the Lord to Cyrus, His anointed one—
Whose right hand He has grasped,
Treading down nations before him . . . So that you may know
   that it is I the Lord,
The God of Israel, who call you by name. . . .
I am the Lord and there is none else. (Is 44:28, 45:1, 3, 5)

In sum, it seems that in all phases of the history of Israel, the same kinds of events must recur; the nations will be called upon to collaborate with Israel in fulfilling the divine will. There are predictions of this kind in Isaiah. Israel will be welcomed by the peoples amidst whom she is exiled. The nations and their kings will take part in the reconstruction of the Temple: "Aliens shall rebuild your walls" (Is 60:10).

The most cursory examination of the layout of the Temple will reveal that there were three principal divisions, the last two of which were subdivided into special areas which did not at all spoil the overall harmony of the building.

The exterior part was called *har ha-bayit*, and Gentiles were allowed there, without reference to their beliefs. That is, they were not required to affirm beforehand that they subscribed to the Noachide religion, which was regarded as necessary for their salvation—perhaps because their very presence in this holy place would have seemed a sufficient token of their religious commitment. There are even certain Psalms which refer to this function of the holy mountain as a destination for the religious visits of Gentiles:

Who may ascend the mountain of the Lord?
Who may stand in His holy place?—
He who has clean hands and a pure heart, who has not
taken a false oath by My life or sworn deceitfully. (Ps 24:3–4)

The absence from this passage of any allusion to particular rituals and beliefs of Judaism, or even to monotheism itself, persuades us that the psalmist is referring to Gentiles, whose proper religion is summarized precisely in the moral precepts which he enumerates. Psalm 15 contains a still more detailed account of those "who may dwell on Your holy mountain," which includes the following very indispensable

308

moral quality: "[He] for whom a contemptible man is abhorrent, but who honors those who fear the Lord" (Ps 15:1, 4). These words confirm our reading, since "fearers of God" was the virtually official Jewish designation of such Gentile believers.

After the area which was accessible to the Gentiles came the parvis, the court of Israel, and this second part was followed by the area reserved for the family of Aaron. Gentiles were not permitted to enter the court of Israel, nor could the ordinary Israelite enter the court of priests. Moreover, the priests themselves were denied access to that part of their court called the Holy of Holies, which was opened but once a year, and for the high priest only. Thus, there were, in a sense, three temples, each with its own distinct purpose, together constituting a unique Sanctuary, a symbol of the community of all believers, an organic unity whose parts coexisted harmoniously.

The fact that a section of this Sanctuary of Jerusalem was reserved for Gentiles who were not asked to commit themselves to Mosaism is perhaps a phenomenon unique in religious history. It demonstrates the close bonds which link the religion of mankind with that of Israel. Solomon's prayer in the ceremony of dedication is justly celebrated, and contains words which deserve to be quoted. After entreating God to grant the prayers of His people in the Temple which is being inaugurated, the king of Israel adds:

> Or if a foreigner who is not of Your people Israel comes from a distant land for the sake of Your name—for they shall hear about Your great name and Your mighty hand and Your outstretched arm—when he comes to pray toward this House, oh, hear in Your heavenly abode and grant all that the foreigner asks You for. Thus all the peoples of the earth will know Your name and revere You, as does Your people Israel; and they will recognize that Your name is attached to this House that I have built. (1 Kgs 8:41–43)

Another part of this prayer appears in Chronicles, and may be translated thus:

> Any prayer or supplication offered by all mankind or by all Your people Israel[25]—each of whom knows his affliction and pain—when he spreads forth his hands toward this House,

may You hear in Your heavenly abode, and pardon. (2 Chr 6:29–30)

Let us note carefully the two conditions declared to be essential for the prayer of Gentiles to be heard by God. First, their worship must be in harmony with that of the Israelites, for it is said: "Thus all the peoples of the earth will know Your name and revere You, as does Your people Israel" (2 Chr 6:33). Then, they must acknowledge the priestly mission of the Jews, for the text adds: "And they will recognize that Your name is attached to this House that I have built" (2 Chr 6:33). The first of these conditions presupposes the existence of a code for the Gentiles, not altogether identical to that of Israel (for in that case there would be no grounds for distinguishing Gentile from Jew) but yet linked to it in a way which corresponds exactly to the character of the Noachide code. The second condition is precisely that which Maimonides, following the Talmud, prescribes for Noachide religion if it is to be considered legitimate: that it be regarded not only as a kind of moral philosophy, or even a natural religion, but as the original Revelation, given to the entire human race, whose custody has been confided to Israel.[26]

Universalism in Mosaic Worship

What was the basic aim of the religion which was practiced in Jerusalem, from the orthodox Jewish perspective? On this point as on all others, the school which seems most individual in its character, the most rigorously particularist, offers answers which are both the most audacious and the most comforting. According to Kabbalah, the object of Hebraic religion was to achieve a harmonious relation between this world and the other realms of being, to establish and maintain a reciprocity of life and influence between our earth and the higher worlds. There is little that is self-centered or ethnic, surely, and much that is noble and grand about such a religious conception. The universal religion, as Judaism conceives it, extends even beyond mankind, beyond the earth; it embraces, in fact, the universe, the infinite.

The material expression of this religion of Jerusalem was the sacrifices, which, apart from their justification of a psychological or mystical order, were in keeping with the general ideas and customs of the time. And just as the Gentiles had their own designated place in the

Temple, they were also allowed to participate in its worship by bringing their own sacrifices.

The Mosaic Law itself provided for this participation on the festival of Sukkot, the feast of Tabernacles. This date is significant, for apart from the Sabbath (which we have already discussed in this connection), Sukkot is the only Israelite festival which, according to Scripture, should be celebrated in the Temple by all nations:

> All who survive of all those nations that came up against Jerusalem shall make a pilgrimage year by year to bow low to the King Lord of Hosts and to observe the Feast of Booths. (Zec 14:16)

This prophecy is accompanied by an assertion that those who abstain from observing Sukkot will be punished, and thus (let us note in passing) forms conclusive proof that the Law will remain unchanged even in messianic times.

We can see in this particular provision, as in so many other details of the Law, that universal religion does not, according to the Jewish conception, consist in a pure and simple conversion of the Gentiles to Mosaic Judaism, but rather in their acceptance of the truth of Israel's doctrine, even while they retain their autonomy and freedom in religious practice. This is a crucial point, which cannot be sufficiently emphasized.

It would be rewarding to gather here all the rabbinical commentaries which address this matter of the future observance of Tabernacles. They are important enough to form the substance of a special study. The essential idea is that during the eight days of Sukkot, Israel offered seventy sacrifices of propitiation on the altar at Jerusalem, on behalf of the seventy nations of the earth.[27] The early rabbinical authors, both those who preceded the Christian era and those of later centuries, are in full agreement with respect to the intention and meaning of these sacrifices. (This is most remarkable when we reflect that the later rabbis of this group lived at a time when we might least expect to find such a receptive attitude toward the Gentiles.)

Well! Let us listen to the voice of Israel speaking through its leaders, the disparaged Pharisees. Although the Bible expressly prescribes the sacrifices under discussion, it says nothing about the reasons for them or their significance, thus following its usual practice

311

with respect to this subject. The Pharisees, however, provide such explanations, and in a notably humanitarian spirit. First, let us quote from Leviticus Rabbah, under the name of R. Joshua ben Levi (a Palestinian amora of the third century):

> If the nations of the world had known how useful the Tent of Meeting was to them, they would have surrounded it with tents and fortified camps [in order to protect it].

And in another, quite similar passage:

> If the nations of the world had known how useful the Temple was to them, they would have surrounded it with fortified camps to protect it, for it was more useful to them than to Israel.[28]

A Midrash on Shir ha-Shirim puts the matter in more measured terms but no less explicitly, while broadening its scope:

> "Your eyes are like doves" (Song of Songs 4:1) means that just as the dove (offered at the Temple) atones for everyone, so Israel atones for all peoples, for the seventy calves which were burned on the altar at the feast of Tabernacles were offered on behalf of the nations, in order that their existence might be maintained in this world, which is why it is written "They answer my love with accusation and I must stand judgment" (Ps 109:4), that is, I pray for them.[29]

In treatise Sukkah of the Talmud, we encounter a similar passage:

> R. Jochanan says, "Woe to the Gentiles for what they have lost (in losing the Temple), for when the Temple was standing, atonement was made for them on the altar (by means of the seventy calves offered in sacrifice), but now how will they atone?"[30]

And here are other passages from the Pesikta:

> God says to Israel: "My children, I know that during the seven preceding days of the festival [of Tabernacles], you

were occupied with sacrifices for the peoples of the world; now [Shemini Azeret, the eighth day of the Solemn Assembly], you and I must celebrate together." . . . R. Alexandri told the parable of a king who had the joy [of marrying his son]. During the entire week of feasting, the king's son was busy doing honor to the guests he had invited. When the marriage week was over, the king said to his son: "I know that during this entire week of the marriage festivities, you were occupied with your guests; now you and I must celebrate together." . . . So, too, during the seven days of Tabernacles, Israel occupies itself with sacrifices for the nations of the world, for, says R. Phinehas, all the seventy bullocks which Israel sacrificed during Sukkot were on behalf of the seventy [heathen] nations of the world, that they might not perish for their sins.[31]

The rabbis are unanimous on this point. But here is a matter which deserves special mention. The seventy sacrifices offered during the course of the festival—this number itself is very significant—were distributed among the seven days in such a way that each day there was one less sacrifice offered than the preceding day. There were thirteen the first day, twelve the second, eleven the third, and so on, until the seventh day when seven calves would be burnt. No doubt there was some hidden significance in this ceremonial order. We sometimes find this sentence in the rabbis: "The number of the nations of the world goes on diminishing like that of the calves of the festival."[32] Is this simply the acknowledgement of a fact, or is it the expression of a magnanimous hope? Both hypotheses have been advanced. The first seems consistent with the commentary of Rashi:

> The sacrifices of the festival are seventy in number, and they diminish in number each day. This is a sign of the nations' destruction, but in the time of the Temple, these sacrifices protected them from punishments they had incurred.[33]

Even this simple assertion of a fact emphasizes the humane character of these burnt offerings.

But other commentators have gone farther in this direction, and declared that the decreasing number of sacrifices signifies the gradual disappearance of the various religions, and their metamorphosis into more legitimate systems.[34] We may observe, however, that the number stops at seven, which still endorses the principle of plurality and variety of religions. Judaism recognizes that the worship of God must take diverse forms adapted to the particular genius of each people and the character of its environment, though without compromising the all-embracing oneness, whose guardian and model is Israel.

The universal component in the celebration of Sukkot appears more clearly still when we reflect on the time of year chosen for the festival. This was the moment when the year began.[35] We know that the Jews had two ways of reckoning the year: the month of Nisan, in the spring, solemnized by the commemoration of the leaving of Egypt, marked the start of Israel's own special religious year; the secular year, however, which began in Tishri, was the possession not of the Jews only but of all peoples. As this cycle of months, starting with the autumnal equinox, was the only calendar recognized by the Gentiles, it was natural that Judaism should consecrate it with rituals that were essentially universal in character.

It is curious to see how Christian belief has reached a similar conclusion by a roundabout route. A Protestant theologian who has studied the Christian rites of Easter and Pentecost, and their relation to Passover and Shavuot, affirms:

> With regard to Tabernacles, we still lack a corresponding festival, but when the years are accomplished and we find ourselves at last in the required conditions, we too will solemnly join in celebrating Tabernacles. Mankind's present life, which is a life of wandering in the desert, like that of the Israelites after their departure from Egypt, has a Passover [i.e., *Paques*, which in French means both Passover and Easter] and a Pentecost [the word is used for both Jewish Shavuot and Christian Whitsunday], but not yet a Tabernacles, since this festival was instituted precisely for the commemoration of that life of wandering in the desert. It follows that the Sukkot of the Gentiles cannot be celebrated until the moment of the Resurrection.[36]

From a Jewish perspective, of course, this "moment" would mean the time of the Messiah.

7

Relations between Mosaic Judaism and Noachism; Jerusalem as Capital of the Faithful

*T*he Torah, Israel's own special religious code, is also the source of Jewish universalism. It is important to set forth the precise relationship between these two complementary aspects of Torah: Mosaism and Noachism.

Symmachus has a comment which expresses very well the Jewish doctrine of the necessity of religious diversity. If it is reasonable to suppose that the entire human race in fact worships a single, identical Being, why then, he asks, do there exist so many different forms of worship? "It is because the mystery is so great that it is impossible to reach it by a single path."[1] Nothing could be more true or profound. Monotheism can become universal only with this understanding: unity in diversity, diversity in unity.

Moreover, this variety of forms, apart from the supreme unity to which it is subordinated, constitutes in its totality the universal religion. For the variety is not arbitrary or accidental, but something necessary and organic, with roots in the depths of human nature. Thus religious unity could not be fully represented without the participation of all these diverse aspects which, when viewed separately, seem mutually exclusive.

But some will object that even if this principle of religious diversity is itself valid, this is not at all the same thing as the duality—Mosaism and Noachism—which it seems to us to imply. Should there

315

not rather be as many religious systems as there are ethnic varieties? However, if Mosaism is the priestly law of Israel as Noachism is the law of mankind, it is evident that plurality must be encountered in this second aspect of the Divine Law. The priesthood is the bond which unites the finite to the infinite, earth to heaven, mankind to the totality of the vast universe; and its special code, which is an expression of this transcendent rapport, is different from all others, and represents by itself one of the dimensions of the Law. By contrast, the various other forms of religion, corresponding to differences of race and nationality, all participate in the Noachide Law, of which they form the specific varieties. Together, they stand in the same relation vis-à-vis the priestly law of Israel. Thus we can explain the coexistence of the two laws. The first, in its unity, expresses the relation between mankind and the universe; the other, in its inevitable plurality, has a role which begins and ends on this earth, and has diverse variations which correspond to the diversity of race, place, and time. The philosopher Cantoni reflects this contrast when he points out the existence both of constant and universal laws and of laws which are provisional and mutable. The first of these endure even in the midst of the transformations of the others, "for what is changeable—indeed, the very law of change itself—is as fundamental to human nature as the unchanging."[2]

An earlier thinker, Marsilio Ficino, reproduces the Hebraic thought exactly, though perhaps without suspecting it, when he tells us that

> there is a natural religion, the heritage of mankind [i.e., what we are calling the Noachide code], but all religions have some merit, and the diversity of worship constitutes a harmony and produces the beauty of the moral world.[3]

Moses Mendelssohn distinguished between the Mosaic laws written in the Torah and the eternal truths proceeding from the human reason.[4] According to him, these truths, because they have a rational basis, do not come within the special compass of Jewish revelation. He thus recognizes the double character of the Divine Law, though it may be debatable to make the Mosaic code the special consequence of Revelation, to the exclusion of the eternal truths which issue only from the reason. In fact, the most superficial scrutiny is enough to disclose in this special law of Israel an impressive assemblage of rational and universal laws. Besides, it is hard to see why divine Revelation would occupy itself with simple rules of justice and be silent with respect to more important truths which, we are told, depend upon the human reason. Is the precept to respect the life and property of others, for example, less rational than the doctrine of the immortality of the soul?

But, objects Mendelssohn, if the eternal truths themselves were also part of the Mosaic Revelation, how could Providence be justified for having allowed all the earlier generations to have remained ignorant of them? This argument can turn against its author, however, for even he acknowledges that there are laws of rational ethics in the Mosaic code.

All these difficulties disappear when we take better account of the relations which exist between the two laws. The eternal truths, practical as well as theoretical, are—like the universal Noachide Law—older than the Revelation to Moses. This does not, however, mean that they are not part of it. Indeed, the entire Noachide code is contained in the Mosaic Revelation, at the same time that (from a different perspective) the one is independent of the other. That is why the rabbis assert that there is nothing which is forbidden to the Noachide which is allowed to the Jew.

The fact remains that for Mendelssohn as for us, there is an entire area of the Mosaic law which concerns only the Jews, and is unknown to Noachism: legislation, ritual, forms of worship. But in addition, we find matter which is common to the two codes: natural virtues and rational doctrines. From the philosophical point of view, all this may be summed up in the concept of a double law: the rational and the suprarational, the knowable and the unknowable, the intelligible and the superintelligible. It is the first of these two dimensions which we find in the Noachide Law; it is the second which corresponds to the Torah.

Jerusalem as Religious Center of the World

It is to Jerusalem and the Holy Land that the rabbinic paraphrase of these words of Moses is addressed:[5]

> It is a land which the Lord your God looks after, on which the Lord your God always keeps His eye, from year's beginning to year's end. (Dt 11:12)

The commentators ask, is this to say that God is concerned only with this single corner of the earth? No, they answer, but it is thanks to the

317

special care that He lavishes on the Holy Land that God extends His Providence toward all the other countries.[6]

It seems to us that the strikingly universalist idea which the sages derive from this text, which is apparently so exclusive in its implication, beautifully characterizes the authentic spirit of Judaism. A country which finds itself chosen to be a means of grace and blessing for the entire world, but is in no way licensed to hold others in contempt: This is the dominating concept of the entire Law, written and oral, beginning with Abraham, in whom all races should be blessed, and finishing with the Messiah, who will bring both deliverance for Israel and the knowledge of truth for all peoples.

Let us note at once, however, a fact which is as important as it is peculiar. In the entire Torah, we do not meet a single reference to Jerusalem as future site of the Sanctuary. This site is simply indicated in a general manner as "the site that the Lord your God will choose" (Dt 12:5, 11, 14). But these words prove immediately that the choice of place is not immaterial, since it is not left to chance or human will, but committed to divine selection. As happens so often in biblical narratives, so too here, human preference must accommodate itself to providential design.

But does the Torah not seem unaware or uncomprehending of the history of Jerusalem and the claims which that city would be able to assert in order to become the religious center of Israel? Hardly. Apart even from prophetic inspiration, it was natural to foresee that during the entire very long period of the conquest, the site of national worship could not be established at Jerusalem, but rather in the places which circumstance must dictate in turn. Thus the sacred author had necessarily to use an expression which would authenticate the veneration due to those places where the Tabernacle must provisionally be set up, at the same time that it would eventually sanctify the legitimacy of worship in the permanent capital of Israel. Furthermore, Maimonides points out that it was important to avoid anything that could be an occasion for jealousy among the tribes of Israel at a time when it was more than ever necessary to maintain harmony among them.[7]

It is reasonable to suppose that Oral Tradition had already designated Jerusalem as the city most worthy of this distinction, and that Moses had given instructions in this sense to his closest confidants, as there are good grounds for believing he did with respect to many other matters. As we read in Exodus after the victory achieved over Amalek at Rephidim:

> Then the Lord said to Moses, "Inscribe this in a document as
> a reminder, and read it aloud to Joshua: I will utterly blot out
> the memory of Amalek from under heaven!" (Ex 17:14)

To write in a document and to read to Joshua seem two quite different things. What must be written down would be either the account of events or the fate in store for Amalek; but the specific directions would have to be specially devised for the instruction of the man who would have the responsibility of executing the divine decree. In all probability, this is how we ought to understand the words relating to "the site that the Lord your God will choose."

We notice, moreover, that in the promises made to Abraham, the Bible observes the same silence with regard to the Holy Land in general.

> Go forth from your native land and from your father's house
> to the land that I will show you. (Gn 12:1)

Abraham immediately heads toward Canaan, although no specific mention has been made of that land.

The same thing happens at the moment of the sacrifice which God asks of the Patriarch in order to test him.

> Take your son, your favored one, Isaac, whom you love, and
> go to the land of Moriah, and offer him there as a burnt
> offering on one of the heights which I will point out to you.
> (Gn 22:2)

Yet Abraham, apparently without receiving any other instruction, knew from afar the mountain to which he must lead Isaac.

Similarly, it is surprising to hear Solomon, in his magnificent prayer, speak of Jerusalem in the *past* tense, just as the Torah does when it is a question of the mysterious place destined to become the seat of divine worship, as if the choice of this city had been fixed for all time.

This indeed is what is most remarkable: that in the Torah itself, the secret designation of Jerusalem and of the Temple is not always in the future. We are struck by these words in the Song of the Exodus:

> You will bring them and plant them in Your own mountain,
> The place You made Your abode, O Lord,

The sanctuary, O Lord, which Your hands established. (Ex
15:17)

But if we object that what we have here is a poetic image, we shall
recall another passage:

I am sending an angel before you to guard you on the way
and to bring you to the place which I have made ready. (Ex
23:20)

There is, then, nothing of chance or arbitrary choice in the election of Jerusalem to be the religious center. It is the divine will intervening directly when that becomes necessary, or, indeed, an old tradition
which has ordained the choice in advance.

If we search in vain in the Torah for an explicit reference to
Jerusalem as the future capital, this simply shows that in the thought of
the ancient Hebrews, the city had long been destined to play its imposing role. It is actually described as the site of worship of the true God
even before the appearance of Israel in the midst of the moral and
religious ruins which paganism had accumulated on all sides. The Jews
believe that their first ancestor and the father of the faithful, Abraham,
had acknowledged the legitimacy of the worship celebrated at Jerusalem and had paid homage to it by honoring its high priest and by
invoking God under the very name by which He was called in that
place, *El Elyon*, "Most High God." Renan, speaking of the ancient
inhabitants of Palestine, recognized that when Abraham arrived there,
he did not find himself the first of his race, since he encountered a
Semitic chief there, like himself a monotheist: Melchizedek, with
whom he contracted an alliance.

Whatever may be the case, it is certain that the Bible gives us
Jerusalem as the location of authentic worship even while it still belongs to the Gentiles. Far from reluctant to endorse this biblical axiom
which is scarcely likely to flatter Jewish self-esteem, the rabbis, with
great daring, emphasize the holiness of Gentile Jerusalem as well as the
knowledge which the Gentiles had of its glorious destiny. In a remarkable passage, Nachmanides says:

Salem is *Jerusalem*. For it is written, "Salem became His abode"
(Ps 76:3), and even in the time of Joshua, its king was called
Adoni Tsedek, "My Lord of Justice," for from that time the

Gentiles knew that this place was the most august of all, that it was at the center of the inhabited world; and Tradition had taught them that it corresponds in this world to the celestial Temple where Divine Majesty, called *Tsedek*, resides.[8]

But how can we be sure that Salem is the same as Jerusalem? The one name is, of course, contained in the other. When the first element *Jeru* is added to the name *Salem*, it is easy to recognize the name which Abraham gave to the place where Isaac was to have been sacrificed: "And Abraham named that site *Adonai-Yireh*," that is, "the Lord will see" (Gn 22:14).

Thus, according to the etymology provided by the rabbis, we have in *Jerusalem* the *Yireh* of Abraham and the *Salem* of Melchizedek. It is a double word, one part belonging to the Gentiles and the other to Israel. In this collaboration, so to speak, of Israel and mankind, we see an intriguing anticipation of the idea of a universal religion whose capital would be the holy city. According to the sages,

> Abraham called this city *Yireh*, and Shem, the son of Noah, called it Salem. The Holy One, blessed be He, said, "I shall call it by those names which both have given it, that is, *Yireh-Salem*."[9]

We must note, moreover, that the Hebrew name, *Yerushalayim*, is grammatically in the dual number. In certain other names of localities, such as *Kiriathayim* (Gn 14:5) and *Mahanayim* (Gn 32:3), the grammatical dual corresponds to an historical duality. If the same be true of Jerusalem, we may wish to inquire as to the identity of this duality. Perhaps the question is insoluble from an historical perspective, but the religious significance of the doubleness, with both Gentile and Jew contributing to the name of the holy city, cannot be doubted.

What is certain is that the name of the king of Jerusalem in the time of Joshua was *Adoni Tsedek*, essentially the same name as that of the priest *Melchizedek*, king of Salem, except for the substitution of *Adon* for *Melech*. (These two words are basically synonymous, and mean "lord" or "king.") Now we know from Jeremiah that the name of the Messiah will be *Adonai Tsidkenu*, or even simply *Tsidkenu*, "Our Justice": that is, *Tsedek* with the possessive suffix (Jer 23:6). This text, together with another where it is predicted that Jerusalem will be called "city of justice" (Is 1:26), ultimately persuades us that its kings, from Melchizedek until the Messiah, bear a title which contains the name *Tsedek*, "justice," "righteousness." Furthermore, we find the prophet Jeremiah calling Jerusalem by the same name that he predicts for its future king:

> In those days shall Judah be delivered and Israel shall dwell secure. And this is what she shall be called: *Adonai Tsidkenu*. (Jer 33:16)

This name of *Tsedek* appears then as a sort of dynastic title for all the kings of Jerusalem, from the time of Abraham to the era of David, exactly comparable to *Pharaoh* in Egypt and *Abimelech* among the Philistines.

So too, the identification of Salem with Jerusalem emerges from virtually categorical statements in Scripture.

> God has made Himself known in Judah,
> His name is great in Israel;
> Salem became His abode;
> Zion, His den. (Ps 76:2–3)

The parallelism of Hebraic style clearly implies that "Salem" and "Zion" are identical. Elsewhere, we read in connection with the exile of Judah:

> Judah is exiled completely,
> *Shlomim* is carried away captive.[10] (Jer 13:19)

Shlomim, a word which derives from *Salem* or *Shalom*, "peace," "the peaceable," can mean nothing other than Jerusalem, and this plural form recalls the grammatical dual of the Hebrew *Yerushalayim*.

Finally, let us compare the name of the spouse in Song of Songs, *Shulamit*, with that of her "husband" Solomon. The explication which Scripture provides for the name of the son of David is well known:

> But you will have a son who will be a man at rest, for I will give him rest from all his enemies on all sides; Solomon will be his name and I shall confer peace and quiet on Israel in his time. (1 Chr 22:9)

It is natural to suppose that the same idea was intended by the name *Shulamit*, given to the spouse in Song of Songs; and the name evidently has reference also to Jerusalem.

Tsedek and *Shalom*, justice and peace, are two words and two things which are readily associated in the language of the Bible. "Justice and peace embrace" (Ps 85:11).[11]

Since Salem and Jerusalem are but one single and identical city, it is impossible that the Israelites, knowing that the worship of the true God had been established there before the appearance of Abraham, and that their ancestor had paid tribute to this worship and to its great priest, Melchizedek, did not expect to see it chosen as the seat of Mosaic worship precisely because of the ancient titles which called attention to it for this glorious role. And if this be the case, how can we fail to recognize here the evidence of Judaic universalism, since the designation of the city which must be its center draws its *raison d'être* from that city's history as seat of Gentile monotheism? Thus the two religions are based upon a single one. Mosaic monotheism reveals itself to be a continuation of earlier monotheism, and Israel, in making Jerusalem its religious capital, has maintained holy worship in its traditional center.

Conclusion

I

No religion has been more misunderstood, more slandered, than Judaism, and the accusation that it is tainted by a narrow national particularism has often been flung at it by its enemies and detractors. The revelation on Sinai, we are told, is unworthy of a God of sovereign goodness. Exclusive religious privileges given to a single people to the prejudice of all others are said to constitute the most flagrant of injustices. It is indeed intolerable that a wise, impartial Creator should act like a capricious, unfeeling father, who enriches his favorite child by depriving all the rest!

I hope I do not delude myself in claiming that the present work, with all its accumulated proofs to the contrary, should have laid this unfair accusation to rest once and for all. In Parts One and Two, we have established that Hebraic beliefs relating to the God of Israel, and those which treat man and the organization of human society, provide all the essential elements of a substantially universal religion. The idea that Judaism predicates a Divine Law and Revelation as much for Gentiles as for Jews, which we have tried to demonstrate in Part Three, plainly confirms our thesis.

Naturally, these doctrines have powerfully influenced the consciousness which Jews have had of the nature and destiny of their religion. It is appropriate to recall that in the ancient world, Judaism was—from a practical as well as theoretical perspective—the only religion to embody a comprehension of universalism in all aspects of its thought and in all manifestations of its life. In this sense, Judaism puts itself into communion with all mankind; and though it indeed fled from contact with other peoples, who at that time often lived in a state of degradation, it separated itself from them only in order to approach

CONCLUSION

humanity itself, the redeemed humanity of the future, which its exalted conceptions enabled it to glimpse.

No doubt, the entire multitude of Israel were not able to grasp with equal understanding these truths which, even in our own day, remain inaccessible to so many. In the comprehension of every religion there is a natural gradation, corresponding to the intellectual and spiritual development of the believers. This must be particularly true with respect to Judaism, whose doctrines rise infinitely above the plane of mere intellect. It is certain that men like Samuel, David, or Isaiah must have embraced an enormously more elevated conception of Israel's mission than the common folk. But of course we judge the worth of a religion according to the ideas which are achieved by its choicest spirits. It is enough for the eternal honor of Judaism that this ideal, incomparably superior to all that surrounded it, had been preserved at its heart, and that the voice of its Prophets and sages did not stop proclaiming it, despite all hostile circumstances.

And so, while all other peoples of antiquity agreed in recognizing only local deities whose authority did not extend beyond their own frontiers, and thus shared a highly fragmentary conception of God, Judaism alone, from top to bottom, believed in the Unity. And with that single magical word, it brought down from heaven to earth the most precious truths. If God is One, if He is sovereign Master of the universe, as Abraham declared; if there is no place of darkness or of light, of suffering or of joy, where He is not present, as David sang; if to Him alone belong praise and adoration, as Moses and the Prophets repeated—how then would His Providence not be universal? This firm belief of the Jew that his God was the only true God did not allow him to claim that other peoples had no part in His paternal solicitude.

But for Judaism, unity is not only of God; it is also of the world and of the entire human race. The image of divinity on earth, the partner of the Creative Spirit, is not the Jew: it is man. Moreover, long before Abraham's divine call, at the very beginnings of the world, the Bible shows us God as concerned with the destiny of the human race which He had created; and when Noah arrives—the just man, as the Bible calls him—he is honored with special revelations, new laws are given to him, and God concludes a solemn covenant with him and all his descendants (Gn 9:8–17). In the very story of Abraham, a certain remarkable, nearly enigmatic person makes a brief appearance, but what light he sheds! From the shadowy depths of the pagan world, from the heart of that corruption and error which already prevailed everywhere, here, in the person of Melchizedek, is an unmistakable trace in heathendom of an ancient and honorable institution, a worship, a monotheistic priesthood, superior even to that of the Hebrew Patriarch, since Abraham receives the benediction of this priest of *El Elyon*, Master of heaven and earth, the most universal God conceivable (Gn 14:18–20). Not only has the Bible preserved the recollection of this memorable encounter, but when it relates the call of Abraham and the resulting election of Israel, it recognizes explicitly that these events have taken place only for the sake of the entire human race:

> And all the families of the earth
> Shall bless themselves by you. (Gn 12:3, 28:14)

The Jew whose spirit was open to the influences which his religion continually exerted upon him thus had the deep-seated conviction that he was submitting to a God who was Creator and Father of all men, and that the faith of Israel was the center, the focus toward which converged, like so many spokes of a wheel, the beliefs of other peoples. He was persuaded that in the great mass of humanity of which he was part and parcel, he had a special role to fill. The roles which the other peoples were called upon to perform in their respective domains were usually enacted without their knowledge. What did the Hellenic world suspect of its own mission? The Jew, however, in order to be equal to his task, must be fully aware of what it is. He found himself in possession of a Law which, in its most exalted conception, identifies itself with the very law of the universe, thus expressing the highest conceivable form of universalism. But from the perspective of intelligent life, this Law is essentially human, both because it may be supposed to have been born with the first man, and because it is intended to educate the entire human race, and because, finally, it appears constantly in the course of history by way of regular and uninterrupted revelation directed to the reason, conscience, and heart of humanity.

Mosaism itself appears as a single episode of this revelation. It marks the most important stage, however, for in the special code which it brought to Israel for the accomplishment of its mission, it also sanctified the Noachide Law, the authentic catholic law or universal religion.

CONCLUSION

II

But how was the Israelite able to reconcile the simultaneous existence of two laws, one proper for Gentiles, the other for Jews, which might be thought of as two sacred religions or two equally legitimate churches?

It was not simply a matter of difference between national religions. Judaism is so little an ethnic religion that Israel alone—that is, a minute part of the Semitic peoples—accepted it; but, on the other hand, a pagan, whatever his race might be, could enter it freely and would then find himself subject to all its obligations, exactly like a Jew from birth. Judaism is so little a local cult that (with the exception of certain regulations relating to the land) it accompanies the Jew to whatever region of the earth he may settle. And yet, far from feeling obliged to convert non-Jews to his practices, he confines himself to preaching to them that *universal religion* whose establishment on earth was, in a sense, the purpose of his own existence. The phenomenon was unique, the problem challenging.

We are undoubtedly in a better position than the ancient Hebrews to form a clear opinion in the matter, for we can tap two springs. We can study not only the original doctrines themselves, but also the interpretations which the most authentic spokesmen of the Synagogue have never ceased to provide. And that is precisely what we have tried to accomplish in this book. The reader who has followed its development carefully will recognize that the key to the question will be found in the opening of the speech which God puts in the mouth of Moses addressing Pharaoh:

Then you shall say to Pharaoh, "Thus says the Lord: Israel is My first-born son." (Ex 4:22)

This title of "firstborn," far from excluding the other children of the Heavenly Father, to the contrary presupposes them. Mankind is conceived as a great family of which God is the supreme Father; and Israel, firstborn among the brother-peoples, was, as in ancient eastern society, the priest of this family, trustee and administrator of holy things, mediator between heaven and earth. He was vested with priestly functions in order to serve all.

In the light of this teaching, we can understand that Judaism is really two doctrines in one. There are two laws, two codes of

327

discipline—in a word, two forms of religion: the lay law, summarized in the seven precepts of the sons of Noah, and the Mosaic or priestly law, whose code is the Torah. The first was destined for all the human race, the second for Israel alone. The one contains only the essential principles of religion and ethics which are in accord with universal reason and conscience; the other, with its dogmas, rites, and priestly precepts, responds to the mystical needs of humanity. It is one Eternal Law, apprehended from two perspectives.

Such is the meaning of the election of Israel. This people was chosen to fill the distinguished office of teacher, preacher, priest to the nations; and the nations in their turn would value Israel for the high merits of its Patriarchs but also for its natural predisposition to welcome religious truth, its essentially monotheistic genius, and above all, that firm, tenacious, indomitable character which was required to resist the pagan world, to vanquish and convert it.

A grand privilege, to be sure, but a dangerous one. How much in tears, blood, suffering, contention, and scorn has it not exacted from those who have received it! And yet, so profound and powerful is the sense of justice which inspires the sages of the Synagogue, that according to them, this crown of thorns was placed on the head of Israel only after God had offered His Law to all the other peoples of the earth. And by a sublime anachronism, they impose upon Mosaic times the situation of the world at the time of the Roman domination, and imagine that it was first of all to Rome itself that God proposed the privileges of the great religious mission.

> I would accept it [said Edom],[1] but what is that which is written in your Law? "Thou shalt not kill." That would not be convenient to me, for it is by my sword that I live.

And it is thus that after having knocked at all doors, and receiving only negative responses, God turned to Israel, who accepted the glorious but arduous task of preserving the world's truth.[2]

History has confirmed the profundity of this rabbinical allegory. The vocation of Israel is endorsed with the divine seal. It is simple fact that this small, obscure people, scorned and detested by the Gentiles, with neither the science of Greece, the power of Rome, nor even the prestige of extreme antiquity (since by contrast with the ancient peoples of the East, it can claim only a relatively recent origin), today sees its religion, Scriptures, traditions, and holy places the objects of universal veneration. Even more astonishing, its very name is fought over by peoples of altogether different race, who formerly professed the most diverse religions, and all of whom have remade themselves to a certain extent according to the pattern traced in Israel, each claiming to be the genuine Israel. Semites and Aryans, orientals and occidentals, simple peoples and highly civilized ones, Roman Catholics and Protestants and Mohammedans—all exert themselves to reproduce, each in its own way, the biblical prototype. And beneath the extreme variety of forms, we can distinguish the common denominator which unites them all: the conviction that they are the legitimate heirs of a chosen people.

Shall we say that this circumstance, which seems to be one of the foremost triumphs of Hebraic ideas, is due to Jesus or Mohammed? Such a conclusion would be justified neither by historic truth nor by the principles of social evolution. Jesus, certainly, had no notion of setting himelf up as founder of a religious movement to be created in his name. Nor does the Prophet or his teaching have greater claim to our attention in this matter, however considerable we reckon his role, like that of Jesus, to have been.

As mankind develops and acquires a better understanding of the working-out of divine revelation, it becomes clearer that though the sudden appearance of truth among men is perhaps a convenient hypothesis, it does not correspond to psychological reality of any kind. God does not proceed in an arbitrary or capricious way, but, rather, things hold together logically, and history is a continuum. What may seem to us a beginning is really a consequence. Men whom we think of as innovators proclaiming a new covenant in place of the old, which is now declared out-of-date, have themselves received impetus from their milieu. We must seek the determining cause of their activity and success in an earlier religious tradition, which they echo with more or less fidelity. Without a healthy and fruitful tree, the fruits we admire could never have been gathered.

So behind Christianity and Islam, with their grandeurs as well as their blemishes, behind Jesus and Mohammed, we find Judaism, with its sacred Law, its blueprint for mankind, it hopes for renewal and universal brotherhood. How different the world would have been if, instead of attaching itself almost exclusively to the problematical personage of Jesus, erecting thus a new mythology on the ruins of the old ones, Christianity had seized and adapted the truths of Hebraism (which the Nazarene, a good Jew who did not dream of founding a rival church, undoubtedly wished to propagate)—if instead of rupturing the natural ties which ought to unite it with Israel, it had worked, together with Israel, to create a great human family whose various peoples are equally dear to the Father in Heaven! How much blood would have been spared. How many painful pages could be torn from the book of history. And how right Judaism has been, in the face of so much shame, so much abuse of power, of iniquitous wars which have ravaged our land, to maintain its protest against the unjustified claims of the religions which have issued from it: "No, no, you are hardly the messianism which I preach and await. You have not given substance to the ideals of my Prophets."

III

After long centuries of prejudices, of hatred and violent persecution, not only at the hands of nonbelievers but also and above all from peoples and religions which make their appeal to the Bible, at last a new era has begun for Judaism. The amends of the Gentile world, foretold by the seers of Israel, have appeared already among thinkers, among philosophers; and the masses, too, are about to be touched by the spirit of tolerance. Thus does the rising sun illuminate first of all the tops of mountains, and its rays extend later into the depths of valleys.

But the changes in mankind's attitude toward the Jews are not limited to these acts of good faith and simple justice. They have assumed, in fact, a more genuinely religious character, if not in their actual motives then at least in their remarkable correspondence with ancient Hebrew prophecies. If Israel has not yet, until this day, been brought back to its ancestral land, this is at least an idea which is making its way, and we may perhaps perceive its true meaning in this modification of public opinion with regard to a restoration of the Jewish nation.[3]

Besides, no attentive observer can fail to notice that the evolution of those religions which have sprung from Hebraism is taking place at present in a Jewish spirit, and fully justifies the age-old attitude of Israel with regard to the ancient Christian dogmas. It has reached the point where some have advocated a coming-together of faiths—a growing sentiment, which always has a place for the people of the Bible. This is a meaningful and encouraging sign.

Thus, "Israel" and "Humanity" are not at all mutually exclusive

CONCLUSION

terms. The ideas of universal law and national privilege, of justice and predestination, of divine Providence concerned with all men equally and the election of a single people—these ideas are by no means in irreducible opposition, like water and fire. There is no real antagonism between the special Jewish vocation and the unity of mankind, between the Jewish homeland and the brotherhood of nations. The priestly calling of the Jews and universal religion, the Law from Sinai and the Revelation common to all men, meet grandly in a higher synthesis.

If logic counts for something in the world, if historical evolution has lessons to teach us, we must conclude that a religion which bears such fruits, which preaches such doctrines and keeps such an ideal, a religion which—without submitting to hostile influences and diverse *milieux*, embraces all ages, yields neither to antipathies nor to pride nor to passions of any sort, but instead speaks steadily the language of reason, of justice, of truth—such a religion must be the greatest of miracles, the miracle par excellence, the one which makes possible and explains all the others.

Have courage, then, people of God. Hold firmly to your faith in the truth which has been entrusted to you. Surrounded by passion and error, you have always found in your pure ideals reasons to fight on and incentives to keep hoping. You have triumphed peaceably over attacks, traps, persecutions. Continue to refute fallacy with the teaching of your simple and luminous Law. If the learned men of today persist in condemning you, you must make your appeal to the wise men of tomorrow. The past has shown you right; the future too will justify your immortal hopes and the predictions of your Prophets.

Notes

FOREWORD

1. The volume was dedicated, in Hebrew and French, to the author's son Alexandre, "young man of great promise, rabbinical student, who died in the flowering of his life at Leghorn in 1878."

2. In his *Avant-Propos* to the original edition, the Grand Rabbi of France acknowledges the editorial contribution of Aimé Pallière "and the worthy editors of this work." At the same time, he credits "the author's son [Emmanuel Benamozegh] and worthy successor, Dr. Samuel Colombo," with bringing the volume to publication. Perhaps these last are also the "worthy editors" who assisted Pallière.

3. *Avant-Propos* to Elijah Benamozegh, *Israël et l'Humanité*, new ed. (Paris: Albin Michel, 1961), pp. 7–8.

TRANSLATOR'S INTRODUCTION

1. *Encyclopaedia Judaica*, s.v. "Morgenthau."

2. Most of this paragraph is drawn from *Encyclopaedia Judaica*, s.v. "Leghorn."

3. For a useful survey of Italian-Jewish history and culture, see David Ruderman, "At the Intersection of Cultures: The Historical Legacy of Italian Jewry," in *Gardens and Ghettos*, ed. Vivian B. Mann (Berkeley: University of California Press, 1989), pp. 1–23.

4. "I cannot be indifferent to anything human." The saying is ascribed to Terence.

5. See *Encyclopaedia Judaica*, s.v. "Benamozegh."

6. See also his *Lettera apologetica* to the rabbis of Damascus (Leghorn: Benamozegh, 1865), and *Tzori Ghil'ad*, his apology to the rabbis

of Jerusalem, in *Kevod ha-Levanon* (Paris, 1871). For details, see A. Guetta's "Bibliografia."

7. "Israel and Humanity; study on the problem of universal religion and its solution."

8. See *Israël et l'Humanité*, new ed. (1961), p. 7.

9. *Israël et l'Humanité*, new ed. (1961), p. 10.

10. See the bibliography in Jéhouda's edition of Benamozegh's *Morale juive et morale chrétienne* (1946). Guetta's more recent bibliography of Benamozegh's publications and MSS does not seem to include this MS. A thorough examination of all the MSS—not least, the MS of the present work—is much needed, and their availability for scholarly study needs to be clarified.

11. *Israël et l'Humanité, Démonstration du cosmopolitanisme dans les dogmes, les lois, le culte, la vocation, l'histoire, et l'idéal de l'hébraïsme. Introduction* (Leghorn: Benamozegh, 1885).

12. A. Guetta, "Elia Benamozegh: Bibliografia," *Rassegna Mensile di Israel* 53 (1987): 72.

13. See below, Pt. 2, chap. 3, p. 168.

14. See, e.g., the writings of Eduard von Hartmann, Joseph Salvador, et al. Cf. Jéhouda's remark, in his Preface to *Morale juive et morale chrétienne* (1946), p. 11: "Successor of Salvador, Benamozegh sought to re-establish the lost basis of universal religion."

15. Quoted in A. Lichtenstein, *The Seven Laws of Noah* (New York: Rabbi Jacob Joseph School Press, 1981), p. 7.

16. Moshe Idel, *Kabbalah/New Perspectives* (New Haven: Yale University Press, 1988), p. 14.

17. See Glossary, below, s.v. "Kabbalah," "Malkhut," "Pleroma," "Sefirot," "Tiferet," "Yihud ha-Shem," "Zohar."

18. *Encyclopaedia Judaica*, s.v. "Benamozegh."

19. Idel, *Kabbalah*, p. 13; also p. 283. In addition, see Gershom Scholem, *Kabbalah* (New York: Quadrangle, 1974), p. 202.

20. See below, Pt. 1, chap. 1, pp. 78–79.

21. See below, Pt. 1, chap. 1 n. 1.

22. See below, Pt. 1, chap. 1, p. 71.

23. See below, Pt. 1, chap. 1, p. 72.

24. See below, Pt. 1, chap. 1, p. 73.

25. See below, Pt. 1, chap. 1, p. 75.

26. See below, Pt. 1, chap. 1, pp. 74–75.

27. See below, Pt. 1, chap. 1, p. 79.

NOTES

28. For an early form of the concept, see the apocryphal Book of Jubilees 7:22 (1st cent. B.C.E.), cited by Robert Gordis, *Jewish Ethics for a Lawless World* (New York: Jewish Theological Seminary of America, 1986), pp. 63–64. See also Tosefta Avodah Zarah 8:4–8.

29. *Hilkhot Melakhim* 9.1, 10.

30. *Hilkhot Melakhim* 8.10–11.

31. See, e.g., *Biblical Archaeology Review* 12 (1986): 47–63.

32. Gordis, *Jewish Ethics for a Lawless World*, p. 65.

33. See below, Introduction, p. 48.

34. See below, Conclusion, p. 331.

35. William Wolf, "Judaism and Christianity in the Light of Noachism," *Judaism* 13 (1964): 220.

36. Quoted by Pallière in his Preface. See below, p. 31.

37. *Israël et l'Humanité*, new ed. (1961), p. 9. Béziers was the site of Jewish settlement as early as C.E. 990. Two hundred Jews are said to have been killed there during the Albigensian massacre in 1209.

38. See A. Lichtenstein, "Who Cares about the Seven Laws of Noah? A Status Report," *Jewish Law Association Studies* [Boston University School of Law] 4 (1990): 181–190.

39. Preface to *Morale juive et morale chrétienne* (1946), p. 10.

40. Paul Vulliaud dissents from this assessment. In *La Kabbale Juive* (Paris: Nourry, 1923), Vol. I, pp. 515–516, he criticizes Benamozegh as "antichrétienne."

41. William Blake, *Marriage of Heaven and Hell*, plate 14.

PREFACE TO THE FIRST EDITION (1914)

1. Guglielmo Lattes, *Vita e opere di Elia Benamozegh* (Leghorn: Belforte, 1901), p. 20.

2. Elie Benamozegh, *Morale juive et morale chrétienne* (Paris: Kauffmann, 1867), pp. 5–6.

3. Yehuda Coriat, *Ma'or va-shemesh* (Leghorn: Ottolenghi, 1839), Preface.

4. Benamozegh, *Lettere dirette a S. D. Luzzatto* (Leghorn, Benamozegh, 1890), p. 78. Samuel David Luzzatto (1800–1865), scholar and poet, was a dominating figure in Jewish intellectual life of nineteenth-century Italy, like Benamozegh. Their differences with respect to Kabbalah and other matters formed the subject of this correspondence and other publications.

5. Pallière's note: "See Benamozegh's 'Tzori Ghil'ad,' *Kevod ha-*

NOTES

Levanon (supplement to *Ha-Levanon*), numbers 14 *et seq.* (Paris, 1871), a successful defense of his *'Em La-Mikra* (Leghorn: Benamozegh, 1862), addressed to the chief rabbis of Jerusalem. It appeared in the journal *Ha-Levanon* after repeated invitations from a number of Palestinian missionaries. See also Benamozegh's French preface to Rabbi Eliahu Hazan's *Zikhron Yerushalayim* (Leghorn: Benamozegh, 1874)." *'Em la-Mikra* ("The Scriptural Text Itself") is a five-volume philosophical and philological commentary on the Torah. In his preface to *Zikhron Yerushalayim*, Benamozegh praises R. Hazan's work in terms that reveal his own perspective (p. 1):

> Enlightened religion, which takes account of scientific ideas, which seeks to persuade and not merely to gain advocates, is all the more welcome when it comes to us from the land which has given us everything, from Palestine, from Jerusalem, our dear and holy mother.

Having himself been condemned by Palestinian rabbis, Benamozegh was perhaps not reluctant to express approval of this work by a sympathetic rabbi of Jerusalem. At the end of this preface, Benamozegh speaks of the accusations against his own book, inspired "by some excessively zealous rabbis of Aleppo" with respect to "certain propositions in their view equivocal and smelling of heresy." He mentions his apologia, "Tzori Ghil'ad," and affirms that he is "in perfect accord with the ancient Israelite orthodoxy."

6. Pallière's note: "When in 1902 and 1903 Frederick Delitzsch presented, at the Singakademie in Berlin, before the emperor and empress of Germany, his two well-known lectures entitled *Babel and Bible*, in which he sought to show that Hebrew law and civilization were but a late version of the civilization and law of Assyria and Babylonia, there were distinguished critics, both German and foreign, such as J. Barth, Fr. Hommel, Alfred Jeremias, D. R. Kittel, M. Knieschke, and many others, to demonstrate the weakness of his conclusions. But it is equally true that a large number of persons, believers and nonbelievers, learned men and ignorant, were profoundly shaken, as though Delitzsch had made a discovery which could ruin the foundations of religion, or at least cause anxiety. Yet those who were familiar and in agreement with the doctrines of Elijah Benamozegh were not at all taken aback, prepared as they were for certain objections. In fact, they even found in Delitzsch's conclusions new and powerful argu-

335

NOTES

ments in support of their faith in the spirit which inspires the entire Hebrew tradition. See Dr. S. Colombo, *Nozze Cave-Franco* (Leghorn: Belforte, 1904)."

7. *Paradiso* 9.139–141. Text and translation from edition of Charles S. Singleton, Bollingen Series LXXX (Princeton: Princeton University Press, 1975).

8. This and the preceding paragraph appear in the French editions as a footnote.

INTRODUCTION

1. Benamozegh uses the word *Tradition* to denote the "Oral Torah," i.e., Talmud and Midrash. "Hebraism" is for him a more comprehensive term than "Judaism," embracing Oral Torah and Kabbalah as well as Tanakh and its tradition. It must be noted, however, that he is not altogether consistent in his distinction between the two words, sometimes using "Judaism" when we would expect "Hebraism." See Pt. 1, chap. 1, n. 1.

2. Benamozegh may have in mind the controversial assertion of Papal Primacy and Infallibility by the first Vatican Council in 1870.

3. Eduard von Hartmann, *La Religion de l'avenir*, trans. from the German (Paris: Baillière, 1881), p. 9. Hartmann (1842–1906), a prolific German philosopher, is invoked by Benamozegh several times.

4. See, e.g., Megillah 15a, Yoma 9b.

PART ONE, CHAPTER 1

1. Pallière's note: "We have thought it proper to respect the meaning which Benamozegh gives to the word 'Hebraism,' which, as we shall see further on, he uses to designate 'the totality of Judaism,' including, as authentic embodiments, the Written and Oral Law—i.e., the Bible and Oral Tradition—as well as the Kabbalah, which is the highest theological expression of both."

2. Benamozegh's note: "We know in fact too little about nature to be able to speak of the supernatural. We ourselves have always asserted, notably in the *Credo* of our *Teologia dogmatica e apologetica* (Leghorn: Vigo, 1877), that miracles enter perfectly into the domain of nature. If it is true that yesterday's utopia can become tomorrow's reality, it is also true what may today appear to be outside the laws of

nature may eventually be embraced by these laws as the result of a deeper understanding of what nature is."

3. Ernest Renan, *L'Église chrétienne*, vol. 6 of *Histoire des origines du christianisme* (Paris: Michel Lévy, 1879), pp. 63–64. Benamozegh had considerable respect for Renan, quotes him often, and corresponded with him.

4. See Abraham Kuenen, *The Religion of Israel to the Fall of the Jewish State*, vol. 1 (London, 1874), p. 277.

5. See, e.g., Sigmund Freud, *Moses and Monotheism*, trans. Katherine Jones (London, 1939).

6. Pallière's note: "We substitute the expressions *Dieu Un* and *Dieu Unique* for the excessively scholastic ones of the author: *unité ad intra* and *unité ad extra.*" *Dieu Un* is here translated "the unity of God" and *Dieu Unique* "the uniqueness of God."

7. Compare the New Translation of the Jewish Publication Society ("JPS 2") (Philadelphia, 1985): "Hear, O Israel! The Lord is our God, the Lord alone."

8. Leone Modena (1571–1648) was an Italian rabbi, scholar, and poet. See his *Magen va-Herev*, ed. S. Simonsohn (Jerusalem, 1960).

9. The Tetragrammaton is the sacred four-letter name of God (JHVH), which Jews are ordinarily forbidden to pronounce. It suggests the meaning "Being." When it occurs in the Bible or elsewhere, it is pronounced *Adonai*. Benamozegh often uses an alternative form, *Avaya* (i.e., *ha-Vaya*). The usual English translation is "Lord" or "Eternal."

10. Pallière's note: "This is one of the conclusions of William James's remarkable book, *The Varieties of Religious Experience* (New York: Collier Macmillan, 1961 [1902]), p. 408."

11. The reference is presumably to Moses ben Jacob Ibn Ezra (ca. 1070–ca. 1138), Spanish philosopher, linguist, and poet.

12. Benamozegh's note: "Notice the words derived from roots belonging to the same group: *berit*, covenant or alliance, on account of the practise of cutting the sacrificial victim in two; *bar*, son, because he has been born of his parents, and in Aramaic, *bar*, outside; *bor*, excavated well, excavation; and the verbs *bara*, *barar*, to express the act of distinguishing or separating one thing from another."

13. Compare Midrash Bereshit Rabbah 97.3. See translation of Midrash Rabbah by H. Freedman and Maurice Simon, 10 vols. (London: Soncino, 1983 [3rd ed.]). See also *Pesikta de-Rab Kahana*, Piska 6. (See below, Pt. 1, chap. 4, n. 11.)

NOTES

14. The Greek name *Pan*, god of shepherds, hunters, and country folk, means "all, every." *Monad* is a philosophical term meaning a unit, something simple and indivisible.

15. "Make two cherubim of gold—make them of hammered work—at the two ends of the cover. Make one cherub at one end and the other cherub at the other end; of one piece with the cover shall you make the cherubim at its two ends. The cherubim shall have their wings spread out above, shielding the cover with their wings. They shall confront each other, the faces of the cherubim being turned toward the cover."

16. Benamozegh's note: "Sacrifices are represented in Scripture as the bread of God (*lehem*), and the altar as His table: these are gross anthropomorphisms in the context of the spirituality of the God of Israel, and they cannot be explained without kabbalistic doctrine. On the other hand, the sages also call the table of man an altar; for there too is performed a transformation, an elevation of the inferior substance, which becomes sustenance for the higher being, and thus rises a degree. This is why those who offered sacrifices ate a certain portion of them, and in thus cooperating in the consumption of the sacrifice, became the sharers and fellows, as it were, of God. Originally, all sacrifice was a meal, and every meal was a sacrifice. This explains why Jews cannot eat meat unless they have made of the animal itself a kind of consecrated sacrifice. Here also is the true reason for the laws of eating, the prohibition of certain foods. It is because man, too, in his own way, is an altar: in eating he accomplishes a function not only physiological but cosmic, and in a way theological. We can thus see how false, how antiscientific, is the maxim 'it is not what enters the mouth of a man that defiles him but rather what goes out'—as if the consumption of food were a trivial and unimportant act!"

17. Zohar I, 28b–29a. The Zohar ("Book of Splendor") is the principal text of Kabbalism. It was given to the world in the second half of the thirteenth century by a Spanish author named Moses ben Shemtov de Leon (ca. 1250–1305). See the incomplete English translation of Harry Sperling and Maurice Simon, 5 vols. (London: Soncino, 1931–1934; second ed., 1984), and the selections translated by Daniel Matt in *Zohar: The Book of Enlightenment*, Classics of Western Spirituality (New York: Paulist Press, 1983).

18. *Pirke de-Rabbi Eliezer*, chap. 40. See the translation by Gerald Friedlander (New York: Sepher-Hermon, 1981 [1916]), pp. 312–313.

19. See, e.g., Gittin 57b, Sanhedrin 96b.

20. Sanhedrin 91b, Pesahim 119a.

21. Pallière's note: "For those who may be surprised by such an expression, it is necessary to say that there is such a thing as a theology of freemasonry in the sense that there exists in freemasonry a secret philosophical and religious doctrine, introduced by the Rosicrucian gnostics at the time of their fusion with the freemasons in 1717. This secret doctrine, or gnosis, is the exclusive prerogative of those freemasons on the highest levels, or philosophical masons." A fairly recent study of this subject is Abrahão Federman, *Maçonaria, Teosofia e Religião* (São Paulo, 1973 [1960]).

22. Benamozegh here reflects the widespread nineteenth-century condescension toward hasidim as miracle-workers.

23. Émile Louis Burnouf, in *Revue des Deux Mondes*, second period, 38th year (1 May 1868). Burnouf (1821–1907) is cited several times by Benamozegh. He was the author of *La Science des religions* (Paris, 1876).

PART ONE, CHAPTER 2

1. Pallière's note: "*Makom*, from the root *qom*, to stand, *Ma'on*, from the root *on*, to reside. The expression of Malebranche's which has been so justly admired—'Dieu est le lieu des esprits comme l'espace est le lieu des corps' [God is the place of spirit as space is the place of body]—merely reproduces an idea familiar to the Bible and to the Rabbis."

2. Compare *Encyclopedia of Philosophy*, vol. 7 (New York: Macmillan, 1967), p. 533.

3. JPS 2: "For I the Lord your God am an impassioned God."

4. *Geography* 16.2.35: "An Egyptian priest named Moses, who possessed a portion of the country called the Lower [Egypt] . . . being dissatisfied with the established institutions there, left it and came to Judaea with a large body of people who worshiped the Divinity. He declared and taught that the Egyptians and Africans entertained erroneous sentiments, in representing the Divinity under the likeness of wild beasts and cattle of the field; that the Greeks also were in error in making images of their gods after the human form. For God [said he] may be this one thing which encompasses us all, land and sea, which we call heaven, or the universe, or the nature of things." See *The Geography of Strabo*, trans. H. C. Hamilton and W. Falconer, vol. 3 (London, 1916), pp. 177–179. Strabo (1st cent. B.C.E.) was the most important geographer of antiquity.

NOTES

5. Raffaele Mariano, *Cristianesimo, cattolicismo e civiltà* (Bologna, 1879), p. 176.

6. Pallière's note: "In verse 7, the contrast is between *shalom* (peace, happiness) and *ra*, which can denote moral evil as well as calamity. According to the principles of Hebrew parallelism, it is the second of these two senses which is relevant in this passage."

7. JPS 2: "Only among you is God."

8. Benamozegh's note: "We must note that in this verse, the comparative 'there is none like Me' appears in conjunction with the superlative 'there is none else' and consequently has the same meaning. It is erroneous to claim that passages like this one, in which a comparison seems to be set up between the God of Israel and other divinities, prove that Judaism, in proclaiming its God superior to all others, thus tacitly admits the existence of other deities."

9. JPS 2: "O Lord of Hosts, / Enthroned on the Cherubim!"

10. Benamozegh's note: "It is thus that these words ought to be translated and not as 'Everlasting God,' as is sometimes done [e.g., JPS 2]. *Elohei Kedem*, 'God of old,' 'God of ancient years,' is more likely to be used to denote His antiquity."

11. Benamozegh's note: "Rashi remarks, in this connection, that the verb meaning 'make' [*asah*] can also mean 'possess.' [See Rashi's gloss on Gn 12:5 and 14:19.] Calling God 'possessor' of the world, in the Hebrew idiom, may suggest that He formed it from chaos. He would therefore have appeared from the start as God the savior, the Aeon Messiah of the gnostic pleroma, the redeemer of the world and of the Aeon Church." See Gershom Scholem, *Kabbalah* (New York: Quadrangle, 1974), p. 21: "In these stages of Jewish mysticism, the descriptions of the Chariot and its world occupy a place which in non-Jewish Gnosticism is filled by the theory of the 'aeons,' the powers and emanations of God which fill the *pleroma*, the divine 'fullness.' The way in which certain *middot*, or qualities of God, like wisdom, understanding, knowledge, truth, faithfulness, righteousness, etc., became the 'aeons' of the Gnostics is paralleled in the tradition of the *ma'aseh bereshit*, although it did not penetrate the basic stages of Merkabah mysticism." Scholem provides exhaustive explanations of all these kabbalistic and gnostic terms. See also the Glossary in the present volume.

12. Benamozegh's note: "The words 'let him dwell in the tents of Shem' (Gn 9:27) can refer to God as well as to Japheth. Although Onkelos, Rashi, Ibn Ezra, and Nachmanides adhere to the first interpretation, we follow the ancient Sages in preferring the second. Gene-

NOTES

sis Rabbah and the two Talmuds mention both, and the Yerushalmi sees here the declaration of the conversion of Japheth's children and their entrance into the tents, or synagogues, of Shem."

13. JPS 2: "For I the Lord your God am an impassioned God."

14. "These things made of wood and plated with gold or silver are like stones from the mountain, and those who attend them will be put to shame. Why then should anyone think them gods, or call them so?" (Bar 6:39–40; see all of chap. 6.) Translation from Edgar J. Goodspeed, trans., *The Apocrypha* (New York: Random House, 1959).

15. JPS 2: "For the Lord your God is God supreme and Lord supreme."

16. See Pt. 1, chap. 1, n. 9.

17. See pp. 66–67 above.

18. E. du Bois-Reymond, "L'Histoire de la civilisation et la science de la nature," *La Revue Scientifique*, 2nd ser., 7th year, no. 29 (19 January 1878): 676.

19. Niccola Marselli, "Politica estera e difesa nazionale," *Nuova Antologia di Scienze, Lettere ed Arti*, 2nd ser. (1 July 1881) 124–125.

20. John Tyndall (1820–1893), important British physicist and chemist.

21. "Monadnoc" 246.

22. Joseph Albo, *Sefer ha-Ikkarim*, book 1, chap. 3. See translation by Isaac Husik, vol. 1 (Philadelphia: Jewish Publication Society, 1929), p. 58. Albo (b. ca. 1380), a Spanish preacher and theologian, is known chiefly for this "Book of Principles" on the fundamentals of Judaism.

23. Moses ben Israel Isserles (ca. 1520–1572) was a Polish halakhist and philosopher, author of an influential Ashkenazic supplement to Joseph Caro's *Shulhan Arukh*. His *Torat ha-Olah* (Prague, 1570) develops a philosophic conception of Judaism.

24. Pallière's note: "This is what the rabbis mean by that aphorism which is cited several times in this work (Isserles on *Orah Hayyim* 156): 'We avoid advising the Gentiles not to associate other divinities in the worship of the unique God.' But this tolerance does not prevent the authentic Jew from experiencing grief at the sight of explicit idolatry. The same rabbis comment thus on Psalm 69:10 ('My zeal for Your house has been my undoing; the reproaches of those who revile You have fallen upon me'): 'Because they associate their idols with the glorious Majesty.' " The *Orah Hayyim* is the first part of Caro's *Shulhan Arukh*.

NOTES

PART ONE, CHAPTER 3

1. David Castelli, *Della Poesia biblica* (Florence, 1878), p. 200.
2. JPS 2: "the Everlasting God."
3. "And to Seth, in turn, a son was born, and he named him Enosh. It was then that men began to invoke the Lord by name" (Gn 4:26).
4. S. Cahen, *La Bible, traduction nouvelle*, vol. 1 (Paris: Cahen, 1832), p. 54.
5. See Berakhot 3a, Tosafot, s.v. "and they answer."
6. Diodorus of Sicily 1.94. See translation by C. H. Oldfather in Loeb Classical Library, vol. 1 (London and New York: G. P. Putnam's Sons, 1933). Diodorus (fl. 1st cent. B.C.E.) was an historian of the ancient world.
7. Plutarch, *Quaestiones Convivales* 4.4.4–6.2. See Menahem Stern, ed., *Greek and Latin Authors on Jews and Judaism*, vol. 1 (Jerusalem: Israel Academy of Sciences and Humanities, 1974), pp. 557–558: "First . . . the time and character of the greatest, most sacred holiday of the Jews clearly befit Dionysus. When they celebrate their so-called Fast, at the height of the vintage, they set out tables of all sorts of fruit under tents and huts plaited for the most part of vines and ivy. They call the first of the days of the feast Tabernacles. A few days later they celebrate another festival, this time identified with Bacchus not through obscure hints but plainly called by his name, a festival that is a sort of 'Procession of Branches' or 'Thyrsus Procession,' in which they enter the Temple each carrying a thyrsus. What they do after entering we do not know, but it is probable that the rite is a Bacchic revelry. . . . I believe that even the feast of the Sabbath is not completely unrelated to Dionysus. Many even now call the Bacchants *Sabi* and utter that cry when celebrating the god." (In Plutarch's dialogue, these words are spoken by Moeragenes, an Athenian.) Plutarch (46–120) was a Greek moralist, historian, and antiquarian.
8. Macrobius, *Saturnalia* 1.18. See translation by P. V. Davies (New York: Columbia, 1969). An Apollonian oracle is said to identify Iao with the greatest of gods. Macrobius (d. 415) was a late Latin commentator and antiquarian.
9. JPS 2: "The Lord is our Vindicator."
10. That is, after the return from Babylonian exile. See Ezra 2:2.
11. Zohar II, 95b–96a.
12. "For in Him we live, and move, and have our being; as certain

342

NOTES

also of your own poets have said, For we are also His offspring" (Acts 17:28). Aratus was a Greek poet of the 3rd cent. B.C.E.

13. *Yalkut Shimoni*, Naso. The *Yalkut* is a medieval compilation of Midrashic materials on the Bible, of uncertain date, though it has been ascribed to R. Simeon Kara, a French rabbi of the eleventh century. Benamozegh refers to it many times. There is a fairly recent edition of the original text (2 vols., Jerusalem, 1967), but the *Yalkut* still awaits translation into English.

14. Midrash Bereshit Rabbah 8.8.

15. "Aaron shall bring forward the goat designated by lot for the Lord, which he is to offer as a sin offering; while the goat designated by lot for Azazel shall be left standing alive before the Lord, to make expiation with it and to send it off to the wilderness for Azazel" (Lv 16:9).

16. Ish-bosheth was a son of Saul and king of Israel for two years (2 Sm 2:10).

17. See Jgs 7:1; 2 Sm 11:21.

18. See *Guide of the Perplexed* 1.164.

19. Kiddushin 71a.

20. Alfred Maury, *Histoire des religions de la Grèce antique*, vol. 1 (Paris: Librairie Philosophique de Ladrange, 1857), p. 51.

PART ONE, CHAPTER 4

1. F. Max Müller, *Leçon d'introduction à la science des religions* (Paris, 1875), p. 81. See also the English version, *Introduction to the Science of Religion* (London: Oxford, 1873). Müller (1823–1900) was a prolific and original British (German-born) philologist. Following Müller, Benamozegh uses instead of "Indo-European" the older, now obsolete term "Aryan."

2. François Laurent, *Études sur l'histoire de l'humanité*, vol. 1 (Paris, 1879), p. 408.

3. See *De Migratione Abrahami* [On the Migration of Abraham] 9.56–60; *Quis Rerum Divinarum Heres* [Who is the Heir of Divine Things] 14.68–70. Philo of Alexandria (ca. 20 B.C.E.–ca. 50 C.E.) was a very influential Jewish philosopher and exegete, whose voluminous work is an extraordinary confluence of Hebraism and Hellenism. Much of it has been published and is usefully available in the Loeb Classical Library.

4. Benamozegh's note: "See R. Nissim on Avodah Zarah 357a."

343

NOTES

R. Nissim ben Reuben Gerondi (ca. 1310–ca. 1375) was a very important Spanish Talmudist, head of the Barcelona yeshiva. The reference
is to his treatise on the *halakhot* of Avodah Zarah.

    5. *First Apology* 46. Justin Martyr (ca. 100–ca. 165) was an early
Christian apologist, born in Samaria.

    6. See Sanhedrin 105a; Maimonides, *Mishneh Torah: Hilkhot
Teshuvah* 3, *Hilkhot Melakhim* 8.11. Maimonides (1135–1204) was the
preeminent Jewish philosopher and halakhist, the *Mishneh Torah* his
magisterial synthesis of halakhah. For translations, see, in progress,
The Code of Maimonides (New Haven: Yale University Press, 1949 et
seq.). *Melakhim* appears in this series in bk. 14, *The Book of Judges*, trans.
A. M. Hershman (New Haven: Yale Univ. Press, 1949); *Teshuvah* is in
The Book of Knowledge, ed. and trans. Moses Hyamson (Jerusalem: Boys
Town, 1962).

    7. Eratosthenes, Greek philosopher and poet (2nd cent. B.C.E.).

    8. Sanhedrin 98b.

    9. Rashi (R. Solomon ben Isaac, 1040–1105) was a French com-
mentator and exegete of enormous influence in subsequent Jewish culture. He wrote extensive commentaries on the Bible and Talmud.

    10. Benamozegh's note: "These judicial assemblies in the Valley
of Jehoshaphat became, in Christianity, the universal judgment to occur at the end of the world. We have here an example of the way
Hebrew doctrines were transformed: i.e., their original meaning was
stripped away and the spiritual sense alone allowed to remain. The
error of Christianity has been to constantly sacrifice the one to the
other. The Rabbis also saw in this passage the idea of the universal
judgment of souls, but without abandoning the original sense, and so
remained faithful to the principle that the external world of society
must correspond to the internal world of the spirit, and that a single
and identical law governs both the spiritual and the physical worlds,
the terrestrial as well as the celestial Jerusalem."

    11. *Pesikta de-Rab Kahana*, trans. William G. Braude and Israel J.
Kapstein (Philadelphia: Jewish Publication Society, 1975), suppl. 2,
sec. 8, p. 472. This is an early collection (5th–7th cent.) of aggadic
Midrashim.

    12. Thomas Hobbes, *Leviathan*, chaps. 11, 13, 17. Hobbes (1588–
1679) was a brilliant though cynical English philosopher.

    13. Plato, *Laws* 1.626.

    14. See Rom 10:12; Gal 3:28.

NOTES

15. *Pesikta de-Rab Kahana*, Sabbath Shekalim, Piska 2, sec. 7.
16. Benamozegh's note: "The best way to translate this particular expression is 'for it is You who have a portion in all the nations.' We must not render it 'You have all the nations as Your portion,' as we would have to do if the verb were followed by the accusative."

PART ONE, CHAPTER 5

1. See Yevamot 61a.
2. Benamozegh's note: "The Kabbalists use this name to designate the transcendent knowledge of God."
3. See *Mekilta de-Rabbi Ishmael*, trans. J. Z. Lauterbach, 3 vols. (Philadelphia: Jewish Publication Society, 1949): tractate Kaspa 4.65–75.
4. JPS 2: "the Lord alone."
5. Benamozegh's note: "De Wette, *Leçons sur le christianisme*, p. 28." See Wilhelm M. L. de Wette, *Lehrbuch der christlichen Dogmatik in ihrer historischen Entwickelung*, 2 vols. (Berlin: Reimer, 1831–1840).
6. See J. D. Michaelis, *Commentaries on the Laws of Moses*, vol. 1 (London, 1814), bk. 1, art. 8, pp. 21–28.

PART TWO, CHAPTER 1

1. Lucius Annaeus Florus, *Epitome of Roman History* 1. Introd., Loeb Classical Library (Cambridge: Harvard, 1966.) Florus was an historian of the 2nd century, whose summary of Roman history extends to the time of Augustus.
2. Hagigah 12a; Sanhedrin 38b.
3. See Aryeh Kaplan, trans., *Sefer Yetzirah* (York Beach, Me.: Weiser, 1990), pp. 36, 353 (n. 79).
4. *Yalkut Shimoni*, Bereshit.
5. François Laurent, *Études sur l'histoire de l'humanité*, vol. 1 (Paris, 1879), p. 408.
6. See Benamozegh, *Morale juive et morale chrétienne* (Paris: Kauffmann, 1867), p. 296.
7. Émile Louis Burnouf, in *Revue des Deux Mondes*, second period, 37th year (1 Oct. 1867).
8. Alfred Maury, in *Revue des Deux Mondes*, second period, 28th year (1858), 636.

NOTES

9. M. B. Friedenthal, *Yesod ha-Dat* (in Hebrew), vol. 2 (Breslau: Loeb Sulzbach, 1823), p. 31.

10. *Yalkut Shimoni*, Bereshit. See also Mishna Sanhedrin 37a.

PART TWO, CHAPTER 2

1. Yevamot 63b; Avodah Zarah 5a.

2. Nachmanides on Gn 1:26. See *The Commentary of Nahmanides on Genesis Chapters 1–6*[8], trans. Jacob Newman (Leiden: Brill, 1960), p. 55. On the same text, see also Midrash Bereshit Rabbah 8.3.

3. Jules Soury, in *La Revue Philosophique* (Paris) 1 (Oct. 1878). See the same author's *Bréviaire de l'histoire du matérialisme* (Paris: Charpentier, 1881).

4. Judah Halevi was born in Castile ca. 1085. His *Kuzari*, a defense of Judaism, became famous. Composed in Arabic, the work was first published in Hebrew translation by Judah ben Saul ibn Tibbon in 1167. See, e.g., *Kuzari* 5.10.

5. Zeno of Citium (ca. 335–ca. 263 B.C.E.), Greek philosopher probably of Phoenician origin, founded the Stoic school. Only fragments of his work remain. See H. D. Sedgwick, *Marcus Aurelius* (New Haven: Yale University Press, 1921), chap. 1.

6. See Demosthenes, *Against Aristogeiton* 1.35.

7. See *Kuzari* 2.44, 50.

8. *Yalkut Shimoni*, Lekh Lekha.

9. Ps 70:3; Is 1:4, 42:17.

10. Yoma 65b.

11. Cp. Zohar III, 113.

12. Midrash Bereshit Rabbah 11.6. R. Hoshaya was a Palestinian amora of the second century.

13. Benamozegh, *De l'âme dans la Bible*, in series "Bibliothèque de l'Hébraïsme" (Leghorn: Belforte, 1897).

14. Benamozegh's note: "The Hebrew here [in the first clause as well as the second] can be understood as a command."

15. Lv 18:5: "You shall keep My laws and My rules, by the pursuit of which man shall live: I am the Lord."

16. Eduard von Hartmann, *Philosophie de l'inconscient*, trans. from the German by D. Nolen (Paris: Baillière, 1877), II, p. 435. This book was translated into English as *Philosophy of the Unconscious*, 3 vols. (New York: Macmillan, 1884).

NOTES

17. JPS 2: "Man does not understand honor; he is like the beasts that perish."

18. JPS 2: "Man does not abide in honor; he is like the beasts that perish."

PART TWO, CHAPTER 3

1. See Zohar I, 12b, 19b, etc.; III, 9.

2. *Pesikta de-Rab Kahana*, Piska 1.1; *Pesikta Rabbati*, Piska 5.18; Midrash Bemidbar Rabbah 12.6, 13.2; Midrash Bereshit Rabbah 19.7.

3. Sanhedrin 97a; Avodah Zarah 9a.

4. Hagigah 14b.

5. Menahot 29b.

6. Benamozegh's note: "R. Jacob Raccah of Tripoli, *Commentary on the Psalms*, Ps. 83." Raccah lived in the eighteenth century.

7. Hagigah 3b.

8. Rosh Hashonah 21b.

9. Pirke Avot, chap. 1.

10. *Tosefot Yom Tov* on Pirke Avot, chap. 1, s.v. "and he gave it to Joshua."

11. See Rashi on Dt 6:6, which cites *Sifrei*.

12. Benamozegh's note: " 'The practical rule stands according to the latter sages.' See *Yad Malachi* [163] by R. Malachi ben Jacob ha-Kohen." This rabbi was an Italian scholar of the eighteenth century. See also Rosh Hashonah 25; Rashi on Dt 17:9.

13. Benamozegh's note: "Reynaud, *Terre et Ciel*, p. 162."

14. Baba Batra 12.

15. François Laurent, *Études sur l'histoire de l'humanité*, vol. 1 (Paris, 1879), p. 74.

16. See Ex 23:10–11; Lv 25:1–22; Dt 15:1–2, 12–15.

17. Laurent, *Études sur l'histoire de l'humanité*, vol. 1, pp. 419–420.

18. Advocate or Comforter.

19. See Eugène Haag, *Histoire des dogmes chrétiens*, vol. 2 (Paris: Cherbuliez, 1862), p. 335.

20. All the names in this paragraph are identified in the Glossary.

21. See T. P. Hughes, *A Dictionary of Islam* (Lahore, 1964), s.v. *al-Mahdi*, lit. "the Directed One," thus, he "who is fit to direct others, Guide, Leader"; a ruler who shall in the last days appear on the earth. Some sects say that he has arrived though he remains concealed; others

NOTES

believe that he has not yet come. "In the history of Mohamedanism, there are numerous instances of imposters having assumed the character of this mysterious personage. According to one tradition, the Prophet affirmed that the world will not end until 'a man of my tribe and of my name shall be master of Arabia. . . . The Mahdi will be descended from me, he will be a man with an open countenance and with a very high nose. He will fill the world with equity and justice, even as it has been filled with tyranny and oppression, and he will reign over the earth seven years.' " The concept and its history have an unmistakable aura of Jewish messianism.

22. Benamozegh's note: "Stefanoni, *Critica delle superstizioni*, II, p. 165."

23. Hagigah 12a.

24. See *The Book of Raziel* 20b. This work is a collection of mystical Hebrew writings first printed in Amsterdam in 1701.

25. Benamozegh's note: "[Vito] Fornari, *Armonia Universale*, p. 15." Fornari is the author also of a life of Christ, 3 vols. (Florence, 1869–1893).

26. See Midrash Bereshit Rabbah 1.15; also, *Yalkut Shimoni*, Bereshit, 4.

27. *Yalkut Shimoni*, Bereshit, 16.

28. Anaximander is the earliest Greek philosopher and scientist whose ideas are known to us in any detail. He was born in Miletus ca. 610 B.C.E., died ca. 546. See Paul Edwards, ed., *The Encyclopedia of Philosophy*, vol. 1 (New York: Macmillan, 1967), p. 117, s.v. "Anaximander": "Land, sea, air, and heavens are . . . all explained [in his work] by a continual process of separating off from the primeval pair of Hot (dry) and Cold (wet). . . . The origin of living things is explained as part of the same process."

29. These kabbalistic terms are explained in the Glossary.

30. Eduard von Hartmann, *Philosophie de l'inconscient*, II, p. 455. (See, in the present work, Pt. 2, chap. 2, n. 16.)

31. Benamozegh's note: "[Vito] Fornari, *Armonia Universale*, p. 46."

32. *Yalkut Shimoni*, Bereshit, 5.

33. Midrash Bereshit Rabbah 2.5.

34. See n. 27 above. R. Abbahu was a Palestinian amora of ca. 300 C.E.

35. See Pt. 1, chap. 2, n. 22.

36. JPS 2: "A wind from God."

NOTES

37. JPS 2: "From eternity to eternity."

38. JPS 2: "An eternal kingship."

39. Benamozegh's note: "See, among other texts, Maimonides, *Hilkhot Teshuvah*, VIII, with the refutations of Rabad; *Ma'amar Tehiyyat ha-Metim* [Treatise on Resurrection]; and Nachmanides, *Sha'ar ha-Gemul.*"

40. *Yalkut Shimoni*, Bereshit. See also Midrash Bereshit Rabbah 1.8.

41. Eugène Haag, *Histoire des dogmes chrétiens*, vol. 2, p. 333.

42. Ernest Renan, *Questions contemporaines* (Paris: Lévy, 1868), pp. 343–344.

43. François Laurent, *Histoire du Droit des Gens et des relations internationales* (Ghent: Hebbelynck, 1850), vol. 2, p. 467.

44. August Heinrich Ritter, *Histoire de la philosophie ancienne*, vol. 3 (Paris: Tissot, 1836), p. 422. See *The History of Ancient Philosophy*, trans. A. J. W. Morrison, vol. 3 (Oxford: Talboys, 1839).

45. Benamozegh's note: "*Religion de l'avenir*, p. 414."

46. Benamozegh's note: "M. [Ernest] Renan, in *La Revue Philosophique* (Paris), vol. 1 (Oct. 1878), p. 372. It is important to remember that in kabbalistic language, the ideal, the Logos, has the name *Tiferet*, beauty." See the Glossary of the present work, s.v. "Tiferet."

47. See Zebahim 62a; Tosafot on Menahot 109.

48. Sanhedrin 52a. See also Zohar I, 80, 81; Zohar II, 247a.

49. Benamozegh's note: "This is the beautiful idea expressed by the Kabbalah, which calls the death of the just *neshika*, the kiss." See Zohar II, 124b.

50. Ernest Renan, in *La Revue Philosophique*, vol. 1 (Oct. 1878).

PART TWO, CHAPTER 4

1. Shabbat 151b.

2. Mo'ed Katan 16b.

3. See Midrash Bemidbar Rabbah 4.8; *Tanhuma* I.133, 181. (This is a collection of aggadic Midrashim of ca. 7th to 9th cent.)

4. Midrash Bereshit Rabbah 10.411.

5. Isaac ben Solomon Luria (1534–1572): preeminent Kabbalist of Safed, known by acronym "ha-Ari," the [sacred] lion.

6. See *L'Shem Yihud* in the liturgy of Shaharit, immediately before the putting on of the tallit.

7. Benamozegh's note: "See *Il mio Credo* [What I Believe], in

NOTES

Teologia dogmatica e apologetica by Elijah Benamozegh (Leghorn: Francesco Vigo, 1877), p. 271." This is the only volume published of what Benamozegh had intended to be a multivolume work on theology.

8. See Ernest Havet, *Le Christianisme et ses origines* (Paris: Calmann Lévy, 1871), 4 vols.

9. Jules Michelet, *Bible de l'humanité* (Paris: Chamerot, 1864), p. 85.

10. Benamozegh's note: "*Destination de l'homme*, pp. 187 *et seq.*" See Johann Gottlieb Fichte, *The Vocation of Man*, trans. William Smith (La Salle, Ill., 1946), Book III (Faith). The original was published in 1800 as *Die Bestimmung des Menschen*.

11. Benamozegh's note: "*Destination de l'homme*, p. 320.*"

12. Berakhot 6a–7a.

13. *Yalkut Shimoni*, Bereshit, 1.2; see also Prv 8.

14. Benamozegh may have been thinking of Voltaire's celebrated *mot*, "Si Dieu n'existait pas, il faudrait l'inventer" (If God did not exist, it would be necessary to invent him), in the *Épitre à l'auteur du nouveau livre des trois imposteurs*, 1769.

15. Vincenzo Gioberti (1801–1852), Italian philosopher and statesman, author of *Del primato morale e civile degli italiani* (1843).

16. Shabbat 10a.

17. Midrash Bereshit Rabbah 43.7.

18. Avodah Zarah 3b.

19. Benamozegh's note: "*Philosophie des écoles italiennes.*"

20. For Epicureanism and Stoicism, see Glossary.

21. I have not been able to find this passage directly in the work ascribed to Epictetus, the Stoic philosopher (fl. ca. 100), but it could be a paraphrase of his *Discourses* II. 10. 5–6.

22. This is a pervasive idea in the *Meditations* of the emperor-philosopher Marcus Aurelius Antoninus (121–180). See, e.g., 5.10; 12.1, 14–15, 23.

23. Baba Batra 10a. Tinneius Rufus was a hostile Roman governor of Judaea under Hadrian, in the second century. He is known in rabbinic sources as Turnus Rufus. According to legend, he had religious discussions with R. Akiba, and his wife became a convert to Judaism. See Rashi on Nedarim 50b. (*Encyc. Judaica*, s.v. "Tinneius Rufus.")

24. Avodah Zarah 54b.

25. See *Tanhuma Buber*, Thazria, 7. The identity of "Rabbi Elghazi" is uncertain.

26. Benamozegh does not identify his source for this quotation, if indeed it is an authentic and not a hypothetical quotation.

27. Benamozegh's note: "*Essai de Théodicée*, I, 7, 11." The passage is probably from Fichte's *Die Anweisung zum seligen Leben* (1844). See Glossary in the present volume, s.v. "Fichte."

28. J. S. Mill, *An Examination of Sir William Hamilton's Philosophy and of the Principal Philosophical Questions Discussed in his Writings*, vol. 2 (Boston: Spencer, 1868), p. 271.

29. See Rashi on Dt 33:26.

30. Benamozegh's note: "*De Deo*, Introd., XLVI." This is puzzling, for Spinoza's *Short Treatise on God, Man, and his Well-Being*, presumably the text cited, has no introduction. If it is indeed by Spinoza himself (rather than an editor or commentator) it would almost certainly have to be from one of his earliest works, for some of its ideas contradict key elements of his mature thought.

PART TWO, CHAPTER 5

1. Benamozegh's note: "See the commentary on the *Zohar Mikdash Melech*, vol. 1, p. 39." See Shalom ben Moses Buzaglio, *Mikdash Melech* (in Hebrew), 5 vols. (Zolkiew, 1793–1794). This work is a compilation of major commentaries on the Zohar.

2. Maimonides, *Guide of the Perplexed* 1.54.

3. JPS II is slightly different here.

4. Benamozegh's note: "See Menahem de Recanati, on Lech Lecha, 43.2." Menahem ben Benjamin Recanati was an Italian Kabbalist and halachic authority of the late thirteenth and fourteenth centuries.

5. Benamozegh's note: "*Eshkol ha-Kofer*, p. 96." Judah ben Elijah Hadassi, the author of this book, was a twelfth-century Karaite scholar of Constantinople. It is a synthesis of contemporary Karaite thought, and explains *mitzvot* and *halakhot* as arranged according to the Ten Commandments. See p. 96b of the 1836 Hebrew edition.

PART THREE, CHAPTER 1

1. Midrash Bereshit Rabbah 1.1.

2. *Yalkut Shimoni*, Mishle, 8; Midrash Bereshit Rabbah 1.8.

3. Midrash Bereshit Rabbah 19.4, 27.

4. *Logos* was Philo's term for the Divine Mind in its diverse

NOTES

aspects. (See David Winston, *Logos and Mystical Theology in Philo of Alexandria* [Cincinnati: Hebrew Union College, 1985], pp. 15–18; Harry A. Wolfson, *Philo/Foundations of Religious Philosophy in Judaism, Christianity, and Islam*, vol. 1 [Cambridge, Mass.: Harvard, 1947], chap. 4.) The concept is central to Philo's thought, representing God's principal power. It occupies a position intermediary between God and creation (though it is not an intermediary between God and man). Human intelligence is a copy of Logos, which is identified with Wisdom and Torah. This is parallel to the identification of Torah, Wisdom, and the Word of God in rabbinic literature, following Scripture. The word is Greek and means speech, organization, rational order, etc., and is common in Greek philosophical writings. "As the Word of God in all its manifestations, it appears in Jewish and Christian theological texts in Greek from the Hellenistic period. Aristobulus of Paneas, the *Wisdom of Solomon*, and Philo are the Jewish sources, and the Gospel of John the earliest representation of the Christian ones. The later history of the term belongs to Christian theology, where, following John, Logos is the Son, or the preexistent Messiah. Logos as an independent entity appeared in Jewish literature suddenly in the writings of Philo" (*Encyc. Judaica*, s.v. "Logos").

5. Berakhot 6a, 7a. Benamozegh's note: "See the Palestinian Talmud's commentary on Lv 18:4 ['My rules alone shall you observe, and faithfully follow My laws: I the Lord am your God']: 'We learn from this that the Holy One, blessed be He, observes all the precepts of the Law.' "

6. Benamozegh's note: "This is the law of *Pikku'ah Nefesh* ['regard for human life'], which the Karaites did not accept." See Yoma 85a; *Mekilta de-Rabbi Ishmael*, vol. 3, tractate Shabbata 1.10.

7. See Porphyry, *On the Life of Plotinus and the Arrangement of his Work* 2. Giordano Bruno is said to have declared "that his soul would rise with the smoke to paradise." See D. W. Singer, *Giordano Bruno: His Life and Thought* (New York: Schuman, 1950), p. 179.

8. Pietro Emilio Tiboni, *Il Misticismo biblico* (Milan, 1853), p. 536.

9. Benamozegh's note: "It is important to note that in Hebrew the word 'wisdom,' *hokhmot*, appears in the plural, the objective case being in the singular, and that in Gnosticism, it is the last of the *aeons*, exactly as in Kabbalah, the last *sefirah* is also called Wisdom." See Prv 1:20, 9:1, 24:7; but cp. 2:10, 8:12. *Hokhma* appears 29 times in Proverbs, always in oblique cases.

10. JPS 2: "Gauged."

NOTES

11. Philo, *De Vita Mosis* 2.17–20.
12. See Megillah 13a, Kiddushin 40a.
13. See Midrash Bereshit Rabbah 14.6.
14. Midrash Bereshit Rabbah 39.16.
15. Nachmanides on Gn 12:8. See his *Commentary*, ed. Charles B. Chavel, I (New York: Shiloh, 1971), 172.
16. Midrash Shir ha-Shirim Rabbah 1.3.3.
17. Cp. Gn 17:4: "You shall be the father of a multitude of nations."
18. Berakhot 13a.
19. *Yalkut Shimoni*, Bereshit; *Eliyyahu Rabbah*, chap. (28)26. *Seder Eliyyahu Rabbah* is the first of the two principal sections of *Tanna debe Eliyyahu*, a Midrashic work of uncertain date (3rd to 10th cent.). See English translation by William G. Braude and Israel J. Kapstein (Philadelphia: Jewish Publication Society, 1981), p. 349. See also Sanhedrin 105a.
20. Abraham Abulafia, *Sefer Hayyei ha-Olam ha-Ba*. Abulafia (1240–after 1291) was a Spanish mystic, proponent of ecstatic Kabbalah.
21. Midrash Vayikra Rabbah 1.12.
22. Plutarch, *De Defectu Oraculorum* 17. This account of "The Obsolescence of Oracles" is part of *Moralia 5*.
23. Midrash Vayikra Rabbah 1.12.
24. See Sanhedrin 106.
25. See Midrash Bemidbar Rabbah 20.12; Bereshit Rabbah 52.5.
26. *Sifrei*, Piska 40, on Dt 11:12; Piska 357, on Dt 34:10. See *Sifre/ A Tannaitic Commentary on the Book of Deuteronomy*, trans. Reuven Hammer (New Haven: Yale, 1986), pp. 79, 340 (n. 4a), 383. See also *Eliyyahu Zuta*, chap. 11.
27. Baba Batra 15. See also *Eliyyahu Rabbah*, chap. (28)26, and *Eliyyahu Zuta*, chap. [10], where it is said that Balaam surpassed Moses in "native Intelligence."
28. *Eliyyahu Rabbah*, chap. (28)26.
29. *Eliyyahu Rabbah*, chaps. (6)7, (28)26; *Eliyyahu Zuta*, chap. 11.
30. Benamozegh's reference is unclear. But see Mt 12:38–42.
31. See Clement of Alexandria, *On Spiritual Perfection* 2.11 (*Stromateis* 7).
32. See Midrash Bereshit Rabbah 65.20; Sanhedrin 105a. Oenomaus was a pagan philosopher friendly to the rabbis. (Midrash Shmot Rabbah 13.1.)

NOTES

33. Charles François Marie, comte de Rémusat (1797–1875), in *Revue des Deux Mondes*, second period, 35th year (Sept. 1865).

PART THREE, CHAPTER 2

1. R. Elijah Mizrahi (ca. 1450–1526) was the greatest rabbinical authority of his time in the Ottoman Empire. His commentary on the Torah was published in Amsterdam in 1718. The quotation is from a commentary on Shofetim (Dt 16:18–21:9).
2. See Rashi on Dt 20:18.
3. M. B. Friedenthal, *Yesod ha-Dat* (in Hebrew), vol. 2 (Breslau: Loeb Sulzbach, 1823), pp. 122, 4.
4. Sanhedrin 57a.
5. Maimonides, *Mishneh Torah*, Hilkhot Melakhim 8.10. (See in the present work Pt. 1, chap. 4, n. 6, for bibliographical information.)
6. Leone Modena, *Magen ve-Zinnah*, ed. A. Geiger (Breslau, 1856), p. 42.
7. Rashi on Ex 24:3.
8. Maimonides, *Mishneh Torah, Hilkhot Melakhim* 10.10.
9. Yevamot 47a.
10. *Kuzari* 1.101. (See in the present work Pt. 2, chap. 2, n. 4.)
11. Isserles on *Orah Hayyim* 156. (See in the present work Pt. 1, chap. 2, n. 24.)

PART THREE, CHAPTER 3

1. See Avodah Zarah 20a.
2. Ernest Renan, *Les Évangiles et la seconde génération chrétienne* (Paris, 1877), p. 231. This work is vol. 5 of Renan's *Histoire des origines du christianisme*. For an English translation, see *The Gospels*, vol. 5 of *History of the Origins of Christianity* (London: Mathieson, 1889–1890).
3. Horace, *Satires* 1.9.69.
4. From Seneca, *De Superstitione*, quoted by St. Augustine in *De Civitate Dei* 6.11. Seneca the philosopher lived from the late first cent. B.C.E. until 65 C.E. See Menahem Stern, ed., *Greek and Latin Authors on Jews and Judaism*, vol. 1 (Jerusalem: Israel Academy of Sciences and Humanities, 1974), pp. 431–434.
5. Benamozegh provides no source in Philo's voluminous works for this quotation.

NOTES

6. Ernest Havet, *Le Christianisme et ses origines*, vol. 3 (Paris: Calmann Lévy, 1884), p. 457.

7. See Hesiod, *Works and Days* 765–828. Modern texts apparently exclude the specific passage Benamozegh quotes. Linus is a legendary poet, variously connected with Apollo, Urania and Amphimarus, and Heracles (Hercules).

8. Benamozegh's note: "Allusion to the *tebillah*, a bath by immersion which accompanied the circumcision of pagans. *Prohibited Marriages*, ch. XIV, 7." See *The Code of Maimonides*, Book 5, *The Book of Holiness* (vol. 16 of Yale Judaica Series), trans. L. I. Rabinowitz and P. Grossman (New Haven: Yale, 1965), 1.14.7. This treatise is one of two on "Forbidden Intercourse."

9. Ernest Renan, *St. Paul* (Paris: Lévy, 1869), p. 90.

10. JSP 2: "Revered."

11. The Rechabites were a small religious sect of ascetic habits, first mentioned in Jer 35:18. See also Ta'anit 26a.

12. The Gibeonites were a Canaanite people with whom Joshua established a friendly pact, later modified (Jos 9:3–27).

13. Havet, *Le Christianisme et ses origines*, vol. 2, p. 150.

14. Renan, *St. Paul*, p. 46.

15. Ibid., p. 87.

16. *Tractatus Theologico-Politicus*, "Preface" (1670).

17. Megillah 13a; Kiddushin 40a.

18. Renan, *Les Évangiles et la seconde generation chrétienne*, p. 161.

19. Ibid., p. 249.

20. See Eusebius, *Praeparatio Evangelica* 8.8, cf. *La Préparation Évangélique*, text ed. and trans. J. Sirinelli and E. des Places (Paris: Éditions du Cerf, 1974 *et seq.*).

21. François Laurent in *La Revue Politique et Littéraire* (Paris), 2nd ser., *année* 2, 15 February 1873; p. 801.

22. *Morale juive et morale chrétienne* (Paris: Kauffmann, 1867); repr. Boudry-Neuchâtel, 1946; trans. E. Blockman as *Jewish and Christian Ethics with a Criticism on Mahomedism* (San Francisco, 1873).

23. Hullin 94a.

24. Lv 19:10; Pe'ah 4.9; Gittin 61a; Shebi'it 4.3; Maimonides, *Hilkhot Mattenot Aniyyim* 7.7; Caro, *Yoreh De'ah*, 335.9, 367.1.

25. Midrash Rut Rabbah 2.13.

26. Oenomaus was a pagan philosopher of the second century who adhered to the school of the younger cynics, and attacked oracles. He is generally identified with Avnimos, who appears in rabbinic

literature as a philosopher friendly to the rabbis. See Heinrich Graetz, *Geschichte der Juden von den Ältesten Zeiten bis auf die Gegenwart* (Leipzig: Leiner, 1853–1876), vol. 4, pp. 435 *et seq*. An abridged English translation of Graetz's *History of the Jews* was published in 6 vols. (Philadelphia: Jewish Publication Society, 1891–1898).

27. Joseph Caro, *Orah Hayyim*, 135; Gittin 59a, 59b.

PART THREE, CHAPTER 4

1. Maimonides, *Mishneh Torah, Hilkhot Melakhim* 8.11.
2. Joseph Caro, *Yoreh De'ah*, 268.2.
3. Caro, *Yoreh De'ah*, 267.3.
4. Isserles on *Yoreh De'ah*, 268.12.
5. Cf. Maimonides, *Sefer ha-Mitzvot*; trans. into English by Charles B. Chavel, 2 vols. (London: Soncino, 1967).
6. Sanhedrin 74b.
7. Maimonides, *Mishneh Torah, Hilkhot Melakhim* 10.10.
8. Sanhedrin 48b.
9. Sanhedrin 56b.
10. Ibid.
11. Sanhedrin 57b.
12. Baba Kamma 91b.
13. Pallière's note: "In order to spare the reader any confusion, we should observe that the Hebraic doctrine of Noachism is somewhat analogous to one in Roman Catholic theology, which distinguishes between *latria* (worship which may be directed to God alone) and *dulia* (worship directed to the angels and saints). This latter mode of worship, allowed to Gentiles so long as it does not dilute their profession of pure monotheism, is rigorously forbidden to Israel. Indeed, Moses himself has never been worshiped by the Jews and the location of his tomb has even been kept secret so that the masses might not be tempted in any way to associate this greatest of prophets with the adoration of the true God."
14. Sanhedrin 57b.
15. R. Ammi bar Nathan was an outstanding Palestinian rabbi of the late third century.
16. A fourth-century Babylonian amora.
17. Abba ben Aivu, founder of the Academy of Sura in the third century, leading Babylonian amora; known as Rav.
18. Sanhedrin 74b, 75a.

NOTES

19. R. Jonah was a fourth-century Palestinian amora.

20. Sanhedrin, 74; Nachmanides, *Milkhamot Adonai*, on Sanhedrin, end of chap. 8; Maimonides, *Mishneh Torah, Hilkhot Melakhim* 10.2.

21. Sanhedrin 57b.

22. Maimonides, *Mishneh Torah, Hilkhot Melakhim* 9.3.

23. Sanhedrin 57a.

24. Kiddushin 42b; Sanhedrin 29a.

25. Maimonides, *Mishneh Torah, Hilkhot Melakhim* 9.4.

26. Makkot 9a.

27. Maimonides, *Mishneh Torah, Hilkhot Roseah* 5.4. See *The Code of Maimonides, Book Eleven, The Book of Torts* [Seder Nezikin], trans. Hyman Klein (New Haven: Yale, 1954), p. 210.

28. R. Hisda was head of the Academy of Sura (third and fourth cent.).

29. R. Abbaye was a fourth-century Babylonian amora.

30. Makkot 9a.

31. Sanhedrin 58a.

32. Sanhedrin 58b; Maimonides, *Mishneh Torah, Hilkhot Melakhim* 9.8.

33. Benamozegh does not identify the source of this quotation in the works of the French historian Jules Michelet (1798–1874). Cf. Pt. 2, chap. 4, n. 9.

34. Benamozegh's note: "This identification of the mother with the Holy Spirit should not seem shocking. We know that certain Christian sects have elevated Mary to the Trinity in place of the Holy Spirit, and that for the Gnostics, the Holy Spirit itself is a feminine principle. In the apocryphal gospels, Jesus speaks of his mother the Holy Spirit. In the Kabbalah, the *aeon Malkhut* embodies this dual motif."

35. Kiddushin (Jerusalem Talmud), chap. 1.

36. Midrash Bereshit Rabbah 8.1.

37. Yoma 23a.

38. Baron de la Brède et Montesquieu, *De l'Esprit des lois*, Book 26, esp. chaps. 13–14.

39. Priscus (d. ca. 471) was a Byzantine historian sent by Theodosius the Younger as ambassador to Attila, of whom he wrote an account.

40. Jean Charles Houzeaux, *Études sur les facultés mentales des animaux comparées à celles de l'homme*, vol. 1 (Mons: Manceaux, 1872), p. 283.

NOTES

41. Megillah 13a.
42. Perhaps Benamozegh's text has been corrupted here, for his meaning is obscure.
43. Sanhedrin 56b.
44. Sanhedrin 57a; Maimonides, *Mishneh Torah, Hilkhot Melakhim* 9.9.
45. Montesquieu, *De l'Esprit des Lois*, Book 12, chap. 4.
46. Sanhedrin 56b, 59a.
47. Sanhedrin 56b.
48. Ibid.
49. Maimonides, *Mishneh Torah, Hilkhot Melakhim* 10.6.
50. See M. B. Friedenthal, *Yesod ha-Dat* (in Hebrew), 2 vols. (Breslau: Loeb Sulzbach, 1823).
51. Sanhedrin 56b.
52. Shabbat 33a.
53. Jacques-Bénigne Bossuet (1627–1704), French bishop and influential religious author, remembered for his eloquent funeral panegyrics for great personages. His *Politique tirée des propres paroles de l'Écriture sainte* (Statecraft drawn from the very words of Holy Scripture), 1709, attempted to construct a political philosophy based on biblical principles.

PART THREE, CHAPTER 5

1. Adolphe Franck, *Philosophie et religion* (Paris, 1867), p. 213.
2. Joseph Salvador, author of *Loi de Moïse ou Système religieux et politique des Hébreux* (Paris: Ridan, 1822).
3. Franck's expression is *impôt du sang*, and is obscure. Perhaps he means the mitzvah of *berit milah*, circumcision.
4. Zebahim 115b; Bekhorot 4b.
5. See Rashi on Nm 3:12.
6. Ta'anit, chap. 4.
7. Dt 33:10; Ez 44:23–24; Mal 2:7.
8. E.g., Dt 6:7.
9. Jer 2:8, 8:8.
10. Mal 2:11–12.
11. Is 58:13; Mal 3:22.
12. See Gn 49:10 and Rashi's commentary.
13. See 1 Chr 12:32 and Rashi's commentary.
14. See Dt 33:18–19 and Rashi's commentary.

NOTES

15. See Gn 49:14; Dt 33:18–19; and Rashi's commentary. See also *Tanhuma* on these texts.

16. See Salvador, *Loi de Moïse*.

17. Judah Halevi, *Kuzari* 3.41 *et seq.*

18. See Ernest Renan, *Études d'histoire religieuse*, 2nd ed. (Paris, 1857); trans. H. F. Gibbons as *Studies of Religious History* (London: Heinemann, 1893).

19. See 1 Kgs 11:29 *et seq.*

20. Maimonides, *Mishneh Torah, Hilkhot Tefillah* 5.10.

21. P. Manfrin, "Antiche assemblee e sistemi di votazione," *Nuova Antologia di Scienze, Lettere ed Arti*, 2nd ser. (15 May 1882): p. 275.

22. "This will be the practice of the king who will rule over you: He will take your sons and appoint them as his charioteers and horsemen, and they will serve as outrunners for his chariots. He will appoint them as his chiefs of thousands and of fifties; or they will have to plow his fields, reap his harvest, and make his weapons and the equipment of his chariots. He will take your daughters as perfumers, cooks, and bakers. He will seize your choice fields, vineyards, and olive groves, and give them to his courtiers. He will take a tenth part of your grain and vintage and give it to his eunuchs and courtiers. He will take your male and female slaves, your choice young men, and your asses, and put them to work for him. He will take a tenth part of your flocks, and you shall become his slaves. The day will come when you will cry out because of the king whom you yourselves have chosen; and the Lord will not answer you on that day" (1 Sm 8:11–18).

23. JPS 1: "Judge"; JPS 2: "Govern."

24. Alfred Maury, *Histoire des religions de la Grèce antique*, vol. 3 (Paris: Librairie Philosophique de Ladrange, 1859), p. 447.

25. See Ex 22:27 and Rashi's commentary; also Ps 82:1,6.

26. See Ex 19:6; Lv 19:2 *et seq.*; Gittin 62a.

27. Sotah 49a.

PART THREE, CHAPTER 6

1. Benamozegh's note: "These four verbs are appropriate representations of the four languages. The etymology of *ba* and *atha* is clear; *zarach* sounds like the Latin *surgo*, and *hofia* seems analogous to the Arabic. The locations are also, in a sense, appropriate to the respective languages: Seir, in the land of Edom, is a fitting symbol of Rome, which has always been identified with Edom, and Paran was the origi-

nal home of Ishmael, father of the Arab peoples." See Baba Batra 25a; *Sifrei*, Piska 343; *Midrash Tannaim* 209. (This last is a Tannaitic work containing fragments of a halakhic Midrash on Deuteronomy.)

2. Midrash Shmot Rabbah 28.6.

3. Megillah 8b, 9b.

4. Megillah 9b.

5. *Yalkut Shimoni*, Yitro, 286. See also *Pesikta de-Rab Kahana*, trans. William G. Braude and Israel J. Kapstein (Philadelphia: Jewish Publication Society, 1975), suppl. 1, pp. 456–457. Also, see Midrash Shmot Rabbah 27.9.

6. Avodah Zarah 2b.

7. *Pesikta de-Rab Kahana*, suppl. 1.15.

8. The friends of Job.

9. *Eliyyahu Rabbah*, chap. 28(26); *Eliyyahu Zuta*, chap. 11. *Eliyyahu Zuta* is the second part of the Midrashic compendium *Tanna debe Eliyyahu*. (See above, Pt. 3, chap. 1, n. 19.) See also *Yalkut Shimoni*, Ve-Zot ha-Berakha, 951.

10. See Rom 1:19–20; Acts 17:23, 28.

11. See Lk 16:8; Jn 12:36; Col 1:12; 1 Thes 5:5.

12. Gottfried Wilhelm von Leibniz, *Monadologia* (1714). Benamozegh's note cites p. 216 of this work on divine justice, presumably in the French translation.

13. Raffaele Mariano, *Cristianesimo, cattolicismo e civiltà* (Bologna, 1879), p. 281.

14. See Rosh Hashanah 21b; Hagigah 3b; Eruvin 13b.

15. Rosh Hashanah 21b.

16. See Hagigah 3b; Eruvin 13a.

17. *Pesikta de-Rab Kahana*, Piska 12, sec. 25. See translation by William G. Braude and Israel J. Kapstein (Philadelphia: Jewish Publication Society, 1975), p. 249.

18. See Midrash Shmot Rabbah 28.2, 29.1; *Yalkut Shimoni*, Yitro, 294.

19. Vito Fornari, *Della vita di Cristo*, vol. 2 (Florence, 1869), p. 549.

20. Benamozegh's note: "Session of the Academy of Riga on 5 December 1864."

21. Benamozegh's note: "The *Magghid*, ann. 5675, p. 390."

22. Nazir (Jerusalem Talmud), 7, 56b; Midrash Bereshit Rabbah 14.8; *Pirke de-Rabbi Eliezer*, chap. 11 (see translation by Gerald Friedlander [New York: Sepher-Hermon Press, 1916]).

23. Rashi on Ex 20:22.

NOTES

24. Shabbat 101b.
25. JPS 2: "Any prayer or supplication offered by any person among all Your people Israel."
26. Maimonides, *Mishneh Torah, Hilkhot Melakhim* 8.11.
27. Rashi on Nm 29:18 *et seq.*
28. Midrash Vayikrah Rabbah 1.11; Midrash Bemidbar Rabbah 1.3.
29. Midrash Shir ha-Shirim Rabbah 4.1–2.
30. Sukkah 55b.
31. *Pesikta de-Rab Kahana*, Piska 28, sec. 7, 9. See translation by William G. Braude and Israel J. Kapstein (Philadelphia: Jewish Publication Society, 1975), pp. 442–443.
32. Rashi on Nm 29:18.
33. See Rashi on Nm 29:18.
34. Sukkah 55b.
35. Ex 23:16, 34:22.
36. Benamozegh's note: "*Les Deux Alliances*, pp. 65–66." I have not been able to identify the Protestant theologian.

PART THREE, CHAPTER 7

1. Symmachus (late 2nd cent.) belonged to the Ebionite sect of Jewish Christians, according to Eusebius and Jerome. He was translator of the Greek version of the Jewish Scriptures reproduced in Origen's *Hexapla*. Details of his life are obscure, and his work exists only in fragments.
2. Carlo Cantoni, in *Nouvelle Anthologie*, June 1869, p. 277.
3. See Marsilio Ficino's chief philosophical work, *Theologia Platonica* (1482). Ficino (1433–1499) was "the most central and most influential representative of Renaissance Platonism . . . in whom the medieval philosophical and religious heritage and the teaching of Greek Platonism are brought together in a novel synthesis" (Paul O. Kristeller, *Renaissance Thought: The Classic, Scholastic, and Humanistic Strains* [New York: Harper, 1961], p. 59).
4. Moses Mendelssohn (1729–1786), grandfather of the composer, was an influential philosopher of the German Enlightenment and a spiritual leader of German Jewry.
5. Cp. Sanhedrin 59a.
6. *Sifre/A Tannaitic Commentary on the Book of Deuteronomy*, trans. Reuven Hammer (New Haven: Yale, 1986): Piska on Deut. 11:12

NOTES

(p. 79). *Sifrei* is a halakhic Midrash on Numbers and Deuteronomy, ca. late fourth century.

7. Maimonides, *Guide of the Perplexed* 3.45.

8. Nachmanides on Lekh Lekhah. In *Commentary on the Torah*, trans. Charles B. Chavel (New York: Shiloh, 1971), pp. 164–225.

9. Midrash Bereshit Rabbah 56.10.

10. JPS 2: "Judah is exiled completely, / All of it exiled."

11. JPS 2: "Justice and well-being kiss."

CONCLUSION

1. "Edom": "A Jewish code-word, since the early Middle Ages, for Christianity" (Gershom Scholem, *Origins of the Kabbalah* [Princeton: Princeton University Press, 1987], p. 296). According to tradition, the Edomites were bitterly hostile neighbors of Israel.

2. *Mekilta de-Rabbi Ishmael*, trans. J. Z. Lauterbach, 3 vols. (Philadelphia: Jewish Publication Society, 1949), Tractate Bahodesh 1.100–105 (vol. 2, pp. 199–200).

3. Four years before Benamozegh's death in 1900, Theodore Herzl published *Der Judenstaat* (The Jewish State), and in August 1897 the First Zionist Congress was convened in Basle. But another half-century, and the eruption of a barbarism that Benamozegh, who lived all his life in the comparatively genial atmosphere of Italy, could perhaps not have imagined, would be required before his cautious prophecy would be realized.

Glossary

(R.) Abbahu. Palestinian amora of ca. 300 C.E. Notable for his wisdom, integrity, and modesty.

(R.) Abbaye. Babylonian amora (278–338), head of important academy in Pumbedita.

Abimelech. King of Gerar (a region in the Negev) who appears in Genesis in several incidents involving Abraham and Isaac. He is regarded by the rabbis as a righteous Gentile.

Abtalyon. Important Pharisee leader (mid-1st cent. B.C.E.), by tradition vice-president of the Great Sanhedrin though of heathen descent, from Sennacherib or Sisera (Gittin 57b). See: "Shemaiah."

Abulafia, Abraham ben Samuel. Spanish mystic (1240–1291), principal exponent of ecstatic Kabbalah.

Aeons. Gnostic term sometimes used in Kabbalah to denote the sefirot. See: "Pleroma."

Aeschylus. Athenian tragic poet (525–456 B.C.E.), author of earliest extant tragedies, invariably embracing religious themes.

Aggadah. That part of Oral Tradition that includes narrative, history, ethical maxims, parables, and the like; aggadah is not directly concerned with the legal sections of the Torah.

Ahura Mazda. Zoroastrian deity believed to be the source of all good.

(R.) Akiba ben Joseph. An outstanding tanna (ca. 50–135 C.E.), scholar, patriot. Said, in one tradition, to be descended from Haman.

Albo, Joseph. Spanish preacher and theologian (b. ca. 1380), best known for his *Sefer ha-Ikkarim* (Book of Principles) on the fundamentals of Judaism.

Alexandria. Hellenistic Egyptian metropolis where a large Greek-speaking community of Jews existed in the period of the Second Temple.

GLOSSARY

Aliyah. Heb. "ascent," signifying the coming of Jews to Eretz Yisroel, and also, more abstractly, spiritual or metaphysical elevation.

Amalek. A people of the Negev and adjacent desert, hereditary enemies of Israel from the time of the battle at Rephidim after the crossing of the Red Sea, when Israel was attacked by the Amalekites.

Amalric. Scholastic philosopher, b. near Chartres, taught in Paris, d. ca. 1207.

(R.) Ammi bar Nathan. An outstanding Palestinian rabbi of late third century.

Amoraim. Torah scholars who were active from the time of the completion of the Mishnah (ca. 200 C.E.) until the completion of the Talmuds (ca. 500 C.E.).

Anaximander. Greek philosopher of Ionian school (610 B.C.E.–after 546).

Apuleius. Philosopher of second century, b. in Africa, educated at Athens in Platonic philosophy; author of allegorical novel *The Golden Ass.*

Areopagus. An ancient judicial council in Athens especially concerned, during Roman imperial times, with religious matters; also, the hill where this council met.

Avnimus ha-Gardi. See: "Oenomaus of Gadara."

Avodah Zarah. A tractate in the Babylonian Talmud, of the order Nezikin.

Baba Batra. A tractate in the Babylonian Talmud, of the order Nezikin.

Baba Kamma. A tractate in the Babylonian Talmud, of the order Nezikin.

Balaam. Gentile soothsayer who was asked by Balak, King of Moab, to curse Israel, but, after consulting God, refused; best known for having been rebuked by his talking ass (Nm 22–24). He was much exalted in certain rabbinical traditions as a prophet.

Baraita (pl. "Beraitot"). An early halakhah, halakhic Midrash, or aggadah that was not included in R. Judah ha-Nasi's Mishnah.

Bavli. Babylonian Talmud, the interpretation and elaboration of the Mishnah as accomplished in the academies of Babylon (ca. 200–500).

Bekhorot. A tractate in the Babylonian Talmud, of the order Kodashim.

Bemidbar. Book of Numbers.

GLOSSARY

Berakhot. A tractate in the Babylonian Talmud, of the order Zera'im.

Bereshit. Book of Genesis.

Bildad the Shuhite. One of Job's three friends (Jb 2:11); regarded in one rabbinical tradition as a Gentile prophet.

Blake, William. English romantic poet and artist (1756–1826), whose works are often mystical and visionary.

Boethius, Anicius. Roman philosopher, ca. 480–ca. 524. A Christian.

Bruno, Giordano. Outstanding Italian philosopher and poet (1548–1600), executed by the Inquisition for his heterodoxy.

Campanella, Tommaso. Italian philosopher (1568–1639), Platonist, Dominican.

Caro, Joseph ben Ephraim. Spanish-born halakhist and Kabbalist (1488–1575), author of *Shulhan Arukh.*

Clement of Alexandria. Christian theologian (ca. 150–ca. 215), probably from Athens; interested in Christian gnosis, or illumination; postulated Christ the Logos as source of human reason and interpreter of God to mankind.

Cyrus the Great. King of Persia (ca. 600 B.C.E.–ca. 530 B.C.E.), conqueror of Babylonia and restorer of Jews to Eretz Yisroel.

Dante Alighieri. Italian poet (1265–1321), author of the *Divine Comedy.*

Darius I. King of Persia (ca. 550 B.C.E.–486 B.C.E.), great reformer and statesman, famous as lawgiver.

Derekh. Heb. "way." *Derekh eretz* means "way of the world," desirable behavior of a man toward his fellows.

Devarim. Book of Deuteronomy.

El Elyon. Heb. "God the Most High." One of the biblical names of God.

Elihu ben Barachel the Buzite. Young man who addresses Job and his three friends (Jb 32–37); regarded by rabbinical tradition as a prophet.

Eliphaz the Temanite. One of Job's friends (Job 2:11); regarded by rabbinical tradition as a leading pagan prophet.

(Seder) Eliyyahu Rabbah. First and larger part of *Tanna debe Eliyyahu.*

(Seder) Eliyyahu Zuta. Second part of *Tanna debe Eliyyahu.*

Elohei-ha-Elohim. Heb. "God of gods," a biblical name of God.

El Olam. Heb. "God of the universe," a biblical name of God.

GLOSSARY

Emanations. See: "Sefirot."

Emor. A scriptural portion for synagogue reading: Lv 21–24:23.

Enosh. Eldest son of Adam's son Seth. In the Aggadah, the generation of Enosh is the "counsel of the wicked" (Ps 1:1).

Epicureanism. Greek philosophical school that taught that the highest good is peace of mind, which comes from cultivation of virtue for its own sake; condemned as libertine by Jews and Christians.

Eruvin. A tractate in the Babylonian Talmud, of the order Mo'ed.

Essenes. A religious Jewish community or brotherhood in latter part of Second Temple period.

Eusebius of Caesaria. Bishop in Palestine (ca. 260–339), influential church leader and historian.

Ex nihilo. Lat. "out of nothing." Expression used especially with reference to theories of creation.

Fichte, Johann Gottlieb. German philosopher (1762–1814), exponent of ethical idealism. His philosophy is notable for its intensity of moral earnestness.

(R.) Gamaliel ha-Zaken. Grandson of Hillel (ca. 1–50 C.E.), president of Sanhedrin; according to Acts 22:3, he was tolerant of first Christians and a teacher of Paul.

Ger-toshav. Heb. "proselyte of the gate." A fellow-citizen but not co-religionist, though, presumably, an observer of the Noachide *mitzvot.*

Ger-tsedek. Heb. "proselyte of the law." A convert to Judaism.

Gibeonites. A Canaanite people with whom Joshua established a friendly pact, later modified (Jos 9:3–27).

Gideon. Usually regarded as one of the Judges; also called Jerubbaal, son of Joash (Jgs 6:32).

Gittin. A tractate in the Babylonian Talmud, of the order Nashim.

Gnosticism. A philosophical and religious movement of ancient times that became prominent in the second century and had several forms, all characterized by the doctrine that emancipation came through special knowledge (Gr. "gnosis"), the possession of which saved initiates from bondage to matter.

God-fearers. Romans who rejected pagan worship, observed Sabbath, had a marginal role in the Synagogue; called Judaizers. See: "Noachide Law."

GLOSSARY

Hagigah. A tractate in the Babylonian Talmud, of the order Mo'ed.

Halakhah. The legal expression of Judaism, going back, according to tradition, to the revelation to Moses on Sinai.

Ham. One of the three sons of Noah, traditional progenitor of Ethiopians and other African peoples.

Hasidism. Popular religious movement that developed in southwest Poland-Lithuania in latter half of the eighteenth century, emphasizing ecstasy, mysticism, and charismatic leadership.

Haskalah. Heb. term for Enlightenment movement and ideology that started in Jewish life in the 1770s and emphasized secular studies as a legitimate part of a Jew's education.

Hebraism. Used by Benamozegh to designate comprehensive Jewish tradition, embracing Bible, Talmud, Midrash, and Kabbalah.

Hegel, Georg Wilhelm Friedrich. German philosopher (1770–1831) of great influence. His philosophy centered about the concept of Spirit (*Geist*) and its realization in history and experience.

Hellenism. The cultural tradition of Greece, especially its philosophy and art, which, directly and by way of the Roman Empire, penetrated the entire Mediterranean world in ancient times, including Israel. This influence has been perceived by many as a threat to Jewish authenticity.

Heller, Yom Tov Lipmann ben Nathan ha-Levi. Moravian rabbi (1579–1654); his most famous work is *Tosefot Yom Tov*, a commentary on the Mishnah (Prague, 1614–1617).

Hercules. A Greek hero, later worshiped as a god.

Herodotus. Earliest of the great Greek historians (5th cent. B.C.E.), of Halicarnassus in Asia Minor.

Hesiod. Very early Greek poet, later than Homer but of uncertain date.

(R.) Hidka. A tanna of mid-second century. He said: "Love the term 'perhaps' and hate the expression 'what of it?' "

(R.) Hisda. Babylonian amora of ca. 217–309; head of academy in Sura.

(R.) Hiyya. Tanna of late second century. Also called "Rabbah" and "the Great."

Horace. Roman poet of Augustan age (65 B.C.E.–8 B.C.E.).

Hullin. A tractate in the Babylonian Talmud, of the order Kodashim.

Hypostases. Gk. "substance." Used by some Christian theologians to refer to the three Persons of the Trinity.

GLOSSARY

Immanence. The presence of God in His creation; by contrast, transcendence denotes God outside creation.

Indo-European. (Also Aryan, Indo-Germanic.) The language family comprising the chief tongues of Europe, as well as Indian and Persian, and some others; by largely hypothetical extension, the civilization and religion of these peoples.

Isis. Egyptian deity, wife of Osiris; identified originally with the earth, later with the moon. Her worship became very popular in the Roman Empire.

Isserles, Moses ben Israel. A Polish halakhist and philosopher (ca. 1520–1572), author of influential Ashkenazic supplement to Caro's *Shulhan Arukh*, as well as *Torat ha-Olah*, a philosophic conception of Judaism. Known as "Ramah."

Japheth. Third son of Noah, brother of Shem and Ham; traditional progenitor of the Greeks and other European peoples.

Javan. Traditional father of the Greeks, son of Noah's son Japheth; his name reflects "Ionia" (Greek settlement on west coast of Asia Minor and Aegean archipelago).

(R.) Jochanan ben Zakkai. Leading tanna of the last years of the Second Temple (later 1st cent. C.E.) and the period after its destruction; he played an important role in reorganizing religious life.

Joachim of Flora. Controversial, influential Cistercian mystic and philosopher of apocalyptic bent (ca. 1132–1202).

John of Parma. Franciscan preacher and teacher (1209–1289).

(R.) Jonah. Palestinian amora of fourth century.

Josephus, Flavius. Jewish historian and a preeminent representative of Jewish-Hellenistic literature (ca. 38–after 100); author of *The Jewish War* and *Jewish Antiquities.*

(R.) Joshua ben Levi. Palestinian amora, highly respected halakhist, of first half of third century.

Judah Halevi. Spanish poet and philosopher (ca. 1085–1141). His *Kuzari*, a defense of Judaism (composed in Arabic), became famous.

(R.) Judah ha-Nasi. Codifier of the Oral Law (Mishnah) ca. 200 C.E. Referred to honorifically as "Rabbi."

Jus gentium. Lat. "law of nations." International law.

Kabbalah. The tradition of Jewish esoteric and theosophical teachings and mysticism, from the period of the Second Temple forward; especially important in Middle Ages, starting with twelfth century.

GLOSSARY

Karaites. A Jewish sect that came into being ca. 700 C.E., professing to follow the Bible to the exclusion of rabbinical traditions and laws, though in fact it adopted a large part of rabbinical Judaism; a counter-movement against Talmudism.

Kiddushin. A tractate in the Babylonian Talmud, of the order Nashim.

Ki Tissa. A scriptural portion for synagogue reading: Ex 30:11–34:35.

Kuzari. See: "Judah Halevi."

Laban. Grandnephew of Abraham, maternal uncle of Rebekah and father-in-law of Jacob.

Lekh Lekha. A scriptural portion for synagogue reading: Gn 12:1–17:27.

Lessing, Gotthold Ephraim. German dramatist and critic (1729–1781), advocate of Jewish emancipation.

Logos. Gk. "speech, organization, rational order," etc. A complex Greek philosophical term, parallel in some respects to the biblical *Devar Adonai* (Word of God); central in Philo's philosophy (denoting Wisdom or God's power), in Gnosticism, in Gospel of John, etc.

Luria, Isaac ben Solomon. Preeminent Kabbalist of Safed (1534–1572), known as *ha-Ari*, "the [sacred] lion," after Heb. initials of "ha-elohi Rabbi Yitzchak."

Luzzatto, Samuel David. Eminent Italian scholar, philosopher, Bible commentator (1800–1865); unsympathetic to Kabbalah.

Macrobius, Ambrosius. Roman antiquarian and grammarian (ca. 400 C.E.).

Magen va-Herev. See: "Modena, Leone."

Magen ve-Zinna. See: "Modena, Leone."

Maggid. Heb. "one who relates." In later Hebrew, the name for a popular, often itinerant, preacher; also, an angel or spirit who enlightens worthy scholars.

Maimonides, Moses. Preeminent rabbinic authority, codifier, philosopher (1135–1204); author of *Mishneh Torah*, *Moreh Nevukhim* (Guide of the Perplexed), *Sefer ha-Mitzvot*, among many other influential works.

Makkot. A tractate in the Babylonian Talmud, of the order Nezikin.

Malkhut. Heb. "kingdom." In Kabbalah, the tenth *sefirah*; identified with the *Shekhinah*, the Divine Presence in the world; God as immanent. In the human soul, the feminine principle ("queen").

369

GLOSSARY

[ha-] Makom. Heb. "the Place." The Omnipresent; a rabbinical name of God.

Megillah. A tractate in the Babylonian Talmud, of the order Mo'ed.

Mekilta de-Rabbi Ishmael. A halakhic Midrash on Exodus. Probably compiled in Eretz Yisroel no earlier than ca. 400 C.E.

Melakhim. The final treatise in Maimonides' *Mishneh Torah,* dealing with the selection and duties of a king over Israel, the conduct of war, the Noachide commandments, and the Messianic age.

Melchizedek. Heb. "righteous (legitimate) king." A Gentile king of Salem, or Jerusalem (Gn 14:18–20) who was "priest of God Most High" and who blessed Abraham.

Menahot. A tractate in the Babylonian Talmud, of the order Kodashim.

Mendelssohn, Moses. Influential philosopher of the German Enlightenment (1729–1786); a spiritual leader of German Jewry. Grandfather of the composer.

Merkavah Mysticism (Ma'aseh Merkavah). Term used by the rabbis to denote the speculations and visions connected with the imagery of Ez 1, especially the Throne of Glory and the chariot (Heb. "merkavah") that bears it.

Midrash. From Heb. root *drsh,* "to search." A type of rabbinical literature embodying traditional biblical exegesis, both halakhic and (especially) aggadic.

Midrash Rabbah. Name that has come to be used for ten quite different Midrashim, some from as early as ca. 400 C.E.

Midrash Tadshe. An aggadic Midrash of tenth century, mainly symbolic, which was traditionally attributed to R. Phinehas ben Jair.

Mill, John Stuart. English liberal philosopher and economist (1806–1873).

Millenarianism. Christian belief in a future millennium, or thousand-year period of triumphant holiness (see Rv 20).

Mishle. Book of Proverbs.

Mishnah. The Oral Law as codified by R. Judah ha-Nasi ca. 200 C.E.

Mishneh Torah. Maimonides' magisterial codification of halakhah, Jewish law.

Mitzvah. A sacred commandment or duty. Traditionally, the Jew is said to be obligated to fulfill 613 biblical *mitzvot,* other men seven. See: "Noachide Law."

Modena, Leone. Italian rabbi, scholar, writer (1571–1648). Author of *Magen va-Herev,* an eloquent religious polemic (ed. S. Simonsohn,

Jerusalem, 1960), and *Magen ve-Zinnah*, a defense of Oral Tradition (ed. A. Geiger, Breslau, 1856).

Mo'ed Katan. A tractate in the Babylonian Talmud, of the order Mo'ed.

Moloch. Ancient Semitic deity whose cult required the sacrifice or passing through fire of children (see Lv 18:21, 20:2–4; Dt 18:10).

Monolatry. Worship of one God though accepting possible existence of other gods.

Montanism. An apocalyptic Christian movement of the late second century, which is traced to a Montanus, in Phrygia, who declared that the Heavenly Jerusalem would soon descend there.

Mosaism. As used by Benamozegh, the term denotes the obligations of the Jew to fulfill 613 *mitzvot;* in contrast to Noachism.

Nachmanides (Moses ben Nachman). Eminent Spanish rabbi (1194–1270); scholar, talmudist, philosopher, Kabbalist, exegete, poet.

Navi. (Heb.) Prophet.

Negev. A totally arid desert in the south of Eretz Yisroel.

(R.) Nissim ben Reuben Gerondi. A very important Spanish talmudist (ca. 1310–ca. 1375), head of the Barcelona yeshiva.

Noachide Law, Noachism. The code of seven *mitzvot* (with amplifications) regarded by rabbinic tradition as enjoined by the Bible on all mankind; the religion of Noachides.

Oenomaus of Gadara. A philosopher who lived during the reign of Hadrian (117–138), of the school of younger Cynics; generally identified with Avnimus ha-Gardi, who appears in rabbinic literature as a philosopher friendly to the rabbis, and is regarded by them as the greatest heathen philosopher (in company with Balaam).

Orah Hayyim. The first part of Caro's *Shulhan Arukh.* Contains daily commandments and those for Sabbaths and festivals.

Oral Tradition (or Law). The amplification and interpretation of the Written Law, both regarded as having been given to Moses on Sinai and of equal authority. It is embodied in Talmud and Midrash.

(R.) Oshaiah. Palestinian amora of ca. 100–150 c.e.

Osiris. Egyptian divinity, husband of Isis.

Ovid. Roman poet (43 b.c.e.–18 c.e.).

Palingenesis. The doctrine of rebirth and regeneration.

Pan. Gk. "all." Greek god of flocks and shepherds, represented as sensual and animal-like.

GLOSSARY

Paracelsus. Influential Swiss physician, chemist, and alchemist (1493–1541), whose real name was Theophrastus Bombastus von Hohenheim. Developed a mystical theology based on Neoplatonism.

Paraclete. Gk. "advocate." Epithet for Holy Spirit first used by John; occasionally used for Christ also. Traditionally translated "comforter."

Parousia. Gk. "presence." Doctrine of future return, in glory, of Christ—the "Second Coming"—to judge the living and dead and to conclude the present world order.

Parsees. Zoroastrians descended from Persian refugees settled in India, especially at Bombay.

Pe'ah. Second tractate of the Mishnah, of the order Zera'im. There is a Gemara in the Jerusalem Talmud but none in the Babylonian.

Pesahim. A tractate in the Babylonian Talmud, of the order Mo'ed.

Pesikta de-Rab Kahana. An early collection (5th to 7th cents.) of aggadic Midrashim.

Pesikta Rabbati. A medieval Midrash on the annual festivals.

Pharisees. Dominant Jewish religious and political party or sect in period of the Second Temple, from which arose the Rabbinic Judaism of the post-Temple period.

Philo of Alexandria. A very influential Jewish philosopher and allegorical exegete (ca. 20 B.C.E.–ca. 50 C.E.), whose voluminous work is an extraordinary confluence of Hebraism and Hellenism.

(R.) Phinehas ben Jair. A tanna of the second century, best known as aggadist, saintly figure, and miracle-worker. (Even his donkey refused to eat untithed corn.) He appears prominently in the Zohar.

Pikku'ah Nefesh. Heb. "regard for human life." Rabbinical term for the Jew's obligation to save human life, even if ritual *mitzvot* must be violated.

Pirke Avot. A treatise in the Mishnah, of the order Nezikin. There is no Gemara in either Talmud.

Pirke de-Rabbi Eliezer. An aggadic work of the eighth century.

Plato. The preeminent philosopher of Athens (ca. 429–347 B.C.E.), some of whose writings have a mystical, visionary character.

Pleroma. "The concept of the pleroma, the divine 'fullness,' occupies a central position in the thought of the ancient Gnostics. This concept has two shades of meaning: sometimes the 'fullness' is the region of the true God himself, and sometimes it is the region to which he descends or in which the hidden God manifests himself in different figures. It is the place 'where God dwells.' The pleroma is a world of perfection and absolute harmony that develops out of a series of essences and divine emanations known in the history of Gnosticism by the name aeons, 'eternities,' supreme realities" (Gershom Scholem, *Origins of the Kabbalah* [Princeton: Princeton University Press, 1987], p. 68).

Plotinus. Egyptian-born founder of Neoplatonism (ca. 205–270).

Plutarch. Greek philosopher and biographer (ca. 46–120).

Porphyry. Greek Neoplatonic philosopher (ca. 232–ca. 303). Author of a Life of Plotinus.

Rabad. R. Abraham ben David of Posquières (ca. 1125–1198), Talmudic authority of Provence; a penetrating critic of Maimonides' *Mishneh Torah.*

Rashi. R. Solomon ben Isaac (1040–1105), enormously influential French commentator and exegete on Bible and Talmud.

Rav. Babylonian amora (3rd cent.), founder of academy at Sura. His name was Abba ben Aivu.

Rava. Babylonian amora (d. 352), head of an influential academy. His name was Abba ben Joseph ben Hama.

[Book of] Raziel. Collection of mystical Hebrew writings, some from Talmudic times, first printed in Amsterdam in 1701.

Rechabites. A small, ascetic religious sect, first mentioned in Jer 35:18.

Renan, Ernest. French author, religious historian, philologist, and critic (1823–1892), briefly professor of Hebrew in the Collège de France. He was heterodox in his personal beliefs.

Rimmon. A name used for the chief Syrian god, Baal-Hadad.

Rosh Hashonah. A tractate in the Babylonian Talmud, of the order Mo'ed.

Ru'ah ha-Kodesh. Heb. "the Holy Spirit." The divine spirit from which, according to rabbinic thought, prophecy comes. According to tradition, the Torah was given directly by God to Moses, but the other canonical writings were produced under the inspiration of the Ru'ah ha-Kodesh.

Rut Rabbah. Aggadic Midrash on the Book of Ruth.

Sadducees. Jewish sect formed ca. 200 B.C.E., composed largely of wealthier elements (priests, merchants, aristocrats). Many Sadducees were in the Sanhedrin, and they dominated the Temple worship.

GLOSSARY

Sanhedrin. The supreme political, religious, and judicial body of Judaea during Roman period, and until ca. 425 C.E. Also, a tractate in the Babylonian Talmud, of the order Nezikin.

Sefer ha-Ikkarim. See: "Albo, Joseph."

Sefer ha-Mitzvot. Book of Commandments, a compendium and discussion of 613 *mitzvot,* by Maimonides.

Sefirot. A fundamental term of Kabbalah. The ten stages of emanation that manifest God in His various attributes.

Seneca, Lucius Annaeus. Roman moral philosopher (late 1st cent. B.C.E.–ca. 65 C.E.), born in Spain.

Sennacherib. King of Assyria and Babylonia (reigned 705–681 B.C.E.). he beseiged Jerusalem but was unable to conquer it (2 Kgs 19:35). Traditionally, ancestor of Abtalyon and Shemaiah.

Septuagint. Oldest translation of the Bible, into Greek. According to legend, it was accomplished ca. 285–244 B.C.E. by some seventy-two translators who were engaged for this purpose by Ptolemy Philadelphus, who desired a copy of the Hebrew Law for his famous library at Alexandria.

Shabbat. A tractate in the Babylonian Talmud, of the order Mo'ed.

Shebi'it. A tractate in the Babylonian Talmud, of the order Zera'im.

Shekalim. A tractate in the Babylonian Talmud, of the order Mo'ed.

Shekhinah. Heb. "dwelling, resting." The divine Presence in the world; the immanence of God.

Shem. Eldest son of Noah; traditional father of "Semites," including the Hebrews.

Shemaiah. Colleague of Abtalyon (late 1st cent. B.C.E.), and like him, said to have been descended from Sennacherib or Sisera.

Shemitta. The sabbatical year, during which all land in Eretz Yisroel had to lie fallow and all debts be remitted (Ex 23:10–11; Lv 25:1–7, 18–22; Dt 15:1–11). In certain Kabbalistic texts, the seven-year cycle was adapted to a scheme of vast cosmic cycles.

Shir ha-Shirim. The biblical book Song of Songs.

Shmot. Book of Exodus.

Shulhan Arukh. Influential codification of Jewish law by Joseph Caro (Venice, 1565). With the amendments of Moses Isserles, it has been accepted as the chief such code.

Sifrei. A halakhic Midrash on Numbers and Deuteronomy, ca. late fourth century.

(R.) Simeon bar Yohai. Important tanna of second century; pupil of Akiba; traditional author or source of the Zohar.

GLOSSARY

(R.) Simeon ben Abba. Babylonian amora of third century.

Sisera. Pagan leader of a coalition hostile to Israel in days of Deborah (Jgs 4–5). According to a tradition, Abtalyon and Shemaiah were descended from him.

Sotah. A tractate in the Babylonian Talmud, of the order Nashim.

Spinoza, Baruch. Celebrated rationalistic philosopher (1632–1677), born in Amsterdam to Portuguese Sephardi parents. He emphasized the role of reason in metaphysics and ethics.

Stoicism. Influential school of ancient philosophy, with a strong ethical bias.

Sukkah. A tractate in the Babylonian Talmud, of the order Mo'ed.

Ta'anit. A tractate in the Babylonian Talmud, of the order Mo'ed.

Tanakh. A Hebrew word for Jewish Bible, cobbled together from the opening syllables of Hebrew words for Torah, Prophets, Writings.

Tanhuma. A collection of aggadic Midrashim of ca. seventh to ninth centuries.

Tanhuma Buber. An Oxford manuscript of Tanhuma as published in 1885 by Solomon Buber.

Tanna debe Eliyyahu. An important Midrashic work of uncertain date (3rd to 10th cents.).

Tannaim. Torah sages of the first and second centuries, up to the completion of the Mishnah.

Tao. The "Way" (fundamental creative process, basic principle of the universe) according to the Chinese religious and philosophical system Taoism.

Targum. Heb. "translation." Aramaic translation of the Bible. Targum Onkelos is especially authoritative.

Tefillah. Heb. "prayer," especially the Amidah prayer (often called the Shemoneh Esrei), which forms the core of the daily service.

Terumah. Heb. "heave offering." Prescribed in the Torah. Israelites were required to separate this from their own crops and give it to the priests (*terumah gedolah*). There was also a *terumat ma'aser*, which the Levites had to give the priests from the tithes they received.

Tetragrammaton. The sacred four-letter name of God (JHVH), which Jews are ordinarily forbidden to pronounce. It suggests the meaning "Being."

Thomas Aquinas. Greatest medieval Christian philosopher (ca. 1225–1274), identified with Scholasticism. Deeply influenced by Aristotle.

GLOSSARY

Tiferet. Heb. "beauty." In Kabbalah, the sixth Sefirah, identified with God's transcendence. In the human soul, the masculine principle ("king").

Tohu va-vohu. Heb. "unformed and void." From the first verse of Genesis: "When God began to create heaven and earth—the earth being unformed and void." Some mystical texts understood the words to signify, respectively, matter and form.

Torat ha-Olah. See: "Isserles, Moses ben Israel."

Tosafot. Heb. "additions." Collections of comments on the Talmud, and especially on Rashi's commentary, by French and German scholars of the generations after Rashi (d. 1105).

Tosefot Yom Tov. See: "Heller, Yom Tov Lipmann ben Nathan ha-Levi."

Tosefta. A collection of tannaitic *beraitot.* The word is the Aramaic form of Tosafot.

[ha-] Vaya. A Talmudic expression denoting the Tetragrammaton; from Hebrew verb for "to be."

Vayikra. Book of Leviticus.

Ve-Zot ha-Berakhah. A scriptural portion for synagogue reading: Dt 33:1–34:12.

Wissenschaft des Judentums. Germ. "science of Judaism." The scientific and critical study of Judaism. The expression was first used ca. 1820.

Yalkut Shimoni. A medieval compilation of Midrashic materials on the Bible, possibly of the thirteenth century though the date is uncertain. The work has been ascribed to R. Simeon Kara, a French rabbi of the eleventh century.

Yerushalmi. Jerusalem or Palestinian Talmud, the interpretation and elaboration of the Mishnah as accomplished in the academies of Palestine (ca. 200–400).

(Sefer) Yetzirah. Heb. "The Book of Creation." Brief, enigmatic, mystical discourse on cosmology and cosmogony, written originally perhaps between third and sixth centuries.

Yevamot. A tractate in the Babylonian Talmud, of the order Nashim.

Yihud ha-Shem. Heb. "Unity of God." In Kabbalah, the conjunction of Tiferet and Malkhut, which is the source of redemption.

GLOSSARY

Yobel. Heb. "jubilee." The fiftieth year following a cycle of seven Sabbatical years (Lv 25:8–16, 23–24).

Yoma. A tractate in the Babylonian Talmud, of the order Mo'ed.

Yoreh De'ah. Second section of Caro's *Shulḥan Arukh*, dealing with a variety of subjects, such as dietary laws, interest, purity, and mourning.

(R.) Yose. Palestinian amora of the early fourth century.

Zebahim. A tractate in the Babylonian Talmud, of the order Kodashim.

Zend-Avesta. Sacred writings of Zoroastrianism.

Zerubbabel. Babylonian name of the son of Shealtiel (Ezr 3:2), who played a significant role in reconstructing the Temple after the return from Babylonian captivity.

Zohar. "Book of Splendor," the principal text of Kabbalism. It was given to the world in the second half of the thirteenth century by the Spanish author Moses ben Shemtov de Leon (ca. 1250–1305), but, according to tradition, is ascribed to R. Simeon bar Yohai, the tanna of the second century.

Zoroastrianism. System of religious doctrines attributed to Zoroaster (Zarathustra), ca. 628–551 B.C.E., and for a time the dominant religion of Persia.

Appendix
Kabbalah in Elijah Benamozegh's Thought

I. Benamozegh: A Kabbalist in Modern Garb?

*E*lijah Benamozegh was a very erudite and prolific writer, whose domains of creativity were broad and multifaceted. However, one major theme permeates most of his important writings: the centrality of kabbalistic ideas, which are conceived of not only as representing a highly evolved form of religiosity, the quintessence of Judaism, but also as the sources for both Christianity and Gnosticism. For him, Kabbalah is "an abundant source of noble and profound doctrines." Time and again these presuppositions inform his historical and phenomenological discussions. His insistence upon these points qualifies him for the title of Kabbalist.[1] But Benamozegh was a rather peculiar type of Kabbalist. In the following, I shall attempt to point out what seem to be the central points related to his views on Kabbalah.

Kabbalah has often been colored by the cultural ambience within which the various Kabbalists have composed their writings. In the East, a kabbalistic-Sufi synthesis can be discerned; in Italy, an openness toward philosophical theories, much more conspicuous and significant than in Spain, or elsewhere in general. This trait is evident in the writings of the first Kabbalist who produced a significant corpus of writings in Italy, Abraham Abulafia. It is also present in the works of Pico della Mirandola's companion, Yohanan Alemanno, and in several sixteenth-century Kabbalists, such as Rabbi Berakhiel Qafman or Abraham Yagel. This trend, which can be described as universalistic,[2] is still evident in some of the writings of Kabbalists in the seventeenth

378

century who, though writing outside Italy, had spent time there and absorbed Renaissance culture.[3]

It is within this context that we can identify the particular attitude to Kabbalah found in the writings of Elijah Benamozegh. Though he did not interpret the mystical lore in accordance with philosophical terms, he repeatedly drew correspondences between the two types of discourse. By doing so, he was confident that he did not impose an alien mode of thinking on Kabbalah, nor did he think that he had discovered its sources. On the contrary, by pointing out the resemblances between kabbalistic ideas on one hand and Neoplatonic and Gnostic ones on the other, he assumed that he was able to make a decisive argument in favor of the traditional claims as to the antiquity of this Jewish lore. Though he made use of philological and comparative arguments, Benamozegh was mainly concerned with an historical question: Is Kabbalah an ancient Jewish wisdom that, at the same time, also faithfully represents the essence of Judaism? Unlike the orthodox Kabbalists, who embraced this view as a matter of fact and attempted to counteract any opposition to it solely by means of material found in classical sources, Benamozegh combined this approach with methods taken from classical studies. He was well acquainted with many of the available texts of antiquity, in their Greek or Latin originals and also in translation, and his writings constitute a *sui generis* type of erudition in Judaism, not only in the nineteenth century. He represents the most substantial instance of the impact Kabbalah had on a significant Jewish thinker who also drew much from the general culture.

A comparison of his unique stand with other forms of Jewish scholarship in his lifetime will bring out his originality. Like his Italian and other Jewish Renaissance predecessors, Benamozegh attempted to introduce the latest developments in European thought into his spiritual horizon. As we shall see below, he integrated Neoplatonic and Gnostic ideas as useful types of material for comparisons to Kabbalah. However, as a nineteenth-century thinker, he also did his best to become acquainted with, and benefit from, later developments in philosophy. The impact of German Idealism and its Italian repercussions is easily visible in many of his books. From this point of view, Benamozegh is an exception in the Jewish orthodox camp, and not only because his knowledge of Kabbalah, and of many other kinds of Jewish lore, surpassed that of the scholars who were his contemporaries.[4]

APPENDIX

II. The Beginnings of Scholarly Approaches to Kabbalah

The second third of the nineteenth century, when Benamozegh started his literary activity, was the period when Jewish studies were founded and the first major projects of some of the early scholars were conceived. In the aftermath of the publications of Leopold Zunz's studies, a long array of students contributed to the emergence of modern scholarship in matters of Jewish poetry, history, Talmud, Midrash, halakhah, interpretation and, last but not least, Jewish mysticism. This last field was treated in a series of studies initiated by Meier H. Landauer, whose work was followed by the more extensive contributions of Adolph Jellinek. These two scholars did not restrict their investigations to the printed sources relating to Jewish mysticism, but they also perused numerous manuscripts in order to offer the first attempts to organize the chaos of the extant materials.

The premature death of Landauer precluded the printing of his studies in his own lifetime. This task was undertaken by Jellinek, who continued some of the investigations started by Landauer. In France another contemporary produced the first complete modern description of Kabbalah by a Jew. Adolphe Franck, a professor of philosophy, wrote a widely read monograph, *La Kabbale*, printed in 1842. It was translated shortly afterward by Jellinek into German. During this middle third of the century, the greatest service to the study of Jewish mysticism was rendered by Jellinek, who printed important texts of early Jewish mysticism, parts of the Hekhalot literature, short texts belonging to thirteenth-century Geronese Kabbalah, two epistles of Abraham Abulafia, and a short but very important monograph on the relationship between Moses de Leon and the book of the Zohar. To these scholars we can also add the name of Nahman Krochmal, a thinker active a little bit earlier in Poland. He devoted some chapters to matters of Jewish mysticism in his classical *More Nevokhei ha-Zeman*.[5] These contributions, which are only rarely permeated by an antagonism to Jewish mysticism, present various historical schemes to explain the history of Kabbalah. We shall return to some of them below.

III. The Critical Theologians

One of the most respected contemporaries and greatest scholars of the generation, Samuel David Luzzatto, an inhabitant of Trieste and Padua, made an unusual contribution to writings on Kabbalah in the form of a dialogue that was intended to demonstrate the late character of the Kabbalah by describing it as a form of medieval lore. Luzzatto himself underwent a change in his position. Although he began as someone who accepted the antiquity of Kabbalah, his studies of medieval Jewish texts convinced him that the theosophical understanding expressed by a key concept of medieval Kabbalah, the *Sefirot* mentioned in the treatise named *Sefer Yetzirah*, was unknown to early medieval authors. This shift in Luzzatto's thought was coupled with a resurgence of interest in the first detailed critique of Kabbalah by another Italian author, a seventeenth-century rabbi of Venice, Yehudah Arieh of Modena, known to his Christian correspondents as Leone da Modena. His *Ari Nohem*, printed for the first time only in our century, attracted the attention of Isaac Samuel Reggio, the editor of Rabbi Elijah del Medigo's *Behinat ha-Dat*. In his 1833 edition of this book Reggio published several fragments from Modena's critique. Luzzatto's findings as a philologist and theologian, some of them expressed as early as 1829, and the interest in the issue of the antiquity of Kabbalah both in del Medigo's book and in the printed fragments of Modena, inspired Luzzatto's Hebrew "dialogue," which was printed in 1852 in French under the title *Dialogues sur la Kabbale et le Zohar et sur l'antiquité de la ponctuation et l'accentuation dans la langue hebraïque*. Another main target of Luzzatto's learned critique, as pointed out in the French introduction, was Franck's view of Kabbalah. This was hinted at when Luzzatto referred to the ignorance of those who called the kabbalistic texts "la Philosophie religieuse des Hébreux" (this was the subtitle of Franck's book).

This lively interest in Kabbalah by scholars, theologians, and intellectuals was only rarely coupled with a religious investment in the contents of Kabbalah. As mentioned above, positive statements about the value of Kabbalah are not missing from the writings of some of these scholars; but their preoccupation with the material was much more historical than religious. It is only in the tone of the critiques that a greater involvement is felt. Landauer, Jellinek, Krochmal, or Franck should not be regarded as immersed in any deep belief in the concepts characteristic of Kabbalah, though they expressed sympathy toward some of these concepts.

The dissemination of the critiques addressed to Kabbalah, as formulated by Reggio and Luzzatto, who reiterated some of the much earlier findings of del Medigo and Modena, provoked a reaction in the form of two books authored by Elijah Benamozegh. In his earlier

APPENDIX

'Eimat Mafgi'a' he attempted to respond to the criticism articulated by Modena, while in his *Ta'am le-Shad* he took issue with the "dialogue" of Luzzatto.[6] Printed in 1855 and 1863 respectively, in the author's own printing house in Leghorn, these works enriched the learned discourse on Kabbalah in the second third of the nineteenth century. What was new in Benamozegh's apology was not so much the defense of Kabbalah's antiquity, a theory already accepted by Franck, as the detailed critical attitude to the arguments he intended to combat. As Benamozegh himself claimed, his second book was a "refutation critique, historique, et théologique" of Luzzatto's dialogues. The triple character of the refutation reflects the approach of Luzzatto, who intended to express in his dialogues not only a "point de vue scientifique, mais aussi du côté religieux."[7]

Luzzatto's half-scientific, half-theological critique of Kabbalah invited a similar mode of response. Thus, though acting as a preacher and rabbi in Leghorn, Benamozegh not only located himself among the pious believers in the validity and antiquity of this mystical lore, but insisted on establishing his response within the new form of critical writing ushered in some few decades before in Germany. It is this synthesis between a deeply traditional spirituality, very sympathetic toward Kabbalah, and a vast knowledge in ancient classical literature, including Patristics and Neoplatonic philosophy, that gives a special flavor to Benamozegh's detailed responses. Written in Hebrew, and therefore intended not only for the tiny audience concerned with learned debates on *Judaica*, but also for more traditional Jewish readers, the two books are unique in their kind. It is especially remarkable that Benamozegh introduced numerous quotes from pagan and Christian sources in order to make his points. This is quite exceptional when compared with Jewish traditional literature written before him. In the same period when he composed these two defenses of Kabbalah, Benamozegh also prepared his Hebrew commentary on the Pentateuch, *'Em la-Mikra*. This was also described by the author as an interpretation based upon "illustrations, et recherches philologiques, critiques, archéologiques et scientifiques."

IV. Kabbalah and Kabbalistic Sources

A strong allegiance to kabbalistic ideas is conspicuous in Benamozegh's writings. It is not only a matter of defending the "ancient lore" against its critics, but also of advancing a more mystical vision of

APPENDIX

Judaism in general. Kabbalah contributed much to Benamozegh's own formulations concerning the nature of religion. Therefore, the questions must be asked: What is Kabbalah in Benamozegh's view? And what were the kabbalistic writings that served as the background for his thought? As far as I could check in Benamozegh's very voluminous writings, he never gives a clear-cut definition of Kabbalah. This situation seems initially rather bizarre, given the polemic situation which provoked the writings that were produced as responses to critiques addressed to this lore. However, the absence of an elaborate definition of Kabbalah may not be so surprising. It is still a question whether modern scholarship has been able to provide a single definition that covers all the variegated types of kabbalistic literature.[8] It is also very frustrating for the scholars who attempt at "summarizing" Kabbalah as a literature in itself to find that most of the Kabbalists themselves defined their lore as being in deep relationship to other bodies of Jewish writings. Many of their definitions have a relative component: Kabbalah is regarded, for example, as the mystical meaning of the Bible, or is conceived of as constituting part of the Oral Law. When envisioning their lore as an interpretation most of the Kabbalists did not assume that it was an additional layer, grafted on the original or canonic text by the Kabbalists, but rather that it was the disclosure of a dimension inherent in, and crucial for, the spiritual meaning implicit in the sources. Therefore, for the Kabbalists (and I consider Benamozegh to be one of them), to define Kabbalah is to define the most spiritual aspects of the texts that constitute classical Judaism.

Like other Kabbalists, Benamozegh operates with rather broad concepts. He is less inclined to base his phenomenological and historical analysis of texts upon the strictly philological approaches adopted by modern scholarship. In other words, it is not the existence of an ancient corpus of writings that use a certain type of uniquely kabbalistic vocabulary that preoccupies Benamozegh, but the existence of more vague sets of ideas, either in Jewish or in non-Jewish ancient writings. For Benamozegh, the recurrence of mystical and mythical ideas in ancient Jewish texts would be conceived of as a proof of the antiquity of Kabbalah. He was not interested in creating or debating proposals concerning historical sources of Kabbalah or distinctions between kabbalistic schools.

A perusal of Benamozegh's writings and the sources he quoted, directly and indirectly, reveals a rather bizarre situation: Despite the great praise he bestows on Kabbalah, he is rather cautious about quot-

APPENDIX

ing kabbalistic texts at length. The book of the Zohar plays a central role in his references to kabbalistic concepts, more than the Lurianic corpus, such as the writings of Rabbi Yisrael Sarug and Moses Cordovero's *Pardes Rimmonim*. Indeed, even in his later writings on Kabbalah, like *Ta'am le-Shad*, Benamozegh sticks to a rather unified view of this lore. A whole decade after the printing of two of Abraham Abulafia's epistles by Jellinek, and two decades after the printing of Landauer's studies on the beginning of Kabbalah, Benamozegh completely ignores, as far as I can see, the developments of scholarship in this domain.[9]

The general manner in which Benamozegh presents Kabbalah does not allow for the concept of a plurality of views. This is a curious fact, since he views diversity in a positive light when discussing other concepts, including theological ones. In some cases, however, the situation is even more surprising. When he attempts to portray a progressive view of Judaism, Benamozegh resorts to the idea of cosmic cycles, known as *Shemitta* and *Yobel*.[10] In this context he states that the difference between the Gentile views of the cosmic cycle and that of the Jews is between a view of unchanged repetitions on one hand, and one of a progressive repetition on the other.[11] However, the different versions of the theory of cosmic cycles in Kabbalah hardly corroborate this statement. On the contrary, in most cases, the first cosmic cycle is conceived as being presided over by the *sefirah* of *Hesed*, namely one of perfect mercy, while the present cycle is one of stern judgment, *Din*. Since Benamozegh mentions precise sources only very rarely, I wonder whether someone will be able to locate a significant theory of cycles in Kabbalah that can fit his view on this topic.

Last but not least: Benamozegh's two books dealing with the defense of Kabbalah were constructed as refutations of the arguments of the critics. Hence, their arguments are quoted *in extenso*, being followed in each case by his own response. Nevertheless, although there are lengthy quotes from the writings of both Modena and Luzzatto, the quotations from kabbalistic sources are relatively rare.

V. Jewish Theurgy

One of the fundamental concepts in Kabbalah can be described as theurgy. Theurgy refers to the operations that are intended to cause a change within the divine realm.[12] This view, which can be traced to statements in Talmudic and Midrashic literature, received much more elaborated formulations in kabbalistic literature. The daring nature of this concept, one that assumes an imperfect deity who can be assisted by human ritualistic acts, provoked the reactions of the opponents of Kabbalah, as is conspicuous from observations found in Elijah del Medigo's *Behinat ha-Dat*[13] and Leone da Modena's *Ari Nohem*.[14] Modena's criticism of the efficacy of prayer gave Benamozegh the opportunity to formulate his attitude to theurgy. Modena did not accept the possibility of introducing any change in the deity. In order to offer an alternative to the theurgical stand of Moshe Cordovero, he mentions a parable of an author referred to as the "least of the preachers."[15] It seems that Modena's source is none other than Pseudo-Dionysius, as we may see from the following:[16]

Modena

Indeed, I heard, but I did not understand, the sin someone commits when he directs his prayer to God without [directing his thought] to the *sefirot* for because of His absolute unity He cannot change His will. But even the least of the preachers can solve this [quandary] for the understanding of the ignoramus, [using] a simple parable. This [problem] is similar to the [situation of] someone on a ship in a river who throws a cable on a pillar or a tree on the shore and strongly draws the ship and so brings it near to the shore. But whoever sees this may say that he draws the banks of the river to the ship and so he comes near to the shore. But the matter is not so, since the ship comes near to the shore by drawing, whereas the shore stands forever. So is the prayer [like] a cable which is seized above on His will, which does not change itself but the one

The Divine Names

Let us then elevate our very selves by our prayers to the higher ascent of the divine and good rays as if a luminous chain being suspended from the celestial heights and reaching down hither, we, by ever clutching this upwards first with one hand and then with the other, seem indeed to draw it, but in reality we do not draw it down, it being both above and below, but ourselves are carried upwards to the higher splendors of the luminous rays. Or, as if, after we have embarked on a ship, and are holding on to cables, reaching from some

385

praying who was at first remote comes near by his prayer to his God.

rock, such as are given out, as it were, for us to seize, we do not draw the rock to us but ourselves in fact and the ship to the rock.

There is something fascinating in the strategy adopted by Modena here. Modena criticized Kabbalah and its theurgical view of prayer because it was instrumental in conversions of Kabbalists to Christianity.[17] Although Kabbalah was theologically suspect because of its affinities with Christianity and Neoplatonism, it was a late antique Christian Neoplatonist, the quintessence of ancient Christian mysticism, who was, anonymously, presented as the true alternative to the kabbalistic understanding of prayer. It was the concept of the perfection of the unchangeable God informing the solution of the Christian Neoplatonic mystic, the very opposite of the main understanding of the nature of the dynamic sefirotic realm, that allowed Modena to appeal to this unlikely source.

What was the reaction of Benamozegh to Modena's "solution"? He did not suspect the alien source of the parable, and states the problem as follows:

The parable of the ship is not sufficient at all in order to negate the change in the essence of God, exalted be He, from the [attribute of] mercy to [stern] judgment or vice versa. We indeed believe that by the virtue of our prayer, God, blessed be He, fulfills our requests, and hears our supplications, and if so we should deny the special quality of prayer to stir the goodness of the great God toward us. Alternatively, we shall have to fall in the pit of admitting the faith that allows change [in God] and we shall have to admit that by the virtue of our prayer God will change from the attribute of judgment to that of mercy, but this would be a deficiency in the essence of the simple and unchangeable substance.[18]

This quandary cannot be easily answered. Benamozegh wishes that the "least of the preachers" would come and solve it, and wonders whether it is possible to offer a reasonable solution without resorting to the principles of Kabbalah. He says that if the preacher could solve the problem, he would be worthy of the title of the "head of the savants."

APPENDIX

Here again, Benamozegh does not develop an original solution, but points out the quandary that can be solved if Kabbalah is accepted as a legitimate way.[19]

While obviously sympathetic with the theurgical solution in this book of his youth, Benamozegh does not elaborate upon it. In his usual vein, he asks more questions than he answers. It is only in his much later *Israel and Humanity* that the topic of theurgy is exposed as an important issue in itself. A whole chapter, the one dealing with man's cooperating with God, expresses the centrality of this notion in Judaism. Here he explicitly speaks about two levels of divinity: one, immanent in this world, that can be affected by human action; the other, transcendent, that cannot be affected by man. The immanent aspect involves what he calls anthropopathism, the emotional response of God to human action, and it represents the impact of the human on the divine. In fact, he adopts a Kabbalistic theology regarding the two levels, one that enables him to accept the importance of human acts and still allows the existence of a perfect aspect of deity. This is in fact the solution to the quandary formulated in *'Eimat Mafgi'a*. However, I wonder whether this use of Kabbalah is to be understood as merely an appropriation. Unlike the Kabbalists, who spoke about theurgy without allowing a role to immanentism, at least in this specific context, Benamozegh envisions the influence of man on God in terms of the influence of the part on the whole. Any change in the part, which is conceived of as engulfed within the whole, means also a change of the whole. Benamozegh compares Fichte's infinite will, which can be affected by man, to the concept of the *Shekhinah*, the divine presence understood as immanent within this world. He understands this idea as one of the supreme achievements of the rabbis:

> Finally we encounter in the rabbis a doctrine which stuns us by its grandeur and gives us the measure of the elevation which the spirit of the Pharisees could reach. According to them, man exerts a certain influence on the universe: he has the power to disturb or advance, to assist or oppose the divine order. This influence extends up to God Himself, at least to the Shekhinah, the divine in the world, and it is in this idea that we must seek the explanation of all the biblical and rabbinical passages in which we see Divinity feeling the effect of good and bad human actions. We should not be sur-

387

prised, then, to find this very conception in the Kabbalah. On this point as on all others, its doctrine is in perfect accord with the doctrines of exoteric Judaism.[20]

Despite the fact that Kabbalah is invoked as the source of this concept of theurgy, we can ponder whether this is really the case. In most of the kabbalistic sources, when speaking of the influence on the divine, the Kabbalists intend the realm of the ten *sefirot*, understood as the revealed aspect of the deity, a realm that is only rarely viewed as immanent in this world.[21] The transferring of the revealed divinity from the bosom of the transcendental realm to that of the immanent realm is not always clear in Kabbalah. It can be found, to a certain extent, in Lurianic Kabbalah, which speaks about the divine sparks engulfed within this world. This seems to be the direct source that inspired Benamozegh.[22] However, I wonder whether it was a certain version of Kabbalah that was the main source for this understanding of theurgy, or the more pantheistic formulations recurrent in Fichte's idealistic philosophy. Benamozegh's last formulation can be seen, at least to a certain degree, as an attempt to attenuate the greater impact of human deeds on the Divinity as understood by the Kabbalists (they went so "far" as to speak about making God).[23] However, despite Benamozegh's weakening of theurgy, and therefore implicitly of theosophy as well, the above passage bears testimony to an openness that is not always found even in modern scholarship. This view of the ancient forms of Judaism as including a theurgical principle, when expressed by a nineteenth-century thinker, constitutes a vision of the history and nature of Jewish mysticism different from that expressed in many modern studies on Kabbalah. Gershom Scholem, for example, described theurgical motifs as "not completely absent from old aggadic literature," noting the "somewhat dubious theological notion that 'the righteous increase the power of the Omnipotence.' "[24]

The divergences between Benamozegh's vision of theurgy in ancient Judaism and that of some modern scholars are not incidental. They reflect different phenomenologies of ancient Judaism, and a different weight given to some elements in Jewish mysticism. It seems that in this case the nineteenth-century thinker has something important to teach modern scholarship. While Benamozegh, influenced as he was by partial parallels to the kabbalistic theurgy found in Idealistic philosophy, was ready to inspect the Talmudic and biblical texts in order to create an organic continuum between kabbalistic theurgy and

APPENDIX

its sources, modern scholars have been concerned with pointing out the differences between the prekabbalistic and kabbalistic attitudes to the topic of theurgy. It seems that both were to a certain extent correct: The continuity between some late antique Jewish sources and kabbalistic theurgy has been accepted by some scholars in recent studies,[25] while others have remained inclined to emphasize the rupture between the various layers of Jewish tradition.

VI. Benamozegh's Theory of Religious Synthesis

It is in the context of the theurgical element in religion that Benamozegh contributed an interesting reflection about the difference between the nature of the magical elements in Judaism and those in Hinduism. According to his view, nature was conceived of by the Semitic magician as an important realm to be perfected by the thaumaturge, who, at the same time, cannot merge with the divine world. On the other hand in India, nature is regarded as an inferior realm, one that should be subdued by the acts of the magician who is able to reach heaven. A nonmonistic view of existence permeates the Hindu view, while the Jew is understood as a much more monistic thinker. Moreover, while the Semitic magician depends on God, the Hindu one is an independent being.[26] This distinction is relevant for the better understanding of another passage in *Israel and Humanity* that praises the children of Israel for their belief in the absolute unity of God, a view that does not depend upon the philosophical considerations that are characteristic of the Aryan nations. The latter are also described as being much more inclined to mythical perceptions, including incarnation, a position that is different from the transcendental and undivided Godhead of nonkabbalistic Judaism.[27] However, Benamozegh thinks of Kabbalah as unifying these two impulses: The transcendental one symbolized by the Tetragrammaton; and the name *Elohim*, which is a plural form. Kabbalah is therefore a "religious synthesis of Hebraism."[28]

Though Benamozegh does not mention a source for his synthetic vision of religion, it seems that there is at least a partial similarity between this theory of transcendentalism and immanentalism and the view of Nahman Krochmal, articulated a half century before. (Krochmal's position was also created under the influence, in his case a little less articulated, of Kabbalistic thought).[29] Like Benamozegh, Krochmal argues that his synthetic theology ensures Judaism's universal status.[30] Moreover, in a short treatise printed in 1897 and dedicated to the concept of *Malkhut* as the Reign of God, Benamozegh mentions a "very ancient" kabbalistic dictum with regard to the emanation of this divine attribute, one that constitutes an antidote to and a protest against pantheism. The dictum is "Malkhut is with the higher *sefirot* in a relationship of emanation, but not [in a relation] of union."[31]

This "ancient" antidote is supposed to solve the problem of pantheism because it describes an entity that though emanated from God is still not part of the divine unity. According to such a view, the last *sefirah* is indeed the immanent part of the divine, while the nine other *sefirot* constitute the divine unity, and implicitly, His transcendence. However, the inspection of the passages where this statement is found does not allow the conclusion drawn by Benamozegh. The first Kabbalist who used this formula seems to be Nachmanides, and, under his influence, the anonymous Kabbalist who wrote *Sefer Ma'arekhet ha-'Elohut*.[32] The commentator of this book, Rabbi Yehudah Hayyat, makes recurrent use of this sentence to mean that the last *sefirah* is the container of all the higher *sefirot*, as a compounded entity whose link to the other *sefirot* is weaker than the links between these nine divine powers.[33] Insofar as I could inspect the pertinent kabbalistic sources, no immanentistic implication should be attached to this view.[34] Benamozegh's forced reading, already formulated in the somewhat earlier *Israel and Humanity*, seems to be informed also by other considerations.

Benamozegh's assumption that kabbalistic thought represents a synthesis between a transcendental theology, as it was presented more eminently by Neoplatonism, and Gnostic impulses, which were conceived as coming from outside Judaism, was later presented as a major finding of modern scholarship.[35] In any case, this synthetic theory is one of the answers Benamozegh offers to the question that recurs so many times in his book: Is Judaism a universal religion? It is this teaching, according to him, that "is capable of restoring harmony between Hebraism and the gentile world."[36] It seems to me that the vision of Kabbalah as a bridge between the Jewish and European world is not merely the idiosyncrasy of our thinker. It is a fact that the impact on European thought of Kabbalah, which indeed has integrated alien elements, has been very great.[37]

This vision of the most sublime religious phenomenon as a synthesis seems to be Hegelian; by integrating the opposites, the highest phenomenon excels its predecessors. Let me compare this way of understanding the nature of Kabbalah with another attempt to present the highest form of religion, as formulated by a contemporary scholar of mysticism: Robert C. Zaehner. Zaehner's assumption about the phenomenology of religion is that there are two basic religious patterns. The first is the Hindu one, explicating a vision of concord and harmony between man and God, one that will culminate in a total fusion between the two in a mystical experience. India is "die Hauptschule der Mystik."[38] On the other hand, the Semites, who assume a basic discord between man and God, represent the prophetic religion par excellence, a religion devoid of mystical elements, at least as crucial components.[39] This sharp distinction between the prophetic and the mystical, which was apparently inherited from M. Weber and F. Heiler,[40] was applied by Zaehner to the ancient classical religions: the Hindu religion belongs on one side; and the biblical, Zoroastrian, and Islamic religions on the other. Christianity, however, he conceived of as the synthesis between the prophetic and the mystical types of religion, a synthesis that is able to overcome the striking divergences between them. Zaehner regards this religion as fulfilling, in an ideal manner, the vision of the Semites and the Zoroastrians on one hand, and of Hinduism and Buddhism on the other.[41]

Different as their approaches and presuppositions were, and also their conclusions, it is interesting to notice the common assumption of both Benamozegh and Zaehner that the synthesis between the Semitic and Aryan religiosities is also the ideal, or perfect, religiosity. Moreover, similarities between the views of the two forms of religious modalities in the two thinkers are fascinating: the Semitic religion is more oriented toward improving this world, prophetic in Zaehner's terms, while the Jewish thinker speaks about the Semitic thaumaturge as striving to improve nature. Both also assume that the Aryan more than the Semitic religiosity allows a union between the human and the divine. I wonder whether Zaehner was acquainted with Benamozegh's theory. We may assume that he arrived at his theory of religious synthesis by following the Hegelian-like theories that apparently had an impact also on Benamozegh. Nevertheless, it is still striking how similar both syntheses of the Aryan and Semitic religious modalities are in formulation.

VII. Renaissance Affinities

Though he wrote in the nineteenth century, Benamozegh's style is much more reminiscent of some of his Italian predecessors among the

Christian Kabbalists who composed their books at the end of the fifteenth and in the early sixteenth centuries. The search for the correspondences between Jewish Talmudic and mystical writings and those non-Jewish views that he considered to be influenced by them was a problematic task for a traditional Jew, as we learn from a discussion in his early *'Eimat Mafgi'a*. When addressing the question of the divine unity that is possible even on the basis of the assumption that there are ten *sefirot*, Benamozegh mentions the fact that Pythagoras asserted that the ten numbers are united to the Monad,[42] while Plato assumed a multiplicity of ideas within the divine wisdom, and presupposed a single Demiurge.[43] This comparison provoked a rather apologetic footnote, where he mentions that Jewish scholars, such as Rabbi Menasseh ben Israel[44] and Abraham Kohen Herrera,[45] had already resorted to pagan authorities so that he should not be blamed for this practice.[46] Therefore, Benamozegh explicitly identified himself, rather early in his literary career, with the style and way of thought of some of his predecessors who wrote under the influence of Renaissance culture.

It seems that Benamozegh's reserve about being too easily identified with Enlightenment openness to general culture, visible in his early writing, dissipated with time. Less than a decade later, both in his commentary on the Pentateuch and in *Ta'am le-Shad*, the number of the Gentile and Christian sources quoted and discussed at length has increased dramatically. This is extremely significant in the case of the commentary on the Pentateuch, composed in Hebrew. It is replete with quotations from general sources, adduced in Latin character, an exceptional case in the nineteenth century.

In his *Ta'am le-Shad*, Benamozegh's arguments against the attempts of Luzzatto to demonstrate that Kabbalah is a medieval forgery are in fact combating a claim that had been formulated by the critiques of Kabbalah since the Renaissance. In the writings of Elijah del Medigo and Modena the similarities between Kabbalistic ideas and Neoplatonic ones were adduced as an irrefutable proof for the influence of the latter on the former. Benamozegh sometimes adopted the implicit assumption that such similitudes are indeed relevant, but his historical explanation differs from that of the critics, since he believes that the similitudes are the result of the influence of the Jewish material on Gentile thought. From this point of view, he is close to some formulations found in Adolphe Franck and Salomon Munk.[47]

The Gentile author who best represents a starting point for comparisons with Kabbalistic concepts is Plotinus. In one interesting case Benamozegh wrote as follows:

> The words of the author of *Sefer Yetzirah* are illuminated and become brighter by what we know from Pythagoras the philosopher and his school, who hinted at the idea that the ten numbers are the principles of all the existent things.[48] And not Pythagoras alone but also Plotinus, who is the closest in time and more similar to Kabbalah,[49] has designated the soul by the name "number." It may be that also in this instance he had some predecessors among the Greek philosophers . . . and also Augustine the Christian is coming closer to us, as he distinguished between sensible numbers and intellectual ones [*carnales et spirituales numeri*], and if it is so, his own hands prove that his hands do not move from underneath the hands of the Kabbalists, and they are [but] two prophets who prophesy in different styles.[50]

Again, as in the above-mentioned note from *'Eimat Mafgi'a*, Benamozegh apologizes for his recourse to alien sources. Following this passage, he turns to some unnamed orthodox persons, referred to as "quasi pietists" (*ha-mithasedim*), who would protest his literary practice, arguing that secular things should not be compared to holy ones: "I shall not listen [to you] and not desire [your view], and let my part be with the sages and the illustrious masters of Israel, including the students of our Rabbi Isaac Luria, who did not consider it a sin to link by links of love Pythagoras and Plato with the Kabbalah."[51]

I assume that Luria's students referred to here are the same Kabbalists mentioned above: Ben Israel and Herrera. Thus, again, Renaissance Jewish sources are invoked as inspiring and buttressing his approach. In several other instances throughout this book the affinity between Kabbalah and philosophy is presented, again as supported by Renaissance Jewish figures.[52]

It is ironical that Isaac Luria, one of the most particularistic of all Kabbalists, is regarded as a source for the most universalistic view of Kabbalah. However, I want to emphasize that my argument concerning Renaissance influence on Benamozegh transcends his reliance on the authority of Renaissance Jewish authors as part of his apologetic

393

strategy. In my opinion Benamozegh's very concept of the antiquity and unity of religion is extracted from Renaissance sources.

Another school of thought that is constantly mentioned in comparison with Kabbalah is the Gnostic one. Benamozegh was acquainted with the ideas of the Gnostics from some patristic writings, and his attitude to their thought is very similar to his evaluation of the Neoplatonists. As ancient sources, the Gnostic fragments bear evidence for the antiquity of the ideas we also find in kabbalistic writings. His attitude to Neoplatonism and his attitude to Gnosticism are both rather positive and contrast with the negative stand found in the sources from which he learned about Gnosticism. Interestingly enough, Benamozegh emphasized the esoteric nature of the Gnostic doctrine, whereas he conceived of ancient Christianity as an exoteric teaching.[53] He articulates this view by claiming:

> I have no doubt that both the secret doctrine, or the name by which it has been designated, stem from the source of the Jews, namely from the Kabbalah that is known by the very name *Hokhmah*, and from it the distorted judgment, done by the first Christians, who have done with it whatever they wanted. As long as there was no distinction between it and the Kabbalah, it [the latter] has been designated positively by the name *Hokhmah*, but after some time, when the distinction between it and its source has been explicated . . . , it has been approached in a negative way.[54]

This statement forms the background of an interesting claim in *Israel and Humanity* to the effect that a passage in the Epistle to the Romans "contains visible traces of gnostic-kabbalistic doctrines which Paul had learned in the Palestinian schools."[55] Is Paul thought of as being part of the first Christians who were earlier portrayed as distorting the kabbalistic views that were accepted by the Gnostics? It is very difficult to answer this question in a conclusive manner. At least in one discussion it seems that the passage in John 15:8 is described as distorting the esoteric understanding of the first word of the Bible, "In the Beginning."[56] Elsewhere, he mentions again the theory that "at its beginnings, Christianity is but a distorted Kabbalah [and this is an argument for the latter's antiquity]. We heard the voice of the books of Kabbalah, which are not mentioned in the writings of the Talmudists [since they were hidden and occulted by them] explicated within the books of the first Christians, since they were slandering and disclosing the secrets."[57] These assumptions, formulated for the first time early in his career in his Hebrew writings, have been elaborated in a much more articulated treatment in *De l'origine des dogmes chrétiens*, printed in Livorno in 1897. This move from early and shorter Hebrew discussions to later and longer ones in Italian and French is a basic pattern in Benamozegh's literary development.

The claim that early Christianity was an exoteric and distorted Kabbalah is not entirely new with Benamozegh. He mentions explicitly M. Salvador's theory, set forth in *Jésus Christ et sa doctrine*.[58] However, already in the fifteenth century the Christian doctrine of the Trinity was presented by a Jewish thinker as a distortion of the kabbalistic theory of the existence of three supernal lights (named *Zahzahot*) within the infinite,[59] while Pico della Mirandola conceived Kabbalah to be a teaching that confirms, better than any other discipline, the tenets of Christianity.[60]

It should also be mentioned that Benamozegh's vision of the history of Gnosticism stems from Renaissance sources. The first to formulate the theory of the Jewish origin of Gnosticism was apparently the notorious Cornelius Agrippa of Nettesheim, and from his book this view reverberated in many other Renaissance sources. While the Christian *magus* proposed this affinity in order to express a negative attitude to both Gnosticism and Kabbalah, Benamozegh's attitude was much more positive. Indeed, in one of his discussions he explicitly states that the "Gnostics, whose affinity to the lore of Kabbalah is very great, were calling the souls [by the name of] the limbs of the wisdom."[61] Elsewhere, an even stronger awareness of the profound similarity was expressed: "The similarity between the Gnostics and the concepts of the Kabbalah is very awesome and sublime."[62] Relegated to the margin by early scholarship of Gnosticism at the beginning of this century, neglected by the founders of the modern study of Kabbalah, Benamozegh's proposals have nevertheless flourished in the last generation of scholars, who have embraced the view of the importance of Jewish sources for the emergence of this form of religion.[63] In the field of the history of Kabbalah as well, more recent studies seem to corroborate, though only partially, Benamozegh's intuitions.[64]

It should, nevertheless, be emphasized that despite the strong resemblance between Benamozegh's pointing out affinities between ancient pagan sources and Jewish mystical ones, and those resemblances put forth by Pico della Mirandola or Johann Reuchlin, he never mentioned these Renaissance predecessors in his polemical writings. I assume that this "ignorance" is a deliberate move, one that attempted to counteract the criticisms of Kabbalah's influence on Christians. Still, to a great extent Benamozegh's project, while structured as a direct answer to the details of the critiques of post-Renaissance authors, betrays the impact of Ficino's translations of Neoplatonic texts for the reinterpretation of Kabbalah, and it does so in a way similar to that found in the Christian Kabbalists. In fact, the philological tradition of the humanistic period, as represented by Luzzatto's writings, encountered in Benamozegh's response the Florentine approach to religious truths as expressed in different versions by various religious systems. From the very beginning of Christianity the philological approach has tended to uncover religious forgeries, to construct more historical schemata, and has been little inclined to seek for conceptual affinities among different religions. The Florentine thinkers and their followers, on the other hand, were less interested in historical sequences and possible forgeries, placing strong emphasis on the unity of truth. In a way quite similar to the Florentine thinkers who wrote in the Renaissance period, Benamozegh saw the *hebraica veritas* as the initiating source that influenced many of the cognate ideas found in various religions.

This Renaissance view assuming the unity of truth seems to me to be the starting point of Benamozegh's more comprehensive and less apologetical theological project: *Israel and Humanity.* It is in this book that the universalistic tendencies that characterized the spiritual life of many of the Italian intellectuals bloomed in a very special manner. The basis of this universalism was, as in the case of the Renaissance thinkers, deeply informed by the religious faith of the author. In this case, Kabbalah, the ancient and undistorted mystical lore, is conceived of as the ideal religiosity that was not only the pristine religion of the Jews, but also the perfect religious solution of the future. In other words, Benamozegh's universalism was of a limited type, one that reflected, nonetheless, a rather uncommon accord in the Jewish orthodox camp. It assumed a static phenomenology, that is, not so much an evolving process, but a synthesis that contains within itself the most perfect form of religion.[65] Unlike the other European Jewish intellectuals of the eighteenth and nineteenth centuries, who saw the sublimity of Judaism in its rationalistic aspects (similar to the Western *Aufklärung*), Benamozegh emphasized the universalistic and unifying aspects of the mythical components of Judaism, understood as constituting the Kab-

APPENDIX

balah. Together with A. Franck and F. Molitor, he adumbrated the twentieth-century reevaluation of Jewish mysticism as a vital constituent of Judaism.[66]

NOTES TO THE APPENDIX

1. See Gershom Scholem's characterization of Benamozegh as constituting, together with Franz Molitor, "the only two scholars of the age to approach the Kabbalah out of a fundamental sympathy and even affinity for its teachings" (*Kabbalah* [Jerusalem, 1974], p. 202); and Alessandro Guetta, "Elia Benamozegh, Un Cabbalista nel secolo dell'Idealismo," *Bailamme*, vol. 4 (Giugno, 1989), pp. 79–94.

2. See Moshe Idel, "Particularism and Universalism in Kabbalah, 1480–1650," and "Major Currents in Italian Kabbalah between 1560–1660," both printed in David B. Ruderman, ed., *Essential Papers on Jewish Culture in Renaissance and Baroque Italy* (New York, 1992), pp. 324–344, 345–368.

3. This is true especially in the case of Herrera (see note 45 below) and Rabbi Joseph Shelomo del Medigo of Kandia; see Moshe Idel, "Differing Conceptions of Kabbalah in the Early 17th Century," *Jewish Thought in the Seventeenth Century*," ed. I. Twersky and B. Septimus (Cambridge, Mass., 1987), pp. 178–197.

4. It was at a very young age, as young as sixteen, that he composed a Hebrew introduction to the collection of kabbalistic treatises printed by his uncle and initiator in matters of Kabbalah, Rabbi Yehudah Coriat's *Ma'or va-Shemesh* (Livorno, 1839).

5. See David Biale, "Kabbalah in Nahman Krochmal's Philosophy of History," *Journal of Jewish Studies* 32 (1981): 85–97. For more on this thinker see below.

6. In his earlier book there are already some observations that address Luzzatto's book. See II, p. 17b. On the controversy see Y. Colombo, "Il dibattito fra Luzzatto e Benamozegh intorno all Kabbala," *Rassegna Mensile di Israel*, vol. VII (1934), p. 471; and *ibid.*, vol. XXXII (1966), pp. 179–204. As to the title of Benamozegh's response to Luzzatto: the phrase *ta'am leshad* stems from the verse in Numbers 11:8, and it points to the taste of the manna, which was like "the taste of the oil-cake." The consonants of *leshad* can be decoded as an acronym to *le-Shad*, namely "to Sh[emuel] D[avid]," the two proper names of Luzzatto. Benamozegh responds to, i.e., he proposes a "tasteful answer to," the arguments of Luzzatto. Moreover, *leshad* can be under-

stood as a permuted form of the consonants that form *Shadal*, the acronym of Luzzatto's names. The choice of the title may imply that Benamozegh is able to invert Luzzatto's arguments against the authenticity of Kabbalah.

7. Luzzatto also acknowledged explicitly that "mes recherches sur la Kabbale ne sont pas le fruit d'une curiosité litteraire, mais du désir et du besoin de fixer mes idées et mes croyances dans les questions théologiques, et de me justifier auprès de quelques chers et respectables amis."

8. See my "Defining Kabbalah: The Kabbalah of the Divine Names," in *Mystics of the Book: Themes, Topics & Typologies*, ed. R. A. Herrera (New York, 1993), pp. 97–122.

9. It seems that he quotes from Abraham Abulafia only very late in his career; see *Israel and Humanity*, p. 233.

10. *Israel and Humanity*, pp. 166–189.

11. Ibid., pp. 175–178, 185, 188.

12. See Moshe Idel, *Kabbalah: New Perspectives* (New Haven, London, 1988), p. 157.

13. See Idel, "Differing Conceptions," p. 175 and note 178.

14. *Ari Nohem*, ed. N. S. Leibowitch (rep. Jerusalem, 1971), pp. 24–29, 93–95.

15. Ibid., p. 27.

16. *The Divine Names*, III, 1, tr. J. Parker, in *The Works of Dionysius the Areopagite* (Oxford, 1897), I, pp. 27–28; and in *Pseudo-Dionysius, The Complete Works*, tr. Colm Luibheid (Mahwah, 1987), pp. 68–69, n. 126. On this passage of the Christian mystic, see René Roques, *L'Univers dionysien* (Paris, 1983), pp. 128–129; and on its presence in other Jewish sources, see Idel, "Differing Conceptions," p. 177, n. 190.

17. See Idel, ibid., pp. 166–168.

18. *'Eimat Mafgi'a*, I, p. 13a. Benamozegh was acquainted with Pseudo-Dionysius's writings, as is seen from a quote from one of his works in *Ta'am le-Shad*, p. 193. There he conceived the views expressed by Pseudo-Dionysius as being close to kabbalistic ones. Nevertheless, it seems that he never discovered the fact that Modena, and indirectly he himself, were debating an illustration taken from this Christian author.

19. *'Eimat Mafgi'a*, I, p. 13a.

20. *Israel and Humanity*, pp. 202, 203.

21. Idel, *Kabbalah: New Perspectives*, pp. 144–146.

APPENDIX

22. For another influence of this view on Jewish modern philosophy, see the end of Franz Rosenzweig's *The Star of Redemption*.

23. See some of the kabbalistic texts discussed in the studies mentioned in note 25.

24. Scholem, *Origins of the Kabbalah*, tr. A. Arkush, ed. R. J. Zwi Werblowsky (Philadelphia, 1987), p. 80. See also Isaiah Tishby, *The Wisdom of the Zohar*, tr. D. Goldstein (Oxford, 1989), I, pp. 234–236. See also Ephraim Gottlieb, *Studies in Kabbalah Literature*, ed. Joseph Hacker (Tel Aviv, 1976), p. 29 [Hebrew].

25. Cf. Idel, *Kabbalah: New Perspectives*, pp. 156–199; Elliot Wolfson, "Mystical-Theurgical Dimensions of Prayer in *Sefer ha-Rimmon*," *Approaches to Judaism in Medieval Times*, III (1988): 41–80; and now the very important volume of Charles Mopsik, *Les grands textes de la Cabale* (Verdier, Lagrasse, 1993).

26. *Israel and Humanity*, pp. 201–202.

27. Ibid., p. 71.

28. Ibid.

29. See Jay M. Harris, *Nachman Krochmal: Guiding the Perplexed of the Modern Age* (New York, London, 1991), pp. 64–65, 77.

30. *Israel and Humanity*, pp. 71, 72.

31. See the Italian translation of the French text Guetta, "Elia Benamozegh" [n. 1 above], p. 92. See also *Israel and Mankind*, pp. 155, 188–189. The unmitigated pantheism, which does not involve a transcendental aspect, is understood by Benamozegh as the basic error of Spinoza; see his "Spinoza et la Kabbalah," ed. E. Zini (Jerusalem, 5348), pp. 44–45. On the concept of *Shekhinah*—apparently identified by Benamozegh with the last *sefirah*—as the divine immanence, see Joshua Abelson, *The Immanence of God in Rabbinic Literature* (London, 1912).

32. *Sefer Ma'arekhet ha-'Elohut* (Mantua, 1558), fol. 190b. This book, as well as the commentary on it, is quoted several times in *Ta'am le-Shad*.

33. *Minhat Yehudah*, as printed in *Sefer Ma'arekhet ha-'Elohut*, fols. 10b, 12a, 14a, 15b, 16b, 177b.

34. See also the opposite view, expressed by Rabbi Joseph Caro, that the last *sefirah* is part of the divine unity but it is not part of His emanation (R. J. Z. Werblowsky, *Joseph Karo, Lawyer and Mystic* [Philadelphia, 1977], p. 218 and n. 3).

35. Scholem, *Origins of the Kabbalah*, p. 210; idem, *The Mystical*

APPENDIX

Shape of the Godhead (New York, 1991), pp. 15–55; Tishby, *The Wisdom of the Zohar* I, pp. 236–237, 252, n. 17. I have my doubts as to the contribution of the theories of synthesis, as expressed by both Benamozegh and Scholem, for a better understanding of Kabbalah. In some kabbalistic theories, the First Cause, which is supposed to represent the transcendental deity, is to be understood esoterically as implying the more ancient concept of *Shi'ur Qomah*. See Moshe Idel, "Une figure d'homme au-dessus des sefirot (à propos de la doctrine des 'éclats' de R. David ben Yehouda he-Hasid et ses développments)," *Pardes* 12 (1990): 131–150.

36. *Israel and Humanity*, p. 71. See also above M. Luria's Introduction, p. 17.

37. On this issue in fifteenth- and sixteenth-century Italian Kabbalah, see Idel, "Particularism and Universalism," pp. 327–328; "Major Currents," pp. 351–360.

38. *Hindu and Muslim Mysticism* (New York, 1972), p. 3.

39. I have some doubts about the originality of this distinction; see Edward Caird, *The Evolution of Theology in Greek Philosophers* (Glasgow, 1904), II, p. 214; and especially Max Weber's *Ancient Judaism*, tr. H. H. Gerth and D. Martindale (Illinois, 1952), p. 314: "The prophet never knew himself emancipated from suffering, be it only from the bondage of sin. There was no room for a *unio mystica*, not to mention the inner oceanic tranquility of the Buddhistic arhat. . . . Likewise his personal majesty as a ruler precluded all thought of mystic communion with God as a quality of man's relation to him. No true Yahwe prophet and no creature at all could even have dared to claim anything of the sort, much less the deification of self. . . . The prophet could never arrive at a permanent inner peace with God. Yahwe's nature precluded it. . . . There is no reason to assume that apathetic-mystic states of Indian stamp have not also been experienced on Palestinian soil." See also ibid., p. 315.

40. I am unable to locate a reference to Weber or Heiler in Zaehner's discussions of the two major forms of religion.

41. *At Sundry Times* (London, 1958), pp. 190–194.

42. This Greek thinker is mentioned several times in *Ta'am le-Shad*, e.g., pp. 96, 138, 154, 168, 180, 182, 184, 186, 223. On Jewish mention of Pythagoras in the context of Renaissance philosophical understanding of Kabbalah, see my introduction to Reuchlin's *De Arte Cabalistica* (Nebraska, 1993).

APPENDIX

43. I, p. 10a.
44. See Moshe Idel, "Kabbalah, Platonism and Prisca Theologia: The Case of R. Menasseh ben Israel," *Menasseh ben Israel and His World*, ed. Y. Kaplan, H. Mechoulan, and R. I. Popkin (Leiden, 1989), pp. 207–219.
45. His book, *Beit 'Elohim*, is quoted in Benamozegh's *Teologia dogmatica e apologetica* (Livorno, 1877), p. 238, n. 19. On the Renaissance background of this Kabbalist, see Alexander Altmann, "Lurianic Kabbala in a Platonic Key; Abraham Cohen Herrera's *Puerta de Cielo*," *Von der mittelalterlichen zur modernen Aufklärung* (Tübingen, 1987), pp. 172–205; and Nissim Yosha, *Abraham Cohen Herrera's Philosophical Interpretation of Lurianic Kabbalah* (Ph.D. Thesis, Hebrew University, Jerusalem, 1991) (Hebrew).
46. I, p. 10a footnote **.
47. However, Benamozegh's erudition in both the Jewish and the ancient sources, pagan and Christian, is far greater than those of his predecessors. It should be emphasized that in his *Storia degli Esseni* (Firenze, 1865), pp. 62–71, Benamozegh distances himself from Franck's theory that the Kabbalah is of Alexandrian origin, holding for a Palestinian extraction. See also below, n. 54.
48. On *Sefer Yetzirah* and Pythagoreanism, see Scholem, *Kabbalah*, p. 25. On the contact between an important ancient rabbi and a Neopythagorean philosopher, see *Israel and Mankind*, p. 259.
49. See also *Ta'am le-Shad*, pp. 141, 159.
50. Ibid., p. 154.
51. Ibid., p. 154. Compare also the stand expressed in *Teologia dogmatica e apologetica* (Livorno, 1877), p. 190, n. 18, where he asserts that the thirty-two paths of *Sefer Yetzirah*, which are compounded of twenty-two letters and ten *sefirot*, reflect the Pythagorean theory of numbers and the Platonic theory of ideas. See also ibid., p. 199, n. 36.
52. Ibid., pp. 146, 158, 223.
53. *Ta'am le-Shad*, pp. 221–222.
54. Ibid., p. 221.
55. P. 203. See also above, n. 47.
56. See his commentary on the Pentateuch named *'Em la-Mikra* (Livorno, 1862) I, p. 1b.
57. Ibid., I, p. 167b. See also *ibid.*, II, p. 9b. Benamozegh's polemic and biased vision of the origin of Christianity as distortion notwithstanding, there is a growing awareness in modern scholarship

as to the importance of ancient Jewish mysticism for the better under-standing of early Christianity; see, e.g., Bernard McGinn, *The Founda-tions of Mysticism* (New York, 1991), p. 22.

58. *Jésus Christ et sa doctrine* (Bruxelles, 1838), discussed in *De l'origine*, pp. 18ff.

59. See Scholem, *Origins of the Kabbalah*, pp. 353–354; idem, "Zur Geschichte des Anfangs des Christlichen Kabbala," in *Essays Presented to Leo Baeck* (London, 1954), pp. 107–108; and Idel, "Differing Con-cepts," p. 166, n. 142. On the affinity between the kabbalistic and Christian concepts of Trinity, see the letter of Aimé Pallière, printed by Alessandro Guetta, "Due lettere di Aimé Pallière a Elia Benamozegh," *Gli Ebrei in Toscana dal Medioevo al Risorgimento, Fatti e Momenti* (Florence, 1980), p. 62. On the impact of Christian trinitarian formulas on Jewish Kabbalah, see Yehuda Liebes, *Studies in the Zohar* (Albany, 1993), pp. 140–146.

60. See Chaim Wirszubski, *Pico della Mirandola's Encounter with Jewish Mysticism* (Cambridge, Mass., 1987), pp. 106, 123–124.

61. *Ta'am le-Shad*, p. 112.

62. Ibid., pp. 130–131. See also the mention of the affinity be-tween the kabbalistic *sefirot* and the Gnostic aeons in his commentary on the Bible, I, p. 166b. For another comparison between Kabbalah and Gnosticism, see Benamozegh's "Spinoza et la Kabbalah," p. 39, n. 23.

63. On this turn in modern scholarship, see the summary of a major student who does not accept it, Simone Pétrement, *A Separate God: The Christian Origins of Gnosticism*, tr. Carol Harrison (San Fran-cisco, 1990), pp. 45–62.

64. See my *Kabbalah: New Perspectives*, pp. 30–32.

65. Unlike the other spiritual universalism, as represented by the much younger contemporary of Benamozegh, Rabbi Abraham Yizhaq ha-Kohen Kook, whose universalism, based also on Kabbalah and He-gelianism, was much more dynamic and evolutive.

66. See A. Franck, *Kabbalah: The Religious Philosophy of the He-brews*, tr. I. Sassmitz (New York, 1940), p. 219. It should be mentioned that these positive attitudes to Jewish mysticism not withstanding, the last phase of this lore, Hasidism, was treated by him rather negatively.

Table of Abbreviations

Am	Amos
Art.	Article
b.	Born; Son of (*ben*)
Bar	Baruch
B.C.E.	Before the Common Era
Bk.	Book
ca.	Approximately
C.E.	Common Era
Cent.	Century
cf.	See
Ch., Chap.	Chapter
Chr	Chronicles
cp.	Compare
d.	Died
Dn	Daniel
Dt	Deuteronomy
Eccl	Ecclesiastes
ed.	Edited by; edition
e.g.	For example
Encyc.	Encyclopedia
esp.	Especially
et seq.	And following
Ex	Exodus
Ez	Ezekiel
Ezr	Ezra
ff.	And following
fl.	Lived
fol.	Folio
Gal	Galatians
Gk.	Greek

TABLE OF ABBREVIATIONS

Gn	Genesis
Hb	Habakkuk
Heb.	Hebrew
ibid.	In the same place
idem	The same
i.e.	That is
Is	Isaiah
Jb	Job
Jer	Jeremiah
Jgs	Judges
Jl	Joel
Jn	John
Jos	Joshua
JPS	Jewish Publication Society
Kgs	Kings
lit.	Literally
Lk	Luke
Lv	Leviticus
M.	Monsieur; Mr.
Mal	Malachi
Mi	Micah
Mt	Matthew
n.	Note
n.d.	No date given
Neh	Nehemiah
Nm	Numbers
Prv	Proverbs
Ps	Psalms
Pt.	Part
R.	Rabbi
rep.	Reprinted
Rom	Romans
Rv	Revelation
sec.	Section
ser.	Series
Sm	Samuel
s.v.	Under the entry
tr., trans.	Translated by
vol.	Volume
Zec	Zechariah

Table of Scriptural References

2:22–24	263, 270	19:14	104
3:5	86	20:4	104, 124
3:15	168	20:7	229
3:17	192	20:11, 13	104
3:22	86, 163	21:33	86, 101
4:14	191	22:2	319
4:26	88	22:14	321
6:11–12	192	23:6	229
9	18	24:31	105
9:1	263	24:50	105
9:2	191	28:10–19	223
9:3	264	28:14	326
9:3–4	276	32:3	98, 321
9:4	264	36:31	290
9:5	263, 268	50:20	123
9:6	264–265, 268–269		
9:7	278	*Habakkuk*	
9:8–17	325	1:13	129
9:9	123	2:14	173
9:12, 15	123		
9:26–27	88	*Isaiah*	
9:27	299	1:26	321
10:5	206	2:4	304
10:20, 31	207	2:17–18	119
12:1	319	3:13	121
12:3	230, 326	6:3	81
12:5	229	11:9	37
12:8	229	13:4	128
14:5	321	19:18	106
14:13	268	19:23–25	132
14:18	108	19:24–25	286
14:18–20	326	30:33	224
14:19	198	31:5	210
14:19–20	86	34:11	182
14:22	91	43:7	187
15:5	158	43:10	80
17:5	230	44:6	80
17:20	230	44:14	85
18–19	231–232	44:24	84
18:25	121, 221	44:28	307

TABLE OF SCRIPTURAL REFERENCES

45	128	28:27	226
45:1, 3, 5	308	28:28	226
45:5	84		
45:5–7	84	*Joel*	
45:18	182	3:1	109, 173
45:18, 21, 22	85	4:14	224
46:9	85		
49:14–15	211	*Joshua*	
54:5	139	5:14	98
55:8–9	221	9	214
56:2	250		
56:3, 6–7	249–250	*1 Kings*	
60:10	308	8:41–43	309
63:16	212	19:15	128
64:7	210	20:16	291
65:17	181	20:23	136
66:1	80, 209	20:28	136
66:12–13	211	20:31–32	215
66:23	250	21	293
		22:48	291
Jeremiah			
2:2	65	*2 Kings*	
2:3	282	5:10, 14, 15	261
3:19	221	5:15, 17	142
4:23–25	182	5:18–19	267
9:24–25	130	6:21–22	215
10:6, 7	110	8:7–15	286
10:11	85	18:33–34	120
12:14–15	130	18:35	120
23:6	108, 321	19:15	85, 120
23:24	80	19:17–19	120–121
25:9	128		
25:18–26	128	*Leviticus*	
29:4–7	286	3:17	143
31:34	173	10:2	189
33:16	322	16	91
33:20–21	227	16:6	273
		16:9	243
Job		16:29	278
26:7	183	18:27	279

TABLE OF SCRIPTURAL REFERENCES

409

TABLE OF SCRIPTURAL REFERENCES

85:11	323	*Zechariah*	
87:4–6	111–112	8:23	232
90:1–4	184	14:9	111
90:4	187	14:16	311
96:7–10	118		
102:16	253		
102:26–28	183	**NEW TESTAMENT**	
102:27–28	80		
103:19	119		
104:29–30	69	*Acts*	
106:48	184	10:11	264
109:4	312	10:13, 15	264
110	231	15:19–25	54
113:3–4	109	17:26	207
117	118	17:28	342–343
118:2–4	253		
119:89	223	*Galatians*	
135:19–20	253	3:28	21
138:4–5	299		
139:7–12	81		
145:13	184	*John*	
145:14–17	123	1:9	178
147:19–20	245	14:6	161
148	119	15:8	394
148:11–13	118	15:26	177
150:6	119		
		Luke	
1 Samuel		12:3	169
8:6–7	293	17:21	155
8:11–18	359		
29:6	107		
		Matthew	
2 Samuel		3:9	127
7:14	211	5:17	171
10	259	12:25	196
10:2	215	22:1–4	150
23:3	191	23:4	266
Song of Songs		*Romans*	
4:1	312	8:22–23	203

Table of Talmudic References

TABLE OF TALMUDIC REFERENCES

TABLE OF TALMUDIC REFERENCES

Table of Midrashic References

TABLE OF MIDRASHIC REFERENCES

Bibliography of
Further Readings

Benamozegh, Elijah. *'Em la-Mikra*. 5 vols. Leghorn: Benamozegh, 1862. A critical, philosophical, and philological commentary on the Torah (in Hebrew).

———. *Israël et l'Humanité; étude sur le problème de la religion universelle et sa solution*. Paris: Leroux, 1914. Posthumous publication of the author's masterpiece; edited by Aimé Pallière. Substantially longer than the second edition (1961), on which the present translation is based.

———. *Jewish and Christian Ethics with a Criticism on Mahomedism*. San Francisco, 1873. Translation by E. Blockman of *Morale juive et morale chrétienne*.

———. "Judaism and Christianity in the Light of Noachism." *Judaism* 13 (1964): 220–227, 346–350. Translations by William Wolf from *Morale juive et morale chrétienne*.

———. *Lettere dirette a S. D. Luzzatto*. Leghorn: Benamozegh, 1890. On Kabbalah and other matters of contention.

———. *Morale juive et morale chrétienne: examen comparatif suivi de quelques réflexions sur les principes de l'Islamisme*. Neuchâtel: Éditions de la Baconnière, 1946. Third edition of work published originally in 1867. Important preface by Josué Jéhouda.

———. "Préface de l'Éditeur" to Eliahu Hazan, *Zikhron Yerushalayim*. Leghorn: Benamozegh, 1874. Autobiographical.

———. *Scritti scelti*. Special volume of the periodical *Rassegna Mensile di Israel*, ed. Alfredo S. Toaff. Rome, 1955. An anthology of selections from Benamozegh's work, with introductory essay by Yoseph Colombo.

————. *Storia degli Esseni*. Florence: Le Monnier, 1865. On Kabbalism as an essential element of historical Judaism.

————. *Teologia dogmatica e apologetica*. Vol. 1, *Dio*. Leghorn: Vigo, 1877. Contains sympathetic letter to Benamozegh from Giuseppe Mazzini.

Colombo, Yoseph. "Il concetto di religione in Benamozegh." Special volume of the periodical *Rassegna Mensile di Israel* in honor of Dante Lattes (Rome, 1938): 58ff.

Gardens and Ghettos: The Art of Jewish Life in Italy, ed. Vivian B. Mann. Berkeley: University of California Press, 1989. Useful essays on Italian-Jewish history and culture.

Guetta, Alessandro. "Elia Benamozegh: Bibliografia." *Rassegna Mensile di Israel* 53 (1987): 67–81. Incorporates and amplifies earlier bibliographies by Umberto Cassuto (1913) and Alfredo S. Toaff (1955).

Pallière, Aimé. *The Unknown Sanctuary: A Pilgrimage from Rome to Israel*. New York, 1928. Translation of *Le Sanctuaire inconnu; ma "conversion" au judaisme* (Paris: Rieder, 1926). An eloquent spiritual autobiography and precious introduction to Benamozegh.

Schwarzschild, Steven S. "Do Noachites Have to Believe in Revelation?" *Jewish Quarterly Review* 52 (1961–1962): 297–308; 53 (1962–1963): 30–68. Analysis of a central theme in Benamozegh's work.

Bibliography of Sources:
Texts, Editions, Translations

Albo, Joseph. *Sefer ha-Ikkarim* (Book of Principles), ed. and trans. Isaac Husik. 4 vols. Philadelphia: Jewish Publication Society, 1946.

Ari Nohem, ed. N. S. Leibowitch. Jerusalem, 1971.

Babylonian Talmud: tractates Avodah Zarah, Baba Batra, Baba Kamma, Bekhorot, Berakhot, Eruvin, Gittin, Hagigah, Hullin, Kiddushin, Makkot, Megillah, Menahot, Mo'ed Katan, Pesahim, Pirke Avot, Rosh Hashonah, Sanhedrin, Shabbat, Shebi'it, Sotah, Sukkah, Ta'anit, Yevamot, Yoma, Zebahim. *The Babylonian Talmud*, ed. I. Epstein. 35 vols. London: Soncino, 1935–1952.

Benamozegh, Elijah. *'Eimat Mafgi'a*. Leghorn: Benamozegh, 1855.

———. *Israël et l'Humanité; étude sur le problème de la religion universelle et sa solution*. Paris: Leroux, 1914.

———. *Israël et l'Humanité*. New ed. entirely rev. Paris: Albin Michel, 1961.

———. *Israele e l'umanità*, trans. M. Morselli. Genoa: Marietti, 1990.

———. *Yisroel v'ha-Enoshut* (Hebrew version of *Israël et l'Humanité*), trans. S. Marcus. Jerusalem: Mossad ha-Rav Kook, 1967.

———. *Morale juive et morale chrétienne: examen comparatif suivi de quelques réflexions sur les principes de l'Islamisme*. 3rd ed. Neuchâtel: Éditions de la Baconnière, 1946.

———. "Préface de l'Éditeur" to Eliahu Hazan, *Zikhron Yerushalayim*. Leghorn: Benamozegh, 1874.

———. *Scritti scelti*. Special volume of the periodical *Rassegna Mensile di Israel*, ed. Alfredo S. Toaff. Rome, 1955.

———. *Spinoza et la Kabbalah*, ed. E. Zini. Jerusalem, 1988.

———. *Ta'am le-Shad*. Leghorn: Benamozegh, 1863.

———. *Teologia dogmatica e apologetica*. Vol. 1, *Dio*. Leghorn: Vigo, 1877.

Caro, Joseph. *Shulhan Arukh*, with commentary by Moses Isserles. Standard editions.

Clement of Alexandria. *Stromateis*. In *Alexandrian Christianity: Selected Translations of Clement and Origen*. Philadelphia: Westminster, 1954.

Coriat, Yehuda. *Ma'or va-Shemesh*. Leghorn, 1839.

Dante Alighieri. *Paradiso*, ed. and trans. Charles Singleton. Bollingen Series LXXX. Princeton: Princeton University Press, 1975.

Demosthenes. *Against Aristogeiton*, ed. and trans. J. H. Vince. Loeb Classical Library. Cambridge, Mass.: Harvard, 1935.

Diodorus Siculus. *Bibliotheca Historica*, ed. C. H. Oldfather. Vol. 1. Loeb Classical Library. New York: Putnam, 1933.

Eusebius, Bishop of Caesarea. *Preparation for the Gospel*, ed. and trans. J. Sirinelli and E. des Places. Paris: Éditions du Cerf, 1974 *et seq.*

Florus, Lucius Annaeus. *Epitome of Roman History*, ed. E. S. Forster. Loeb Classical Library. Cambridge, Mass.: Harvard University Press, 1966.

Friedenthal, M. B. *Yesod ha-Dat*. 2 vols. Breslau: Loeb Sulzbach, 1823.

Hesiod. *Works and Days*, trans. M. L. West. New York: Oxford University Press, 1988.

Hobbes, Thomas. *Leviathan*. Intro. by A. D. Lindsay. London: Dent, 1965.

Horace. *Satires, Epistles, and Ars Poetica*, ed. H. R. Fairclough. Loeb Classical Library. Cambridge, Mass.: Harvard University Press, 1970.

Josephus, Flavius. *Jewish Antiquities*. Vol. 7. Loeb Classical Library. Cambridge, Mass.: Harvard University Press, 1957.

Judah Halevi. *The Kuzari*, trans. H. Hirschfeld. New York: Schocken, 1964.

Justin Martyr. *The Apologies of Justin Martyr*. Cambridge: Cambridge University Press, 1910.

Kara, Simeon. *Yalkut Shimoni*. 2 vols. Jerusalem, 1967.

Koran: *Al-Qur'an: A Contemporary Translation*, trans. Ahmed Ali. Princeton: Princeton University Press, 1988.

Macrobius, Ambrosius. *Saturnalia*, trans. P. V. Davies. New York: Columbia University Press, 1969.

Maimonides, Moses. *The Book of Adoration* [Book 2 of *Mishneh Torah*], ed. and trans. Moses Hyamson. Jerusalem: Boys Town, 1962. *Hilkhot Tefillah* is on pp. 98a–119b.

———. *The Book of Knowledge* [Book 1 of *Mishneh Torah*], ed. and trans.

Moses Hyamson. Jerusalem: Boys Town, 1962. *Hilkhot Teshuvah* is on pp. 81b–93a.

———. *The Code of Maimonides*, series of translations that will include the entire *Mishneh Torah*, in progress. New Haven: Yale University Press, 1949 et seq. *Hilkhot Issure Bi'ah* is in Book 5, *The Book of Holiness*, trans. L. I. Rabinowitz and P. Grossman, 1965. *Hilkhot Mattenot Aniyyim* is in Book 7, *The Book of Seeds. Hilkhot Roseah* is in Book 11, *The Book of Torts*, trans. Hyman Klein, 1954. *Hilkhot Melakhim* is in Book 14, *The Book of Judges*, trans. A. M. Hershman, 1949.

———. *The Guide of the Perplexed* (Moreh Nevukhim), trans. Shlomo Pines. Chicago: University of Chicago Press, 1963.

———. *Sefer ha-Mitzvot, The Commandments*, trans. Charles B. Chavel. 2 vols. London: Soncino, 1967.

Marcus Aurelius. *The Meditations of the Emperor Marcus Aurelius*. Oxford: Oxford University Press, 1944.

Mekilta de-Rabbi Ishmael, trans. J. Z. Lauterbach. 3 vols. Philadelphia: Jewish Publication Society, 1949.

Midrash Rabbah, ed. and trans. H. Freedman and Maurice Simon. 10 vols. 3rd ed. London: Soncino, 1983.

Nachmanides, Moses. *The Commentary of Nahmanides on Genesis Chapters 1–6⁸*, trans. Jacob Newman. Leiden: Brill, 1960.

Pallière, Aimé. *The Unknown Sanctuary: A Pilgrimage from Rome to Israel*, trans. Louise Waterman Wise. New York: Bloch, 1928.

Pesikta de-Rab Kahana, trans. William G. Braude and Israel J. Kapstein. Philadelphia: Jewish Publication Society, 1975.

Pesikta Rabbati, trans. William G. Braude. 2 vols. New Haven: Yale University Press, 1968.

Philo of Alexandria. *Works*, with translation by F. H. Colson. 12 vols. Cambridge, Mass.: Harvard University Press, 1932–1968.

Pirke de-Rabbi Eliezer, trans. Gerald Friedlander. 4th ed. New York: Sepher-Hermon Press, 1981.

Plato. *Laws*, ed. R. G. Bury. 2 vols. Loeb Classical Library. Cambridge, Mass.: Harvard University Press, 1967–1968.

Plutarch. *Quaestiones Convivales*. Vols. 8 and 9 of *Moralia*, ed. P. A. Clement et al. Loeb Classical Library. Cambridge, Mass.: Harvard University Press, 1961–1969.

Porphyry. *On the Life of Plotinus and the Arrangement of His Work*. In Plotinus, *The Enneads*, trans. Stephen MacKenna. New York: Pantheon, n.d., pp. 1–20.

BIBLIOGRAPHY OF SOURCES

Pseudo-Dionysius. *The Complete Works*, trans. Colm Luibheid. Mahwah, 1987.

———. *The Works of Dionysius the Areopagite*. Vol. 1. Oxford, 1897.

Rashi. *Commentary on the Torah*. In *The Pentateuch and Rashi's Commentary*, ed. Abraham ben Isaiah and Benjamin Sharfman. 7 vols. Brooklyn: S. S. and R. Publishing Co., 1949.

Scriptures: Christian. Authorized [King James] Version.

Scriptures: Jewish. *Tanakh: A New Translation of the Holy Scriptures*. Philadelphia: Jewish Publication Society, 1985.

Sifrei: *Sifre: A Tannaitic Commentary on the Book of Deuteronomy*, trans. Reuven Hammer. New Haven: Yale University Press, 1986.

Spinoza, Baruch. *A Theologico-Political Treatise*. In *The Chief Works of Benedict de Spinoza*, ed. and trans. R. H. M. Elwes. Vol. 1. Bohn's Philosophical Library. London: Bell, 1883.

Strabo. *Geography*, trans. H. C. Hamilton and W. Falconer. 3 vols. London, 1912–1916.

The Talmud of the Land of Israel [Yerushalmi], trans. Jacob Neusner. Vol. 24, Nazir. Chicago: University of Chicago Press, 1985.

Tanna debe Eliyyahu: The Lore of the School of Elijah, trans. William G. Braude and Israel J. Kapstein. Philadelphia: Jewish Publication Society, 1981.

Zohar, trans. Harry Sperling and Maurice Simon. 5 vols. London: Soncino, 1931–1934. 2nd ed., 1984. (Complete text with Hebrew trans., ed. Yehuda Ashlag. 22 vols. Jerusalem: 1945–1958.)

Bibliography of Sources: Monographs, Articles, and Reference Works

Abelson, Joshua. *The Immanence of God in Rabbinic Liturgy*. London, 1912.

Altmann, Alexander. "Lurianic Kabbala in a Platonic Key: Abraham Cohen Herrera's *Puerta de Cielo*." In *Von der mittelalterlichen zur modernen Aufklärung*, pp. 172–205. Tübingen, 1987.

Biale, David. "Kabbalah in Nahman Krochmal's Philosophy of History." *Journal of Jewish Studies* 32 (1981): 85–97.

Caird, Edward. *The Evolution of Theology in Greek Philosophers*. Vol. 2. Glasgow, 1904.

Colombo, Yoseph. "Il dibattito tra Luzzatto e Benamozegh intorno alle Kabbala." *Rassegna Mensile di Israel* 8 (1934): 471–497.

Dumézil, George. *Mitra-Varuna*. Paris, 1948.

Encyclopaedia Judaica, ed. Cecil Roth. 16 vols. Jerusalem: Encyclopaedia Judaica, 1972.

Encyclopedia of Philosophy. 8 vols. New York: Macmillan, 1967.

Feldman, Louis H. "The Omnipresence of the God-Fearers." *Biblical Archaeology Review* 12 (1986): 58–63.

Fichte, Johann Gottlieb. *The Vocation of Man* (Die Bestimmung des Menschen), trans. William Smith. La Salle, Illinois, 1946.

Franck, A. *Kabbalah: The Religious Philosophy of the Hebrews*, trans. I. Sassmitz. New York, 1940.

Freud, Sigmund. *Moses and Monotheism*, trans. Katherine Jones. London, 1939.

Gordis, Robert. *Jewish Ethics for a Lawless World*. New York: Jewish Theological Seminary of America, 1986.

Gottlieb, Ephraim. *Studies in Kabbalah Literature*, ed. Joseph Hacker. Tel Aviv, 1976. [In Hebrew.]

Graetz, Heinrich. *Geschichte der Juden von den Ältesten Zeiten bis auf die Gegenwart*. Vol. 4. Leipzig: Leiner, 1853–1876.

Guetta, Alessandro. "Contributo alla lettera dell'opera filosofica di Elia Benamozegh." *Rassegna Mensile di Israel* 49 (1983): 565–572.

———. "Due lettere di Aimé Pallière a Elia Benamozegh." In *Gli Ebrei in Toscana dal Medioevo al Risorgimento, Fatti e Momenti*. Florence, 1980.

———. "Elia Benamozegh: Bibliografia." *Rassegna Mensile di Israel* 53 (1987): 67–81.

———. "Elia Benamozegh, un Cabbalista nel secolo dell'Idealismo." *Bailamme* 4 (June 1989): 79–94.

Harris, Jay M. *Nachman Krochmal: Guiding the Perplexed of the Modern Age*. New York and London, 1991.

von Hartmann, Eduard. *Philosophy of the Unconscious* [trans. from the German]. 3 vols. New York: Macmillan, 1884.

Houzeau, Jean Charles. *Études sur les Facultés Mentales des animaux comparées a celles de l'homme*. 2 vols. Mons: Manceaux, 1872.

Hughes, T. P. *A Dictionary of Islam*. Lahore, 1964.

Idel, Moshe. "Defining Kabbalah: The Kabbalah of the Divine Names." In *Mystics of the Book: Themes, Topics, and Typologies*, ed. R. A. Herrera, pp. 97–122. New York, 1993.

———. "Differing Conceptions of Kabbalah in the Early 17th Century." In *Jewish Thought in the Seventeenth Century*, ed. I. Twersky and B. Septimus, pp. 137–200. Cambridge, Mass.: Harvard University Press, 1986.

———. Intro. to Johann Reuchlin, *De Arte Cabalistica*. Nebraska, 1993.

———. *Kabbalah: New Perspectives*. New Haven: Yale University Press, 1988.

———. "Kabbalah, Platonism and Prisca Theologia: The Case of R. Menasseh ben Israel." In *Menasseh ben Israel and His World*, ed. Y. Kaplan, H. Mechoulan, and R. I. Popkin, pp. 207–219. Leiden, 1989.

———. "Particularism and Universalism in Kabbalah, 1480–1650" and "Major Currents in Italian Kabbalah between 1560–1660." In *Essential Papers on Jewish Culture in Renaissance and Baroque Italy*, ed. David B. Ruderman, pp. 324–344, 345–368. New York, 1992.

———. "Une figure d'homme au-dessus des sefirot (à propos de la doctrine des 'éclats' de R. David ben Yehouda he-Hasid et ses développements." *Pardes* (1990): 131–150.

Jacob, Walter. *Christianity through Jewish Eyes: The Quest for Common Ground.* N.P.: Hebrew Union College Press, 1974.

James, William. *The Varieties of Religious Experience.* New York: Collier Macmillan, 1961 [pub. 1902].

The Jewish Encyclopedia, ed. Isidore Singer. 12 vols. New York, 1901–1906.

Katz, Jacob. *Exclusiveness and Tolerance: Studies in Jewish-Gentile Relations in Medieval and Modern Times.* Oxford: Oxford University Press, 1961.

Kristeller, Paul Oskar. *Renaissance Thought: The Classic, Scholastic, and Humanist Strains.* New York: Harper, 1961.

Lattes, Dante. *Aspetti e problemi dell'ebraismo Torino.* Turin: Borla, 1970.

Lattes, Guglielmo. *Vita e opere di Elia Benamozegh.* Leghorn: Belforte, 1901.

Lichtenstein, Aaron. *The Seven Laws of Noah.* New York: Rabbi Jacob Joseph School Press, 1981.

———. "Who Cares about the Seven Laws of Noah? A Status Report." *Jewish Law Association Studies* [Boston University School of Law] 4 (1990): 181–190.

Liebes, Yehuda. *Studies in the Zohar.* Albany, 1993.

MacLennan, R. S., and A. Thomas Kraabel. "The God-Fearers—A Literary and Theological Invention." *Biblical Archaeology Review* 12 (1986): 47–53.

McGinn, Bernard. *The Foundations of Mysticism.* New York, 1991.

Mendelssohn, Moses. *Moses Mendelssohn: Selections from His Writings,* ed. Eva Jospe. New York: Viking, 1985.

Michaelis, J. D. *Commentaries on the Laws of Moses.* Vol. 1. London, 1814.

Mill, John Stuart. *An Examination of Sir William Hamilton's Philosophy and of the Principal Philosophical Questions Discussed in his Writings.* Vol. 2. Boston: Spencer, 1868.

Mopsik, Charles. *Les grands textes de la Cabale.* Verdier: Lagrasse, 1993.

The Oxford Dictionary of the Christian Church, ed. F. L. Cross and E. A. Livingstone. 2nd ed. Oxford: Oxford University Press, 1983.

Pallière, Aimé. *Bergson et le Judaïsme.* Paris: Alcan, 1933.

Pétrement, Simone. *A Separate God: The Christian Origins of Gnosticism,* trans. Carol Harrison. San Francisco, 1990.

Renan, Ernest. *Études d'Histoire Religieuse.* Paris: Michel Lévy, 1864.

MONOGRAPHS, ARTICLES, AND REFERENCE WORKS

"Rome ou Jérusalem." Symposium in *L'Arche* 30 (1959): 20ff.

Roques, René. *L'Univers dionysien.* Paris, 1983.

Roth, Cecil. *The History of the Jews of Italy.* Philadelphia: Jewish Publication Society, 1946.

Salvador, Joseph. *Loi de Moïse ou Système Religieux et Politique des Hébreux.* Paris: Riden, 1822.

Salvador, M. *Jésus Christ et sa doctrine.* Brussels, 1838.

Scholem, Gershom. *Kabbalah.* New York: Quadrangle, 1974.

———. *Major Trends in Jewish Mysticism.* New York: Schocken, 1961.

———. *The Mystical Shape of the Godhead.* New York, 1991.

———. *Origins of the Kabbalah.* Princeton: Princeton University Press, 1987.

———. "Zur Geschichte des Anfangs des Christlichen Kabbala." In *Essays Presented to Leo Baeck,* pp. 108–109. London, 1954.

———*Sefer Ma'arekhet ha-'Elohut.* Mantua, 1558.

Singer, D. W. *Giordano Bruno: His Life and Thought.* New York: Schuman, 1950.

Stern, Menahem. *Greek and Latin Authors on Jews and Judaism.* 3 vols. Jerusalem: Israel Academy of Sciences and Humanities, 1974–1984.

Tannenbaum, R. F. "Jews and God-Fearers in the Holy City of Aphrodite." *Biblical Archaeology Review* 12 (1986): 55–57.

Tishby, Isaiah. *The Wisdom of the Zohar,* trans. D. Goldstein. Vol. 2. Oxford, 1989.

Toynbee, Arnold. "Le Diaspora: est-elle une condition nécessaire à la survie du judaïsme?" *L'Arche* 30 (1959): 30ff.

Twersky, Isadore. *Introduction to the Code of Maimonides* (Mishneh Torah). New Haven: Yale University Press, 1980.

Vulliaud, Paul. *La Kabbale Juive: histoire et doctrine.* 2 vols. Paris: Nourry, 1923.

Weber, Max. *Ancient Judaism,* trans. H. H. Gerth and D. Martindale. Illinois, 1952.

Werblowsky, R. J. Z. *Joseph Karo, Lawyer and Mystic.* Philadelphia, 1977.

Winston, David. *Logos and Mystical Theology in Philo of Alexandria.* Cincinnati: Hebrew Union College, 1985.

Wirszubski, Chaim. *Pico della Mirandola's Encounter with Jewish Mysticism.* Cambridge, Mass., 1987.

Wolfson, Elliot. "Mystical-Theurgical Dimensions of Prayer in *Sefer ha-Rimmon.*" *Approaches to Judaism in Medieval Times* 3 (1988): 41–80.

425

Wolfson, Harry A. *Philo: Foundations of Religious Philosophy in Judaism, Christianity, and Islam.* Vol. 1. Cambridge, Mass.: Harvard University Press, 1947.

Yosha, Nissim. *Abraham Cohen Herrera's Philosophical Interpretation of Lurianic Kabbalah.* Ph.D. thesis, Hebrew University, Jerusalem, 1991. [In Hebrew.]

Zaehner, Robert C. *At Sundry Times.* London, 1958.

———. *Hindu and Muslim Mysticism.* New York, 1972.

Zarka, Christian. "Sur le syncrétisme culturel entre Livourne et Tunis: l'alimentation." *Rassegna Mensile di Israel* 50 (1984): 766–784.

Index

Aaron: 113, 189, 193, 273, 281, 283, 305, 309
Abbahu, R.: 181
Abbaye: 270
Abimelech: 104, 109, 124, 229, 232, 286, 322
Abraham: 86, 91, 104, 109, 158, 169, 193, 257, 260, 286, 318–321, 325, 326; as apostle to Gentiles, 227–236
Abulafia, Abraham: xix, 233, 353n20, 384
Achish, King of Gath: 107
Adam: 87, 142, 148, 149, 153, 163, 164, 165, 167, 174, 178, 190, 191, 193, 205, 228, 242, 263, 264, 272, 275, 303, 304; mystical conception of, 178, 179, 184
Adonai: 114. *See also* God, names of
Adoni Tsedek: 320–322
Aeschylus: 121, 187
Aggadah: 51, 78, 148, 203, 228, 234
Ahab: 215
Ahura-Mazda: 187
Akiba, R.: 74, 170, 171, 200
Albigensian massacre: 334n37
Albo, Joseph: 99, 181

Alemanno, Yohanan: xix
Aleppo: 335n5
Alexandria: 195
Aliyah: 161, 188
Allievo, Giuseppe: 199
Alma: 142
Amalek: 214, 318, 319
Amalric: 177
Ammon: 214, 215, 259
Anaximander: 180, 348n28
Aner: 286
Angels: 70, 97
Anthropopathy: 196
Apollo, oracle of at Claros: 107
Apuleius: 112
Arabic: 297
Arabs: 241, 299
Aram: 215
Aramaic: 86, 106, 297, 298
Aravna: 304
Ari Nohem: 381, 385
Aristotle: 3, 154, 269, 294
Articulated Word: 226
Assyria: 286
Attila: 274
Augustine: 393
Avnimos ha-Gardi. See Oenomaus of Gadara
Azazel: 91, 114, 343n15

427

INDEX

Baal: 114, 115
Babel, Tower of: 102, 190
Babylon: 206, 214, 252, 286, 307
Balaam: 93, 105–106, 208, 233–235, 300
Baptism: 252, 261
B'chor: 167
Benamozegh, Elijah ben Abraham: composition of *Israël et l'Humanité*, xiii, 4, 5, 6, 7, 8; contemporary influences, 10, 11, 12, 13; and Kabbalah, 13–17, 32–35, 378, 379, 382–393; life of, 2–5, 14, 31, 32, 36; manuscripts of, 333n10; and Noachism, 18–21; philosophy of, xix–xxiii, 3–9, 11, 14–18, 21, 27, 28, 32–37, 378, 379; writings of, 8–10, 25
Benamozegh, Emmanuel: 1, 2
Ben-hadad: 215, 291
Bergson, Henri: 4
Berit: 337n12
Béziers: 334n37
Bildad: 233, 300
Blake, William: 28, 29
B'nei ha-nechar: 250
Boethius: 7
Bossuet, Jacques-Bénigne: 3, 280, 358n53
Bruno, Giordano: 221
Buddha: 148, 400
Buddhism: 201
Burnouf, Émile Louis: 79

Cahen, S.: 104
Cain: 167, 191, 263
Canaanites: 214, 242, 243, 277, 278, 298

Cantoni, Carlo: 316
Castelli, David: 101
Chaldeans: 252
Cherubim of the Tabernacle: 71
Christianity: 39, 40, 43, 45–52, 54–57, 68, 79, 86, 97, 164, 166, 169, 173, 177, 188, 194, 200, 202, 203, 209, 210, 231, 238, 243, 244, 246, 251, 252, 254, 258, 261, 264, 266, 268, 277, 298, 314, 329, 330, 344n10, 391, 392, 394, 396; relation to Judaism, 45–48, 51–54, 56–59, 104
Circumcision: 78, 252, 254, 257
Clement of Alexandria: 235
Cordovero, Moses: 384, 385
Coriat, Yehuda: 31, 32
Cosmos: 148, 178, 296
Cyrus, King of Persia: 306, 307
Cyrus the Zoroastrian: 84

Dante Alighieri: 3, 36, 113, 177
Darius, King of Persia: 307
David: 259, 304
Day of Atonement: 91, 251, 261, 273, 274
Decalogue: 91, 275, 297
Delitzsch, Frederick: 335n6
De l'origine des dogmes chrétiens: 395
Descartes, René: 197
Diodorus Siculus: 107
Dionysus: 342n7
duBois-Reymond, E.: 94

Easter: 314
Eber: 232
Eden: 191, 275, 306
Edom: 212, 213, 230, 290, 291, 328, 362n1

INDEX

Gordis, Robert: 20, 21
Gospels: 51, 127, 150, 155, 169, 170, 177, 178, 210
Great Year: 176
Greece: 206, 298, 299, 328
Greek mythology: 175
G'ulah: 203

Haag, Eugène: 186, 187
Hadassi, Judah ben Elijah: 215, 351n5
Haeckel, E. H.: 83
Hagar: 272
Ham: 206, 207
Hanania ben Gamaliel: 277
Hanina: 268
Hanun: 215, 259
Hartmann, Eduard von: 49, 180
Hasidism: 15, 78, 274
Haskalah: 3, 12
Havet, Ernest: 195, 251, 254
Hayyat, Yehudah: 390
Hazan, Eliahu: 5, 335n5
"Heaven of Heavens": 95
Hebraism: 15, 238, 258, 286
Hegel, G. W. F.: 83, 98, 180, 390, 391
Heikhal: 209
Hellenism: 156
Heraclitus: 126
Hercules: 150
Herrera, A. K.: xxi, 392
Hesiod: 252
Hezekiah, King of Israel: 120
Hiddush: 171
Hidka: 277, 279
Hinduism: 389, 391
Hinnom, Valley of: 224

Hiram, King of Tyre: 107, 214, 286, 305, 306
Hisda: 270
Hittites: 229
Hiyya: 181
Hobbes, Thomas: 132
Hokhmah: 394
Holy Land: 319; importance to Israel, 142–144
"Holy of Holies": 95
Horace: 251
Houzeaux, Jean Charles: 274, 275
Hugo, Victor: 3, 132

Ibn Ezra, Moses ben Jacob: 254, 303, 340n12
Idel, Moshe: 14
Ilan: 205
Il mio Credo: 349–350n7. *See also* Benamozegh, writings of
Image-worship, 88, 89
Incas: 275
India: 201, 281, 389
Inner Word: 226
Isaac: 260, 272, 321
Isaiah: 286
Ishmael: 167, 230
Islam: 46, 50, 178, 206, 250, 304, 329, 347–348n21
Israël et l'Humanité: editing of original publication, xi, 23, 24, 37–38; editions, xi–xiv, 24; theme and contents, 4–8, 10, 13, 18, 21–25, 27, 28, 387. *See also* Benamozegh
Issachar: 284
Isserles, Moses ben Israel: 99, 247, 341n23
Italy: xix, 3, 4, 332n3

INDEX

Jacob: 212, 260, 272, 281; dream, 223

James: 53, 244

James, William: 10, 337n10

Japheth: 206, 299, 340n12

Javan: 299

Jehoshaphat, Valley of: 129, 223, 224, 344n10

Jéhouda, Josué: 9, 26, 27

Jellinek, Adolph: 380

Jeremiah: 286

Jerusalem: 223, 303, 317–323

Jesus: 155, 169, 171, 177, 202, 211, 233, 244, 257, 329

Jethro: 74, 105

Jewish Christians: 244

Joachim of Flora: 177

Job: 105, 233, 249, 300

John of Parma: 177

Joseph: 123

Josephus: 126, 257, 289, 303

Joshua: 254, 319, 321

Judah: 284

Judah Halevi: 155, 157, 182, 247, 286

Judaism: attitudes toward idols, 96; baptismal rite, 261; brotherhood of peoples, 207–209, 212–215; dominion of man over nature, 190, 198; eldest son, role of, 282–283; endurance, 55, 58; ethical obligations to Gentiles, 259; freedom, 157, 158; God, conception of, 63–71, 80–83, 91, 121, 154, 220–222, 289, 293; as creator, 83–86, 101, 102; as father, 209–213; as judge, 87; as loving the poor, 200; as universal, 109–124, 135–140, 151; human dignity, 153; international law, 206, 207; man, conception of, 86, 148–152, 154–156; man as collaborator with God, 191, 194–202, 220; man as creator, 202–204; man in God's image, 154, 196; imitation of God, 156, 160, 161; man as priest of nature, 193, 194; and modern science, 70; Jews as priests of mankind, 239; nobility of body, 156; mystical concept of humanity, 296; national god incompatible with Judaism, 140–142; pre-Mosaic, 141; monotheism in, 83–95, 97, 98, 100–102, 106, 108; monarchy, ideas of, 285, 287–289, 291–294; pagan ideas, influence of, 77, 78, 106, 107; priesthood, 281–289; prophets, role of, 284–287; proselytism, 72, 74–76; sacrifices, 281, 282; separation from other peoples, 92, 93; soul, immortality of, 163; two parts of, 139–141, 237–248; ultimate aims, 44, 53, 54; unity of mankind, concept of, 205; universalist ethics, 258, 259, 280; universality, 43–46, 48, 49, 58, 228, 259, 297–303, 308, 311, 314, 315–327, 329–331; virtuous Gentiles, ideas of, 249, 250

Jus Gentium: 128

INDEX

Menasseh ben Israel: xxi, 392
Mendelssohn, Moses: 4, 151,
    152, 316, 317, 361n4
Merkavah: 137, 170, 340n11
Messiah: 50, 166, 185, 255, 314,
    318, 322
Michelet, Jules: 195, 271
Mill, J.S.: 10, 204
Millenarianism: 177
Mizrahi, Elijah: 242, 354n1
Moab: 131, 214
Molech: 279
Molitor, F.: xxiii, 393
Monolatry: 89, 90, 92
Monotheism: 228, 229, 241, 257,
    267, 308, 323, 328
Montanists: 177
Montesquieu, Baron, de: 274,
    276
Morale juive et morale chrétienne: 8,
    31, 258. *See also*
    Benamozegh, writings of
Morgenthau, Henry, Sr.: 1
Morselli, Marco: xii
Mosaic Law: 18–20, 43–46, 52–
    54, 82, 91, 93, 123, 136,
    140–144, 157, 158, 227, 228,
    237–242, 244–248, 249, 250,
    252–258, 260–262, 264, 269,
    273, 274, 277, 281, 291, 292,
    300, 302–304, 309, 311, 315,
    316, 326–328. *See also* Moses
Moses: 73–76, 78, 89, 91, 92,
    105, 115, 153, 157, 169,
    170–172, 183, 192, 193, 223,
    234, 253, 254, 257, 258, 260,
    273, 279, 280, 282, 285, 290,
    291, 305, 314, 318, 339n4,
    356n13. *See also* Mosaic Law
Müller, F. Max: 10, 121, 343n1

Munk, Salomon: 392
Mysticism: *See* Kabbalah

Naaman: 142, 261, 267
Naboth's Vineyard: 293
Nachmanides: 154, 229, 243,
    303, 320, 340n12, 390
Nank, Dr.: 303
Nasi: 290
Nasi Elohim: 229
Nebuchadrezzar: 128, 130
Neoplatonism: 390, 394
New Moon: 250
Nir le-David: 8. *See also*
    Benamozegh, writings of
Nissim ben Reuben Gerondi:
    344n4
Noachism: 6, 13, 18, 19, 20–22,
    24–27, 29, 48, 53, 54, 100,
    144, 237–239, 243–248,
    250–258, 260–280, 288, 310,
    315, 316, 326–328, 356n13.
    See also Ger-Toshav
Noah: 123, 169, 191, 192, 208,
    243, 252, 260, 263–265, 272,
    325

Oenomaus of Gadara: 235, 259,
    355–356n26
Onkelos: 74, 340n12
Orah Hayyim: 341n24
Oraita: 142
Oral Tradition: 252, 261, 262,
    273, 276, 278, 286, 318
Original Sin: 164
Osiris: 150
Ovid: 251

Pagan Mysteries: *See* Judaism, pa-
    gan ideas, influence of

INDEX

INDEX

Other Volumes in this Series